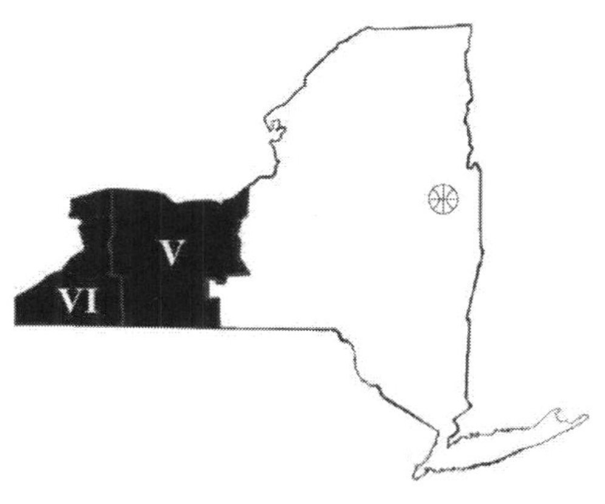

To Sara
Thank you for your support,
and it was nice meeting you.
Your ATTITUDE determines
your ALTITUDE!

[signature]
2025

To see the print and video promotional content created for *The Engineers: A Western New York Basketball Story*, scan the QR code above or visit this URL:
www.bigwordsauthors.com/theengineersawnybasketballstory

Contributors to The Engineers: A Western New York Basketball Story

The following are the many contributors to *The Engineers: A Western New York Basketball Story* who were gracious enough to each tell their stories to me as I crafted my own. To tell this story the way I want to tell it with depth and substance, I could not have done it on my own. Telling this story was a long process, and there were times when I felt self-doubt and wondered if this was a big waste of time. Each contributor reminded me in their own way that I was creating something worthwhile and to stay the course. Thank you all again.

"At the time we were playing, I would put the Yale Cup up against any league. There was talent across the board. I think we had the best team, but I can go through every school, and I can name two or three guys who I thought were really good. But it was very renegade-ish [laughing]. We should have gone to the states three years in a row. Jason and Damien went twice, but I went once, which was my senior year. We would get to the Far West Regional game. We had way more talent, but all the teams did was slow the ball down. They were patient, and we didn't have anything at that time—those first two years to combat that."

—Adrian Baugh, Player, Buffalo Traditional High School

"Our whole family, including my cousins, was a basketball family, and I just grew up watching basketball. My Dad used to take us to high school games when Trott Vocational was really good back in the day. We would go to see

Trott and Niagara Falls play. That is what really got me going, and it was just a family thing. Basketball was it for my cousins and me. My cousins always played, so I was always playing with them."

—Carlos Bradberry, Player, LaSalle Senior High School

"For me it was a skill set of hit the open jumper, play some defense, don't over dribble, and if the man is open, give it to him. The ball travels ten times faster than you can run, so it was more of those little things. Because you didn't get a shot that game, did you get the W? A lot of times on the basketball court, guys say, 'I didn't get to shoot!' Who cares? Did you WIN?"

—Curtis Brooks, Player, Hutch-Tech High School

"Ken Jones' style was extremely structured, and I would only scale it back just a bit. There were really no complaints from me on how he ran the system."

—Adonis 'AD' Coble, Player, Hutch-Tech High School

"Basketball taught me that you can learn a lot from losing. Losing is a part of life. When I say losing, I don't mean losing all the time but instead being able to take that failure and create some sort of success out of that failure and use it as a learning tool. It taught me that. It taught me how to work well with others, to count on people, to trust other people too, and as we talked about, the accountability piece."

—Ryan Cochrane, Player, Cardinal O'Hara High School

"I think anyone would be naïve not to think a coach does not know who he wants on his team. They have a certain idea, but you have to have tryouts and go through the process. And if you find a gem, a diamond in the rough, then, hey, that is great, but pretty much the rosters are already set. And at a school like ours where you did not necessarily have the best talent, you basically got the kids from the neighborhoods, and they played football, so most of the football players played basketball."

—Samuel 'Quin' Coffey, Player, Kensington High School

"I learned the game at a young age. There was a Boys Club two blocks over from our house. That was the place where all the kids went. Whether you wanted to play sports or just hang out, it was the spot that everybody went to. Obviously, I was attracted to basketball. I think I got attracted to it when my uncle would have his friends come over. They would watch it on the old black-and-white TVs—the NBA games. I would be in the background, kind of just peeking in and looking at certain things. They would be doing their thing. I think that is where my love for the game started. My skills were honed at the 13th Street Boys Club, and that is where it all started for me."

—Modie Cox, Player, LaSalle Senior High School

"Me and Ric are talking, Ricardo Jackon. I said, 'We are going to win it all this year, Ric.' Our first game was against Riverside. I said we are not losing to them. Something happened with Ben Rice. He was there at the game, but he could not play. He was ineligible. They told him he could not play. They still had Shawn Hargrove, Ed Harris, and, I think, Shawndel Planter. We played them in the first game of the year, and I had 27 points against them. It took some wind out of their sails, if I am being totally honest, Ben Rice not being there. He could shoot that ball. So it says, 'Seneca stuns Riverside,' I don't know what the caption was. Everybody knew they would beat us because we stunk the year before. That victory might have been one of the most important victories in the history of that school. It started something because nobody believed it. 'Yeah, we are going to win.' You say it, but it is different when people start buying in and believing it."

—Demoan Daniels, Player, Seneca Vocational High School

"I was teaching at Hutch, and my head was always in athletics, and I came down, and he [Coach Ken Jones] was always shooting the breeze with me. He was a fascinating guy. Do you understand that man—how old was he, sixty-three years old, when he retired? He would get to Hutch-Tech at 6 a.m. in the morning, run whatever before-school programs he ran, teach all day, run three miles at lunch, and then, during the season, run a practice from 3 p.m. to 6 p.m., and then go home. Try doing that for four months in a row. That is one of the reasons I couldn't do it. Emotionally and physically, I tried, but it just killed me!"

—Francis Daumen, Coach, Hutch-Tech High School

"It was tough one year. It was Thanksgiving break or Christmas break. Tim Winn came back to the gym one day. It was Modie Cox. It was Jody Crymes [laughing]. It was Terry Rich, and it was—who else came back? I think Mike Starks came back, too [laughing]. You are talking about getting beat up? Coach Monti did not blow the whistle, and he did not call fouls [laughing]. We got beaten up the entire scrimmage, but we learned and got better from it, as it made us tougher. And they always poured into you. They always knocked you down but picked you back up and said, 'Hey, man, you have to keep fighting, pushing, and getting better.' That's how we built up toughness over the years, and I think that is how they came back and poured into us, and I think it was just great."

—Dewitt Doss, Player, LaSalle Senior High School

"When players get cut, the thought process is that you could be next if you do not get to work! It is one thing if a player decides they do not want to be on the team, but it is another if you get cut. For anybody that is left, you are grateful that you did not get cut, and then you have to keep working at it because someone can take your spot!"

—Carlton Ford, Player, Hutch-Tech High School

"Eventually, it went from the backyard to running into one of my now mentors, Garcia Leonard. I met him at twelve years old at the Masten Boys & Girls Club. At the Boys Club, I learned the culture. The Boys Club back then was considered the 'Mecca' of basketball for all the people who came out of Buffalo. The type of people that were coming through the Boys Club at that time were some big names, including Glen Taplin, Ray Hall, Trevor Ruffin—you name it—and those guys were coming through there, and that was just the pick-up games. At that age, I was playing with them and catching on. I was also tall for my age back then."

—Damien Foster, Player, Buffalo Traditional High School

"I think we went 3–15. It was miserable in the sense that you never want to be part of a losing team. That was the year—I played against Ritchie Campbell and Marcus Whitfield—we played Burgard at home that year, and I think we lost by 60 points [laughing]. Man, these cats—Ritchie was throwing it off the backboard, and 'Ice Cream' was catching it and dunking it. They KILLED us. Ice Cream was Marcus Whitfield. They waxed us, but that was a memorable game for me because that was the first time I ever played in a varsity game. I got in the game because we were getting blown out, and that is when I scored my first 2 points."

—Dion Frasier, Player, Hutch-Tech High School

"Yes, I played on the junior varsity team as a freshman but did not make the varsity team. Very close! Yes, I finally made varsity my sophomore year. That 1990–91 team was a classic. There were some Buffalo legends on that team. They always gave us something to strive for in our junior and senior years, but going undefeated in the Yale Cup series…unheard of!"

—Jermaine Fuller, Player, Hutch-Tech High School

"We used to sneak into Alumni Arena up at the University at Buffalo's north campus. I remember one time some homeboys I played with from the neighborhood, we all snuck in together. We ran into some boys who, I think, played at Williamsville South. We got a pickup game going, and me and my friends are playing pickup-style basketball, and these guys are running plays! They've got five guys from their school, and they're running presses. So that was interesting to me, and what I learned from that was that the more organization you can have in a sport and earlier, the more acclimated you become playing it because you know from your experiences. Playing at Delaware Park and playing at Williamsville North or South is a whole different type of way of playing basketball. They were being taught discipline and structure earlier, and they were just in the habit of practicing it more."

—Carlos James Gant, Player, City Honors High School

"I don't think I tried out freshman year, but I tried out sophomore year. I didn't make it, and it was an eye-opener for me because it showed me that I did not have what it took to play. I didn't know about offensive plays. Hell, I didn't know what a '2-3' was, let alone a '1-2-2', a '2-1-2', a '2-2-1', a '1-3-1', or what a press was, nothing. I didn't know any of that stuff. I didn't know what a 'stack' was. I didn't know what a 'motion' play was. I was completely raw, so it was basic raw talent running up and down the floor. I had the talent to play the game, but I didn't have the mental capacity to know what I was playing."

—George Gayles, Player, Bennett High School

"People were going to school, and they were playing sports. The way people were getting ahead was going through school through athletics. It was competitive, and like you said, there was a lot of stuff you learned about through organized sports. You learned camaraderie. You learned how to be responsible, do not let them down. You had pride, this and that. It was nothing like it is today. The thing today is do not squeal. Do not snitch. But it was a different type of respect back then. You learn a lot through sports. You get mad, and you do not go beat them up. The coach says, 'They just practiced harder than you guys, so they deserved the win.' So, you just go back and practice harder. And I know it sounds corny, but back then, it worked. You just worked hard, and you tried to move on. Some guys did not make it. Everybody doesn't win in everything nowadays. It taught you how to win humbly and how to lose gracefully. Don't get mad. Sports teach you camaraderie and how to accept defeat, because life, life—you don't go through life winning everything. There are setbacks and defeats, and sports teach you how to handle that. And that's something I got from that. And nephews and grandkids should be into sports. It's a part of education. It's a part of learning, and it teaches you a whole lot. And that's the way I feel about it."

—Anthony 'Tony' Harris, Player, Burgard Vocational High School

"Walter was there as a freshman. He played on the junior varsity team. Billy was there with me during my freshman year. Ben came that year. Shawndel was there with me as a freshman. And Emmanuel Parker came that year as well. Emmanuel and Ben were additions for us that year. That, to me, was the passing of the torch that year. My sophomore year, Willie and Pooch were our guys, and that was his senior year. In my junior year, Pooch was gone. Willie was gone, and it's… You've been a starter since you were a freshman, and so now it's like junior year. It's a passing of the torch. It's your turn to lead these guys. So, Russ put that on me, and I took it. So, Ben was an addition, as was Emmanuel Parker. Billy, Shawndel Planter, and Walter Gravely—they were all there as freshmen, but they played junior varsity basketball."

—Edmond Harris, Player, Riverside High School

"At the beginning, you could tell that we weren't good but that we were getting better. And then, you have to remember, the teams we were playing against, they had way more experience. These are guys who, even though I didn't play against them, I heard about them. Burgard, they had 'Ice Cream' and Ritchie Campbell. And they weren't even considered the best team. In my junior year, Performing Arts was ranked No. 1 in the states at the beginning of the year. Performing Arts was. Traditional was good. We might've had the least experienced team. It was only Flash, Pep, and Quincy that had played. Everybody else was new. But as the season went on, you could see we were getting better. We weren't winning that much, but we were getting better, and at the end of that season, I had confidence that we were going to be good going into my senior year. I knew we were going to be much better."

—Frankie Harris, Player, Hutch-Tech High School

"Like Jones, I think he set the tone in terms of brainwashing because it was that more than anything. Every coach after that I compared to Coach Jones. If they didn't stand up in terms of his structure, I didn't gel with them. Coach Jones helped me out and got me to 'JUCO' (a junior college) down in Texas, and that's where I played for the next two years. The coach was structured, but he wasn't different from Jones. Then I went to Birmingham and played, and the coach was totally unorthodox and just totally willy-nilly, and I couldn't thrive. I couldn't do it, and I stopped playing. That level of coaching wasn't good for my development and wasn't what I needed. So, Jones developed a whole pathway for me as far as the way I looked at coaching and stuff like that as far as good or bad. That was really fundamental in my development in terms of my growth as a person and where I am now."

—Keith Hearon, Player, Hutch-Tech High School

Continued in the backcourt of this book…

The Engineers: A Western New York Basketball Story Part One

The Engineers: A Western New York Basketball Story Part One

Innocent Basketball Dreams

Anwar Y. Dunbar

The Engineers: A Western New York Basketball Story Part One
Innocent Basketball Dreams

Published by the Big Words LLC

2620 Redcoat Drive, 1D
Alexandria, VA 22303

ISBN: 979-8-218-44315-3 (paperback)
ISBN: 979-8-218-47398-3 (hardcover)
ISBN: 979-8-218-47484-3 (eBook)

Book Artwork and Cover Design: Amahl Dunbar, Coach Ken Jones and FreePik.com (the cover basketball image)

The Author's Photograph: Myron S. Ottley Photography

Printed in the United States of America

Dedications and Remembrances

I want to thank the Creator first. Regardless of your spiritual beliefs (or lack thereof), a key theme of this story is that while we have our own plans in life, multiple forces are always at work driving the outcomes we see and experience, both cosmically and in our corporeal realm. Efforts such as playing on basketball teams or writing books can either coalesce and be successful or fall apart. All of this underscores the importance of prayer.

I want to thank my mother, Wendy C. Anderson, a veteran writer and the best mother a son could have. Thank you for the unconditional love you always gave us and for editing my articles and blog posts. Thank you also for the important question you asked me when I shared in your living room that I was setting out to do this, which was, "Have you considered taking a writing class?" It was after sharing one of my early creative writing samples with you that I subsequently took some writing classes. It's one thing to say that you want to write a book, but quality writing requires some learning and lots of practice. I had lots of personal practice up to that point, but I needed some formal education and training. Thank you for all your motherly and grammatical guidance in my life and on this journey. In writing your own book, you, in part, paved the way for mine.[1]

I want to thank my father, Rodney L. Dunbar, for telling me at an early age that I had a gift for writing. The rest of our father-son relationship has been quite complicated over the years, but those powerful words stayed with me. You helped motivate me to become successful in your own unique ways numerous times throughout my journey throughout life. Elements of your own complicated life story, in addition to those of us *SOFT* Buffalo boys and others like us, are also shared in this story.

I want to acknowledge my older brother Amahl, a true artist and creator. We did quarrel a little bit throughout the years as most siblings do, and we are in many ways opposites. I was fortunate to have you as an older sibling, and you've been a critical contributor to my own creations as my visual arts consultant. This book is just one example of that. Oh, and I may have never seriously considered attending Hutch-Tech High School if not for you. I also want to acknowledge Gabriel DePriest Smith, my 'brother from another mother' as said in hip hop culture. You also left a critical imprint on my life and this story. We are truly kindred spirits, and you've also helped me make sense of our lives and this complicated world in your own way. Dorian Johnson, thank you for your contributions as well.

I want to thank all the other relatives, friends, and acquaintances who provided moral support during this journey. There are too many other people to name, and

---

[1] (Anderson, 1998)

you know who you are. Even the critics and doubters who questioned this project, you also played a valuable role in this journey. You helped motivate me to keep going, and you caused me to ponder why this story matters. This is a critical question for an unknown first-time author.

I want to thank those of you from the Hutch-Tech alumni community who shared pictures and resources that I did not have access to. I want to thank Laura Kennedy Lama from my class of 1994 for sharing pictures of the Hutch-Tech boys' basketball teams from yearbooks I no longer had. Also, thank you to Michael T. Rivera from the great class of 1991 for sharing images and stories of the late Kevin Roberson, one of the bases for this story.

I want to thank the veteran published authors who lent their coaching and experience. Two that come to mind are Rom Wills, who confirmed that one can be successful as a self-publisher and that people still read books today. I also want to acknowledge fellow Johnson C. Smith University alumnus and published author Tyrell Hughes for his coaching through this process and for his continuous and infectious enthusiasm and optimism.

I want to acknowledge those who transitioned from this Earthly plane as I worked my way through this project. Dr. Kenneth Leon Jones was a critical part of this whole thing, and his wife, Mrs. Alice Jones was too. Without you, Coach, there would be no story. That's literally true, as depicted in this story. Your love for the game of basketball, your players, and your life underpin this entire project.

There were several Hutch-Tech basketball players who passed away during the finalization of part one of this project. Two were Quincy Lee and Paul Saunders of the class of 1991, affectionately known as 'Q-Lee' and 'PA', respectively. Jason Holman from the class of 1993 passed away as well. These are just players from the boys' basketball team who I have knowledge of or played with in the early '90s. There were other Hutch-Tech alumni who passed away as I worked to bring this story to life.

Raheem Gaines, a hardcore sports fan from my 1994 Hutch-Tech class, passed away within months of my submitting this manuscript for what I thought was its final editing and processing as we transitioned from 2023 to 2024. He was also a friend and a brother. Raheem was a true Ohio State Buckeye fan, and he was very gracious following the annual Michigan vs. Ohio State Football games, regardless of the outcome.

My Uncle John Harris, who appears in this story, passed during the Covid-19 pandemic along with so many others. There were many others who passed away during the crafting of this book, both naturally and seemingly prematurely, again depending on your philosophical and spiritual beliefs. I must also acknowledge the late Kobe Bryant from the basketball world, also known as the 'Black Mamba', who tragically passed away early in 2020 with his daughter Gianna. A central theme of this project involves learning *how* to compete in life. You learned that at an early age Kobe, and you taught us all about it during your professional basketball career through your infamous 'Mamba Mentality'. Salute and rest in power.

Thank you to Mother Eva M. Doyle, my first-ever science teacher in life at the Campus West/College Learning Laboratory at Buffalo State College. You later took up your own personal call as an author, investigator, and teacher of Black History and histories of all kinds. You reminded me in your own way during this process that our history matters.

I finally want to thank Starbucks and all the other coffee shops for providing public spaces for us, as authors and creators, to work on our ideas. Also thank you to the technology innovators for designing these modern tools for creating our art. I honestly don't know how people did this years ago. Writing your first book is not easy. It occurred to me that this one story is just one of many from our high school, and it was one little speck in the entire human population on the planet Earth. Though its themes and underlying meanings are timeless, I hope someone gets value out of it. Best regards, and yours in good sports!

Foreword

One day, strolling through Facebook, I came across the post from my old coach Pat Monti. It was an interview by Dr. Anwar Dunbar regarding LaSalle basketball (pronounced LAY-Salle by many alumni and former players). It discussed our dynasty, which started in the late '80s and lasted until the school closed in the late '90s. There happened to be a series of interviews. Two others were of the great Carlos Bradberry and the great Tim Winn, also known as 'Fat Jack'. Due to my alias, the 'Controversial Counselor', I was thinking, hold up, wait a minute, how do you start talking about a dynasty without starting with our great 1988 New York State Class B Federation Championship Team? I felt someone from the 1988 team should have been interviewed.

Now, granted, that person would not have been me because I had little to do on the court with us winning the championship. Our star players that season were No. 54, Eric Gore, and No. 11, Michael Starks. I became the team's emotional leader during that run. I became a great locker room presence and a voice of reason. I kept a balance and emphasized that we had all the talent in the world but that we needed to channel our emotions so we could make a run and win it all.

We notched great wins that season. In our league, we defeated Christian Laettner's Nichols teams. After winning the Class B sectional in Western New York, we defeated teams including Gloversville, Syracuse-Nottingham, and Samuel Gompers on the way to the New York State Class B Federation Championship. We finished that season 27–0, and LaSalle basketball was dominant for the next decade.

So, I reached out to Dr. Anwar Dunbar to see if he wanted to interview someone from the 1988 team and that I would be willing to be that person. Now my success was nowhere near the accomplishments of Carlos Bradberry or Tim Winn, but I just wanted our team to get its just do. I am a firm believer that once you are a champion, you are always a champion. I also believe that championships are won through collaboration and teamwork.

A funny thing happened. Dr. Dunbar didn't know that I was making myself available to be interviewed on behalf of the 1988 team, but a collaboration started and gradually unfolded between us. During the time of reaching out to Dr. Anwar Dunbar, I started following his posts, and we became friends on social media. Just like me, he created a YouTube channel, and I subscribed to it.

With me being a published author, we collaborated on several broadcasts in his spaces and in mine. He also sought my advice numerous times regarding authorship. We have collaborated for multiple years, and I really enjoy Dr. Anwar Dunbar's platforms. I believe he is a forward thinker, and he has a lot to offer. He now has four YouTube channels, and his platforms are diverse and talk about education, general topics, sports, science, and media. They basically run the gamut.

Kudos to Dr. Anwar Dunbar for taking on that challenge. We both know trying to build a brand and create something separate from our day jobs is not easy. It all depends on your followers and what people do to help you along the way. I believe we are two like-minded individuals with the same goals. I wish nothing but the best for him, and I think he feels the same about me.

I am from Niagara Falls, NY, and Dr. Dunbar is from nearby Buffalo. That is how he knew of our great basketball dynasty at LaSalle Senior High School. He saw and faced at least one of our teams firsthand. I think it was the 1991–92 Carlos Bradberry-led team.

Growing up on North Avenue in Niagara Falls was not peaches and cream, as they say. I faced many situations. I dealt with a vicious cycle involving my Dad, for example. Once my grandmother Glover died, my father made a turn for the worse. Once I reached the age to get into sports, I felt I could have achieved more if my father had been present, which is an important parallel to Dr. Dunbar's story and the stories of many boys from our background.

Relationships with fathers are important but can be tricky as well. During the times my Dad lived in the household, I remember him being critical of me for the close relationship I had with my mother. I strongly feel he was missing that closeness once my grandmother died. He also experienced the lack of a relationship with his father, which affected our relationship.

I just know that growing up playing youth sports, it is important to have your Dad (or a male mentor, ideally) as an advocate. Growing up on North Avenue with so many boys, I was able to grow and maintain my competitive spirit. But like I said, if my father had been around, it would have given me more confidence. I always played well as far as football games in the neighborhood or pickup basketball games. During organized game situations, though, I lacked confidence when it was time to perform, again, something that's common for boys from our background.

From what I observed when playing football, kids whose fathers were more active seemed to play the more *skilled* positions, such as quarterback, wide receiver, running back, and cornerback, where you could score touchdowns. I grew up primarily playing defensive end where the biggest pleasure was sacking the quarterback. Deep down inside, I knew I could play wide receiver as I had good hands. I could also play running back as I had moves, and I for damn sure could play cornerback! I knew I could play a skilled position, but see, when you have an advocate such as your Dad speaking up for you, the results will be different.

Around ninth grade I started playing competitive team basketball due to the motivation and encouragement of our former point guard from the 1988 team, the legendary Michael Starks mentioned above. Mike helped me with some basic skills, such as learning how to go off the right foot for a left-handed layup and dribbling with my left hand. I wanted to get better, and I knew Mike had the goods to lead me in that direction. I finally joined the Boys and Girls Club and played for their team in the 12–14 age group. I won the Most Valuable Player Award for the team that season because of my character, being respectful and responsible, attending all practices, being a team player, and providing maximum effort.

Through sports, my character as a counselor started taking shape and I was always an advocate of doing the right thing. I supported people who were in the role of an underdog. I was a champion for anti-bullying. I had the innate ability to realize when someone was hurting and take them under my wing to support them. I grew up with so much self-doubt, and I knew I did not want anyone else to experience the pain.

I discovered that counseling was right down my alley, and I have been in education for the past twenty-six years. I have served as a school counselor with the Baltimore County Public School System for the last sixteen years. For ten of those years, I have served as the Department Chair of School Counseling. I am also the author of the original book *Cocktail Conversations by the Controversial Counselor*.[2] The revised edition led me to win the 2017 Indie Author Legacy Award for Author on the Rise. My most recent book is *NO Friday Foolishness* was published in November of 2019.[3] I also have been a part of several blog talk and podcast shows during the past six years.

Growing up on North Avenue in Niagara Falls, experiencing the absence of my father, and then getting to participate in sports, I can relate to the story Dr. Dunbar is telling in *The Engineers: A Western New York Basketball Story*. It is a story not just about his basketball journey at Hutch-Tech High School in Buffalo but also about his teammates and other kids who played basketball from Western New York in that magical time spanning from the late ‘80s to the early ‘90s. Having competed myself and now working with kids, I know firsthand the excitement of participating in athletics as a young person and what sports teach us.

I know how sports impact the self-esteem of young people and both the elation and disappointment sports can bring at that age. I understand the innocent basketball dreams we all start off with, which is the first part of Dr. Dunbar's story. Furthermore, though I was fortunate to win multiple championships my senior year on a team that went 27–0, I understand many other student-athletes learn about life's harsh realities, which Dr. Dunbar depicts in part two of his story.

I was one of the fortunate kids to win a state federation title, but as described, there were adversities in my journey. I further know what those experiences in sports teach us as we transition into adulthood, especially boys transitioning into

---

[2] (Glover D. L., Cocktail Conversations, 2014)

[3] (Glover D. L., No Friday Foolishness, 2019)

manhood. Finally, as a counselor myself, I understand the importance of coaches, father figures, and mentors—and what happens when you do not have them. There's so much that sports teach us about life, and we use those lessons even after we stop playing and transition into the adult world. This is what is important about Dr. Dunbar's story.

Writing this foreword has brought me much excitement because I think of myself around this time six years ago, getting ready to publish my own book. The feeling is surreal and being a part of this journey with Dr. Anwar Dunbar makes it special to be able to speak on sports, my childhood, and the trials and tribulations, along with counseling. These subject matters speak to who I am, and knowing I was and am a part of this soon-to-be-great publication, *The Engineers: A Western New York Basketball Story*, is what great memories are all about. Good luck, Dr. Anwar Dunbar. I wish you much success as an author and any other endeavors you set out to accomplish.

David Lorenzo Glover, aka 'The Controversial Counselor', Author, Counselor, and YouTube Content Creator

Disclaimer. *The Engineers: A Western New York Basketball Story* is based upon real life events. The real names are used for those who gave their consent and those mentioned in game summaries and box scores captured in newspapers like the *Buffalo News* and the *Rochester Democrat and Chronicle,* sectional books, *etc.* Most other names have been changed to protect the personal identities of those who did not agree to be directly mentioned. The games and scores are further based upon those reported in these periodicals. The college and professional basketball and football scores of that time period are considered common knowledge and for the most part, are not referenced. Finally, this story is being told by the writer, and not Hutch-Tech High School, the Buffalo Public Schools, or any other school, interscholastic sports league, or organization. Best regards and yours in good sports.

Table of Contents

Preface

Who This Story Speaks to Today, a Second Dream and Becoming a Writer

As I finished parts one and two of *The Engineers: A Western New York Basketball Story*, I was in a season where I was watching Robert Greene's content on YouTube. Robert authored masterpieces including: *The 48 Laws of Power*, *Mastery*, and most recently, *The Laws of Human Nature*.[4,5,6] I recently experienced an adverse family situation in the fall of 2021. Afterward, I wanted to learn more about controlling my emotions and navigating life's inevitable chaotic situations more effectively, developing a level of stoicism, if you will. It was something I had to work on throughout my life consistently. Coincidentally, some of the experiences I discuss in *The Engineers* reflect that early on in my life and in the lives of others. Coaches of any sport will tell you that getting groups of players to move in one direction can be very chaotic, and a significant part of that is managing egos and emotions.

It was 2022, approximately eight to nine years after I started working on *The Engineers*. In interviews, Robert admitted that his books took years to craft and finalize, which made me feel better. We, as writers, sometimes get criticized for taking too long to complete our art. Something else he shared spoke to me as a young author looking to publish his first book. He stated during an interview that authors must think hard about relating their work to the people of the era they are living through. That is, it is one thing to have a story to tell, but how does it relate to young readers who may be going through their own unique challenges in their modern era?

I thought I had done an excellent job discussing the themes of the story and learning points in earlier drafts. Still, I never thought about relating the books directly to a generation growing up in a world vastly different from that of those of us who grew up in earlier eras. I was living through some of those same changes as a late member of Generation X. Some were difficult, perplexing, and, in some ways, angering for myself and those around me, including some relatives. Some expected our lives to be like theirs in an unrecognizable world in many ways.

Society was now more digital and more diverse in every way, and there were many change agents seeking to create equality of all kinds without thinking about the greater ramifications for society, prior family cultures and traditions, and our species as human beings. Economics and gender were two big ones regarding

---

[4] (Greene, The 48 Laws of Power; First Edition, 2023)

[5] (Greene, Mastery; Reprint Edition, 2013)

[6] (Greene, The Laws of Human Nature; Reprint Edition, 2019)

establishing equality (or equity). There were efforts to create more than two genders now. Men and women did not get along the same way they had before. Things had become faster, and in some instances, expectations for life had become unrealistic. There were also factions who thought there were too many human beings on our planet Earth and wanted to see our species' numbers shrink. It was a less innocent time than the late '80s and early '90s.

In the final stages of finishing *The Engineers*, I was once again reminded that things happen in their own time, and sometimes there is one more thing you need. I described some of the themes of the books with Alice Jones, the wife of the late Coach Ken Jones, over lunch near the transition from 2023 to 2024, four years after his passing. Coach Jones is a key figure in this story and very much helped lay the groundwork for it in addition to others.

I described my revelation to Alice that the story I wrote was a proxy for the United States itself, in addition to being a mere story about the game of basketball. That is, while Coach Ken Jones built a great basketball program at Hutch-Tech High School, it ultimately did not work well without players who embodied its codes and values. It was like today's United States, which many speculate is declining and arguably crumbling from within. I know this is a sobering way to start a book, but it's what people are discussing in 2024. Author and podcaster Aaron Clarey discussed this in his book entitled, *Enjoy the Decline: Accepting and Living with the Death of the United States*.[7]

While I harkened back to days past, Alice reminded me that there were things about the United States that were not good and not perfect in terms of the history of the country. There were, in fact, things that were crooked and wayward throughout its history. While there were aspects that worked well for some, there were many aspects that did not work well for others. The same was true for the basketball program her late husband built, despite how perfect it looked on the outside. It was a powerful revelation.

Going back to Robert Greene's advice for authors, I asked a mentor, whom I'll call Mark, about lessons young people need to hear in modern times. Over the years, we have had many talks about the world, society, economics, and how culture and our social mores have changed. I figured he would have ideas about what young people today need to know. He made three points. Two were what I expected, and the third surprised me, and I wondered how I would relate it to my story. The following are three overarching points younger people should keep in mind when reading parts one and two of *The Engineers: A Western New York Basketball Story*.

The first is that life isn't perfect. My mentor stated that today's younger people expect life to be perfect, and all of us with experience know that it is far from it.

---

[7] (Clarey, 2013)

This principle comes up throughout my story. The second is that you can have either equality of opportunity or outcome, but not both. Equality of opportunity/outcome is a common debate today, and I think this is something sports show us time and again. I believe this also comes up throughout my story. Even with similar opportunities, will our outcomes be the same or different? Why or why not in either case? In life, there are winners and losers, and falling into either group could result for any number of reasons.

His final comment was that you can breed prosperity or wealth equality, but not both. There's an apparent financial meaning in this, but at a higher level, it means that life is about choices. There are choices and *tradeoffs* where you can seldom have everything. Furthermore, there are consequences for pretty much everything and every choice in life. This principle is depicted throughout *The Engineers: A Western New York Basketball Story* as well.

Finally, I'll say some words about manhood. If you read *The Engineers*, one thing subtly touched upon throughout the story is the consequences of not having men around, especially for young boys. In the third decade of the twenty-first century, amongst its many other problems, the United States is facing a crisis when it comes to boys and men. There is lots of content out there for those interested in learning more about this. I decided to mention this here after a discussion I hosted on YouTube on the book entitled, *Why Should White Guys Have All The Fun?*[8] The book is the biography of Reginald F. Lewis, the United States' first black billionaire. I hosted the discussion for Black History Month 2022.

It's not a long passage, but towards the end of his biography, one of his closest friends mentions that Lewis, who was born to a single mother himself, was concerned about black boys going forward. This would have been in the late '80s and early '90s, just before he died from brain cancer. The book doesn't go into specifics, so readers are left to speculate about his concerns. I suspect it had something to do with a dearth of positive male figures and those boys being left to figure things out on their own due to decisions that were out of their hands. Again, this is a key underlying theme of *The Engineers: A Western New York Basketball Story*. I was in my teens and on my basketball journey at that time and experiencing this very thing.

In good faith, I must extend this to all boys in the United States, especially those of Generation Z and those coming after them who are facing unprecedented challenges and circumstances. I created numerous teaser materials to promote *The Engineers: A Western New York Basketball Story*. Some of those materials involved excerpts from the forty-three interviews I conducted with players and coaches from Western New York. Someone left an interesting comment underneath my first offering, sharing some of the quotes from my contributors. It involved a

---

[8] (Walker, 2005)

challenge/dynamic of our modern era described above, and it relates to the genders.

"This was a great piece. It would be nice to see a piece written about female basketball players as well," a commenter named Pamela said. It wasn't a surprising comment in 2023. This reader, in some ways understandably, wanted to see something similar for girls. Like many consumers of content though, I don't think she recognized that I was setting out to tell a specific story, while she focused on her particular wants. I likewise did not necessarily create this art with the specific intent of gender equality. I was telling my story, and it was from a man's perspective, something which has been lost in modern times. This occurrence reaffirms the importance of this work, as many essential components of our society are being discarded, homogenized, or transformed altogether.

That said, I want to acknowledge that women's basketball has come a long way at the time of the publishing of this book, and more people are watching women's basketball than ever before. I recently witnessed Head Coach Dawn Staley's University of South Carolina Lady Gamecocks defeat Head Coach Lisa Bulder's Iowa Lady Hawkeyes, led by Caitlin Clark, to win the 2024 Women's College Basketball National Championship. That game did something that we hadn't seen on the men's side in years, and that was that it created a rivalry with people fervently pulling for either side for various reasons. There was lots of emotion surrounding that national championship game.

Likewise, while this story is written from a young man's perspective, there too are young women who have set out on the basketball path, just like Angel Reese, Caitlin Clark, and Raven Johnson. There are also girls who have had life happen to them in various ways, in some instances having their dreams altered and their lives sent on vastly different trajectories than those they dreamed about. Girls are likewise facing unprecedented challenges in our brave new world.

Modern young men and older men and society could use a story like this about growing up and having to figure out life without all the tools you need to succeed. I first read about this in Dr. Robert Glover's timeless work entitled, *No More Mr. Nice Guy.*[9] I was interested in the book to help figure out how to navigate the dating world like many men. There were several important historical aspects in the book though, which shed light on how our culture and society had changed. Glover, for example, pointed out environmental and systemic changes in society, such as the transition from an *agrarian* to an *industrial* society, which led to boys spending less time with their fathers and older men daily and not being able to model their behaviors as much.

Numerous people are looking at this right now in greater detail. Some names include: Dr. T. Hasan Johnson, Aaron Clarey, Dr. Warren Farrell, Nicholas

---

[9] (Glover R. , 2003)

Eberstadt, Professor Scott Galloway, Richard Reeves, Dr. Jawanza Kunjufu, and others. Many have written books on boys falling behind in our society and the long-term ramifications of such a thing. I understand if these words are controversial and cause angst for some, but these are highly relevant issues for everyone at the time of the finalization of this book.

Dr. T. Hasan Johnson is one of the voices of a digital collective on YouTube called the 'Black Manosphere' who is from the academy, and who is doing a lot of important work in this area. In his teaching at the academy, his video content creation, and in his book, in particular, entitled, *Solutions For Anti-Black Misandry, Flat Blackness, and Black Male Death,* he has done considerable work highlighting the modern plight of black boys.[10] Women such as Suzanne Venker are stepping up and asking uncomfortable questions about the consequences of the breakdown of the nuclear family. In her book entitled, *Reclaiming The Black Feminine*, Kendra Davis highlights and reminds her black female readers about their natural power in terms of partnering with men in a complimentary way in the formation of families.[11] Many of these discussions and questions are analogous to the great game of basketball, and they address some of the cultural changes in our modern society. Many involve the concept of teamwork, and the idea of putting the team's best interests over the needs and wants of the individual team members.

Questions must be asked about what happens to a society where boys are ill-equipped to compete and mature into men. What happens to such societies? What happens to that country's once-mighty military? What is the result for societies that don't adequately prepare their boys to compete, lead, and succeed?

In one of the early chapters of the above-mentioned Nicholas Eberstadt's book entitled, *Men Without Work*, he does, in fact, state something to the effect of, "A country can be no more successful than the success of its men!"[12] This verbiage will likely offend some people in today's world, but that's good. Furthermore, it's important to consider what's true and false, despite feelings to the contrary. Culture and the latest fads, after all, cannot undo biology. For all these reasons, *The Engineers: A Western New York Basketball Story* is a microcosm of life, as will be discussed later.

* * *

Dreams are integral and sometimes mysterious parts of all our lives. They visit us when we sleep. They speak to us in our subconscious minds, and they also formulate when we are conscious. Those that visit us when we sleep are sometimes

---

[10] (Johnson, 2023)
[11] (Davis, 2022)
[12] (Eberstadt, 2022)

very random things, reminders of experiences in our lives both good and bad, and sometimes they foreshadow things to come. In some instances, they take us back to experiences that we will forever wish we could relive and do over—things we sometimes long and yearn for afterward, especially if that dream goes unfulfilled. In the best-case scenarios, they give us things to aspire to and to shoot for.

I have secretly always dreamed of being a writer. Being a basketball player preceded that dream. In middle school, I recall telling everyone, "I want to be a chemist." Being a scientist was something I foresaw as a 'tween', but it wasn't something I ever obsessed over until I got into graduate school. There I faced daily the dual possibilities of not finishing my PhD, and potentially earning it one day. In my current career as a pharmacologist, I have not landed far from that goal. As early as elementary school, my father also told me that I had a gift for writing and that always lingered in the back of my mind.

"Yeah. And you aspired to be financially free by the time you turned 40 years old!" Dreams can also be destroyed by any number of parties, relatives and friends, and the world in general. Roughly 30 years after telling me that I had the gift of writing, Dad mocked me for a more recent dream I had of becoming financially free by 40 years of age. After finishing my PhD, I started studying the financial teachings of writers like Robert Kiyosaki, author of the *Rich Dad Poor Dad* series.[13] Kiyosaki and other financial coaches and teachers encouraged writing your dreams down and posting them somewhere in a place where you could see them every day.

Unfortunately, I did not have the privacy of my own room during that period, and my father saw my aspiration, probably daily as well. He mentally tucked it away and weaponized it against me one fateful night after I did not achieve the goal. A lifelong employee who had only known disappointments for most of his life and probably seeing most of his own dreams crushed, he saw fit to mock me. I hated him for it, and I was devastated at the time. This event sets up a couple of themes in this story. One theme is perseverance, which is taking blows and jabs from critics but continuing to move forward.

Another theme is the importance of exposure, that is, having exposure and training for a given area of interest, and how the lack of that exposure can hinder your success. Without immersing yourself in your craft and finding support systems for the things you want to do, you likely won't reach your goals. I've learned this lesson repeatedly throughout life.

* * *

[13] (Kiyosaki, Rich Dad Poor Dad What The Rich Teach Their Kids About Money--That The Poor & The Middle Class Do Not, 2000)

The Engineers: A Western New York Basketball Story is just that, a story. I have likewise always enjoyed hearing the stories of others and telling my own. Over time I came to view them as tools for passing on knowledge and wisdom and vehicles for laughs. Jonah Berger discussed the former in his book entitled, *Contagious*.[14] One of the biggest joys of the holidays for me was always listening to stories about people from my late Grandmother Lena McKinney and other elders. Her stories usually involved her relatives, her children, or people from our church, the Tried Stone Baptist Church on Humboldt Parkway in Buffalo, NY.

My Uncle Tony could tell some good stories, too, when he was both sober and after he had a few drinks. The best ones were about his brothers and sisters, our cousins, or the different *lowlifes* from the projects. He and his siblings (my mother included) grew up on the west side of Buffalo in the neighborhood known as 'Black Rock'. My Uncle Scottie, also known as the 'Iceman', could tell some good stories too. Like those of my Uncle Tony, his stories were also about his brothers and sisters, and folks from the projects. Most of his stories involved the Banks family. His best friend, John 'Boola' Banks, was from that family. He always told the same stories repeatedly and laughed at them even if no one else did.

Dad always had great but bizarre stories, too, such as the one about his cousin who ate so much pork that he eventually began to look like a hog. He further stated that he noticed that those relatives put mayonnaise on everything. Yes, Dad told that one on repeated occasions, and he believed it too. There was also the story from his youth in the New York City subway system, where he thought a mysterious man was following him and was about to shoot him due to mistaken identity. When Dad turned around in the stairwell, he saw the man put something back into his overcoat, which he thought was a gun. It was one of those chance things. Had Dad been murdered that day, my older brother, Amahl, and I would never have been born. I always visualized that story in my mind like a movie whenever he told it to me.

There was also the older female tenant who lived in the lower unit of Dad's home in Schenectady, NY. One day he went downstairs to ask her for her rent, and he said, "Something demonic or other-worldly seemed to take over her. Her eyes rolled back into her head, and her ears turned up!" That experience forever soured him on being a landlord—one of many in a lifetime of experiences that corroborated his superstitions and led to his distrusting many of the things he would encounter in general. And then there was the story of the woman who got him arrested because he didn't want to date her anymore. He was intimate with her, resulting in her becoming a *jilted* ex-lover. He insisted that had he not had enough money saved up, he wouldn't have been able to post his own bail.

---

[14] (Berger, 2013)

I'm saying all of this to say that I've always enjoyed hearing stories, the humor and wisdom from those stories, and writing stories. Stories not only tell us about our pasts, but in some instances, they also tell us how and how not to move throughout life. I have always been a natural teacher and have always wanted to tell my own stories about the people I've known, the experiences I've had, and the lessons I've learned during my journey through life.

* * *

I first thought about writing *The Engineers: A Western New York Basketball Story* during my first year of graduate school at the University of Michigan in the fall of 1999. I was in a seminar for our first-year Program in the Biomedical Sciences curriculum. I should have been paying attention to that day's science lecture, which was why I was there, but instead, I got to writing about my years on the Hutch-Tech boys' basketball team back in high school. Those experiences were still alive and inside of me. I was five to six years removed from my last game.

After a brief stop at the State University of New York College at Brockport, I had since completed another chapter of life, my undergraduate studies at Johnson C. Smith University. Being a Hutch-Tech Engineer was my first and perhaps my greatest adventure up to that point, and arguably of my lifetime. It was my very first major success and failure lesson in life, one which I have thought about both consciously and in my dreams over the years.

Writing *The Engineers* is something that I wanted to do for a while, and settling into a federal career twenty years later with a good work-life balance allowed me the time to devote to this second dream. Being a basketball player was my first dream. It was also my first teacher in life, one that would impact all my endeavors that followed it.

* * *

Over the 2011 holiday season, I started doing the actual research for *The Engineers*, a project conceived in my mind twelve years earlier. Much of the book would be written from my memory and those of others around that time. It would also need real-life events to tell the story in a meaningful way. It would need pieces of history in the way of actual game write-ups and box scores to properly anchor the story in time and place.

I worked remotely in Buffalo on my job in the federal government. I used the downtown Buffalo Public Library as my workstation for its wireless internet access. I speculated about it for a while, and I discovered, in fact, that the library had archived issues of the *Buffalo News* going all the way back to the 1990s and beyond, all on microfiche. They were in the 'Grosvenor Room', which held much of Buffalo's history in the form of documents, maps, and periodicals. It became my second home on visits back to Buffalo.

During that holiday season, I began going to the January and February months of 1994 to copy the box scores and write-ups of the high school basketball games, particularly my games at Hutchinson Central Technical High School, or Hutch-Tech for short. Scrolling through paper after paper, I passed over the larger newsworthy events of that era, such as Bill Clinton's first presidential election and the Buffalo Bills' four Super Bowl runs. There were articles about Donald J. Trump (long before becoming President) and TV shows that were just getting started at the time, like *The Real World* on Music Television (MTV). Me and my brother Amahl watched that show religiously early on in addition to other shows like Jerry *Seinfeld.*

Scrolling through reels and reels of microfiche was tiring. I became quite familiar with the vinegar-like smell of the reels of microfiche as the years went on. An acetic acid mixture was probably used to prepare or preserve those reels of film. I also became familiar with the sound of the scrolling devices at high and low speeds. Each copy was $0.20, and I made lots of copies. It was well worth it in the end, though. Later, the library digitized its systems, allowing users to take snapshots of the periodicals electronically to save them on removable USB thumb drives. This was more green and environmentally friendly.

Looking at those box scores made me feel like we were all a part of history, and we were. Every win and loss that the Hutch-Tech Engineers had over the years was carefully and methodically documented, as were all the games in Section VI. We were small specks of history on a world and in a galaxy that was billions of years old.

* * *

The underlying principle/theme of *The Engineers: A Western New York Basketball Story* is Creating Ecosystems of Success. Even though I knew there was an abundance of teachable lessons in the story as I was writing it, I didn't have a name for this very important principle/theme when I first conceived of it. It was later given to me by my previously discussed mentor Mark. For me, he was like the *Rich Dad* Robert Kiyosaki referred to in his *Rich Dad Poor Dad* series—a man whom many skeptics argued was a fictional character Kiyosaki made up.

I cannot say whether Robert's Rich Dad is real or fake, but I *can* say that mine is real, as is his son Matt, collectively my financial team. In addition to the principle described in the previous paragraph, he gave me an abundance of others, and he underscores an especially important component of my writings, mentoring. After adopting me one day on a Northwest Airlines flight from Detroit to Washington, DC, Mark proceeded to pour things into me that I did not receive back in Buffalo.

This is not blaming my parents, but many of the things fell outside of their knowledge sets and world views. He poured into me key aspects of manhood and taught me lessons about investing money that would have taken me many more years to learn and incorporate on my own, if at all. He also taught me a lot of valuable lessons about politics, history, and society, which I would not have learned within my own bloodline.

He did not charge me for any of it either. He simply saw a desire to learn, a need to transfer his knowledge, and he allowed me to benefit from what he knew. It was like my relationship with Coach Ken Jones, again a key figure in *The Engineers*. I was one of many of his protégés—vessels looking to be filled with his knowledge and wisdom. This, again, is not to say that my parents were bad parents—they were quite the opposite. It is just to say that sometimes the expertise we need to achieve our dreams or to become successful may come from outside our bloodlines. The same was true for my basketball dream in my teens and some of my later endeavors in life.

Creating Ecosystems of Success is the central principle of *The Big Words Blog Site*, which I created to continue to build my presence as a writer as I worked on *The Engineers* and a science fiction novel I wrote called *The Second Star*. When *The Engineers* is finished and ready to present to the world, I hope that my blog will still be in existence and will have grown. Again, in most of my writings, there is a core theme of mentoring, something I hope comes out in *The Engineers*. Mentors are critical. For the thing we're interested in, they can point us in the direction in which we should go and allow us to benefit from their knowledge and wisdom. Having them and not having them can vastly alter the course of our lives.

"Excellence is grounded in specific environments!" The last thing I'll say about Creating Ecosystems of Success is that *The Engineers* is a 'Gladwellian' story. It was in part inspired by the works of the great Malcolm Gladwell, one of my heroes. Gladwell is a master of explaining things and understanding historical events, in some instances sharing *revisionist* history. The above-mentioned mentor introduced me to Creating Ecosystems of Success and turned me onto Malcolm Gladwell by giving me a copy of *David and Goliath,* which dealt with how personal disadvantages can be turned into advantages, something my work will challenge readers to do.[15]

You will see hints of one of Malcolm's other great works, *Outliers* in *The Engineers*.[16] In *Outliers*, Malcolm discusses how environments impacted the successes of some of the world's most notable people. In other words, they were positioned in those environments to be who they became and didn't do everything

---

[15] (Gladwell, David and Goliath: Underdogs, Misfits, and the Art of Battling Giants; Reprint Edition, 2015)

[16] (Gladwell, Outliers: The Story of Success; Reprint Edition, 2011)

on their own. Furthermore, environments change. You can thus be assured that this isn't a story strictly about basketball and there are deeper meanings.

This is a good place to note another theme of *The Engineers*, and that's that people are different things to different people, and even our heroes have critics and faults. I wrote an essay discussing this involving Coach Jones. Like Coach Jones, Malcolm has his critics and detractors too. Malcolm drew considerable ire following a debate with another thought leader, Douglas Murray, whom I've also come to respect. His latest book at the time of this writing is entitled, *The War on the West*.[17] Our heroes are not always right, and I actually sided with Murray in that debate which involved whether we could trust traditional media in our modern age. Again, our heroes are not infallible, and they aren't always right.

* * *

There were several inspirations for *The Engineers: A Western New York Basketball Story*. During my one year at the State University of New York College at Brockport, author Dr. Gerald Early presented his book entitled, *Daughters* one evening.[18] At eighteen years of age, I sensed that I might one day want to be a writer just like him. Maybe it was an epiphany or something natural within my spirit. After he finished speaking, my curiosity took over, and I approached him. I asked him what it took to become a writer.

"What did you just ask him?" My friend Schwizer Phinazee, a Rochester native, inquired with his signature sarcasm after watching me talk to Dr. Early for a few minutes. Schwizer was a good friend that year, and we unfortunately lost contact after I transferred from Brockport to Johnson C. Smith University in Charlotte, NC.

"I asked him about the keys to becoming a writer. He told me, 'You have to *read* a lot, and you have to *write* a lot!'" I never forgot Dr. Early's words. I didn't know how I would start writing for our school newspaper though at the time, something he recommended to start gaining experience. I had not written anything for public consumption before. What I did do was keep a journal both by hand and then digitally, starting in the mid-1990s. I'd also read numerous books on a variety of topics aside from my science training. I continued reading.

I have always loved narrative stories, which is what *The Engineers: A Western New York Basketball Story* is. *The Autobiography of Malcolm X*, which I coincidently read for the first time in an English class at Hutch-Tech High School, made a lasting impression on me. The book was based upon the experiences and reflections of the grown-up, older Malcolm X, looking back at the peaks and valleys of his life

---

[17] (Murray, 2022)

[18] (Early, 1994)

with clarity, understanding, and wisdom. *The Engineers* may thus read a lot like *The Autobiography of Malcolm X*.[19]

It may also read like the television (TV) show *The Wonder Years*, which was my favorite show growing up. I loved watching the adult Kevin Arnold look back at his younger self's journey toward manhood. He did not understand the deeper significance of those years until he was older. At a young age, I could relate to Kevin's journey. The ending sequence of the show stirs something inside me every time I watch it, even now. It is like the feeling I get when watching the ending of the movie *The Outsiders* when Pony Boy finds Johnny's letter in his book and reads his deceased friend's words about innocence and life's simple beauties and things being new and golden, like sunsets.

One of my favorite movies is *The Shawshank Redemption*. As Morgan Freeman's character, Red narrates the movie, it always makes me feel like I'm in Kindergarten, listening to an old record while lying on a carpet or watching an old film in the early 1980s. It was a prison movie, but it had a strong friendship component and dealt with the strength and resiliency of the human spirit, one of Stephen King's storytelling hallmarks.

The same is true for *The Green Mile*, also originally written by Stephen King and then directed by Frank Darabont, just like *The Shawshank Redemption*. Other favorite narrative movies are *American Beauty*, *Forrest Gump*, *Goodfellas*, *Casino* and *Paid in Full*. The latter three movies were all based on real-life events, and once again, all dealt with people and the strength and resiliency of the human spirit.

I was also inspired by John U. Bacon's book entitled, *Three and Out: Rich Rodriguez and the Michigan Wolverines in the Crucible of College Football* and the many stories about Michigan sports.[20] What better and more storied sports school is there than my alma mater, the University of Michigan? There were many older, grizzled football coaches like Fritz Crisler, Fielding Yost, Bo Schembechler, Gary Moeller, and Lloyd Carr who undergird the lore of the football program. That's just the coaches. There are also legions of players who have worn the maize and blue over the years. I'm not just saying this because I'm an alumnus, but in the book (and others), Bacon clearly lays out the heritage of the school's storied football program, which is inspiring to learn about.

There were so many subplots and conspiracies that led to Coach Rodriguez's lack of success at Michigan. In anything, there is always a lot going on behind the scenes that the layperson cannot see. By nature, the fans in the stands focus on the results on the field and typically not on what is happening behind the scenes. Bacon's most recent book entitled, *Endzone: The Rise, The Fall, and The Return of*

---

[19] (Haley, 1990)

[20] (Bacon, Three and Out: Rich Rodriguez and Michigan Wolverines in the Crucible of , 2011)

Michigan Football, touched upon the difference one man can make for countless others, in this case Head Coach Jim Harbaugh.[21] Mitch Albom's book *The Fab Five* was powerful, too, which chronicled Michigan's storied five freshmen who briefly lifted the school's basketball program to the top of the college basketball world.[22] The Fab Five is mentioned in *The Engineers* for how they forever changed the basketball world.

Another significant inspiration was *Hoop Dreams*, the documentary based on the high school basketball careers and dreams of Arthur Agee and William Gates from Chicago. Though I was nowhere near as talented as Agee and Gates, I could sympathize with what they went through. Both had dreams of going to the National Basketball Association (NBA), but life happened to them as it does everyone. Arthur had no control over the decisions his father Bo made or the nation's economics of the time, which ultimately affected his playing career. William suffered a career-threatening knee injury his junior year of high school, and when he returned as a senior, he wasn't the same player. Each time I watch *Hoop Dreams*, I feel something inside. If possible, I would love to meet the two stars of the movie one day.

And finally, I want to acknowledge Robert T. Kiyosaki of *Rich Dad Technologies*, whom I discussed earlier in this preface. Robert has received a lot of flak over the years from a lot of people. Two of the main questions that come up when discussing him are whether his Rich Dad is fictional or real and whether he owns the real estate that he said he owns in his books. In my own desire to get involved in real estate investing, I was faced with those same scrutinizing questions, and believe me, they weren't pleasant.

I'm acknowledging him and his efforts for attempting to reveal the secrets of wealth to the rest of us who have never conceived of such things, for causing some of us to dream, and for encouraging us to follow our personal talents and missions. Many of us were taught to simply live to work for someone else, which is the normal trajectory of life for much of the population. I also want to thank him for introducing the concept of making multiple derivatives of oneself, a simple but valuable concept discussed in his book *Conspiracy of the Rich*.[23]

In the fall of 2011, I was blessed to be able to take Stephen Covey's *The 7 Habits of Highly Effective People* training through my day job. One of the key teachings of that training is the creation of a personal mission statement. One of the bullets of my mission statement is to "Improve the lives of others through monetary gifts or through the giving of my time." One of the ways to do that is to tell stories through

---

[21] (Bacon, Endzone: The Rise, Fall, and Return of Michigan Football; Reprint Edition, 2016)

[22] (Albom, 1993)

[23] (Kiyosaki, Rich Dad's Conspiracy of the Rich: The 8 New Rules of Money, 2014)

writing, and this all wraps back into the principle of Creating Ecosystems of Success.

The Engineers: A Western New York Basketball Story is thus an extension of that part of my personal mission statement. Through sharing this story, which people close to me have never heard, I will be able to teach others, particularly young black males and young males in general, about life in an era where it's needed more than ever. I will teach them what it takes to succeed in this competitive and unfair world where there are many gray areas, and where there are often tradeoffs for our desired outcomes. Young males of all cultures could use these lessons. Hell, I'll go a step further and say that everyone could use the lessons and themes undergirding my story.

There are a lot of lessons about basketball as well, but the deeper lessons are about life and how to persevere through the hard times and ultimately succeed. It is an up-and-down story of hope and perseverance, something all people in the United States could use today. And with that, I hope that you, the reader, enjoy part one of *The Engineers: A Western New York Basketball Story*. I also hope that there is something in it for you or someone you know.

Writing this story and seeing the project through to the end was a huge piece of my second dream, and I pray that this one will come to fruition. There wasn't room in the dedications, so I'm going to thank you all here. Thank you to Dr. Gerald Early for your aforementioned advice in this preface. It led to me starting my own blog, and that led to the generation of the investment capital for this project. Thank you also to the search engine optimization company that partnered with me so that I could generate that capital. Finally, thank you to my financial team for your expert guidance on this project and in other endeavors.

A Mid-1990s Battle of Bulls and Engineers

This year could have been different though. With the Hutch-Tech boys basketball team's returning class of 1995 senior core, and the returning highly talented group from Buffalo Traditional, there was a lot of anticipation for that game. There was a lot of experience on both sides and the Engineers were talented in their own right. I was excited to see what they could do against the Bulls. The class of 1995 players had ascended as their own group just the way Coach Jones intended for all the classes to do, and it was now their time. What they were doing was the exact thing I hoped to experience as a senior a year earlier with my class of 1994. It was what I innocently dreamed about several years earlier. Life had its own plans for all of us though…

Prologue. My First Success and Failure Lesson, My First Great Adventure, and Innocent Basketball Dreams

"I just cannot imagine how much work it would take to write something like that!" **—Coach Francis Daumen, Head Coach, the Hutch-Tech boys' basketball team, 1993-94, 2015 on Facebook**

"So, what is this book about, Anwar?" In her soft and motherly voice, Alice Jones, Coach Ken Jones' wife, asked me one of the most important questions at that time about my book project. It was one of my many visits with the Joneses to their Amherst, NY home. The first was twenty years earlier, in the 1990s. They spent most of their year in San Antonio, TX now. I reunited with them there about a year and a half earlier in the fall of 2012. Just south of the north campus of the University at Buffalo on Millersport Highway, their suburban neighborhood was more tranquil than the east side of Buffalo where I was from, only miles away.

In the fall of 2012, it had been just under twenty years since I had last spoken to them. They looked the same, a testament to their excellent genes, health habits, or both. I had not interacted with Alice much then, but I remembered her at Coach Jones' basketball camp. I also remembered her briefly stopping into our tiny Hutch-Tech gym during random practices in the winter afternoons. She was of Mexican descent, and just like then, she had the same tanned-brownish complexion and curly-bushy hair, which was now a little grayer. She wore glasses and looked professorial, consistent with being a retired educator. She was petite and had a gentle way about her.

Coach Jones still wore his sweatsuits and had his birdlike facial features. He had a sharp nose and chin. He also still had a little bit of hair on the top of his head with longer curly hair on the sides, which was now completely gray. He still looked like an older white college professor from any university. With two knee replacements, he moved slower now, though he was still quite active. This was part of his secret to managing and beating his Parkinson's Disease. If no one said anything, you would not know he had it.

In addition to staying physically active, his other key to managing his condition was something called deep brain stimulation. There were two subtle lumps on the top of his head. Underneath the skin, there were electrodes that penetrated his brain, stimulating his Dopaminergic neurons. This region of the brain loses function, causing Parkinson's characteristic symptoms. Coach Jones was a fighter, though, and was doing everything he could to stay physically active. Sitting still was not natural for people like him.

Coach Jones wrote his own book entitled, *Fighting Back* to educate others about how he dealt with his Parkinson's Disease. It was one of many books he wrote.[24,25] The cover of the book featured a picture of him lifting weights with a determined look. It discussed his deep brain stimulation, as well as his rigorous daily stretching and weightlifting routines. It also contained words from his doctor, who administered the treatment, and some of his poetry. He gave copies of the book to me, Michael Mann, and Adonis Coble, two other former players from the class of 1992. They were seniors on the 1991–92 Hutch-Tech boys' basketball team. That was my sophomore year and my first season on the team. In the fall of 2014, the four of us had lunch at Louie's on Transit Road in Tonawanda, NY, along with Michael Mann's two kids. Coach Jones loved Louie's.

Coach Jones developed a love for poetry in his retirement and wrote a poem about me the first time I visited San Antonio. It was entitled, *What A Guy*. The Joneses let me stay at their house for my final night there. It was a bit of a restless sleep for me, and I heard him stirring around late at night in his Wayside Drive home as I lay in their guest bedroom. Just before leaving for the airport early that morning, he gave it to me. He handed me a piece of paper in the hallway of his home, just looking at me without saying anything. As I scanned it and realized what it was, I slowly smiled in happy disbelief. It was one of the greatest gifts I will ever receive. We hugged, and I departed for the airport and my life in Washington, DC.

"It is going to be about a bunch of different things," I replied vaguely, looking around the backyard and not wanting to sound like a bullshitter. Many people say they are going to do things and do not finish them. Many people had set out to write books but never followed through. After visiting them initially in San Antonio, I had made only minimal progress.

I knew the fabric of the story itself in terms of events, but the themes of the book would not become clear to me until later in the process. At that point, I just knew that it was something I had to do. The season to pursue this dream had come, and I was there to take action. I was wide open, looking at the proverbial basket, just like a player on the court. I just had to shoot life's ball at my dream.

"I foresee the book being kind of like the '80s TV series *The Wonder Years*," I said, choosing my words carefully, sipping on a beer Coach Jones had gotten me. At some point I would have to be able to concisely discuss the book, and this was good practice. "In the TV show, Kevin Arnold looks back to his childhood years as an adult, gleaning the lessons from his experiences and making sense of what

---

[24] (Jones, FIGHTING BACK: A WAY OF DEALING WITH NEUROLOGICAL DISORDERS, 2013)

[25] (Jones, DEFENSE: The Greatest Equalizer in the Game, 2018)

he didn't understand then. It was a powerful show for me. I look back at those years on the team in much the same way."

"Oh, by the way, the scrapbooks I gave you, I have a story to tell you about them," Coach interjected, which startled me as Alice started saying something about my synopsis of *The Engineers*. I thought Coach might want his beloved scrapbooks back. They were archives of Buffalo and Rochester high school basketball which he methodically captured starting in the 1960s from issues of the *Buffalo News* and the *Rochester Democrat and Chronicle* newspapers.

Coach Jones loved high school basketball. He was both a curator and a keeper of the history of the high school *Cage* battles on the hardwood floors in the many Western New York gymnasiums. 'Cage' and 'Cagers' were frequently used by the *Buffalo News* sports writers when referring to the high school basketball games they covered. The term originated from the early professional games (1910-1915) played in actual cages to separate the audiences from the playing court to speed up the games by keeping the balls in bounds.

He also saved clippings in his personal archive from smaller town-specific publications and other materials from across the state relating to high school basketball. I would have taken the entire collection, but based upon space and how heavy they were, I only kept them starting in the late 1980s when Duke University legend Christian Laettner attended the Nichols School near Delaware Park.

"Many of those life lessons have repeated in different situations after high school and into my adult life," I continued.

"So those are the kinds of things the book will be about," I said, turning back to Alice.

"Okay," Alice smiled, easing my angst. "Sometimes we do not know what books are about until we are deep into them or even until they are finished."

"As I tell my narrative story about what happened during my years on the Hutch-Tech boys' basketball team, the life lessons I learned will be infused into it and will hopefully benefit someone else," I said, turning to Coach. "Coach, you had a story about the scrapbooks?"

"Oh, yes, I do. It is a good thing you came and took them when you did," Coach said, sipping his beer. "Our basement flooded soon after you left, and the rest were ruined. I took them out and dumped them in the trash. My son Lee saw them in the dumpster and went in to try to salvage what he could get. So, you now have all that is left of them!"

We talked for a little while longer. Eventually, Coach and I shot baskets on the hoop in his driveway until around 5 or 6 p.m. that day. It was a Saturday. We could have been two kids on a playground. The Joneses offered to take me to dinner that evening, but I told my girlfriend at the time that I would meet up with her for dinner after her 6 p.m. broadcast on TV. I felt bad about not going with them that night. They had given me so much. That was in August of 2013 or 2014, I believe. Coach and Alice went back to San Antonio shortly thereafter, and I returned to my life in Washington, DC.

* * *

So, what is *The Engineers: A Western New York Basketball Story* about? Alice Jones was spot on. Though I felt what the book was about in an innate way, the underlying themes and messages did not become clear until after my third and fourth revisions. Interviewing other coaches and players, which I will discuss later, gave me additional clarity. As I conducted my forty-three interviews, key themes emerged. Many were like my own. They transcended players, coaches, schools, and life. With that, I will start with what *The Engineers* isn't about.

First, everyone thinks they are an *expert* on basketball, even people who have never played an organized game, ran a play, or done a drill. Teaching a younger sibling to dribble and put the ball through the hoop is enough to be an expert for some people. While *The Engineers* is a basketball story, it is not entirely about teaching one to become a great basketball player. It does, however, contain many secrets to excelling on the hardwood and in any craft in life. It is not a book about making it to the NBA. If you are a lucky kid with God-given physical gifts though, and blessed to have everything lined up just right for you, this story can help you. The significance of things 'lining up just right', is discussed throughout the story.

Simply put, *The Engineers* is my first success and failure lesson in life—my first great adventure, which set the stage for all that came after it. My home was my first ecosystem in life where values and some success and failure lessons were instilled. There was much more to learn though, and I could only get those lessons outside with other kids and adults.

The story of *The Engineers* was my first *big* life lesson. Winning our city and sectional titles, like our 1990–91 Hutch-Tech boys' basketball team, was something I hoped for and agonized over as a teen. I did dream about the NBA and being like Michael Jordan before that, but eventually my eyes settled on success at the high school level.

As you will see in the story if you read it, I did not understand all that went into achieving those goals. On the front end, I did not understand all the pieces that needed to come together to win a city title and a sectional title. There were so many aspects of preparation and things that needed to line up just right, as is often the case in sports and life itself. I have thought about it for years afterward and will probably always look back on those years, wondering about how things might have been different if the proverbial basketball of life had bounced a little differently for my teammates and me. Wondering about the 'what if' is a curse and an eternal question that plagues many athletes and, in some instances, fans.

Prologue. My First Success and Failure Lesson, My First Great Adventure, and Innocent Basketball Dreams

Is it a long book? Yes, it is, and it is not for everybody. *The Engineers* chronicles the six-year stretch spanning from the seventh to the twelfth grades, a bit of a cocoon where I started in one form and emerged on the back end as someone (and something) else. I start my narrative story with the seminal moment that made me dream about the great game of basketball, the 1988–89 NBA Eastern Conference playoffs. It was game five of the opening quarterfinal round where the great Michael Jordan single-handedly lifted his Chicago Bulls over the Cleveland Cavaliers with 'The Shot'.

I start my narrative story with a 30,000-foot look at the basketball ecosystem in which *The Engineers* takes place, Section VI within the New York State Public High School Athletic Association. Section VI was composed of all the city and suburban public high schools in Western New York. There were also private schools in our area. I discuss how every team's basketball quest started each year with high hopes and ended with varying results. Furthermore, I discuss how the fortunes of each team, their players, and coaches were in part impacted by factors both in and out of their control. Some were personal, environmental, systemic, and unique to the locale and municipality. In hindsight, it is the phenomenon of equal opportunities with varying outcomes described in the preface of this book.

The Engineers is a long and windy road of discovery, innocence, and heartbreak, but a fun one. It will surely spark nostalgia in players and coaches alike, retired and current. The early stages track my quest to play basketball for my middle school team. For a kid who wanted to play, I knew nothing about playing the game in a meaningful and competitive way. I just wanted to be a part of my school team.

Transitioning from the seventh to the eighth grade, with little to no male supervision, I had little guidance regarding my development and returned essentially the same player skill-wise. Major themes of *The Engineers* are thus mentoring and skills development—what happens when you have them and when you do not. I underpin the story with the significance of who is around you helping you develop your craft at a young age and how kids excel when they have early mentorship in comparison to the kids who do not. I also discuss how kids develop differently both physically and mentally depending upon a multitude of factors, including genetics and environment.

The bulk of the story takes place at Hutchinson Technical High School, or Hutch-Tech for short, the home of the maroon and gold Engineers. Throughout the story, I refer to Coach Jones' 1990–91 team with reverence as they created a magic that engulfed the entire school during my freshman year. It caused some of us to dream and set a standard that some of us hoped to follow. In the aftermath of the 1990–91 team's magical season, my story arc merges with Coach Jones' and other Hutch-Tech boys' basketball players.

The remainder of the story chronicles the journeys of the 1991–92, the 1992–93, and the 1993–94 teams. I specifically capture the unique personalities of each group, how the players fit together, the challenges of each team, and each team's fate using a narrative story. I also look back at the 1994–95 team after graduating. The journey becomes a *Lord of the Rings*-type of story where characters come and go for any number of reasons, some tragic and some due simply to life's circumstances.

The themes of *The Engineers* further emerge through the stories of each team. I will name a few. While the power of dreams was emphasized in the preface, it is important to also have perseverance and toughness, as life often isn't always a smooth ride. In addition to the 'Xs and Os' Coach Jones taught us, he talked to us regularly about perseverance through the difficult stretches in games and in life. As one clergyman said at his memorial service, he ministered to us through the game. His one quote that has stayed with me over the years is, "Your *ATTITUDE* determines your *ALTITUDE*!" That being said, there were many more.

Dealing with change is another major theme in *The Engineers,* as things do not always stay the same and often deviate from what and where we thought they would be. Life is not always a straight line either. It is not always fair, nor is it perfect in terms of its intended outcomes and its subsequent results. Life further requires personal adjustments and resilience depending upon what you encounter. Going back to the preface, my mentor discussed the concept of life not being perfect when I asked his opinion about what the book should say to today's young people. Making peace with the outcomes of life is also a critical theme.

Friendship and leadership are major themes as well. In some instances, we start down the paths of life with our friends, and at certain junctures in the road, life separates us. If it is something we really want to do and a specific road we are traveling on, we must find ways to keep going, even when those we have started off with fall away. This is not something that is easy to do, especially if the original plan was to make it to the destination together.

Leadership is another theme for which there are multiple contexts. The first of which is leading oneself. Another context involves leading others. It is a crucial element in everything as leadership and leadership styles can be the difference between teams winning and losing, members of the team becoming their best selves, or becoming disillusioned and losing hope altogether. This goes for both the sports and adult work worlds. It is a key aspect of life.

Another context of leadership is, once again, mentoring, perhaps the most critical context for it. As described in the preface, mentors can make all the difference in the world through their experience and wisdom. In any craft, mentors can help their mentees reach never-imagined heights. Likewise, the lack of mentors can leave those in need left to figure things out on their own, if at all. A young person might have the desire to do something, but without proper guidance, achieving that goal becomes exponentially more difficult. Mentors can come from anywhere. They can come from inside or outside of a family's bloodlines, but they are critical.

The story of each Engineers team coincides with my own personal journey through high school, the challenges of puberty and adolescence, and my learning to become a solid student. A good portion of the story also looks at some of the other programs and players in Section VI, some of which seemed to win every year and in different ways than how we did it at Hutch-Tech. The story concludes with me looking back on the journey and understanding what it all meant, and how those experiences have translated into the adult world, numerous workplaces, and the other arenas of life.

* * *

"You went to San Antonio to visit Coach Jones? Why did you do that?" My best friend Gabriel Smith questioned me over the phone from Phoenix, AZ.

I guess it sounded odd that I would journey to Texas to see my high school basketball coach with me being in my thirties at the time. Just like Coach Jones, my best friend Gabe is a central character in *The Engineers*. Some of the dynamics described in the last section about the themes of the book played out in our friendship as teens, and it is a brotherhood that has survived many circumstances over the years, and it has remarkably lasted into our adult lives.

Early on, I understood this narrative story would be more effective if I drew upon the accounts and experiences of other teammates, players, and coaches who were there with me at that time. I thus tracked down forty-three players and coaches with varying degrees of success. A former teammate I saw regularly when visiting Buffalo was the above-mentioned Adonis Coble, one of our seniors from the 1991–92 team, my beloved sophomore season. Adonis was in my brother's class of 1992, and I had fond memories of being teammates with him that season. He attended the Mount Olive Baptist Church, my mother's church near Delavan Avenue and Grider Street on the east side of Buffalo.

In early August of 2012, I saw Adonis at Sunday service after not seeing him on previous visits. He looked about the same. He was slightly shorter than me and had a little more bulk on his frame now. His face filled out just like all of ours had, and he still had the same soft and high-pitched voice. I approached him about an interview for my book project, and he agreed. Having a short temper during our playing days, he now evolved into a mellow and even-keeled family man. He was always a *character* guy, but I never considered us to be close. I was actually a little afraid of him when we were teammates, but some things change with time.

Surprisingly, he knew where to find Coach Jones and Michael Mann, and he gave me both their phone numbers. I was able to immediately contact Coach Jones. Tracking Michael Mann down was a little trickier. I originally gave an account of my reconnecting with Coach Jones in this prologue, but for the sake of brevity, I moved it to the bonus chapter entitled, *A True Student of the Game*, which is at the end of part two of *The Engineers.*

While the final version of *The Engineers: A Western New York Basketball Story Part One* is lengthy (but efficient), it was almost twice as long before making my third and fourth revisions. I realized the story had too much *fat* in some places, some of which disrupted the flow of it. I needed to do more *showing* and less *telling*, as they say in the writing world. The material that slowed down the main story was too valuable to leave on the cutting room floor though, as they say in the movie business. It is thus captured in bonus chapters at the end of the main story for both parts one and two of *The Engineers*. There are three bonus chapters for part one. In addition to a tribute to the 1990–91 team, there are bonus chapters on the program Coach Jones established and a story about our little old box of a gym.

* * *

The original title for this book was simply *The Engineers*. I added the second half because I wanted Western New Yorkers all around the country and the world to see and identify with it. Western New Yorkers as a population of people have spread out across the United States. As you will also see, this narrative story is not just about me, but it's also about others from that time–teams, coaches, and our basketball ecosystem, Section VI. To some degree it also touches upon Section V in the Rochester area as well, our sister city and its surrounding towns.

Crafting this story was hard but fun work, just like the great game of basketball. The first draft was raggedy, as most are. Once Coach Jones gifted me his scrapbooks, I grounded the story in the actual games I discussed, giving it authenticity. I also continued interviewing teammates, players from other schools, coaches, and even relatives. I want to thank those of you who shared your stories with me and added depth to this project (see the front and back of this book).

Who is *The Engineers* for in terms of audience? I struggled with this question after participating in a writing advance in the spring of 2018 hosted by the lovely veteran writer Kamryn Adams, but the answers eventually came to me. This story is for a lot of people. It is for sports fans. It is also for athletes who once dreamed and saw their dreams crash and burn but who were also made better by their experiences.

It is for individuals who want to do something but do not have mentors. I am particularly thinking about boys who have had to figure things out without the guidance of father figures or older men, a prevalent theme in our modern Western world, one which may be causing a larger crisis. It is an uncomfortable theme for some in our modern progressive era in the United States, but it is an important one. *The Engineers: A Western New York Basketball Story* is likewise a story for young people who are pursuing interscholastic athletics and competition beyond that level. Finally, it is for people who like stories about the human spirit.

I thus present to you *The Engineers: A Western New York Basketball Story*, a tale about basketball, but more importantly, a tale about life that contains lessons and themes that translate far beyond the basketball court into every other arena of life. Going back to my guiding principle in the preface of Creating Ecosystems of Success, it is my hope that this work, while being therapeutic and entertaining for me, will help others. With that, I will start the story with a discussion of the ecosystem in which *The Engineers* takes place, Section VI within the New York State Public High School Athletic Association, the first training ground and learning laboratory for many of us who were blessed to participate in interscholastic athletics. It was a training ground that would impact and shape us for years to come.

Part one of *The Engineers: A Western New York Basketball Story* is entitled, *Innocent Basketball Dreams*. The name embodies the feeling I got when I saw Michael Jordan hit his magical shot against the Cleveland Cavaliers. It also embodies the feeling I got when I saw the 1990–91 Hutch-Tech boys' varsity basketball team play and when I heard about their many victories. It further embodies the feelings inside of me when I earned a spot on the varsity basketball team as a sophomore and received my jersey/uniform. I dreamt of being like Michael Jordan and his Chicago Bulls, and I dreamt of being like the 1990–91 Hutch-Tech boys' basketball team, who were just a few years older than me.

Everything was fresh and new, and the sky was the limit in middle school and my freshman year at Hutch-Tech. Anything was possible. Going back to the concept of dreams, they are important things for young people and adults alike. They give us ideas and create visions. Our journeys in life start though, when we step out onto the road in pursuit of them. Once we do, life becomes like the great game of basketball itself, where the outcomes can be anything on any given night, depending upon any number of variables. In some instances, our pathways toward those dreams are a clear and straight line. In other instances, they are squiggly and convoluted lines that we must figure out gradually as our journeys unfold. This was the case in my basketball story and my life.

Finally, parts one and two of *The Engineers* are stories about life, success, learning perseverance, and dealing with potential failures in life where the outcomes of everything are uncertain. This is a story not just about the great game of basketball, but it is also a story about people from different backgrounds and different personality makeups, and how they fit together when working towards common goals and missions. It is a story about innocence, learning to strive, and redemption after dealing with hardships. It is a story needed now more than ever in our modern society, our country, and our world.

Chapter 1. The Yale Cup, Section VI, and the Far West Region: Our Basketball Ecosystem

"The Yale Cup wasn't represented in Section VI—there was no state championship eligibility or anything like that. My graduating class and the class after us—were really upset that in 1971 or 1972, they finally allowed the Buffalo Public Schools to play in Section VI!"
—Phillip R. Richardson, Head Coach, the Hutch-Tech boys' basketball team, the mid-1990s, September 2016

"I wish New York State did what they do down here in Florida. In Florida, they don't call them 'sectionals', they call them 'districts'," said Coach Pat Monti, the coach of arguably the most dominant boys' basketball program ever in Western New York, the LaSalle Explorers of Niagara Falls. "When you play in your district championship game, win or lose, you're not out of the tournament. The winner hosts the loser from the district next to you, and your district loser goes to play the other winner so that the two teams could end up meeting again to see who advances to the final four." Coach Monti had retired in Florida with his wife, Kathleen. He was still immersed in the great game of basketball even in retirement, but the rules for postseason play were slightly different in Florida than in New York State.

The story world for *The Engineers: A Western New York Basketball Story* is the westernmost region of New York State, but most of the story was physically crafted and revised in the Washington DC area, specifically Northern Virginia. The 'DMV' (DC, Maryland, and Virginia) likewise has its own unique basketball history and lineage of great players and those who never made it beyond the lower levels of the game, just like many other regions. Some names that come to mind are: Adrian Dantley, Derrick Wittenberg, Len Bias, Adrian Branch, Juan Dixon, Michael Beasley, and Kevin Durant. That's just a short list. Chicago and New York City have their own unique basketball histories, in addition to many small towns and municipalities across the United States.

I wanted to share with you the reader that you likely have experienced or observed the themes in this story play out where you're from, if you haven't experienced them personally yourself. This story is thus universal and relatable to other geographic regions. The great game of basketball is the same everywhere, as are the dynamics around it, no matter where it is played. These themes have also played out in non-sports arenas and contexts, as myself and my interviewees collectively acknowledged.

* * *

Every year around late October and early November something special happens in gymnasiums across the United States. Basketball season starts. Coaches ponder their upcoming schedule and how to get their team prepared for the four-month journey that lies ahead. They ponder the players they'll keep on their rosters. Veteran players return to repeat or build upon the successes or failures of the previous year. Prospective players hope to earn a spot on their school's varsity basketball team and to wear their school colors in competition on the hardwood. A roster spot on one's varsity basketball team was an elite and prestigious position in the early '90s.

* * *

Dr. James Naismith invented the great game of basketball in 1891 in Springfield, MA. The game spread across the United States and the world over the next century and beyond. In the United States basketball was a way of life for much of the population. Basketball ecosystems were in every municipality, county, city, and state. Whether you were from Arizona, California, Georgia, Ohio, Texas, Wyoming, or any of the 50 states, there were basketball ecosystems where you grew up. Orange leather and rubber basketballs manufactured by companies like Baden, Rawlings, Spalding, and Wilson were dribbled and shot at basketball hoops everywhere, both indoors and outdoors.

Our basketball ecosystem was called Section VI. The New York Public High School Athletic Association (NYPHSAA) was comprised of 11 sections for its multiple interscholastic sports leagues and conferences. Each represented the many beautiful geographical regions that comprised New York State, spanning from the Great Lakes to the Adirondack Mountains, down to Long Island on the Atlantic Coast. Section VI was comprised of Erie, Niagara, Orleans, Chautauqua, and Cattaraugus counties.

While New York State had its very rural areas, it also had four medium-sized upstate cities along the Interstate 90 corridor. They were Buffalo, Rochester, Syracuse and Albany. All four were dwarfed by New York City. High school basketball-wise, most urban areas had city leagues surrounded by suburban leagues. These were peppered by a private school league or two. Most of the kids of color played in their city leagues. In cities like Buffalo and Rochester there was usually one city league, while there were several in major cities like Chicago and New York.

Chapter 1. The Yale Cup, Section VI, and the Far West Region: Our Basketball Ecosystem

***

By the late '80s Western New York had undergone significant changes since my grandparents' generation migrated north thirty or forty years earlier. Most of us born in the '70s and beyond heard stories of our fathers, uncles, and grandfathers working at the Bethlehem Steel Plant, earning solid wages doing backbreaking and, in some cases, hazardous work. The steel industry made Western New York, and particularly Buffalo, a thriving metropolitan area. By the late '80s and early '90s, all we had left were the abandoned steel mills in the City of Lackawanna, which was south of downtown. They were one of the few remnants of that fabled time when significant Italian, Jewish, and Polish populations still lived within the borders of the city.

The loss of those steel jobs created a service-oriented city, one with economic shortages manifesting in the city's public and private school systems. The shifted demographics played a role too, particularly the movement of the city's white residents out to the suburbs and the northern and southern parts of the city. It was a much different Buffalo for my generation, where the east and west sides of the city became predominantly Black and Puerto Rican. In *our* Buffalo, the 33 Expressway, also known as the Kensington Expressway, connected many of the suburbs directly to downtown. This critical artery ran through the former Humboldt Park, which is another *ghost* of our city only heard about in stories.

Our Buffalo missed out on something else the previous generations had enjoyed, professional basketball. In addition to having the Buffalo Bills and the Buffalo Sabres, there was a professional basketball franchise called the Buffalo Braves. They played downtown in the Buffalo Memorial Auditorium. We affectionately referred to it as 'The Aud', and its hardwood floors were once graced by such players as Bob McAdoo, Adrian Dantley, Randy Smith and many legendary opponents. Randy Smith founded the basketball league named after him, the Randy Smith Basketball League. It was still around in the early '90s, and many players affectionately referred to it as 'The Randy'.

It was said that before the NBA allowed our beloved Braves to move out to San Diego and Los Angeles to be remade into the Clippers, the professional basketball presence created an abundance of summer basketball leagues. This made Buffalo a fertile ground for growing basketball talent. It was a much different time, one my generation, and those after us, only heard about in stories and when seeing the Braves logo in pictures and on throwback sports apparel.

The Buffalo City high school basketball league was called the Yale Cup, which some of my peers now fondly refer to as 'The Yale'. I can't tell you when it was chartered, but it was probably as old as the schools which comprised it. I also can't tell you why it was named after an Ivy League school. Most of the schools comprising it were the opposite of the Ivy League, in terms of quality, by the early '90s. The same was true for our city football league, the Harvard Cup.

The Yale Cup league of the '90s was made up of fourteen schools. Some of the schools no longer exist due to economics, shifting demographics, or some combination of the two. Ours was a much different lineup of schools than in my mother and her peers' teen years or that of the kids today. East High School, for example, which I had heard about in numerous stories, was transformed into the Buffalo Vocational Technical Center (BVTC).

Hutchinson Central Technical High School, or Hutch-Tech, was the lone technical high school in the system. Some of the other schools were vocational high schools where the students learned skill trades. Others had pure academic curricula. There was one culinary arts school and one school for the visual and performing arts. The fourteen high schools were all interconnected with the same superintendent and the same athletic director, and all operated under the same anemic budget. In the early '90s, it was rumored that Buffalo Alternative, the school for the most ill-behaved students in our city, would get to compete in the Yale Cup, something that didn't come to fruition. The fourteen-school lineup and their respective nicknames and school colors included:

- Academy for the Visual and Performing Arts (aka Buffalo Arts or Performing Arts High School), the Cavaliers, black and gold
- Bennett High School, the Tigers, orange and blue
- Buffalo Traditional High School, the Bulls, navy blue and gold
- Burgard Vocational High School, the Bulldogs, red, blue and white
- City Honors High School, the Centaurs, burgundy and gray
- Emerson High School, the Eagles, red and white
- Grover Cleveland High School, the Presidents, green and white
- Hutch-Tech High School, the Engineers, maroon and gold
- Kensington High School, the Knights, green and gold
- Lafayette High School, the Violets, violet and white
- McKinley Vocational High School, the Macks, orange and black
- Riverside High School, the Frontiersman, purple and gold
- Seneca Vocational High School, the Indians, dark green and white
- South Park High School, the Sparks, red, black and white

In the '80s and '90s, the Buffalo Traditional Bulls, Burgard Bulldogs, McKinley Macks, Bennett Tigers, Grover Cleveland Presidents and the Kensington Knights ruled the Yale Cup. Other teams that stepped up to make runs were the Riverside

Frontiersman, the Hutch-Tech Engineers, the Seneca Indians, the City Honors Centaurs and the South Park Sparks. The teams that weren't very successful in those times were the Lafayette Violets, the Performing Arts Cavaliers, and the Emerson Eagles.

The Yale Cup was not an ideal league. It was under-budgeted and lacked the frills that the suburban and private schools had, including modern facilities, an athletic trainer for every school, and a 'feeder system' for its varsity programs. Feeder systems consisted of organized freshman and junior varsity programs designed to develop players at younger ages. The lack of these programs meant most of the players from the city were not well-trained prior to competition on the varsity level. As a result, most got started learning the fundamentals of the game late, if at all. Only a few of the Yale Cup schools had junior varsity programs, and those were voluntarily run by coaches who didn't get paid anything extra.

While most of the Yale Cup basketball players learned to play the game on neighborhood courts, city playgrounds, and hubs where the great players once congregated like Delaware Park, the suburban and private school players formally learned the game through developing in the aforementioned feeder systems. They also attended summer camps where they learned and reinforced the fundamentals of the game. This produced two distinctly different styles of basketball. There was the freelance, isolation-based, undisciplined *street* game from the city. Then there was the patient and methodical, fundamentals-based *suburban* style.

This training was evident when suburban players would set screens and picks, run plays, and readily shoot long-range jump shots in pickup games, things not emphasized in city community centers and on playgrounds. For us, it was about ball handling and going up strong to the hole. You were lucky if you figured out these two styles existed, or if you had someone to explain these nuances to you early in your development. The same is true in terms of realizing that the great players figured out how to blend both styles, something many kids didn't figure out until much later.

The Yale Cup league games were immediately after school. For road games, players left their last classes early to get to their opponents' gyms on time which were often across town, and they had to use public transportation to get there. Coaches often drove their starters to the games who were usually already dressed as the rest of the team gradually arrived. Except for pre- and postseason play, there was typically no riding together to the games on one bus.

There was no time to rest before the games as was done in the suburban and private schools where tipoffs were later in the evenings. In those environments, Mom, Dad, Grandma, and the entire community could consistently come to support their teams. There was no time for the players to sit in silence to focus their minds on the opponent and the game plan. In Buffalo, there were concerns about crime and safety after hours, and with good reason. Security would be needed for the league's fourteen schools after hours, a service with an additional price tag.

Back then the Yale Cup schools only played each other once a year in league play, meaning you only saw the inside of an opponent's gym every two years. This also meant that you only got one shot at opponents unless you played each other in non-league play, or if you were in the same sectional class where you could face each other again in postseason play. In most other leagues in Western New York, teams played each other twice in league play.

While we could easily be distinguished by our school colors, few if any of the Yale Cup teams had jerseys that displayed the name of the school. Our uniforms were made by the sports apparel manufacturer, Champion, out in Rochester, NY. Their slogan was, "It takes a little bit more to be a Champion!" Our uniforms were made with 100% nylon with block numbers on the front and back. Our home uniforms were mostly white, with the other colors of the school on the waistline of the trunks and along the edges of our uniforms. They were simple, but beautiful.

Yale Cup teams were known for having very little discipline and structure, and not playing any defense. The athletic talent was there though, as our league was full of tall and quick *thoroughbreds*, as my uncles called them. They were seldom coached in structured programs, and they often faltered in sectional play against lesser talented, but more disciplined teams. Running fast and jumping high were attributes often nullified by coaches who could 'X and O'. They were neutralized by teams that used patient and methodical offenses run by players possessing high 'basketball IQs' and highly developed fundamentals.

Coaching in the Yale Cup was an exclusive club. For a long time there were restrictions on who coached in the league. It was a duty reserved only for city school faculty members. Some coaches knew very little about basketball, had no passion for the game, and weren't driven to learn more. Some were simply gym teachers or English or history teachers appointed to the post by default. Only the players and other coaches knew who the quality coaches were. Talented players could often mask a coach's ineptitude for the casual onlooker.

Poor coaching could further be overcome to some degree with the help of fathers, uncles, older brothers, or mentors who could develop players outside of school. But what if they were not there to help? Players were left to figure things out on their own. Despite it all, the Yale Cup of the '80s and '90s was a magical league, one which gives me butterflies to this day when thinking about it.

* * *

A handful of Yale Cup basketball players made it to the NBA. Potentially the most famous of all was Bob Lanier of Bennett High School, who played his college basketball at St. Bonaventure University before becoming a star player for the Detroit Pistons. Trevor Ruffin, also of Bennett High School, made it to the NBA after playing at the University of Hawaii. He played for the Philadelphia 76ers and the Phoenix Suns. Cliff Robinson played at Riverside High School before helping to put the basketball program at the University of Connecticut on the map under legendary Head Coach Jim Calhoun. In the NBA he played for the Portland Trail Blazers and several other teams. Another player, Jason Rowe from Buffalo Traditional High School, had a lengthy professional career overseas.

There were numerous other great Yale Cup players in the 80s who didn't make it to college or the NBA. The most legendary of them all is probably No. 13, Ritchie Campbell, who played at DeSales and then Burgard. He was a legendary guard who could do whatever he wanted to do on the basketball court. He was Western New York's all-time scoring leader in the '90s with 2,355 points. There was also Marcus 'Ice Cream' Whitfield of Burgard, Ray Hall of McKinley, Curtis Aiken of Bennett, Keith Robinson of Grover Cleveland and Adrian Mitchell of Emerson.

* * *

The Yale Cup was just one piece of the entire mosaic that was Section VI basketball. There were also public suburban schools in Erie, Niagara, Orleans, Chautauqua and Cattaraugus Counties. In each county there were suburban cities and rural towns, each with their own conferences/leagues. They formed a proverbial ring around the Yale Cup League, and they played suburban-style basketball.

There were four Erie County Interscholastic Conferences (ECIC) where the suburban schools played. Jamestown, Lancaster, Orchard Park, and Sweet Home comprised the ECIC I. Williamsville North, Hamburg, Clarence, and Depew comprised the ECIC II. Williamsville South, Lackawanna, Cheektowaga Central, Amherst, and Pioneer comprised the ECIC III. Finally, John F. Kennedy (JFK), East Aurora, Cleveland Hill, and Alden comprised the ECIC IV. In the '90s, the dominant teams from the ECIC conferences were Lackawanna, Williamsville South and Clarence. Other teams made runs during that time, including Williamsville North, John F. Kennedy and Hamburg.

Some leagues contained schools from multiple counties and municipalities, such as the Niagara Frontier League which encompassed Niagara Falls, Grand Island, and even the towns of Kenmore and Tonawanda, both in Erie County. The Niagara-Orleans League encompassed schools in the western portion of Niagara and rural Orleans Counties. There were also leagues from the other more rural farm areas like those in Chautauqua and Cattaraugus Counties.

LaSalle Senior High School, Kenmore West, Lockport, the Nichols School and North Tonawanda made up the A Division of the Niagara Frontier League. Grand Island, Kenmore East, Lewiston-Porter, Niagara Falls Senior High School, and Niagara-Wheatfield comprised the B Division. Akron, Albion, Wilson, Medina, Starpoint, Barker, Royalton-Hartland and Newfane were the schools that made up the Niagara-Orleans League. These were towns most of us city kids never knew existed, and they felt like they were worlds away from our east-side neighborhoods, though they were only slightly northeast of Buffalo.

Finally, there were the conferences far south of Erie County, bordering Pennsylvania. There were the Chautauqua Conferences I-III and the Cattaraugus D. These were the schools in what is referred to in Western New York as the Southern Tier, the mountainous and rural areas that were typically hit the hardest by the lake effect snow during the wintertime.

These were the yearly battles in Section VI. Teams played non-league games starting in November throughout December. Everyone battled it out in their respective leagues from early January to the middle of February when sectional postseason play began and with it, the quest for the state tournament. It was a quest that took place across New York State in the aforementioned cities and regions.

In sectional play schools from each league competed in single-elimination tournaments that were divided into four classes based on school size: Classes A, B, C, and D, in descending order of enrollment. The Yale Cup teams didn't compete in postseason play until the early '70s. My generation, likewise, didn't know anything else besides competing in Section VI.

Up until the 1993–94 season, you had to win more than half of your league games to qualify for postseason play. In the Yale Cup that meant winning at least seven games. All Western New York teams were eventually allowed to compete in this final and most magical phase of the season, taking away some of its luster. It was called an *open* format, something some of the other sections were already doing.

In early March the Section VI winners squared off against the winners from Section V, from the Rochester area in the far West Regionals, for the right to go to the state tournament in Glens Falls, NY. There they would compete for the state championship with public schools from across New York State. With every game the competition stiffened and the stakes rose higher and higher.

The NYSPHSAA Championship wasn't the final stop though. The public school state champions competed in another four-team bracket the next week with the champions from the Catholic Schools State Tournament, the Independent Schools State Tournament, and finally, the Public School Athletic League Champions from New York City. From these four teams, Federation Champions were crowned in their respective classes. These teams and players got the ultimate bragging rights, nationwide recognition and top offers to play college basketball. Kids who weren't originally on college scouts' radars also benefited tremendously.

While not in Section VI, the area private schools also factored heavily into the Western New York high school basketball scene. Many of the private schools that were abundant just two decades earlier had closed, leaving only a handful. Interviews with some of the area coaches revealed that there were once ten private Catholic/Jesuit high schools. Some of these schools were Bishop Newman, Cardinal Doherty and Father Baker. Schools that remained open included Bishop Timon, Canisius, Cardinal O'Hara, Niagara Catholic, St. Joe's, St. Francis, St. Mary's/Lancaster, and Turner/Carroll. They made up the Monsignor Martin league.

The Monsignor Martin League schools matched up against the Section VI public schools in non-league play, whether it was in pre-season tournaments or individual games. They further competed in their own post-season playoffs. If a Monsignor Martin team made it through their playoffs, they could potentially meet up with one of the Section IV teams in the federation championship in Glens Falls. The same was true for Western New York's independent private schools such as the Nichols school, which Christian Laettner attended, the Park School, the Gow School, West Seneca Christian, St. Mary's School for the Deaf, and Christian Central.

In the early to mid-90s, Section V was much stronger than Section VI and dominated the Far West Regional games. They went on a run for about five to six years with a firm grasp on the matchups. At halftime of the 1992 Class A Far West Regional matchup between LaSalle and Greece Athena, Mike Harrington of the *Buffalo News* stated, "From top to bottom, the Section V schools face tougher competition night to night, competition that the Section VI schools don't see!"

Going back to our Yale Cup League, in addition to the lack of feeder systems, continuity wasn't always a given. With a few exceptions, the Yale Cup Champions were usually the best team that particular year in terms of athleticism and talent, and received a few favorable bounces. If these teams advanced to the Far West Regionals, they were often bested by teams that were used to stiffer competition and that had been together for a series of years. Another difference between the sections was that the private schools in Section V participated in sectional play with the public schools.

* * *

Every year shortly after the season concluded, the All-Western New York First Team was presented in the *Buffalo News* on the second Saturday of April. It was quite an honor for a high school student-athlete to receive such recognition for all to see. Deeper in the sports section were the second, third, and fourth teams, and the all-league teams for each conference. They all paid the price to get there, and for some of them, the ball bounced in the right direction, so to speak, on the court and in life as well.

Many players wanted to excel on that level, but didn't due to things like program/team instability and decisions made by peers, teammates, and faculty. Familial ecosystems factored in heavily too. Some players had plans of being special basketball players. Unforeseen circumstances however, derailed those plans, such as injuries, puberty, and other random life decisions and situations.

* * *

The next fall, the whole cycle would start over again. The coaches and players who really wanted to win didn't wait until the fall to get ready. Preparations started immediately after the previous season ended through spring sports, practices, camps, and summer leagues. Seniors obviously didn't return due to graduation. Sometimes underclassmen, often promising talents, didn't return or could not contribute the next year due to injuries which were particularly damaging if the player was lost for the whole year. Many players likewise never recovered mentally or physically after significant injuries.

There was also attrition due to poor grades, a lack of individual skills development over the summertime, a lack of focus, a lack of desire, family/life situations, or just being a teen and making the inevitable poor teen decisions. Some kids were not brought back the next year because the coach didn't foresee playing them much, and a fear of that kid poisoning the locker room. The kids who played even just a little bit were fortunate though, as there were other youth who never got the opportunity to put on a jersey and watched enviously from the stands, wondering what if?

Some coaches retired for greener pastures, burnout, or even fear of being unable to control the group of kids returning the following year. In some instances, the exact same coach and group of kids couldn't repeat their successful year because of any of the aforementioned reasons. Sometimes hungrier and more talented competition emerged in their league or their section.

This was the world of high school basketball in the late 80s and early 90s in Western New York, prior to the dawn of the Amateur Athletic Union (AAU) basketball as we know it today. Some would argue that it has usurped the importance of traditional high school basketball, however. None of this was unique to the Far West Region of New York State. Across the country, in every city and every town, and every gym, these scenarios played out.

Some kids dreamt of being great basketball players, winning their leagues, making deep sectional runs, and leaving high school as heroes. A select few reached that summit and beyond, while others did not. All were forever impacted by their high school basketball experiences. All look back with wonder for the rest of their lives, some lying in bed at night thinking about that missed shot, that injury, that low grade, that promising season that came off the rails—all of it. It's something that only those who competed could truly understand. For some student-athletes, these same experiences helped shape their lives and paradigms going forward into the many other arenas of life.

Chapter 2. The Birth of a Hoop Dream

"You better eat your Wheaties!" **—Michael Jordan, Wheaties Commercials, the late 1980s**

So how does an inner-city kid from the east side of Buffalo earn a PhD in a STEM (science, technology, engineering, and mathematics) field from one of the world's greatest universities? Depending on your spiritual beliefs, it involved some luck, but it also involved a set of values and experiences that were laid in place several years prior. The key experiences didn't involve science at all, but instead, the great game of basketball.

It involved a journey starting in middle school and ending early in college. It involved a long and winding road of discovery, innocent dreams, heartbreak, mentors (or lack of), complicated family dynamics, and learning about people and life. The classrooms for all this were the City of Buffalo, a gymnasium on the western part of the campus of Buffalo State College, and finally, an old box of a gym on the corner of South Elmwood Avenue and Chippewa Street in downtown Buffalo.

* * *

"...And Jordan takes the inbound pass. He dribbles it to the top of the key and gets a shot off on Ehlo...and YEAH, THE BULLS WIN IT! THE BULLS WIN IT!" These were the exact words of the Chicago commentators in the closing seconds of game five of the NBA's 1989 Eastern Conference quarterfinal series between the No. 6-seeded Chicago Bulls and the No. 3-seeded Cleveland Cavaliers. The other analyst laughed saying, "They've just upset the Cleveland Cavaliers," as the Richfield Coliseum in suburban Cleveland lay silent.

We had just witnessed 'The Shot'. It was one of many highlights from No. 23, Michael Jordan's storied basketball career; it was just the latest one at that time. This one was special, not just because of the drama surrounding it, but because it was also the next step in the Chicago Bulls' ascension to being one of the NBA's elite franchises. It further established Michael as the new face of the NBA and galvanized legions of No. 23's fans. It might be blasphemy, but for some of us, he became our God, at least for a time.

The Bulls' then head coach, Doug Collins, ran onto the court, smiling in disbelief, both fists extended up above his head and his curly bush flowing in the air. Just after scoring his game-winning forty-fourth point, Michael leaped up into the air pumping his fists multiple times as his teammates swarmed him, celebrating their 101–100 victory. It was a swarm of red, black, and white; the Chicago Bulls' colors. With the help of No. 33, Scottie Pippen, Jordan single-handedly lifted his team past an arguably deeper and superior Cleveland team that had bested them numerous times during that regular season. Cleveland's colors were light blue and red, and I felt like they were barbarians trying to defeat my beloved Bulls.

The Bulls advanced to the Eastern Conference semifinals, where they matched up against Coach Rick Pitino's No. 2—seeded blue and orange New York Knicks. They were another stronger team who had dominated the regular season series. They were also a young team, but deeper and more balanced. They were led by their young star center, No. 33, Patrick Ewing, and No. 13, Mark Jackson. Like Cleveland, the Bulls upset the Knicks, winning the series in six games before running up against the No. 1—seeded red, white, and blue Detroit Pistons in the second of their four legendary playoff clashes. This was the first of three in the Eastern Conference finals.

My best friend, Gabriel Smith, and myself both knocked on the door of puberty at the time. We were two young, round, and chunky black kids from the east side of Buffalo. We were best friends since the second or third grade, and we were inseparable. Like our peers, we were both growing, maturing and evolving, though I had already passed Gabe in terms of height.

We both felt the magic of Michael's shot that evening. We simultaneously jumped up from the floor yelling in front of our living room TV on Harriett Street. We were both ecstatic that the Bulls had pulled out the win over Cleveland, a win which seemed unlikely at times over the previous four games. Anyone watching the two of us chubby middle schoolers celebrate might have thought that we hit the shot ourselves.

We both wore our Chicago Bulls jackets. Mine was an all-white Swingster off-brand jacket with the team logo over the heart. I also wore my red corduroy Chicago Bulls baseball cap. Gabe's jacket was a more popular Starter brand. It was solid red with 'BULLS' spelled in a slight arc across the chest in large black letters with white trim. The starter jackets also had the Bulls' logo stitched on the wrist on the left-hand cuff. Red, black and white. There was something magical and enchanting about the Chicago Bulls' red, black, and white jerseys and seeing Michael and his teammates compete in them against the other NBA teams.

I had just started following the NBA seriously a year earlier. It was just after my brother, Amahl, graduated from our elementary school, the College Learning Laboratory/Campus West, or Campus West for short. It was during that time that I saw the ending of game 6 of the 1988 NBA Eastern Conference finals between the Boston Celtics and the Detroit Pistons. I was in my father's hotel room, the Travel Lodge on Main Street in Buffalo, as the final seconds slowly ticked away.

"That is Dennis Johnson, the point guard for the green and white Celtics. It doesn't look like the Celtics are coming back," Dad said. The Celtics' No. 3, Dennis Johnson, was shooting some inconsequential free throws as the Celtics were on the verge of being eliminated 6–2 by the younger Detroit Pistons in the world-famous Pontiac Silverdome. After a series of battles in the preceding years, Detroit had finally unseated the older Celtics. It was just before the iconic footage of Kevin McHale and Isiah Thomas slapping hands as McHale told Thomas, "Don't be happy just to get there [the NBA Finals]. Go and win it!"

These were my very first memories of NBA basketball. It was right in the middle of what many call the Golden Age of the league. It was the era that starred Ervin 'Magic' Johnson and Larry Bird. The two rivals and stars rescued their teams, the Los Angeles Lakers and the Boston Celtics, as well as the rest of the NBA from its 1970s abyss. Typical of my life, I was coming to the party late as I missed most of Magic and Larry's classic duels and the rest of the 1980s renaissance of the NBA. I also missed all the great college basketball in the National Collegiate Athletic Association (NCAA) of that era which created the wave of talent coming in under Magic and Larry. I had not the slightest clue that Buffalo once had its own NBA franchise. In 1978, our Buffalo Braves moved to San Diego to become the Clippers. Six years later, in 1984, they moved slightly north to become the Los Angeles Clippers, the laughingstock of the league for decades.

"Man, I HATE Bill Laimbeer," my cousin Marcus said in his high-pitched whiny voice. After eliminating the Boston Celtics, the Pistons advanced to the 1988 NBA finals to play the purple and gold Los Angeles Lakers for the NBA World Championship. We were at an early summer gathering over my Auntie Debbie's house. It might have been Game 5 at the Pontiac Silverdome because I remember Bill Laimbeer's father being interviewed courtside. Auntie Debbie's son, Marcus, voiced a disgust for the Detroit Pistons' No. 40, Bill Laimbeer, who many disliked because of his physical play, and his bullying persona, the hallmark of the 'Bad Boys'. There was also No. 44, Rick Mahorn, who portrayed the same energy and image. The *Bad Boys* were the persona and identity that the Pistons took on to mirror the Oakland Raiders from the NFL. The entire City of Detroit got behind and embraced their bullying renegade team.

Even for a novice like me, it was a classic clash—the red, white and blue Pistons vs. the purple and gold Lakers. They were the 'Showtime' Lakers. The two teams battled each other on CBS as Dick Stockton and Hubie Brown commentated the game. It was my first time seeing not only the Pistons play, but also the Lakers' star-studded starting five consisting of No. 32, Magic Johnson, No. 33, Kareem Abdul-Jabbar, No. 42, James Worthy, No. 4, Byron Scott, and No. 45, A.C. Green. They were backed up by players like No. 21, Michael Cooper, No. 43, Mychal

Thompson, and No. 31, Kurt Rambis, who was white and wore a mullet and goggles just like Abdul-Jabbar and Worthy.

It was also my first time really seeing the Lakers' head coach, Pat Riley, work the sidelines. He was known for his slicked-back hair and suave appearance. I saw him in numerous commercials for men's hair care products. These were all household names I had seen or heard in passing through the media and through classmates up to that point.

In this legendary Game 6, No.11, Isiah Thomas, sprained his ankle before magically scoring 40-plus points (in spite of the pain), 25 in the third quarter—an NBA Finals record. In front of the crowd at the 'Fabulous Great Western Forum' of Inglewood, CA, the Pistons almost pulled out the victory and the world championship. A suspect foul called on Bill Laimbeer as Kareem Abdul-Jabbar turned to shoot his signature 'skyhook' on the lower left block cost them the game. Abdul-Jabbar sank both free throws sealing the win for the Lakers and tying the series 3–3. The Lakers went on to win Game 7 to secure the repeat.

At the start of the 1988–89 season the next year, I couldn't tell you many specifics about Michael 'Air' Jordan and the Chicago Bulls. I somehow gravitated towards them over the other 25 teams in the league at that time. I had seen Michael dunking in commercials and on magazine covers. WTBS in Atlanta featured him in their NBA ads along with its other stars. One commercial that I vividly remember was soundtracked to the song *Let's Go to the Hoop*, a parody of the classic rock and roll song *At the Hop* by the group Danny and the Juniors. In one ad the Chicago mascot, Benny the Bull, danced in the middle of a montage of dunks and fancy passes. There were also Michael's commercials with Spike Lee's Mars Blackman character and the Wheaties commercials. Michael was everywhere.

Now feeling the Michael Jordan *fever*, I followed the Bulls religiously, gradually learning more and more about their other players. 'No. 23 in red', as the Pistons later referred to him, stood 6'6" and was just under 200 pounds. He was tall and lean, and he ran up and down the floor like a gazelle. He had tremendous leaping ability, and he seemed to float in the air during his jump shots. He glided through the air when he drove to the basket, hence the nickname 'Air'. He was highly skilled on offense and his game was continuing to evolve. He played both sides of the floor as he was as tenacious a defender as he was skilled on offense. With his bald head and ears poking out at the sides, he was the undisputed leader of the Bulls and the heart and soul of the franchise. Finally, *Sports Illustrated* released *Come Fly With Me 1990* in tribute to him which I watched repeatedly.

Michael's supporting cast on the 1988–89 team consisted of the young forwards, the 6'8" No. 33, Scottie Pippen and the 6'10" No. 54, Horace Grant, and the veteran 7' No. 24, Bill Cartwright at center, who had a strange-looking jump shot. The Bulls had traded a player named Charles Oakley to the New York Knicks for him. They also had three smaller point guards—No. 5, John Paxson,

No. 11, Sam Vincent, and No. 14, Craig Hodges. All were 6' to 6'2". Finally, coming off the bench that year were veteran big men No. 2, Brad Sellers, No. 40, Dave Corzine, and rookie No. 32, Will Purdue, out of a school called Vanderbilt University. All three were seven feet tall.

The Bulls' head coach was Doug Collins. One of their assistants was a guy named Phil Jackson, a former New York Knick whose picture I'd seen in the book *Rockin' Steady* which is based upon the legendary Walt 'Clyde' Frazier, the floor general for the New York Knicks' 1970s two world championship teams.[26] The book belonged to one of my uncles, and I found it in our basement in some boxes one day.

At the start of the 1988–89 season I bought an NBA yearbook from a local supermarket chain, Tops Friendly Markets, and followed the Bulls game by game. If I didn't watch them play live on TV I would see the highlights on the cable TV Headline News, which ran sports updates twenty minutes into every half hour. I wrote a 'W' or an 'L' next to each of their games in my magazine. On Sundays there was a show called *This Week in the NBA,* hosted by Fred Hickman, on the same station which I religiously watched. I loved its opening music and montage, which included Michael Jordan, Magic Johnson, Larry Bird and other players like Charles Barkley and Dominique Wilkins.

I was a true fan, though I would never own an authentic Michael Jordan jersey, a Chicago Bulls Starter jacket, or a pair of Nike 'Air Jordans' as a youth. I lived on every win and loss during those years. Like so many other kids in the United States and eventually around the world, Michael Jordan inspired a basketball dream within me. After Michael hit that shot against Cleveland, I likewise set out to pursue my own basketball dream.

* * *

I was born in the City of Albany, the capital of New York State. My parents met at the State University of New York at Albany, then referred to as 'Albany State'. My older brother, Amahl, was born in Tacoma, Washington where Dad was temporarily stationed in the United States Army two years earlier. My first three years of life were spent in Albany before my folks divorced. I considered them a bit of an odd couple as I got older and started to understand the world more. Mom moved us back to her hometown of Buffalo, the westernmost major city in New York, which sat on the eastern banks of the Niagara River between Lake Erie and Lake Ontario. She planted her roots there and never left.

---

[26] (Frazier, 2013)

Mom was the third of eight children born to my grandmother, Lena McKinney. Grandma and her sisters were Buchanans, and they moved to Buffalo from Louisiana and Missouri as a part of the Great Migration, where southern blacks moved northward to take advantage of the abundance of industrial jobs and escape the Jim Crow South.

Steel was king in cities like Buffalo and Pittsburgh, while the automobile industry was king in cities like Detroit. It was a prosperous time for Buffalo, and it was a very different city than the one that my peers and I grew up in. The Buffalo we knew was a shell of its former self. It was a deindustrialized, service-oriented northern city known mostly for pizza, chicken wings, four seasons, and long winters. Reminders of what the city once was were all around us in the form of old buildings, abandoned train tracks and pictures and stories. It is also considered to be a racially segregated and non-progressive city.

My mother is an attractive, brown-skinned woman. Mom wore her hair mid-length for most of my childhood. Her glasses gave her a studious appearance which was indicative of who she was. She graduated from Riverside High School in 1968 and earned her bachelor's degree in Business Administration at State University College at Buffalo, or 'Buff State' for short in the early 1980s when we moved back to Buffalo.

"No one loves you and your brother more than I do!" Someone later described her as the 'salt of the earth' in that she was relatively simple in terms of needs and lifestyle. She cooked for us most of the time. They were mostly healthy meals, many from scratch, and they were all scrumptious, especially the breakfasts. She further provided a safe and loving home. She wasn't an extravagant shopper, nor was she prissy. She also didn't party much except on special occasions. Motherhood was her utmost desire in life, and she was one of the last of her kind. Again, it was motherhood and not her career or college degree that was her greatest aspiration.

Mom was always quite physically active and I have vivid memories from my youth of her jogging around Delaware Park on Saturday mornings. She also ran in the 'Turkey Trot' on Thanksgiving mornings before making dinner for all of us. Finally, she worked out many mornings to her Mary Decker videos. The album featured Neil Diamond's hit song *America.* I can still envision her in her headband, Tee-shirt, shorts, and sneakers, working out in the living room. She also interestingly smoked a cigarette at times in the evenings after work as she watched TV and unwound from her day.

Mine was an innocent childhood full of birthdays, holidays, cartoons and toys. I particularly loved model toy train sets. We were *Star Wars* and *Star Trek* kids who fantasized about outer space and superheroes. Hours upon hours were spent after school watching *Challenge of Superfriends*, *The Transformers*, *G.I. Joe*, *Voltron*, and other cartoons. I was also a *Rocky* kid who fell in love with the series after seeing *Rocky*

III when I was around six years old. Something about Sylvester Stallone's fictional Italian boxer and his world connected with my soul as a youngster.

There was time spent outside on bicycles, walking around the neighborhoods and at playgrounds like most kids, but there were also hours upon hours spent indoors playing video games. Gabe had a Nintendo Entertainment System, while we had a Sega Master System. We played those systems for long hours on sleepovers and visits to each other's house. Mom was ahead of the curve in terms of technology, because we had computers in our house at a young age. While we played some games on our Tandy Home Computer, she insisted that we learn correct word processing form and technique, something we didn't understand at the time regarding its importance.

"Each of my children is different, Anwar," Grandma Lena used to say during our talks. She was a beautiful, light-skinned woman with black hair and a distinct streak of gray in the middle of the front of her head, which steadily grew as the years went on. Even at an early age, I sought the wisdom of my elders. My grandmother had five boys and three girls. As a child, there were numerous times when they were all together in one place. One was during Christmas in the early 1980s, and it was captured in a picture taken in the Jasper Parish Housing Projects in north Buffalo, where they all grew up.

The previous two generations of my family experienced some part of the Civil Rights Movement and the events surrounding those tumultuous times. Each of the eight siblings and their cousins went to the various high schools in the Buffalo Public Schools system. Bennett, Burgard, East, Hutch-Tech and Riverside to name a few. Most of my aunts and uncles eventually left Buffalo, occasionally returning for short periods, and left again for other parts of the United States. My Uncle Tony stayed permanently, just like Mom.

"Sister Dunbar, your boys are so well-behaved!" Mom kept Dad's last name after they split. I have vivid memories of members of the Tried Stone Baptist Church, on Humboldt Parkway, telling my mother this, often astonished as though many of the kids they met were not well-behaved. Mom and Grandma raised us in a house full of love, instilling us with values and raising us for society. We weren't problem kids and were taught traditional morals and values–the importance of hard work, sharing, playing fair and square, and understanding the difference between right and wrong.

Our work ethics were taught in part by the household chores we became responsible for both inside and outside of the house, whether it was mopping, vacuuming, washing the dishes, yardwork, or shoveling snow in the long Buffalo winters. We were kept off the streets and all of its dangers for the most part, and education and reading were encouraged. Attending college was an expectation for both me and Amahl, as both our parents earned college degrees. Amahl and I were thus both intellectually curious, and we spoke articulately. We stood out at school in our preppy attire and the nicely cut parts in our hair.

It was an ideal childhood, except that there was no male presence in our home 24/7, as my father lived five hours east in the City of Schenectady, NY. Amahl and I were blessed though, in that he made an effort to remain in contact with us and sent for us several times a year. Later I realized that many of my black peers across the United States did not even have that. They did not know who their fathers were, or they knew who they were and were estranged.

The lack of men didn't become very noticeable until puberty and adolescence. In multiple areas, my brother and I had to figure things out on our own. One area was girls, a lifelong quest. Another was athletics. I have few memories of my uncles participating in sports except for my Uncle Scottie. I might've seen him play basketball when I was four or five years old when he still lived in Buffalo. I also recall pictures of him playing shirtless and wearing those 1980s-style short shorts with his socks pulled up over his calves in collages my Auntie Melva made.

He called himself the 'Iceman', probably in tribute to the silky-smooth guard from the NBA, No. 21, George Gervin, not the Marvel superhero. The nickname embodied my uncle's signature cockiness and self-confidence. These qualities surely would have rubbed off on me and my brother had we spent more time with him. The youngest of eight children, he left Buffalo in his late teens and was gone for most of our childhood. The same was true for three of our other uncles.

Uncle Tony, whom I considered the *rock* of our family as I got older, was Mom's oldest brother. Everyone went to him when they needed financial help. He was tough-minded but forgiving, and his generosity was sometimes taken advantage of. He was brave too, as he took on a career as a firefighter. He was always very generous towards me and my brother financially, regularly giving us monetary gifts around the holidays and on our birthdays.

Even though Uncle Tony lived in Buffalo, we mostly saw him on special occasions, in addition to the random times when he would pop up at our house. He spent lots of time hanging out in the old neighborhood, Black Rock, as they called it. He often showed up with a bottle of Tropicana grapefruit juice in an excited mood and sometimes with red eyes, wearing his signature Kangol hat, trench coat, jeans or khakis, and sneakers. A running joke later between me and my best friend, Gabe, was that there was more than just grapefruit juice sloshing around in his bottle. Uncle Tony talked fast and openly made fun of people from the projects or relatives. I loved it when he came around.

I did not have any inkling that Uncle Tony played sports at any point in his life, until I grew up. He had strong opinions about sports that he enjoyed like basketball and football, as did most of my uncles when I heard them talking amongst themselves. Uncle Tony bet on games regularly with guys from Black Rock. Once I overheard him talking about this guy and that guy owing him money. We played a game of pickup basketball in my Auntie Melva's driveway in Atlanta one Thanksgiving. I think Amahl, Uncle John, and Uncle Scottie played in that game also. It was an absolute fun time spent with our uncles.

As a child, Uncle Scottie took us to see the world-famous Harlem Globetrotters one night. They were so smooth, and I remember their sneakers screeching on the hardwood floor that evening in addition to their comedy and skill with the basketball, hallmarks of their act. It was the only time I remember seeing a basketball game as a child.

"Guide the ball with your left hand and follow through with your right hand, AD Number Two! You want to raise straight up and release the ball at the top of your jump," my Uncle John said to me at our house on Harriet Street. He affectionately referred to Amahl and me as 'AD Number One' and 'AD Number Two'. A basket was mounted on the garage when Mom and Grandma bought the house on Harriet Street. On one of his visits from Alabama, I think I asked him to show me something, and he took me out into the backyard.

"You also want to stop that Dick Van-Dyke leg kick shit you are doing," he continued. Uncle John was slender in stature and wore a beard. His glasses gave him a college campus activist/professorial look in combination with his beard. He also had gruffness about him and a short temper. For some reason, I kicked my right leg backward as I shot the ball, but not afterward, as I heeded his heavy-handed instruction. My uncle's words mattered to me, and I valued his experience and mentorship.

"You want to practice dribbling with your right hand and your left hand," my Uncle Scottie sternly instructed me on one of his visits. Uncle Scottie was dark-skinned and bowlegged. He wore his hair close like Uncle John, with a mustache at the time. We moved to Hastings Avenue, and one morning he took me to nearby Roosevelt Park. He had me dribble the ball there and back.

He poured what he could into me regarding shooting and offense that morning. It was an isolated occurrence, and it was mentoring I wish I could have had it on a regular basis. He aggressively pushed me that day, which I was not used to, though I was grateful for it. When I whimpered due to his firm and aggressive tone when teaching me, he scolded me and assured me that getting personally pushed and being tough were parts of playing basketball. I just wasn't used to that type of teaching, but it was good. These collectively are the basketball memories I have with my uncles.

"You Buffalo boys are SOFT!" Dad was an only child who grew up in upper Manhattan in New York City. One of my most vivid memories is of him deriding me and my brother one scorching summer day in New York City when he made us walk from Midtown Manhattan back to my grandmother's apartment in upper Manhattan. Neither I nor my brother were used to walking that many city blocks, so, in that regard, he was probably right. That day stands out to me, because I thought Dad was exceptionally tough on us by forcing us to walk in that excruciating heat. We *had* our father to toughen us up, as my mother would say years later, in that we knew who he was and saw him somewhat regularly, even though he lived on the other part of the state.

"I'm proud of you son." Dad gave supportive words often when we were younger. They became less and less as we got older and gave way to the bullying style of fathering, at times and mentoring, described on that scorching day in New York City. He stood around 5'11", and he was an average-looking, brown-skinned man with slight bowlegs. His hair started thinning in the early '80s. There was some debate through the years about who favored him more looks-wise, but most people said I did more so than my brother. We picked up parts of his personality, both good and not so good.

Dad was a smart guy early on academically. He earned his bachelor's degree in physics and then later his master's degree in education. He was a middle school teacher. He served in the Army for several years and then in the Air Force Reserves to make extra money for most of my childhood. Dad had a very distinct diction and way of communicating. He was not very suave or charismatic, but he liked to dance. He was very particular and liked things done a certain way, whether it was his money, his schedule, or his life in general. He was haunted by the divorce from my mother and may never have gotten completely over it. I looked up to him in those times, something that changed and evolved over the years.

Dad never completely lost his New York City accent and still pronounced his words like a downstater. His father, my grandfather, died when he was 18 years old, and I only saw him in pictures. I don't think Dad found any other male figures or mentors for the rest of his life, which led to a life of figuring things out on *his* own, arguably the legacy of his line.

Dad joined something called a fraternity in our pre-middle school years. It was called 'Omega Psi Phi', and their colors were purple and gold. I recall Dad and some of his fraternity brothers doing some sort of stepping routine late one night in the park at the school across from his apartment on McClyman Street in Schenectady. The main chant during the step was something about, "♫We're going to BOP to Omega!♫". I noticed paraphernalia with a coat of arms or seal around his home over the years on my visits. He mentioned his fraternity in passing at times and not in great detail. Otherwise, there was little exposure to it as his sons.

"Dunbars like to dance," Dad said often. He told me many stories about attending dances and social functions in his area. It didn't come easily to me as a youngster, because we didn't do much of it on my mother's side of the family. It was actually a little scary for me, especially around my peers at school dances. Dad had a good time at social functions, and I admired seeing him dance and socialize when he took us with him to functions. One such function was a boat party on

Lake George, NY one summer. Our paternal grandmother, Grandma Evelyn Dunbar from New York City, whom we only saw on summer visits to the Albany area, was there having a good time too. Grandma Dunbar was a happy and talkative, shapely brown-skinned woman. She cooked for Amahl and me and fed us like kings when we were together on our summer visits with Dad.

There was some basketball on visits with Dad once or twice a year. He would beat us up on the basketball court, as fathers often do their sons who are smaller and less physically able early in life. There were two years in middle school when Gabe went out to visit him with me, and we both got a taste of how good basketball was outside of Buffalo. One day at Scotia Park stands out in my memory. Scotia Park, a vast park near the Mohawk River, had white Reebok half-moon backboards and baskets during that time. I recall an older, darker-skinned man named Paul, who Dad knew. He ran us all off the court in a game of 'Twenty-One' and then a couple of games of pickup basketball. He deceptively appeared to be quiet and unassuming, but he had a lot of game. It was an early lesson on appearances being deceptive, especially in the great game of basketball.

Summer visits were part of the visitation agreement in my parents' divorce settlement. Dad's background was baseball, a popular game for kids in New York City with multiple major league teams in his era. There were pictures of him playing baseball in his hometown as a teen. At one time I believe there were the Brooklyn Dodgers, the New York Giants and the New York Yankees, and they were all in the city simultaneously. Later, it was the New York Mets when the Dodgers and the Giants departed for the West Coast.

On visits to the Albany area, I found that Dad was into something called *judo*. Based on what I had seen on TV and the movies, I associated the gi and colored belts with kicks and punches. This martial art that Dad was involved in, interestingly, dealt more with throwing opponents and properly landing on the ground after being thrown or taken down.

Baseball was not widely popular with me as a youth. I have wondered numerous times if I would have taken to it more had I grown up under my father's tutelage. (The same is true for music.) Mom and my Uncle Tony enlisted my brother and me in T-ball and in a baseball league, but neither took root in us.

"Football is a barbaric sport," Mom said, and I soon began echoing that sentiment. It was a physical and, in some instances, a violent game, but there were lots of great things about it. It taught young men a lot of important lessons. There were only two professional sports teams in Buffalo back then—the Buffalo Bills from the National Football League (NFL) and the Buffalo Sabres from the National Hockey League (NHL). Few black kids in Buffalo took an interest in hockey. Football, however, was different and many other boys had some exposure to it early on.

"The Bills STINK!" Larry Garmon said this numerous times in my younger years in his strong and base-filled voice, partially joking and partially serious. He was a bit of an *alpha-male* and a tough guy who Mom dated on and off after divorcing my father. He was also from the Black Rock neighborhood, and everyone knew each other growing up. He also attended Riverside High School, like my mother. He was a bit of a jokester and he was always reading the newspaper and keeping up with world events which made him a multidimensional man. Larry was a football player himself, and what I considered to be a real *man's man,* looking back. I gravitated towards him and I looked up to him. Things didn't work out between him and my mother, and he was gone after a while. Continually being in his presence probably would have rubbed off on us, not just in terms of football but in other areas as well. The same is true for our Uncle Scottie.

Larry was right about the Bills. In the early- to mid-1980s, in the post-O.J. Simpson era, they were a laughingstock around town and in the NFL. They did stink until the mid-to late-'80s when they drafted players like Jim Kelly, Thurman Thomas, Andre Reed, Bruce Smith and others. This led to the franchise's resurgence under Head Coach Marv Levy's leadership. My brother and I didn't get involved in playing football for most of our childhood, with no real interest in the game and with a perpetually losing professional franchise.

Aside from a stint where we both took Isshinryu Karate before Amahl went started high school, there was not much participation in athletic competition besides the time when we dabbled in baseball and T-ball. There were also summers where we participated in summer programs at the Salvation Army, and then in a sports program at Canisius College. Otherwise, there was no formal involvement to a team sport until I fell in love with the game of basketball in middle school. As such, there was a lot for me to learn.

"Don't get your hopes up! A lot of young men want to go to the pros, but few of them get there." Mom said this several times throughout my childhood. These words usually came when I was getting my sights set on something, such as a goal or an objective, and she usually said them in passing. In hindsight, I don't think her intent was discouragement. Instead, it was her innate motherly love and protection. Perhaps it was her reminiscing on some of her personal disappointments in life and wanting to shield me from my own. Regardless, my innocent basketball dream was ignited, and after getting caught up in the magic of the NBA of the late 1980s, I wanted to do what I could do to fulfill it.

Chapter 3. A Basketball Player-Manager: The 1988–89 Campus West Bengal Tigers Boys' Basketball Team

"Okay Dunbar, here's the deal. I'm going to keep you as a player-manager! I'm not going to play you much, but you'll be on the team!" **—Walter James Cook, Head Coach, the Campus West College Learning Laboratory/Campus West boys' basketball team, November 1988**

I attended the College Learning Laboratory/Campus West, or 'Campus West' for short, from grades one through eight. The school sat on the westernmost side of the State University of New York College at Buffalo or 'Buff-State'—my mother's alma mater. I was one of the lucky kids to win the lottery and get accepted into the charter school. Amahl was accepted a year later. Mom valued education, and she thought it was a superior school compared to PS#66, where he had previously attended. I attended pre-k and kindergarten there.

Grades one through five were innocent times. Prayer has since been taken out of public schools, but standing and reciting the Pledge of Allegiance and acknowledging God in the mornings was still normal at that time. Middle school was the period in which the transitioning out of childhood started. It was the first time in my life that I noticed things became different. I started noticing girls, many of whom I had been in class with for years, but somehow had not paid attention in *that* way. Now, magically, I did. Both genders were also starting to blossom and develop, each in different ways and at different speeds. It would be years before I developed any comfort and confidence in terms of talking to girls.

When I looked in our bathroom mirror at the beginning of grades six and seven, a brown-skinned, chubby kid with full lips and little to no facial hair, stared back at me. I was round in the middle with large and healthy thighs that spread out when I sat down. My hair was short and parted, and our barbers were always sure to cut it according to my mother's preferences at the barber shop. Amahl and I shared similar features for the most part, except for our weights. I got the *round* genes while he got the *thin* genes in terms of weight. Many people asked Mom if we were twins growing up.

In terms of my height, I knocked on the door of 6', though I was just under that number at 5'10" or 5'11". Fashion-wise, we dressed somewhat clean-cut and preppy. We had no fashion sense at all, something highly emphasized in our culture as black people in the United States. Left to our mother's tastes, Amahl and I had

Hawaiian shirts, for example. Mine was blue and white, while his was red and white. Many of our classmates didn't know what to make of them, and some voiced it, while others kept their thoughts to themselves.

That year, I also remember desiring to identify with my blackness culturally. It was a switch that suddenly got flicked on when I started noticing certain trends and behaviors in the other black kids, and I wanted to be like them and mix with them. I think I asked for Bobby Brown's *Don't Be Cruel* record that Christmas of 1988. It was a sharp departure from the hair rock bands we had listened to in previous years like Bon Jovi and Mötley Crüe. We took a strong interest in rap music then as well, which was still relatively new as a genre. When I say *we*, I'm referring to myself, Amahl and my best friend Gabe. While my brother Amahl was two years older than us, the three of us were inseparable.

I had not mastered being a student yet. Most of the time I would do just enough work to get by, but never enough to consistently excel. I got in trouble for my grades once and did my best never to get a talking-to like the one my mother gave me in the fourth or fifth grade. I hated disappointing people, especially her.

At the start of my seventh-grade year, Amahl went off to some school called Hutchinson-Central Technical High School, or 'Hutch-Tech' for short. It was a science and technology school and one of the best high schools in the city. I still remember Mom doting over him as he left our Harriett Street house that fall morning in 1988. He wore his glasses, a powder blue jacket, jeans or khakis, and sneakers. He too had a studious look image-wise. It was the second time in our lives when we were at different schools, and I was now the only remaining Dunbar at Campus West.

Physically, my body started changing. At some point during the middle of elementary school, I gained weight and became a round kid. Mom put me on a diet because Dr. Rusi Udwadia, my pediatrician, said that if my weight continued trending upward, I would become obese. He showed us a plot depicting how my weight would increase if certain steps were not taken. The conversation made me feel ashamed. He also said that I was going to be tall.

"He has flat feet," Dr. Udwadia noted during one of our visits. He was a studious-looking, middle-aged East Indian man with glasses, upright, bushy hair, and a strong accent. "You have to make sure his shoes have arches!" *Bad* flat feet? I did not understand the significance of this until much later. Feet were feet, right? Mom was diligent about my shoes and sneakers from that point on, and she vigilantly checked them for arch support before purchasing them.

My being put on a diet made me feel singled out, especially at home where my brother could eat as much as he wanted to while my portions were now tightly regulated. Amahl was always thinner than me in terms of build, so none of this was a concern for him. Mom also made me go to Delaware Park with her on

Saturday mornings just to do something active. She ran around the park while I shot baskets on the basketball courts along Parkside Avenue.

The outdoor courts in Buffalo went through four seasons as is customary for the region itself. During the summertime the city put fresh nylon or chain nets on the outdoor hoops. By the end of the summer they were torn up, and by the next spring you were lucky if anything was left to slow the ball from sailing through the basket. There was something about seeing it drop through the net that made making baskets more worthwhile versus hoops with no net. The hallmark of those Delaware Park courts was the surrounding grass and trees, the red and green pavement, and finally, the metal backboards (which are no longer there). On cold and rainy Buffalo days, water pooled on parts of the courts which eventually helped warp and crack them. The four-to-five-month-long winters contributed also.

On one of those cold wet mornings something profound happened. While Mom jogged around the park, I shot baskets. I had not been formally trained in terms of the fundamentals of basketball yet, so I didn't clearly understand the difference between a layup, a jump shot, a hook shot, a free throw, etc. So I just shot up any and everything. From the top of the key in one instance, I took a couple of dribbles, two steps, and launched a two-handed shot from the foul line, which banked off the backboard and ricocheted into the hoop. I had made a basket, and it was the coolest thing. I stood proudly marveling at my basket for a couple of seconds.

"DO IT AGAIN!" A voice yelled from the road circling the park, suddenly diverting my attention. It was an older black man in a sweatsuit who saw me make the shot. He walked at a brisk pace. I stared at him briefly, smiling. "Go ahead. Let me see you do that again!"

DO it again? Could I do it again? Could I make another basket? Pausing momentarily, I accepted the man's challenge. I took the ball back to the top of the key and reset myself. I dribbled the ball back towards the foul line and launched another off-balance running two-hander. This time it clanked off the rim. I turned and looked at the man who smiled at me and just kept on walking. I kept shooting until Mom finished her jogging. *Do it again…*

* * *

Mr. Walter James Cook was the first coach to give me a chance to play 'organized' basketball. I think he went by *Jim* Cook, if I am being exact. He was in his late thirties or early forties at the time. He was a tall, slim white man with thinning black hair. He wore a beard in my early years at the school, but he switched to a clean-shaven look as the years went on. *Mr.* Cook is how we all referred to him. I can't think of any of us referring to him as *Coach* Cook.

Mr. Cook always wore sweatsuits and low-top sneakers, Converse, I believe. He was involved in the Empire State Games, because he frequently wore blue and gold sweatsuits with the official logo on them. He had also coached the Campus West boys' basketball team since I had been at the school. He was the face of our team as far as I was concerned.

I started paying attention to the boys' basketball team when I was in the fifth or sixth grade. Some of the names that come to mind during that time include Paul Saunders, Quincy Lee, Charles Thompson and Dion Frasier. Other names that I remember are Colin Rhodes, Taj Collison, Menaleak Brown, Tremaine Hardin, Jamel Brown, Darius McClamb, David Hamilton, Sean Harwell, Douglas Croomer, and Ronald Jennings. These guys were not necessarily all on the team together at one time, but I remember them being Mr. Cook's players. A notable name I heard a lot about before that group of players was Carlin Hartman. I must have been in the fourth or fifth grade when he was in the eighth grade, and I remember hearing his name quite a bit in association with our basketball team.

Our team nickname was the Bengals, which was the Buffalo State College mascot. Before becoming old enough to play on the team, I remember Mr. Cook having his teams put on demonstrations for Parents Night—an evening for parents to come into the school to meet the teachers and discuss their kids academic progress and behavior in class.

"It's good for the parents to get to know each other," Mr. Kenneth Bernard Smith said to my mother. Mr. Smith had a deep hoarse sounding voice. He was a dark-skinned stocky man who usually wore a stylish top hat, a sweater, slacks and shoes. His wife, Sally Smith, was a beautiful light-skinned woman who reminded me of Coretta Scott-King. I believe it was at a parents' night one year that Gabe's parents met my mother for the first time while Gabe, Amahl, and I ran around the school having fun.

In addition to the academic exchanges on Parents Night, there were athletic demonstrations in the gymnasium. The Campus West gym was a large facility with two window-style backboards at each end, several half-moon baskets throughout the gym, a regulation-sized basketball court with wooden bleachers on both sides. There were climbing ropes and a skylight on the ceiling allowing natural light to shine in.

This particular night the older students performed demonstrations of all kinds while the audience watched. My cousin, Amir Willis, for example, did some gymnastic exercises on the pommel horse. Mr. Cook had the boys' basketball team do dribbling drills, layup drills, and passing drills; all to the Harlem Globetrotters' classic theme, *Sweet Georgia Brown* by Brother Bones and His Shadows. I was impressed by the basketball team and I wanted to be like them. They made basketball look fun.

Chapter 3. A Basketball Player-Manager: The 1988-89 Campus West Bengal Tigers Boys' Basketball Team

* * *

I decided to try out for the boys' basketball team in the seventh grade. I was still a round and chubby kid, and I was very raw in terms of fundamentals. Wanting to be on the team as badly as I did, I knew very little about the game other than the fact that the ball was supposed to go into the hoop. I had not been to any camps or gone through any formal training up to that point other than playing random pickup games and 'street' basketball, and even that was rare. I also learned from the few NBA games that I watched on TV and the small amount of information I had gotten from my uncles during their visits.

I do not remember Mr. Cook's format for tryouts. I don't recall academic standards for trying out either, but that doesn't mean there were none. I do remember feeling out of place and getting easily winded running up and down the court with the other guys. Running the stairs outside of the gym for conditioning was difficult too. I breathed hard and sweated buckets, trying to keep up my chubby with the other guys. I had never challenged my body like that before. It was scary to feel my lungs and muscles burn and like my limbs would fall off. Mostly, it was fun and I desperately wanted to be part of the team. I wanted to be a part of the group. I just wanted to make the team and be one of the guys.

"Now listen, Dunbar," Mr. Cook said in his stern and low-pitched voice one day after tryouts. He knew me from years and years of gym class. He looked at me out of the corner of his eyes in a serious way. "I'm going to *keep* you on the team as a *player-manager*! I'm not going to play you a whole lot, but you'll be on the team, you'll practice, and potentially get into *some* games." He had watched me struggle during tryouts and mercifully gave me a roster spot. It is something I remember to this day, and I'll always be grateful to him.

While I did not really understand what a *player-manager* was, I knew that I was not cut from the team and that I was a part of the group of guys. In hindsight, he wanted to give me a chance to learn, though I was not ready to get on the floor to play competitively. Perhaps being on the team, practicing with the guys, and being on the sidelines for the games would accelerate my growth in some way. I would at least get to be one of the guys, and I really wanted to be a part of the group.

Ronald Jennings, John Benson, Jackie Crump, Marcus Perkins, John Rustevio, Vance LaGrange, Germaine Holton, Basheer Crawford, Jason Hellerman and Clarence Miles also made the team. The last two guys were eighth graders. Clarence was our tallest player at 6'3", which at that time seemed huge to me.

Jason Hellerman was one of the few white kids on the team, and he openly looked up to the Boston Celtics' No. 33, Larry Bird. Few of the black kids looked up to Larry Bird, probably due to color and race. Few of us liked the Celtics. Up to that point, I admittedly never watched Bird play much. I just knew that he was the antithesis of Magic Johnson, and that he played on the *white* team, even though he had several black teammates. Jason was tall, kind of chubby, and had a distinct jump shot. He cocked it almost behind his head and then brought it forward, seemingly in slow motion. It always looked like a shot put from track and field or a heave of some sort to me.

I still remember my very first basketball jersey. It was blue and white and said Bengals or Campus West on the front. Campus West did not have a collection of jerseys for us, so we had to order them from an outside vendor. That meant that we had to get money from home, bring it in, and order our uniforms. Mr. Cook gave us a deadline, and we all brought our money in one day, maybe $20–$30. We all sat on the floor of the gym filling out forms capturing our sizes, jersey numbers, and the names that would go on the back of our tank tops.

I picked No. 3 after Dennis Johnson who ironically was the point guard for Larry Bird's Boston Celtics. I remembered the Celtics getting eliminated by the Detroit Pistons the previous year. Ronald Jennings chose No. 21 for Dominique Wilkins, and I think Jackie Crump chose No. 23 for Michael Jordan. Jason Hellerman chose the No. 33 for Larry Bird. John Benson looked up to Magic Johnson, but chose the No. 4.

Mr. Cook encouraged us to go with nicknames on the back of our jerseys instead of our real names. I went with the nickname that my Uncle Scottie had given me at a young age, 'Dr. A'. It was a salute to Julius Erving, also known as 'Dr. J'. Dr. J wore No. 6 for the Philadelphia 76ers and was one of the well known faces of the NBA before he retired, like Magic Johnson and Larry Bird. Uncle Scottie had taken his nickname 'Iceman' from the NBA's George Gervin. Like Dr. J, No. 21, Gervin was a star in an older defunct league called the American Basketball Association and had continued his career in the NBA with the San Antonio Spurs.

We received our uniforms within a few weeks. I had never had a uniform for a team before, so it was magical for me. In my limited time watching basketball, I saw the NBA players wear them, and now I had one signifying that I was a part of a team. On the same court where we filled out our order forms and gave Mr. Cook our money, we sat and watched as he unloaded several cardboard boxes with beautiful blue and white jerseys for each of us. It was like Christmas. We all examined our uniforms front and back and then tried them on.

"Waar's name is 'DRA'! What's going on DRA?" The manufacturer did not add the period to signify the abbreviation of a doctor, so the name on my back literally said DRA. Basheer Crawford loved it and poked at me frequently about it that year. He was a light-skinned kid who wore glasses and looked studious, but he also had a larger-than-life personality.

"We're starting to click a little bit now," Mr. Cook said at practice after a loss and then started going into one of many discussions that I did not understand. He had a slow and methodical cadence when he spoke, and he paced back and forth in his Tee-shirt and sweatpants. The court made a sharp creaking noise with each step of his Converse sneakers. I do not remember practices under Mr. Cook being very in-depth other than him teaching us some iteration of the 'Motion' offense, the 'Three-Man Weave Drill', conditioning, etc. One time I got knocked on the ground during a drill and laid there for a few seconds. Mr. Cook looked at me with disgust and his whistle in his mouth and slowly said, "Get up off the floor Dunbar, and toughen up!"

I recall Mr. Cook frequently saying, "When you get to high school and play on the *varsity* basketball team–." I did not understand what exactly a *varsity* team was and how it was different from what we were doing there at Campus West. I assumed I would keep playing basketball as the years went on, even though I had no exposure to this varsity basketball. I assumed we would all keep playing into our teens.

"Mr. Cook is an asshole," Ronald Jennings grumbled one day after practice as a group of us walked to the bus stop. Interestingly, not all the players liked Mr. Cook, who seemed like a nice enough guy to me. After all, he did give me the chance to be on the team. Ronald, who was our star, felt differently that day. Something must have happened between the two of them.

We played in the Public School Athletic League (PSAL), and our games were right after school, just like our practices, with no games on the weekends. Some of the other teams in our league included North Park, Campus East, Campus North, West Hertel, and some of the public schools. It was all so new to me, and it was exciting to be playing basketball.

It was my first ever taste of organized basketball. I loved it. For our home games we would dress in our uniforms and start our warmups. Mr. Cook did not give us a specific stretching or warmup routine. We simply performed jump shots and layups to have us break a sweat. We also did some layup lines.

Gradually the other teams would show up at our school. When they appeared, we would look at them, and they would look at us, which usually caused a sense of fear within me in a primal way. Perhaps it was just the unknown and sensing some sort of battle was about to take place. The same was true when we went to our opponent's gyms. Upon arrival you could hear the echo of the basketballs bouncing in the gym as you approached it. When we would enter our opponent's gyms in our street clothes, we were greeted with ominous stares as our hosts perhaps wondered what kind of game we were going to give them.

"They're playing a zone defense against us," some of my teammates said watching our opponents' strategy on defense during one game. Their defenders were not following our players around individually. Instead, they stood in a formation of some sort and shifted to face the ball wherever it went. I didn't know what a *zone* defense was, and now I had a lot of time to watch and pick up new tips as I sat on the bench. True to Mr. Cook's words, I did not play. I simply sat on the end of the bench, watched, and studied. Some of what I saw went over my head, while other stuff, like what a zone defense was, sunk in.

Because I did not really know *how* to play, getting into the game scared me a little bit. What would I do if I got in on either side of the ball? Oftentimes the actual play within the lines was only steps away from where I sat. It also felt like it was galaxies away in terms of my skill level and the potential of my getting on the floor and playing in a meaningful way.

As a coach, Mr. Cook was not much of a yeller, nor was he very animated. He was kind of laid back. That was an average season for us. With Ronald Jennings leading the way at the point guard position, our record was roughly 0.500. Jason Hellerman, John Benson, Marcus Perkins, and our anchor in the middle that year, Clarence Miles, all logged significant minutes for us. Though he was our tallest player, Clarence did not look comfortable on the court. Sometimes he struggled to secure rebounds when the ball bounced off the rim. He would grab at it multiple times like he was trying to catch a butterfly or a ping-pong ball.

"Clarence needs to be more aggressive than that," or, "Clarence isn't very coordinated," some teammates mumbled during games. Clarence lived down the street from me on Harriet Avenue. He was the *man* of his female-dominated home. His mother and grandmother took him to church several times a week, which seemed to be the main priority for them.

"That kid looks like a TERRORIST!" There were always lots of jokes on the bench during the games from players like Basheer Crawford. In one of the games played in our gym, there was a player from the visiting team whose hair was overgrown, giving him a feral appearance. He wore sweatpants instead of shorts and played very aggressively, especially when going for rebounds, often getting called for fouls. He was fair-skinned, giving him an Arabic appearance. Nothing was off-limits for the clowns on our team. I vividly recall Mr. Cook giving a stern and silent look of disapproval towards the end of the bench when he heard that joke. Mr. Cook was true to his word in that I didn't play much that season, but it was still lots of fun being on the team.

* * *

Shortly after the season ended, there was the faculty game. It was customary for the faculty to play against the boys and the girls teams. We dressed up in our uniforms while the faculty wore their gym clothes. It was funny seeing them not in teaching attire, but in shorts and sneakers, running around just like us kids. In alternating quarters, the boys and girls teams competed against the faculty as the rest of the school watched and cheered. The gym was electric for those games, and our classmates erupted with every play, whether it was a basket, steal, or turnover. Mr. Cook played on the faculty team. He returned to our sideline in between quarters and pointed out who would play. Mr. Christman or Ms. Coghlan did the same for the girls. I attentively watched each of the six to seven periods wondering if I might get on the floor.

In my blue uniform, my matching blue and white socks pulled all the way up, and my matching blue and white Converse high-tops, I was a bundle of nerves in the buzzing gym. Would I get into the game in front of everyone? Mr. Cook finally ran over and put me in the game in one of the final periods. I wanted to score just one basket. It was all I wanted. I got winded just running up and down the floor though, and was unable to take advantage of any potential opportunities. When the final buzzer sounded, I huffed and puffed and sweated like I played the entire game. I felt like I failed or missed out on something great in some way. Mom showed up to that game after leaving work early. She took pictures of us out there running around. She took one of me walking off the court with an angry look on my face. It looked like I was flexing what little muscles I had on my twelve-year-old left arm.

"Waar was mad and is flexing his muscles in this picture," Basheer Crawford said. Once again, he made fun of me when I brought the pictures to school to show everyone. Waar became my nickname. My classmates simply cut the first two letters off the front of my name and went with what was left. I liked it though. It gave me another sense of belonging to the group. Most of the team had nicknames.

The season ended and we didn't qualify for any type of postseason play. I must confess that after our season was over I was proud of my dark blue and white Campus West basketball jersey. I wore it at every opportunity. One Sunday there was a celebration at the Emslie Street YMCA, perhaps a Black History or Dr. Martin Luther King, Jr. celebration. I was there front and center with my jersey, blue and white socks, and my white Converse sneakers. I was a basketball player, and I wanted to show it.

Later that evening we were allowed to go into the gym and play basketball. Gabe and I teamed up and played a kid by the name of Dorian Willis from Hutch-Tech High School. He was tall, slim, and fair-skinned and I had not seen him in pictures of the Hutch-Tech boys' basketball team. Much to my surprise he was pretty good as he, and whoever he teamed up with, ran Gabe and me off the court.

Skill-wise, I was powerless to make any meaningful difference in that game and got frustrated. Offensively I didn't know how to effectively score the ball, and defensively, I didn't know how to stop my man. Gabe and I could not get on the same page and bickered, something that would continue happening when we teamed up in the coming years. I was deflated and embarrassed afterward.

That night I realized that just having a jersey didn't mean that I could play the game. Furthermore, Mr. Cook making me a player-manager on our boys' basketball team didn't mean that I was any good. Having a jersey did not mean anything if I did not have the game to back it up. But where was I going to get that game from? How was I going to get better? I wandered into that summer of 1989 not knowing how to develop my game, but I played whenever and wherever I could. I wanted to get better, but I just didn't know how.

* * *

I still dreamed about being a basketball player and I got completely caught up in the aura and the magic of the NBA. My bedroom in the back of our house had become a bit of a shrine to the league and its players. I collected NBA posters from K-Mart and similar stores, which I hung on the walls with thumbtacks and marveled at them. One was entitled 'Sultans of Slam', which featured a young Michael Jordan, Dominique Wilkins, Clyde 'The Glide' Drexler, Charles Barkley, Spud Webb, Gerald Wilkins, and Larry Nance. There was the 'Magic Show' poster which featured a collection of images of Magic Johnson.

"I recognize Michael Jordan and Magic Johnson, but who is number twenty-one?" Mom asked me about another poster that featured No. 23, Michael Jordan, dunking at the Great Western Forum with No. 32, Magic Johnson, and No. 21, Michael Cooper, looking at him in awe. At the time I didn't know who the dark-complexioned role player was; only that his nickname was 'Coop'. The versatile Coop came off the bench for the Los Angeles Lakers and could do most things highly skilled, but he served as a defensive specialist and a shooter for the *Showtime* Lakers when necessary. I wasn't familiar with the Lakers' roster or history and told Mom it was Mark Aguirre who played for the Detroit Pistons. I also had a second Michael Jordan poster where he was dunking during what looked like a slam dunk contest, because he was wearing a gold chain.

The two other notable posters I had were of Michael Jordan and his Chicago Bulls teammates, Scottie Pippen, Horace Grant, Bill Cartwright, John Paxson and, I believe, Craig Hodges. Finally, I had a poster entitled, 'NBA All-Stars', which had 16 players on it. Among them were Michael Jordan, Dominique Wilkins, Magic Johnson, Kareem Abul-Jabbar, Larry Bird, Isiah Thomas, Patrick Ewing, Chuck Person, Xavier McDaniel, Tom Chambers and others.

I looked at those posters daily during my comings and goings. In the morning when I woke up, I looked at them. At nighttime, before going to sleep, I looked at them. I dreamt of being like them. I wanted to be like them. I just didn't know how or what all went into getting to where they were.

"I don't understand how these players can get paid so much money to play these games! It's just a game!" It was during those times of discovering the NBA, slam dunk contests, three-point shootouts, all-star games, NBA finals, posters, and sneakers that Mom voiced her confusion over the whole thing. What was the big deal? Why was it so important? It was a magical time for the game which swept many boys away. The 1990 NBA All-Star Game captured that magic as the coaches and the East and West players were introduced to a montage of highlights played over Janet Jackson's *Rhythm Nation*, Rob Base & DJ EZ Rock's *It Takes Two*, and Wreck's-n-Effect's *New Jack Swing*. The final player introduced that night was none other than Michael Jordan himself. It was a truly magical time.

Later in life, once entering the working world myself, I understood Mom's point about the players' salaries and the value the game added to society. What I also learned as an adult is that it provided an escape from real life, like going to the movies. For those who indulged in playing sports it was a connection to those innocent times of dreaming of playing professional sports before the real world set in and took hold. For the young people just discovering the world, the NBA and its players inspired us to dream. Whether or not we knew how to get there or what it all entailed, many of us dreamed.

"I *LOVE* Derrick Coleman from Syracuse. I tell you, I just *LOVE* Derrick Coleman," said Mr. Amoroso. Mr. Amoroso was a short, bearded, muscular Italian teacher. He taught at Campus West and he was very talkative and playfully beat up on some of the boys, including me, to the degree that a faculty member could do so. It was good for us. He learned that I had taken an interest in basketball and started talking to me about a player from Syracuse University. The highly talented 6'10", No. 44, Derrick Coleman was the star player for the Syracuse Orangemen at the time. Coleman eventually ascended to the NBA.

I recall hearing about the Syracuse University basketball program and its matchups with schools like Georgetown, St. John's and Villanova. They were on TV at times, just like the NBA. However, I didn't take the time to stop and look at the games or the players. These younger players would go on to become NBA players, at least the elite ones. A few years earlier I recall my father asking me if I had watched a great game between Georgetown and Villanova where the latter team magically emerged as the winner. Around that time, other teams that were making enough noise for a novice like me to hear about them were schools named Duke, North Carolina, and another school out west called the University of Nevada, Las Vegas (UNLV). There was much more basketball to be watched and studied other than the NBA.

Chapter 4. A Basketball Player: The 1989–90 Campus West Bengal Tigers Boys' Basketball Team's Run

"Just go up strong, Anwar!" —**Ronald Jennings, Captain and Player, the 1988–90 Campus West boys' basketball team, our eighth-grade year**

In the fall of 1989, I saw No. 23, Michael Jordan, play live for the only time in my life. It was a preseason exhibition game, and the Chicago Bulls were matching up with the Miami Heat. As a franchise, the Heat was in its infancy as the NBA had just expanded to 25 teams the previous year. The league added both the Miami Heat and the Charlotte Hornets. The game was in Buffalo and Mr. Smith took Gabe and me to the Memorial Auditorium to see it. Gabe had a beautiful sister named Kensela. She was several years older than us to the point where Gabe basically lived like an only child. As such, he received lots of goodies from his parents which I too was able to partake in, like going to NBA games.

The Detroit Pistons, also known as the Bad Boys, eliminated the Bulls from the 1989 NBA playoffs in six games the previous season. The Pistons then swept the older and injury-riddled Los Angeles Lakers, who had beaten them in the 1988 NBA Finals. The Bulls returned their core players including No. 23, Michael Jordan, No. 33, Scottie Pippen, No. 54, Horace Grant and No. 24, Bill Cartwright; in addition to guards No. 5, John Paxson and No. 14, Craig Hodges. In the 1989 NBA Draft, they added rookies No. 34, Stacey King, and No. 10, BJ Armstrong from the Universities of Oklahoma and Iowa, respectively. I wasn't familiar with either of them as I hadn't followed the college game in a meaningful way in my limited time being interested in basketball.

There was another change in the NBA. Phil Jackson, who was an assistant on Doug Collins' staff the previous year, was promoted as the new head coach. Jackson was a role player on the legendary 1970s New York Knicks team. I knew of him because of the book *Rockin Steady,* based on the life of Walt 'Clyde' Frazier, which one of my uncles owned and left at my house.[27] In the 1989 *Sports Illustrated* NBA preview issue, there was a picture of Jackson, Armstrong, King and another rookie named Jeff Sanders, all grinning for the camera. Jackson wore a black sweatsuit and a pair of the 1988–89 Air Jordans. His face was clean-shaven, and he stood with one leg bent on the podium where the rookies sat. They drafted No.

---

[27] (Frazier, 2013)

42, Sanders, out of Georgia Southern University. I don't think he had a long career with the Bulls. Later that year, they also signed a key, but temporary player, No. 45, Ed Nealy.

Before going to the Bulls, Jackson served as the head coach for the Albany Patroons of the Continental Basketball Association after making other coaching stops. Leading up to that season, there was lots of talk about Jackson moving Michael Jordan back on the wing and *off* the ball. Doug Collins played Michael at the point guard position down the stretch of the 1988–89 season, which worked until matching up against the Pistons. Being relatively new to competitive athletics, I did not realize the significance of the Bulls' coaching change or that coaching changes were a part of sports in general. Coaching changes could likewise occur for any number of reasons and sometimes unexpectedly.

I started collecting *NBA Hoops* basketball cards that year, and I knew the background information of some of the players on the court any given night. The Heat was coached by Ron Rothstein, who had a young lineup of players including No. 41, Glen Rice from the University of Michigan, No. 4, Ronny Seikaly who was Lebanese, and No. 31, Dwayne 'Pearl' Washington, both from Syracuse University. Though Syracuse was only three hours away from Buffalo, I was oblivious to the legend of Pearl Washington, or his namesake, the legendary Earl 'The Pearl' Monroe. Washington was a magician with the ball just like Monroe. It turned out that many basketball nicknames were recycled and reused by successive generations. They were a sign of respect to the younger players and a way to pay homage to previous generations.

I learned all kinds of trivial information about the NBA through collecting the *NBA Hoops* basketball cards, such as the backgrounds of players like the Charlotte Hornets' No. 7, Kelly Tripucka. Tripucka attended the University of Notre Dame and he even played for the Detroit Pistons alongside Isiah Thomas for a stint. The NBA was full of lesser-known players who were traded multiple times, in addition to the stars who were the faces of the league.

Gabe and I wore our Chicago Bulls jackets and apparel to the game along with a lot of other kids. 'The Aud' was electric when we walked in. It was my second time ever attending an event there. My first time was not to see the Buffalo Sabres, but instead an evening of wrestling courtesy of the World Wrestling Federation. Mom's coworker from the United Way, Dennis Wilkerson, took us.

Every time the Bulls did something in warmups, the crowd erupted with "OOOOHS" and "AHHHHHS." Michael, Scottie Pippen, and Horace Grant gave us a couple of dunks during warm-ups and during the game itself. There were rumors leading up to tipoff that No. 23 was not going to play at all, but Michael did not disappoint us. He and the starters played most of the first half, but not much afterward so as not to risk injuries. The Bulls won the game 115–107, led by John Paxson's 17 points. The Heat rallied after Phil Jackson sat his starters and BJ Armstrong finished with 8 of the Bulls' final 14 points to save the win. Gabe and I were blessed to have his father take us to that game. It would be years before I would see another live NBA game.

* * *

During my eighth-grade year, I continued growing and maturing physically. I was not thin yet, but I was not as round as I was the year before. I now stood around 5'10" or 5'11". That year I tried fitting in socially and identifying with my *blackness* culturally more so than before. I emulated hip-hop and R&B cultures and largely listened to songs by the group 'Guy', who were just coming into their own. Some of the black girls were amused when I sang the chorus from Guy's hit song *Let's Chill.*

I updated my look as well. That year, I started off with a low-top *faded* haircut like the Atlanta Hawks guard, No. 4 Spud Webb, but I eventually grew a high-top fade. As the year went on, I got an 'S-curl' like Webb's teammate No. 21, Dominique Wilkins. Gabe got the S-curl first. I wanted to do something new and exciting after seeing Kid, from the rap duo Kid and Play, spray something into his hair during the movie *House Party*. I cared more about my fashion also. I wore my share of sports apparel, but I tried to dress up on some days in sweaters, khakis, and shoes like Ronald Jennings from my class.

That first quarter of my eighth-grade year, I made the Honor Roll, something I had never done before. It was one of the few times in my K–12 years that I would earn one of the pink certificates signifying that I'd earned a 90% or better average in all my classes. I carried that average for another semester before dropping back down into the Merit Roll, which earned a similar blue certificate. For most of elementary school, I regularly earned the white Perfect Attendance certificates, the importance of which I did not understand at the time.

One of the best students in the eighth grade was the above-mentioned Ronald Jennings. Ronald seemed to have it all together with his A-average and smooth, dapper demeanor/image. He just oozed confidence. He was dark-skinned and slightly shorter than me with bow legs. That year he started off with a high-top fade, but he transitioned to what we called a 'Gumby', a triangular-shaped haircut made famous at the time by the recording artist Bobby Brown. On some days Ronald wore steel-tipped dress shoes in addition to sweaters and the MC Hammer-type pants, which were the in thing at the time.

Ronald's resting face had a level of intensity to it. As an eighth grader there was something mature and masculine about him. It might have had something to do with his playing football for a little league team called the Buffalo Vets. One day he brought in a set of trading cards of the Vets team with his picture wearing his uniform. He could've easily been one of the Buffalo Bills.

Some of the other boys went with a dressy look on some days and mixed in sports apparel on other days. John Benson, another black boy for example, wore a lot of Adidas sweatsuits, sneakers and jewelry. John really looked up to rap artists like Run DMC and emulated the hip-hop images of the time, something that started transcending race. The girls dressed in the styles of the day as they were maturing and transitioning into womanhood.

"You can have an A average too, if you just study and do your work," Ronald nonchalantly said as a group of us walked down the hallways of Campus West. I had made a joke or comment about him and his *good* grades, pretty much revering him. I did not understand how much control I had over my academics at the time. Ronald understood that the secret was simply focus and dedication. Later that year, he earned the 'Jesse Ketchum Award', which was given to the most accomplished student/leader in class.

* * *

I returned for my eighth-grade year hoping to be more than a player-manager on the Campus West boys' basketball team. Unfortunately, going into the summer of 1989, there was no formal plan for my off-season development. A specific plan to attend a basketball camp, to strengthen my offensive and defensive fundamentals or working with a coach or a trainer would have increased the likelihood of me getting on the court. Thus, I did not come back with anything new skill-wise, such as a reliable jump shot, a dribble move, or any defensive fundamentals. I likewise do not remember Mr. Cook talking to any of us about offseason development at all.

"I've got Batman," a kid said at nearby Roosevelt Park. We were choosing teams to play pickup basketball on a 1989 Friday summer evening. I wandered over there to see if I could get into a game. I think most of the guys that evening lived in the Langfield Projects across the 33 Kensington expressway, and I did not know any of them personally. One by one, the players were picked up, and the teams were created. I was identified as *Batman* because of the black Tee-shirt I wore, one of my favorite shirts at the time. It had the traditional black and yellow symbol, and I also wore black jeans and black Nikes. Earlier that summer, Warner Brothers released the classic Batman film, which starred Michael Keaton and Jack Nicholson and was directed by Tim Burton.

This was the extent of my offseason development. It involved pickup basketball games at Roosevelt Park or wherever else I could find opportunities to play. We played games of Twenty-One also known as 'Rochester', a game of individual skill where it was every man for himself and where the first player to score 21 points won. I also played some pickup basketball at the Edison Street Baptist Church around the corner from our home on Harriet Street before we moved to Hastings Avenue. There was a basketball court in the church, and they would let some of us in to play on weeknights. I did my best with what I knew, but I still had no real direction, so my greatest benefit was simply breaking a sweat and playing with the other kids. I did not know how to create shots for myself or affect the game meaningfully.

* * *

After the summer of 1989, I expected to come back to Campus West to play for Mr. Cook again, but to my surprise, he left. Like the Chicago Bulls, we had a new coach, Mr. Dennis Rozlowski. Mr. Cook looked more like a gym teacher. He conservatively wore his sweatsuits and had a bit of an icy demeanor. Mr. Rozlowski, on the other hand, looked like the Los Angeles Lakers' Kurt Rambis—a bit of a hippie-type with his glasses, a mustache, and longer hair. Another difference was that Mr. Rozlowski wore shorts instead of sweatpants. He was looser than Mr. Cook personality-wise, and our team felt that way under him.

"Just go up strong, Anwar," Ronald Jennings told me during gym class. We were playing a game of five-on-five on two of the half-moon baskets in our vast gym. 'Going up *STRONG*' meant aggressively shooting the ball, usually in the paint, and not being afraid of contact by defenders. It was asserting oneself with the ball. On that play, I grabbed an offensive rebound and scored off a 'put back' or a shot from right next to the basket. I timidly 'pump faked' multiple times, and Ronald encouraged me to play with less fear and more strength—something he had already learned to do. It was my first time hearing that term, and because it came from him, it held special significance.

The 1989–90 CLL/CW Bengals featured many of the same players from the previous year, but some new faces as well. From our eighth-grade class, there was Ronald Jennings, John Benson, Marcus Perkins, Germaine Holton, Basheer Crawford, Vance Lagrange, John Rustevio, John Adamzyack, Cary McAllister, Josue Arroyo and me. From the seventh-grade class there was Ronald's younger brother, Jermaine Jennings, and Muhajer Alwakil.

Basheer and some of the guys jokingly called Josue 'Paco', who was on our team and class clown. Germaine Holton jokingly called John Adamzyack, 'Zachary Adams', making fun of his Polish name. The blonde-haired Cary McAllister was nicknamed 'Droopy' because of his eyes. Because of the personalities on that team, it was a fun group to play with, and the laughs were nonstop. A player absent from our roster and quietly sprouting up height-wise was James McClewer, an awkward black-haired clown of a white kid, also from our class.

I do not remember how Mr. Rozlowski conducted tryouts, but when the dust settled, I was a player on the team and not a player-manager. I might have asked him about it, wondering if I would still have my special designation, to which he told me, "No." We had to order team jerseys once again. Our 1989–90 jerseys were orange and white and the tank tops were a breathable mesh material just like the college and professional teams.

Although the team was more relaxed under Mr. Rozlowski, he did not allow us to put nicknames on our jerseys. Instead, he insisted that we use our real last names giving us more of a businesslike feel. Thus, the name on the back of my jersey was now Dunbar. Instead of taking the No. 3 as I did the year before, I took the No. 54 for the Chicago Bulls' young power forward, Horace Grant. While I wore a pair of blue and white Converse sneakers the previous year, I opted for a pair of black Nike Flights inspired by the Chicago Bulls' who wore black sneakers during the playoffs based on superstition and tradition.

We were a much stronger team than we were the previous year. The undisputed leader of the team was Ronald Jennings. He was the point guard and emerged as the leading scorer. He wore No. 21 again in honor of the Atlanta Hawks' Dominique Wilkins. Ronald was not much of a shooter from long-range, but he had a way of slashing to the basket for layups, which is how he usually scored. In some instances, he got fouled and got to the free-throw line.

Our team was also powered by the rebounding of Vance Lagrange and Basheer Crawford, as well as the outside shooting of John Benson. Other players logging significant minutes were Muhajer Alwakil, John Rustevio, Marvcus Perkins, and John Adamzyack. Early on, I noticed that Muhajer, who was not on the team the previous year, was getting playing time, and I wasn't. Though a year younger, he was somehow more comfortable on the floor than I was.

"Jermaine, STOP crying! KNOCK IT OFF," Ronald said, reprimanding his younger brother during a game. It hurt Jermaine that he also was not playing. We both watched most of that season from the bench. I was not bitter about it, though, and I was once again just happy to be on the team and to be one of the guys.

"Anwar, go in!" My first-ever basket came in a home game. We were up by so many points that Mr. Rozlowski looked down at the bench and casually put me in. When you do not get much playing time, you get butterflies when you finally get onto the floor. Once you step out between the lines, it feels like another world, and you just don't want to mess anything up. On that play I recall running the baseline back and forth and flashing with my hands, calling for the ball, which Mr. Rozlowski taught us. I felt loose, and I was not nervous that day.

On the biggest play of my life, I ran to the right side of the lane on the baseline just outside of the low block. Ronald dribbled at the top of the key, analyzing our opponents' zone defense. He saw me and without hesitation threw me a two-handed over-the-head pass. It was thrown with enough force to get to me quickly, but not so hard that it slid through my nervous hands out of bounds. Without thinking, I caught the ball in one motion and threw up a shot on pure instinct. It dropped into the cylinder, rattled around, and then fell through the net for me.

"WAAR! WAAR! WAAR!" Our bench erupted as I ran down the court. I high-fived Ronald and Vance, feeling like a million dollars. I had finally scored a basket which was my only goal then. I might as well have scored 100 points that day. Mr. Rozlowski left me in the game for just a little while longer before pulling me out. Once, I was out of the game, and then later that night, visions of the basket kept running through my mind. I can still see it today. I scored a basket!

* * *

"What are you doing here?" After surprisingly recognizing him, I questioned the opposing coach before one of our games. It was my Cousin Phillip Richardson from Aunt Rosemary's wing of the family. He was the coach for the School 45 boys' basketball team. I approached him after emerging from our locker room.

"No. What are *you* doing here?" He jokingly replied to my question. That day they came over to our gym for a scrimmage. I recognized him immediately. He was a large, muscular black man with a beard, curly coarse hair, and a round nose. He was hard to miss. We were *blood*, but I was not exposed to his side of the Buchanan family much, and I had no idea that he was into athletics or that he coached. We beat School 45 that day, and I would not see Phil again anytime soon. I would see him only sparsely over the coming years.

* * *

"It's not a Starter jacket! What kind of jacket is this? Is it a Chalk Line brand jacket?" Some of my teammates mischievously asked questions about my Chicago Bulls jacket while grabbing at the collar and trying to read the tag behind my neck. I leaned my head to the side as they aggressively grabbed at my collar and turned it so they could see the tag. I hoped they would eventually stop. "It's a Swingster brand? What's a *Swingster*?" Basheer Crawford jokingly asked out loud. We were all waiting at the bus stop on Grant Street after practice or it could have been on our way to another game.

No, my Chicago Bulls jacket was not a Starter brand. Chalk Line was the next brand under Starter. None of them had heard of a Swingster before. Being the most sheltered member of the team and one of the last to catch onto more mature things, I was often the butt of jokes, but there was camaraderie within our group of players, and I never took offense. I could tell that Basheer did not mean any real harm and again, I was happy to be one of the guys.

* * *

By the time we played Campus East, we were on a roll. Campus East was located near Delavan and Fillmore Avenues, just behind Chelsea Street, where my Great Aunt Rosemary lived. Once again, there was the angst and anticipation of walking into an opponent's gym. There was the sound of the basketballs bouncing and the ominous looks from our hosts on the way to the locker room. It was the essence of competition, the anticipation before the actual game, and then the feeling of potentially winning or losing. There is nothing like it.

That game was a total team effort. Campus East kept it close in the first half and made me think that our eight-game winning streak would end. They played a zone defense which limited Ronald's penetration. I wondered where our offense was going to come from. In the second half I watched from the bench as Vance Lagrange's offensive rebounding and John Benson's timely three-point shooting kept us close and eventually pushed us ahead. On some shots John squared up and released the ball right in front of the bench where I sat. It was one of our toughest tests of the season, but we won. Winning was a great feeling.

* * *

Our first season loss came against either North Park or one of the numbered schools. I remember that they had two incredibly talented players. Their colors were green and white. One of them was the point guard, who had a wiry frame, sleepy Asian eyes, and a lower lip that poked out. The other player was about 6'7" tall. He towered over his teammates, but still had a look of eighth grade innocence about him. He was brown-skinned, had a sharp nose and closely cut hair. I personally had a sense of intimidation by the sight of him and was unsure how Ronald and the guys would work their magic against him. While the magical combination of Ronald's penetration, John Benson's shooting and Vance LaGrange's rebounding was enough to take us this far, how would we fare against this team in this game?

As the game unfolded, the tall kid's height provided a definite advantage for our opponents in the middle of the game, offensively and defensively. He held his right arm up, slightly cocked, watching as any of our players tried to bring the ball close to the basket for layups, and he swatted everything away. In this game the referees also started calling Ronald for traveling violations, something they had not done before. Ronald shook off the first couple of whistles, but his frustration steadily mounted as each of his baskets were swiped away. He eventually lost his composure and openly contested the officiating. We lost that game and felt defeat for the first time that year.

Chapter 4. A Basketball Player: The 1989-90 Campus West Bengal Tigers Boys' Basketball Team's Run

"Man, we lost one game and everyone is doubting us," Ronald said, as we walked through the hallways of Campus West. It was my first time that year hearing our leader shaken up. I recall some girls, like Nideara Hawkins, who played on the girls' team, joking about it. It's what middle school kids did.

Even though we had just lost our first game, we had such a good record that we qualified for the Gold Dome Tournament, to be held at one of the other PSAL schools. Interestingly, our opening-round opponent was the same team we had just lost to, with the young guard and the tower in the middle. Could we beat them this time?

Even though we came out fighting hard, the green and white team eventually wore us down. Their young guard sliced our defense with precision and skill again, penetrating to the basket, and their big man stagnated our offense. Once again, the referees called Ronald for traveling, which gradually caused his frustrations to mount. He eventually stormed out of the gymnasium with his fists balled up. It was a physical game too. Marvcus Perkins eventually had to come out of the game with a bloody mouth. In the end, we lost to them again, ending our season.

We received participation trophies, and something else cool happened after the game. Mr. Rozlowski treated our entire team to a meal at McDonald's. It was a very welcome treat for a kid like me who rarely got to eat there. Ordering a quarter pounder with cheese meal was an easy choice for me. John Benson ordered a filet of fish meal, which caused me to ponder why someone would go to McDonald's and not order one of their beef burgers.

That year, at our end-of-the-year sports assembly, we all received trophies. On the front, they were inscribed with '19-CLL-CW-90' and underneath 'CHAMPS'. Ronald received the Most Valuable Player Award and then something unforgettable happened. I received the Most Improved Player Award. I did not play much, and I was shocked to receive it. I walked slowly across the stage, smiling in an embarrassed kind of way. Maybe some of my teammates, like John Benson, Marvcus Perkins, or Ronald Jennings himself, saw improvement in my game and recommended me. Maybe it was one of the other Physical Education teachers who looked on from the sidelines and thought I had improved. Perhaps Mr. Rozlowski genuinely saw me improve under his watch.

* * *

The young guard from the team that beat us twice didn't live far from my home. He lived in the Langfield Projects which was a couple of blocks from my street. Sometime after that game we met at the Roosevelt Park basketball courts on a cold, windy day when no one else was around. I was shooting and saw a figure wander over the bridge dressed in a hoodie, jeans, and sneakers. I could not see his face, and I was initially afraid after hearing stories of violence in the projects. It turned out he just wanted to shoot with me.

"What's your name man?" I asked him his name, striking up a conversation as we sat down on one of the benches between shooting baskets.

"Jeremiah," he said.

"My name is Anwar," I replied, shaking his hand.

I told him that I recognized him from our two losses to his team. He was laid back about it and humble. He said that the tall kid's name was Shareef and that he and Jeremiah talked about how they wanted to go to the NBA. He also told me that he played basketball at the Bailey Doat Boys Club, which I later joined myself, hoping to get some of the game that he had. I never saw Jeremiah there, however.

After the season ended that year, I once again did not have a plan for developing my game besides playing pickup street basketball around town. I also did not have any drills to practice over the summertime. Nor was I close enough with any of the other guys on the team to go out and play pickup basketball outside of school, which would have boosted my basketball IQ and skill level.

Most of the basketball I played was either at Roosevelt Park, other neighborhood courts, or in my backyard on a hoop on our garage that was not regulation height. Much of what I tried to do was to go up strong, as Ronald Jennings encouraged me to do. I was an empty vessel that would have willingly learned from anyone. I was oblivious to the ways to learn the game that were available to me locally.

Eventually Mom bought me an instructional basketball video by the Boston Celtics. I think it was called *Winning Basketball.* It starred Red Auerbach, Larry Bird, Kevin McHale, and some of the other Celtics. It had drills for dribbling, shooting, and some aspects of defense. I recall Kevin McHale specifically noting *not* to block shots out of bounds, but instead to keep the ball in play after gently deflecting opponents' shots. It was a good video, but how would I put it all together?

"Kevin McHale is a *bad* white boy," my Uncle Jeff said numerous times about the Celtics' No. 32, Kevin McHale, in those days. It was a huge compliment for a Celtics player, as they were largely considered a *white* team. No. 33, Larry Bird was, of course, the face of that team. *Bad,* in this instance, meant that he was highly skilled and was tough for any opponent to guard.

Looking back, one of my biggest takeaways from the video was Red Auerbach stating that the overarching objective of basketball was to put the ball through the hoop more than your opponent. There were also dribbling demonstrations by guards No. 12, Jerry Sichting and No. 5, Sam Vincent, but what was the key to putting everything together to play the game competitively there in Buffalo?

* * *

Chapter 4. A Basketball Player: The 1989-90 Campus West Bengal Tigers Boys' Basketball Team's Run

Amahl went to Hutchinson Central Technical High School, or Hutch-Tech for short, in the fall of 1988; a school my Uncle Jeff and Auntie Tracey also attended. My Uncle Scottie also attended Hutch-Tech, but did not graduate from there. My biggest motivation for attending the school was making everyone as proud of me as they were proud of Amahl. Had he gone to another high school, I would have followed him there.

Amahl brought his yearbooks home those first two years, and I studied them. I asked him about this new school he went to every day. Hutch-Tech was also on Elmwood Avenue, like the Campus Learning Lab, but it was downtown and it felt far away. Wanting to play the varsity basketball Mr. Cook discussed, I turned to the back of the yearbooks to the Hutch-Tech boys' basketball team.

The pictures were in black and white, so I could not see the school colors. The Engineers were coached by Ken Jones, a middle-aged white man with glasses. Coach Jones balding on the top of his head and had short, curly black hair around the sides. In the team photos he wore a suit, a shirt, tie and shoes, not sneakers. He looked very professorial and mild-mannered. I immediately started dreaming about playing for this Coach Jones, though I hadn't gone to any of their games.

Coach Jones stood at attention like a military sergeant next to half of his players who stood in the back row while the other half knelt in front of them. They wore all-white uniforms and looked like a college or professional team. I recognized three of their players—Charles Thompson, Quincy Lee and Dion Frasier. They were Bengal Tigers under Mr. Cook at Campus West, and they now looked older and more mature. Abraham Mungro and Adrian Brice were the lone seniors on that team. Derrick Herbert, Ed Lenard, Frankie Harris and Jerome Freeman were juniors. Charles Thompson, Curtis Brooks, Jerrold Skillon, and Quincy Lee were sophomores. Finally, Dion Frasier, Jermaine Skillon, Michael Mann and Chris Souter (the only white kid on the team), were freshman. They wore warmup shirts over their jerseys, covering up their numbers. There were four or five team managers in those pictures as well. One was Monica Peterson from my church, Tried Stone Baptist Church on Humboldt Parkway.

In addition to the team picture I saw in the yearbook, there were several action shots with captions beneath them. The team they were playing in the picture was primarily African American. 'Youth and Inexperience' was the title of the team's summary. In Amahl's first year at Hutch-Tech he, in fact, told me that the boys' basketball team lost a lot of games.

For the 1989-90 season, the Hutch-Tech team had improved and qualified for the sectionals, which was a big deal. The title for that yearbook summary was 'A Slow Start', suggesting that it was a mixed season for them with an unimpressive start, but a strong finish. The yearbook contained action pictures of players like No. 20, Derrick Herbert, handling the ball, and No. 13, Curtis Brooks, shooting the ball. Another guy, No. 33, Michael Brundige, dunked the ball and hyped up the crowd. Interestingly, I noticed that he wasn't on the team the previous year. No. 22, Jerome Freeman, played defense and worked hard to prevent the opposite team's offensive player from advancing the ball, which was captured in another picture. No. 55, Charles 'Chuck' Thompson, battled for a rebound in another picture. Another addition to the team was No. 30, Paul Saunders, from Campus West. Paul, Curtis Brooks and Jerome Freeman all wore a pair of 1988-89 Air Jordans. They looked like a strong team, and it looked like a good place to play basketball.

At a Hutch-Tech open house the boys' basketball team scrimmaged in the gym. It was not a large gym like the one we had at Campus West, but instead it was small and boxy, located in the basement of the old H-shaped building. I did not recognize any of the players. Although I did recognize Coach Jones. He energetically ran up and down the floor with team, blowing his whistle and stopping to instruct them before resuming play. It all confirmed my wanting to play for him.

You had to academically qualify to attend Hutch-Tech. You could not just attend without taking the entrance exam. Gabe and I took the Hutch-Tech entrance exam on the same day. His father, Bernie, was an alumnus, just like my relatives. Gabe started attending Cleveland Hill Elementary School when his family moved to Cheektowaga. He was in the fifth or sixth grade. Our friendship remained intact and I really wanted us to reunite in high school.

Gabe and I entered Hutch-Tech High School wearing our Chicago Bulls jackets surrounded by a sea of other kids that I did not recognize. It was the day before Thanksgiving and none of the Hutch-Tech students were there, just faculty members and volunteers. Gabe took his exam in different room than I did, and I felt some angst about us being split up. Because we finished at different times, I did not see him afterward. The exam asked a variety questions from numerous subjects, most notably math and science. When I turned in my exam I wondered how I had done. I did not apply to any other schools. Where would I go if I did not get into Hutch-Tech High School?

* * *

As opposed to thinking about my next steps in life, many of my thoughts back then were about fitting in socially. I started the year on the honor roll (a 90% overall average and upward), but my grades gradually slid back into the merit roll (an average of 80-89%). My favorite class that year was probably English with Dr. David Sylveres, a middle-aged bearded, Ivy League type. His teaching method was dry, but he exposed us to some great stories, including *The Ransom of Red Chief*, *The Most Dangerous Game*, and *Flowers for Algernon*. I still remember those stories.

Chapter 4. A Basketball Player: The 1989-90 Campus West Bengal Tigers Boys' Basketball Team's Run

I studied American History with Mr. Lee, who was previously an administrator, and Physical Science with Dr. Sinatra. Physical Science was the precursor to Physics, the *grandfather* of all the sciences. I did not take to it like I took to Life Science the previous year with Mr. Radamaker. His class was fun and I absorbed the material easily. Physical Science did not appeal to me then, or at least not the way Dr. Sinatra taught it.

In my freshman year I discovered girls. A year earlier, I developed a big crush on a girl named Tamekia Toller, but that did not go anywhere. In the eighth grade I strongly liked the previously mentioned Nideara Hawkins, whom I had barely noticed before. I was taken by her brown skin, thick lips and overall beauty. I noticed her shape too. She had round, voluptuous hips, a curvy backside and healthy thighs. She gave me her phone number towards the end of the year, even though she was talking to some guy at another school. Later, I realized that she didn't take me seriously. The same could be said about most of the other black kids in my class.

"Anwar, why do you always use those *big words*?" Some of my classmates, the girls in particular, asked me this question repeatedly. It was mostly the black girls. With my big words I think they saw me as a little awkward and nerdy, and I felt that way. My vocabulary was simply a byproduct of reading being encouraged at my home.

* * *

On June 6, 1990, I graduated from grade school at Rockwell Hall, on the Buffalo State College campus. It was an exciting, but sad time. Most of my friends were moving on to different high schools, and we would not be classmates anymore. I was admitted to Hutch-Tech after passing the entrance exam, as were five or six classmates from Campus West. Some students were going to Seneca Vocational High School, some went to the Buffalo Academy for the Visual and Performing Arts. Still others went to Riverside High School. One classmate was going to Kenmore West High School in the suburbs. And even though he met the entrance requirements for Hutch-Tech, Ronald Jennings chose to attend a private school called Turner/Carroll. I was disappointed, as I had hoped we would continue as teammates on the basketball court.

It was a beautiful ceremony. The boys wore blue caps and gowns, while the girls wore gold. We were all so young and innocent. We sang a song called *Responsibility*, and they played the song *That's What Friends Are For,* by Dionne Warwick, Gladys Knight, Elton John and Stevie Wonder over a montage of photographs of our eighth-grade class.

Dad drove to the ceremony from Schenectady and he took multiple pictures that night with one of his large old-school cameras. Some of those pictures were of Amahl, Gabe and me goofing off in the parking lot behind my mother and grandmother as we made our way to the ceremony. I took a picture with Tamekia Toller and Tamara Johnson. I did not know how to put my arms around them, so I just stood with them with my hands at my sides, smiling. Dad made fun of me about it later. I also took pictures with my teammates. I shed some tears during and after the ceremony, knowing that I would not see many classmates anymore who had become such a familiar part of my life.

The night was not over. After the ceremony, Mom and Grandma went home while Dad took Amahl, Gabe and me out to get something to eat and hang out. Later, I stayed with Dad in his room at the Travelodge Motel in downtown Buffalo.

"You don't have to hide your chest from me, son," Dad said as I removed my shirt with my back turned. "You don't have to be ashamed of how your body looks."

"Okay," I responded. The ridicule from my classmates was still fresh in my mind. I was ashamed of how my 13-year-old body looked. Because I was plump, I had male breasts in seventh and eighth grades, which made me the brunt of jokes, especially by the black girls who called me 'Titty-Man'. It rattled an already fragile self-esteem. Most kids had something they were made fun of over, so I wasn't alone. Like Nideara Hawkins, kids made fun of her because of her large forehead. Marcus Perkins had strong breath most of the time and the kids were relentless. The running joke about LaDedra Morton was that she looked like the boxer, Mike Tyson. Finally, Martina Marinelli was continuously called 'Butch', a slur that I was slow to understand in terms of the implication.

I can't believe it's over, I constantly thought to myself as I laid in bed at the Travelodge. The next morning, Dad took us to Gi Gi's, a black-owned soul food restaurant on East Ferry Street. It was his favorite eatery in Buffalo. I think Amahl and I got into trouble that day because Mom wanted us back home at a certain time. Dad defiantly brought us back later than he was supposed to.

Dad parked his blue Buick on Hastings Avenue a couple of houses down from our house. We took a couple of pictures in front of his car, father and sons. Dad wore one of his button-down short-sleeved shirts, brown slacks and brown shoes. Amahl wore his blue jacket, khakis, and glossy steel-tipped shoes. I had on my white Chicago Bulls Swingster jacket, shorts and black Nike Flights with the S-curl on top of my head.

My eyes were red and watery because Dad was about to leave. I did not completely cry this time like I used to, as I was now older. Shortly after taking the pictures he got into his car and headed east back to his life in Schenectady. That fall of 1990, a new chapter would start for me, high school—a four-year journey after which my innocent basketball dreams and life would never be the same.

Chapter 5. Skill, Knowledge, Power: The Old H-Shaped Building

"I remember when we were teenagers, we thought we knew everything. We thought we were grown, and we really weren't." —**Mom and my Uncle Tony at family gatherings in the late 1980s and early 1990s**

At thirteen to fourteen years of age, I could not fathom life in my twenties and beyond. I could only see the four years ahead of me, and I had no idea who I would be on the back end. My motivation for attending Hutch-Tech High School was simply to make my family proud of me. It was through Amahl attending Hutch-Tech that I learned of Coach Ken Jones and the Hutch-Tech boys' basketball team. I had only seen them in the black-and-white pictures in Amahl's yearbooks. As the fall of 1990 approached, I dreamt of playing for Coach Jones. It was an exciting time, and the world was changing on many fronts. Towards the end of the summer of 1990, I pondered entering high school and playing basketball there, but that was just one of many events happening in our world.

***

Around the time of Amahl's birthday in August 1990, the dictator Saddam Hussein of Iraq in the Middle East, invaded a neighboring country called Kuwait. His face was all over the television stations and newspapers. He was brown skinned with short black hair, a bushy mustache and a stone face. He wore a military uniform with a matching beret, often smoking a cigar. President George Herbert Walker Bush condemned the invasion and promised a response by the United States. In his addresses, he pronounced Saddam like he was saying Adam, but with an S at the front. I had yet to take a world history course, and I was unfamiliar with either country.

Over the next four months a coalition force led by the United States and member countries of the United Nations assembled and embarked on two campaigns to liberate Kuwait. The first was 'Operation Desert Shield' which established the forces in the Persian Gulf. The second was 'Operation Desert Storm', an offensive campaign against Iraq itself. Critics thought the conflict was only about securing the oil in the region, though President Bush insisted it was about liberating Kuwait. It was the first major military conflict I was aware of in my lifetime.

Neither I, Amahl, nor any of our close friends were old enough to participate in the war. For us it was something we would only see on TV. That is, until we found out that our father was being sent to the Persian Gulf that winter as a part of his duties in the Air Force Reserves. He would be part of a medical unit, not in combat. I do not know how my brother took it, but it gave me feelings of uncertainty, as my father and I were close. It was in the back of my mind when my first year of high school started.

* * *

The early '90s were a special time, even in an old 'Rust Belt' city like Buffalo, which had seen better days. For me, it was still a relatively innocent time. It was prior to cell phones, the internet, social media, and reality TV. On my first day of high school in the fall of 1990, I woke up and turned on the 'Breakfast Club' on Power 94-93.7 WBLK FM, the only 24/7 black radio station in Buffalo, if I recall correctly. I listened to the show on the cassette radio Dad gave me one Christmas. Gabe's parents gave him one, and I wanted one myself. Gabe and I were like *twins* or *shadows* as my cousin, Monica Willis from Atlanta, referred to us once. If he did or had something, I wanted to do it or have it as well.

The Breakfast Club was a show hosted by Brian Scott, Kim Fox and Lou St. James. They had probably gotten the name from the famous 1980s teen movie, *The Breakfast Club*. Emilio Estevez, Molly Ringwald, Anthony Michael Hall, and Judd Nelson all starred in the movie. If you were black in Buffalo, the Breakfast Club radio show probably got you started in the morning. They played songs like *Love Crazy* by Atlantic Starr, *Tender Kisses* by Tracie Spencer, or some other hip hop or R&B grooves. They also discussed what was happening in the general news and in black media. The James Lofton Report ran once or twice a week around the Buffalo Bills' games. Lofton was one of the Bills' star wide receivers.

A popular song that year was *I Want to Sex You Up* by Color Me Badd, which was on the *New Jack City* soundtrack, along with tracks like *New Jack Hustler* by Ice-T, *I'm Dreaming* by Christopher Williams, *There You Go Telling Me No* by Keith Sweat, and an interpretation of *For the Love of Money* by Troop featuring Queen Latifah. That year I listened to the *Mo Money* soundtrack quite a bit, which had songs on it like *The Best Things in Life Are Free* by Janet Jackson and Luther Vandross, *Let's Just Run Away* by Johnny Gill, and *A Job Ain't Nothing But Work* by a new group called Lo-Key featuring the popular rapper, Big Daddy Kane. Gabe bought the soundtrack, and I dubbed it on a cassette tape for myself.

Before the school year started I regularly listened to the album, *Edutainment,* by the rapper KRS-One, who was the leader of the group Boogie Down Productions out of the South Bronx. He had a conscious/historic focus, rapping about everything from African History to African American History, to socioeconomics and politics. As with most of my music, I got *Edutainment* from Gabe. Again, whatever Gabe did, I did or tried to do too.

* * *

I began my freshman year at Hutch-Tech still wearing my S-curl haircut. Looking in the mirror that first morning I could not see it, but my body had matured further from early summer. Comparing my seventh and eighth-grade pictures from Campus West to my freshman year, it was clear. I wore my Detroit Pistons World Championship tee shirt from the 1989–90 season which they repeated the following year, beating the Portland Trail Blazers. I was a Bulls fan, but I loved the caricatured championship tee shirts. I put on a pair of jeans and a new pair of low-top black Nikes Mom bought for me. Tee shirts, sweatshirts, jeans, and sneakers with occasional sweaters, khakis, and shoes made up my wardrobe that year.

The three of us (Mom, Amahl and me) ate breakfast together as we did most of the time. It was cold or hot cereal on some days and eggs and homemade pancakes on others; usually the weekends. After breakfast, Amahl and I departed for one of the Niagara Frontier Transportation Authority (NFTA) Metrobus stops on Eggert Road. Before high school my trips to and from school were on the 'cheese' or yellow buses, but not anymore. Buffalo Public School students received bus passes and rode public transportation. We caught the #12 Utica 'Special' bus, which made its way from the Buffalo-Cheektowaga border on the east side to the 33 Expressway exiting at Utica Street and Humboldt Parkway in the city. It let us off at the Theater Place Station on Main Street near Chippewa Street.

We sat in the back of the bus where the seats faced each other. With his glasses, blue jacket, button-down shirt, khakis and black steel-tipped shoes, which were in style for black youth, Amahl looked kind of preppy. Paisley and polka dot button-down shirts were also in style. The boys mostly wore a high-top fade or forward or sideways slope cuts; while the girls mostly wore mushroom cuts. The fashion in Buffalo was very much influenced by the hip-hop and R&B culture from the 'New Jack' era, which originated in New York City.

As we got on the expressway, two upperclassmen recognized Amahl. They looked at us, pointed, and snickered, recognizing that we were brothers. I just looked on, nervously thinking about this new world that I was entering. It was scary, but exciting at the same time.

From Theater Place Station we walked west on Chippewa Street, passing a strip of adult shops and pornography stores. At the corner of South Elmwood and Chippewa stood the H-shaped building, which was dark brown from years and years of pollution in the air, probably from the steel mills south of the city in

Lackawanna. Waves of students flocked to the school from all directions, most of whom I did not recognize.

The enormity of entering this new world slowly sunk in. Hutch-Tech was an older structure than Campus West. It both looked different and it felt different. Instead of a carpeted and comfortable small building on a college campus, this was a massive factory-like structure with an industrial chemical smell on the inside. On many days, that smell was mixed with the odor of wood dust on the lowest floor due to the presence of the shop classrooms. Likewise, the smell of chlorine was strong coming from the swimming pool.

After entering the front wooden doors of the school, Amahl took me to the auditorium and then quickly disappeared with his backpack in tow over his right shoulder. He was a junior, so this was all routine for him. I looked with discomfort at the auditorium full of faces I did not recognize. Because the Smiths lived in Cheektowaga Gabe could not attend Hutch-Tech unless he used his grandmother's address on Best Street, a common loophole used by many families. His parents ultimately decided to keep him at Cleveland Hill High School, and we were destined to never be classmates again.

All throughout my brother's first two years of high school, I heard stories about Mr. Joseph Gentile, the stern-looking, tan-colored man with short hair, big glasses and a black beard. There were so many stories about his leading Hutch-Tech to the 'National School of Excellence' status two years earlier and how he ruled the school with an iron fist. Vivid in my mind was the story about my brother's best friend Dorian Johnson, who thought he had escaped detention the previous year, only to have Mr. Gentile call off a list of the names of students who still had to pay their debt.

It seemed like our class, and those behind us, would never know Hutch-Tech under Mr. Gentile's watch. He departed Hutch-Tech and was replaced by Ms. Barbara Schnell, a petite middle-aged white woman with short, graying blonde hair. What most of the students would remember about her are the pink slippers that many of them joked about. The senior and junior classes she had inherited from Mr. Gentile, the classes of 1991 and 1992, were stellar in every way and were very well-behaved. What would come after them remained to be seen.

* * *

Skill, Knowledge, and Power were the three maroon words on the official seal or coat of arms of Hutch-Tech High School. The words were wrapped around a maroon inverted triangle with a T on the inside. The triangle was surrounded by a maroon circle. This seal embodied the principles of Hutch-Tech, principles which some of the students took seriously throughout their four years.

Chapter 5. Skill, Knowledge, Power: The Old H-Shaped Building

My core classes as a freshman were like the ones I had at Campus West such as language arts, history, math, and science courses. My other classes were electives, including a foreign language (Spanish) and a computer class. I also took a pre-architecture course and a career/occupations course. And finally, a required physical education class, which for all incoming freshmen, was swimming.

My homeroom teacher that year was Mr. Augello. It was room 207 on the second floor. Room 207 overlooked the front courtyard of the building, the front of the H. Mr. Augello was a middle-aged Italian man with glasses. He had no hair on the top of his head, but there was gray hair on the sides of his head. He was a little round in the stomach, rarely smiled, and had a gritty voice. He usually wore a polo shirt, khakis and shoes. He taught Global Studies.

What I remember most about that class was how unruly we were at times. When Mr. Augello was not teaching us about the Empress Dowager, Indira Gandhi, or Jawaharlal Nehru, the class always became rowdy to the point where it felt like a zoo. Order was restored when a sharp slamming noise came from the front of the room. We would all turn to see Mr. Augello standing there staring at us stone-faced, holding his metal rod against the board. This ritual became so common that, at times, I would turn to see him looking at us, hoping to avoid the shock of it, but I never did. You knew it was coming, and he startled us every time.

As with elementary school, the class that came easiest for me was General Biology, taught by Mr. Lee, a graying middle-aged, roundly-shaped man with glasses who spoke in a monotone voice. My hand shot up at every opportunity, answering questions about the classification of different organisms, cells, or the basic molecules of life. The class started off differently than my Life Science class in elementary school, which was taught by the young and enthusiastic Mr. Radamaker two years earlier. Mr. Lee started his class by giving us an overview of the basic organic molecules of life: proteins, sugars, fats, and nucleic acids. Then he proceeded into greater detail.

In the back of the classroom sat a dark-skinned, energetic, conspicuous and mischievous-looking kid named Charles Huggins. I still remember seeing 'Chucky' for the first time and wondering what his deal was. We made eye contact a few times. I had never seen anyone like him before. He was hyperactive as he chewed his gum and squirmed in his seat.

In general, I was unfocused academically as a freshman. The two classes that came easiest to me were General Biology and English, both of which I had a natural inclination. A studious looking middle-aged man with glasses and thin black hair named Mr. Kerr taught my English class that year. He always wore a white button-down shirt with black slacks and he never failed to bring his coffee thermos to class. English class was immediately after lunch that year, and I recall being tired and sometimes confused, because he would give us very simple and dispassionate instructions such as how to craft an essay. My grades in other classes depended upon whatever attention span I had left after English class. I did not understand the need for some of my classes, like computer programming for instance. I had no interest in programming computers. Consistently excelling in every class would be a challenge for me over the next four years. There were occasional flashes of brilliance, but no consistency.

* * *

With roughly 1,000 students, Hutch-Tech was much bigger than Campus West. There were so many pretty girls in my class. If they read this, they will know who they are. At the time I lacked social confidence, which hindered me from forming any meaningful friendships with them. That said, my black female classmates were not the only ones I considered beautiful. I also noticed the white and Puerto Rican girls. And that was just in my class. There were many, many females in the upper classes of 1991, '92 and '93 who would not have given me the time of day as a freshman, but whom I secretly admired and desired.

All the upperclassmen, especially the class of '91 seniors, seemed so mature and adult-like. They had developed physically and mentally. Having been at the top of the hierarchy at Campus West, I was now at the bottom socially in this new high school world. Having faithfully studied my brother's yearbooks I recognized the members of the boys' basketball team immediately, and I was in awe when I saw them in the hallways. I recognized Curtis Brooks, Jerrold 'Pep' Skillon, Charles 'Chuck' Thompson, Quincy Lee and Paul Saunders.

Lee, Saunders and Thompson were now bigger and more grown-up versions of the kids I saw years ago at Campus West. Chuck Thompson reached the height of 6'5" and had a hulk-like physique. Paul Saunders had a bit of a babyface and was about 6'1". The same was true for the wiry Quincy Lee. Shorter than Chuck Thompson at 6'2", Pep Skillon also had a Hulk-like build. Curtis Brooks was also well built at 5'11". The latter three played football that year.

Seeing them around the halls of Hutch-Tech that year, they always looked like they were having fun, but they were not loud and obnoxious guys in terms of harassing other students. They wore the typical attire for young black men in that era: paisley or polka dot button-down shirts, jeans, khakis, boots, and sneakers. Like most kids, they wore sweatshirts and hoodies from their favorite colleges and universities on some days. Their whole class looked like that. They were a close and powerful group but not loud, arrogant, and gaudy.

My brother's class of 1992 was a different story. They were loaded with a whole cast of characters like Jermaine 'J-Bird' Skillon, Pep's younger brother. Amahl had talked about him, and I had also seen him in the boys' basketball team's yearbook pictures. J-Bird had a commanding presence and was very confident in the hallways. He was much stockier than his brother. Then there was Jason Paris, who was nicknamed 'J-Paris'. I had heard my brother mention him also. He was a suave guy who wore glasses and had short, curly hair. There was a skinny junior named Adonis Coble whom Amahl also mentioned. These guys and others were all larger-than-life personalities who made their presence known throughout the hallways.

There were many more characters in the class of 1992 whose names I will not mention. A group of them called themselves the 'Cock Diesel Crew' or the 'CDC', many of which were football players. Some of the guys in that class did not talk as much, who weren't as noticeable, and who you could easily miss. Overall, the class of 1992 was a great group.

The class of 1993 had more than its fair share of personalities and characters, perhaps more than any other class. One was Roderick Peoples who was nicknamed 'Spanky'. He was a muscular kid who wore glasses and lived in the Langfield Projects. A group of guys called themselves the 'Mack Daddies', which gave them an identity within the student body like the class of 1992's CDC. These were all guys who stood out as they walked down the hallways, cracking jokes, causing mischief, and in some cases, picking on us freshmen as they did one time when some of them sprayed my classmate David Lees with water guns. Like the class of 1992, there was another set of more studious guys in the class of 1993 whom you could easily miss.

Amahl jokingly classified the student body into the 'A crowd', the 'B crowd', and the 'C crowd', suggesting there was a social hierarchy at the school. Socially speaking, there were definite tiers in the student body, and he was right in that there were 'stars' in our little high school world. Most people fell into one of them, and some fell into none. In the end the crowd that mattered most was that which was always on the Honor Roll. I could not see that at the time.

Like Campus West, I found myself looking at some of the other guys in my class and thinking that they had it going on, a form of 'hero worship'. They seemed to be at peace with themselves and outwardly appeared to have confidence with the opposite sex. Someone I would classify as my new 'Ronald Jennings' was Shaun Willis. He and some of the other guys seemed to know exactly what to say to the girls and how to get along with them.

I put Ranald Davison from Campus West in this class as well, though he was what I would have called an undercover gangster. He was down with a lot of the guys from the gang 'BSP', which was an acronym for 'Bailey Style Posse' or 'Bailey Street Posse'. We were cool at Campus West, but I did not associate with him as much at Hutch-Tech. A guy by the name of Jared Hiddleston and a classmate named Terrance Collison also came from Campus West. I saw them from a distance, but did not get to know well that year.

"Hestin, Anwar has been doing really good work lately, and I don't want to see you distracting him," said Mr. Dicorzo, reprimanding one of my new friends named Hestin Brown in our Mechanical Drawing class. Hestin was another black kid, albeit a chunky one, who was musically gifted. I originally hung out with Hestin Brown and the fast-talking Chucky Huggins, who turned out to be two of the biggest clowns in our class. Chucky nicknamed himself the 'Smack Daddy' because he talked so much *smack*. They already knew each other, and I became the group's third member.

"You *ribbing* on me? You *breaking* on me?" Chucky asked this of anyone who engaged him in one of his comical battles of wits. Hestin, and especially Chucky, would probably be best remembered for 'ribbing' or what some circles would call 'playing the dozens'. It was a way of playfully making fun of people for their unchangeable physical attributes, some of which were naturally evolving. Sometimes I engaged with them, but often quit early because my feelings would easily get hurt. They also clowned around with a tall and skinny kid named Gary Lane, who came to Hutch-Tech from City Honors, and tiny Roger Crowler.

Watching all of them interact and make fun of one another, and sometimes getting involved myself, were good times. There were other people in our class who, just like the rest of the school, fell in between the cracks of the A, B and C crowds or did not fit in with any of them. Two of these were Alim and Raheem Gaines, fraternal twins who looked very studious on the outside, because they both wore glasses, but didn't say much. I did not get to know them, initially.

Most of the kids I have discussed were black, but Hutch-Tech was, and is, a multicultural school. By default, I spent more time with the black kids based on comfort level. There was a significant Puerto Rican population, and a small number of Asians. I do not have memories of any middle eastern classmates.

* * *

There were many clubs and extracurricular activities available at Hutch-Tech including the Student Government, the Intra-Class Council, and the honor fraternities and sororities, 'Kappa Sigma Phi' and 'Beta Sigma Phi', respectively, both of which I had no insight. You had to be on top of your academic game to join these groups. Looking at the 1990–'91 picture(s), only one of the twenty-plus boys in the club was black. I only saw was a bunch of preppy guys and not future societal leaders, which is what they were on track to become.

There were many other intellectual and arts-related clubs at Hutch-Tech. Among them was the Student Council, the National Honor Society, the Chess Club, the Debate Team, the Mock Trial Team, Math Team, Writing Club, the Community Leadership Team, Building Enhancement Society, BEAM (Buffalo Engineering Awareness for Minorities) and the Architectural Design Society, among others. There were opportunities to be library tutors/monitors. The girls (mostly black) had the Hutch-Tech Drill Team. There was a choir, which was primarily made up of black students; and the school band, which, I believe, went to Busch Gardens in Virginia every year.

And of course, there were the sports teams. Hutch-Tech competed in pretty much everything a student could want, except boys' volleyball and wrestling, which the Buffalo Public Schools did not offer. Our football team was allegedly solid during my brother's freshman year. Somehow it fell into mediocrity. Many blamed it on the new coach, Bill Boyleston, a gregarious larger-than-life older white gentleman who wore glasses and had thinning gray hair and bowlegs. Mr. Boyleston had a distinct dramatic Broadway stage-like personality and voice. He was the overseer of the football team when I arrived at Hutch-Tech. He also coached the girls' basketball team and its star player, No. 34, Latoya Crumpton. Latoya was an athletic slender brown complexioned girl from the class of 1993. She wore a short 'Jheri curl' hairstyle. She was a basketball phenom and often fearlessly played with boys at every opportunity. Latoya was the top player on Mr. Bolyeston's basketball team every year.

Mr. Girard coached both the boys' and girls' swimming teams. He was a pleasant older white gentleman with gray hair who had been on staff since my brother, Amahl, started at Hutch-Tech two years earlier. Ms. Kathy Garcenea, or more respectfully, *Coach* Garcenea, coached the boys' baseball team and assisted Coach Boyleston with the football team. She wore her hair short and she wore Adidas, Nike or Reebok sweatsuits most of the time; and sunglasses and baseball caps when coaching outside. She was a short athletically built woman who had a bit of a New York City-like swagger about her and spoke like one of the guys. All the students loved Coach Garcenea. I think she was of Italian descent. Mr. Galluciano, who taught history, coached the bowling teams. Mr. Shea, who taught social studies, coached the cross country team, which my brother participated in, and Mr. Pressley coached the track and field teams.

The boys' basketball team was headed by none other than Coach Jones. In addition to the varsity team, Coach Jones organized an intramural program for the boys of the school so that they could participate in semi-organized play with team names, records, etc. It was a well-oiled machine where teams were chosen in a draft-like format and scores were kept. We had student volunteer referees blowing whistles and calling fouls, most of which the players contested. There was something there for boys who just wanted to play noncompetitively. For boys who wanted to play on the varsity team, it was a good way to make themselves known.

Upperclassmen played on Tuesdays and Thursdays, while freshmen played on Fridays. I would go in early on Tuesdays and Thursdays to watch the games. They took place on both halves of the tiny court; teams played shirts and skins. Sitting in the stands, I witnessed Coach Jones patrol the sidelines and watch the games himself.

"JUST PLAY AND LET THE REFEREES DO THEIR JOBS!" He yelled at the players, seemingly protecting the student referees. It was the first time I heard his raspy and thunderous voice. Remembering the pictures of Coach Jones in Amahl's yearbooks, he was the opposite of what I expected. He was in good shape for an older man. He had a sharp chin and nose and he was balding on the top of his head, with short curly black hair on the sides. He took long, powerful strides with his bowlegs and looked as though he was floating, but with a slight bounce. Finally, he was dressed similarly to how I saw him at the open house the previous year—in his polo shirt, short shorts, and sneakers with striped socks.

As I watched the games, I recognized many of the upperclassmen. Curtis Brooks was amazingly fast as he advanced the ball up the floor, his head up all the time, looking to make a play. Many of the other football players participated as well. I remember seeing Amahl play once, and the guys from his class of 1992 were particularly vocal during the games, complaining to the refs and trash-talking during the contests in the early morning hours.

For my class of 1994 on those Friday mornings, I do not recall us having formal teams. I didn't enjoy playing skins because I was still uncomfortable with my body. Not having formally developed my game, I was unable to score consistently. One player in my class who stood out was the previously mentioned Shaun Willis. He was a little shorter than me, but had large hands and huge calves. He could easily rise up and dunk the ball, usually off two feet like Spud Webb from the Atlanta Hawks in the NBA. I admired that. I immediately thought he was our best player. Since freshmen had to take swimming, Friday intramurals presented the best opportunities for me to play basketball at the school that year.

"SOME OF YOU GUYS ARE GOING TO BE STINKING BY SIXTH PERIOD," someone from my class jokingly yelled out in the visitor's locker room after intramurals one day. The visitor's locker room wasn't much of a locker room, there were no lockers. It was a vast dark room with benches and coat hooks along the walls. Adjacent to it was what I'll call a prison-like shower room because there was no privacy, if you know what I mean. Coach Jones gave participants the option of showering after intramurals. Hutch-Tech was indeed like an older industrial building. The lever for the showers was in the shared coaches' offices, as was their own personal shower. I later noticed that Coach Jones himself and the other coaches regularly showered after workouts. At first I didn't shower, but later I opted for good personal hygiene throughout my school day.

It was a good time to be at Hutch-Tech, and if you liked basketball there was a lot of opportunities available to you, particularly in 1990–91. Consistent with our school's core principles of Skill, Knowledge and Power, we were there to be students first. Unfortunately, it would take some of us a little bit of trial and error to learn how to juggle our coursework and the extracurricular activities.

Chapter 6. Unqualified For the Junior Varsity Team

"I was pretty much an A-average student in the second half of high school. I came out roughly a B student considering how rough the first two years were."
—Carlton Ford, Player, the Hutch-Tech boys' basketball team, 1991-93, August 2018

My Uncle Wesley J. McKinney, living in Buffalo, made my freshman year very special. The middle initial 'J' in his name stood for Jeffrey. Uncle Jeff was the sixth of my grandmother's eight children. His siblings gave him the nickname 'Bodine' after the *Beverley Hillbillies* character Jethro Bodine.

He attended Hutch-Tech in the 1970s. Afterward, he entered the United States Air Force, where he served overseas. He later settled in Omaha, NE. I had no knowledge of Nebraska, but I kept hearing my mother and grandmother talk about it. It could've been a foreign country as far as I was concerned.

After Uncle Jeff was discharged from the Air Force, like many people who left Buffalo, Uncle Jeff returned to regroup and figure out his next moves in life. He found a job at one of the Tops Friendly Markets stores, our major local supermarket chain, and worked in the bakery. It was a logical fit as he was always interested in the culinary arts and was unofficially our family chef.

What was great was that he stopped over to our house regularly. We would sit and watch sports as he sipped on his beer and told stories about the Air Force. He insisted that they made *real* beer in Germany, for example, unlike the watered-down beer in the United States. I was too young to know what he meant. Any beer that I sipped tasted terrible. It was cool, though, because I could bond with a male figure and partake in his experiences.

I was most impressed with his knowledge of sports. Uncle Jeff knew a lot about college and professional football, basketball and baseball. We never went out and played anything like I did with Uncle John and Uncle Scottie on their visits, but I learned so much just listening to Uncle Jeff. He was an invaluable resource, and for that short period of time, he filled in something that had been missing in my basketball journey. Sitting and talking sports with my Uncle Jeff was one of the best times of my life.

"Anwar, Lenny Bias was supposed to continue the Boston Celtics' dynasty! He was going to take over for Larry Bird, and those guys and the Celtics were going to keep winning," Uncle Jeff said passionately one day. I had seen a picture of a guy named Len Bias in one of the NBA yearbooks I purchased from Tops. It was on his draft night. He wore a gray and white striped suit, with a shirt and black tie and his new Boston Celtics baseball cap. The year was 1986. It was immediately after Commissioner David Stern announced that the Celtics picked him early in the first round of the NBA draft. He sat smiling and looking away, knowing that he had made it to the NBA, the dream for so many youngsters that was only achieved by a select few. His entire life and professional career were ahead of him. He was destined to impact the future of the NBA and everything basketball-related, its fans, businesses endorsements, everything.

No. 34, Len Bias, was ultra-talented, and I heard he went toe to toe with Michael Jordan when the University of Maryland played the University of North Carolina. One of the stories I heard about them was that Bias held his own against Michael and did not back down. Some argued that he was better than Michael, something I couldn't fathom. He died tragically of a cocaine overdose in a dorm room on the University of Maryland at College Park campus shortly after being drafted. Again, some said he was better than Michael or would have been better had he lived.

"Michael Jordan isn't the best player in the world, Anwar," Uncle Jeff said, something that confused me based on what I had been seeing on TV and the magic surrounding Michael and the NBA. It was something Dad and I also discussed. The significance of the statement was that Michael, while great, was simply the best player who stayed in school, stayed healthy, did not get snatched away by violent crime, and made it all the way to the proverbial basketball mountain top.

There were countless other players who did not make it for many reasons. For young black men, two of the main hindrances were poor academics and criminal behavior. It was around that time when I first heard of a player named Ritchie Campbell, a local phenom who was arguably the best basketball player Buffalo had ever produced. He did not reach his full potential due to academics and crime-related activities. He had a reputation of being like a basketball God.

Uncle Jeff hung around Buffalo for about a year before leaving again. He went down south to New Orleans. While I wish he had been around longer to pour more of his knowledge into me, the times that we sat and watched sports were special. For young people like me who were still relatively new to athletics and competition, hearing stories about players like Len Bias from people who had seen him play was very valuable. There was value in knowing *about* basketball and its history, in addition to playing it.

* * *

My lack of academic focus came back to bite me for the first time when our first-quarter grades came out during my freshman year. My highest grade was 96% in General Biology, the class that excited me the most. For most of my other classes, my grades were somewhere between 70% and 85%. In Global Studies, I earned a measly 67%. With just a little more focus, I could have gotten my grade above the 70% threshold, which was necessary to participate in the basketball program and all the interscholastic athletics at Hutch-Tech.

Sometime after Coach Jones put the call out over the morning announcements for the tryouts for the varsity team, he made a similar announcement for freshmen and sophomores to try out for the junior varsity team. The announcement specifically said that a 70% average was needed in one's core courses to participate. I had not completely developed an understanding of academic requirements and self-accountability yet and wondered if the rules could be bent for me.

I remember approaching Coach Jones about it afterward, hoping that he had let me slide somehow. We had little history together and he only knew me in passing. He might have also known me as Amahl Dunbar's younger brother. It was down by the coaches' offices, and he stood by the bulletin boards when I approached him.

"Excuse me, Coach Jones," I said, walking over to him sheepishly. "I'd like to come out for the junior varsity team."

"Dunbar, is it?" He responded to my statement with a question in his raspy and scratchy voice. He was much more relaxed in comparison to the angry shouting person I saw at intramurals. He wore his signature polo shirt, shorts, socks and sneakers. He stood bow-legged with his hairy arms folded, peering at me from behind his glasses. *Dr.* Jones, as Coach Garcenea often referred to him, looked very professorial with his sharp nose and chin, his thick, slightly gray, and black curly hair on the sides of his head, and with thinner threads on the top.

"Yes," I replied to him, holding my little secret, which I was hoping he would give me a pass on.

"Well, how do your grades look?" He then got to the heart of the matter.

"Good, it's just that I got a 67% in Global Studies," I told him.

"Ohhhhhh… Well, you cannot play then. I'm sorry," he said slowly, as though it was as painful for him as it was for me.

"Okay, thank you," I said, turning and walking away with my head down, not attempting to contest it.

It was an important early lesson about accountability and personal responsibility, perhaps the first major one in my life outside of the home. Like so many schools and jobs later in life, there were requirements for participation in the athletics programs at Hutch-Tech, and I had not made the grades that were required. I had not done what I was supposed to do. It felt bad even if it was a learning experience.

Why did I get that 67% in Global Studies? There are several reasons. One was a general lack of focus. I was in this new world and a new social ecosystem with beautiful girls everywhere. Some were my age, and many were older. It was all a little bit overwhelming in a way, and there was an ongoing social adjustment in addition to the academic rigors. I will go to a higher level and state that early on, I did not understand that I was there to be a student first and foremost. I did not understand that those four years were only temporary and that I was there to prepare for my next phase of life.

Another piece is that I do not remember Mom really 'cracking the whip' and establishing an academic standard of her own with consequences and punishments. That wasn't her style; she was more encouraging than critical. This is not blaming her as she had enough to do with keeping food on the table and the lights on. Dad did not get particularly fired up over my 67% Global Studies grade either. So, in a way, I was figuring all of it out on my own, which arguably may have been the most meaningful way to do it, though it had definite consequences.

At Hutch-Tech, we were expected to be 'student-athletes'. We were there to be students first and then participate in any extracurricular activities second. There were requirements for doing so; requirements that were not necessarily set in stone back at Campus West. It was all new for me.

I went back to the drawing board and worked to bring my grade in Global Studies over the 70% threshold. It was not because it was the best thing for my academic future, but because I wanted to be eligible for the junior varsity basketball team in the second quarter. Instead of participating on the junior varsity team in the short term, I focused on my schoolwork as best as I could. I also watched with the rest of the school as Coach Jones and the Hutch-Tech boys' basketball team embarked on their 1990–91 season.

Chapter 7. The 1990–91 Engineers: The Non-League Schedule

"I didn't have a freaky handle or nothing like that. Jones didn't teach us that. The moves that I learned were from watching basketball on TV and rewinding and copying what I saw. Jones didn't give you that. He didn't teach you how to be a good one-on-one player. He didn't. He didn't teach you how to be a great individual scorer. He taught you fundamentals and how to work in the *team* structure. That's what you got from Jones–discipline, team structure, and execution! But I appreciated it." —**Jerrold 'Pep' Skillon, Player, the Hutch-Tech boys' basketball team, 1987-91, May 2017**

During my freshman year, my time would have been best spent getting my Global Studies grade above 70%. Another valuable investment would have been closely following the 1990–91 Hutch-Tech boys' varsity basketball team. This is especially true with my wanting to play basketball at Hutch-Tech as badly as I thought I did. Having followed Michael Jordan and the Chicago Bulls the previous two years religiously, the smart thing would have been to observe what Coach Jones had built at Hutch-Tech in person for myself.

I had never seen the Hutch-Tech varsity team play in person. I had only seen the pictures in Amahl's yearbooks and heard his stories about players like Curtis Brooks, Pep Skillon, Chuck Thompson and Michael Brundige from the class of 1989. The same was true for all the high school basketball teams in Western New York. It was not because of a lack of interest. I simply did not understand the importance of going to watch the games as a middle schooler. Had Amahl been a basketball player himself, I likely would have had the exposure firsthand. Sadly, I didn't know what I didn't know.

I was still very influenced by what those around me were doing. Amahl did not closely follow the basketball team, so I didn't either. He ran cross country after school in the fall. Our lives consisted of going home, doing homework, playing video games, and watching TV. I only heard about the team in the morning announcements with the rest of the student body. The announcements came like clockwork in the morning after every game.

The 1990–91 Hutch-Tech boys' basketball team kicked off its season with non-league play in its own Hutch-Tech Tip-Off Tournament. It was held at McKinley Vocational High School, which was further north on Elmwood Avenue near Buffalo State College. The other three participating schools were Cathedral Boys High School from Toronto, ON, Niagara Falls Senior High School and the host, McKinley Vocational High School.

The tournament started on November 29, 1990, just after the Thanksgiving holiday. The Engineers opened with a win, defeating Boys' Cathedral 66–55.[28] Niagara Falls Senior High School awaited them in the final game of the tournament after defeating McKinley 69–49.[29] They were led by their star, a 6'6" player named Willie Cauley, who scored 26 points and grabbed 19 rebounds.

In the tournament final, according to the morning announcement, the Engineers were in control for most of the game before the score was tied 64–64 with approximately three and a half minutes remaining in the game. Once again, according to the announcement, the Engineers failed to execute offensively and could not contain Niagara Falls, ultimately succumbing to them 83–70; taking home the second-place trophy.[30] Coming out of the tournament, their record was 1–1.

In addition to the morning announcements, the team's schedule was posted near the coaches' offices on the bulletin board for all the students to see. Their next two opponents were Turner/Carroll High School and Depew High School. The only thing that I knew about Turner/Carroll was that it was a predominantly black Catholic school on the east side of Buffalo, located behind the Genesee Street Tops Supermarket. Ronald Jennings, from Campus West, chose to attend Turner/ Carroll instead of coming to Hutch-Tech. I did not know much about Depew High School other than that it was a suburban town.

The Turner/Carroll game took place on a Friday night. I heard that the Engineers won the game 80–67 on the morning announcements the following Monday.[31] I did not go to the game. However, hearing conversations in the hallways from those who went, they seemed to have had a really good time. It sounded like a social function or party as much as it was a basketball game. The victory seemed to be a big deal for the school and the student body, especially the black students. The students were very pumped up about the victory, as were the players, who walked around with extra swagger. There was something special about defeating Turner/Carroll High School.

The Engineers followed up their victory at Turner/Carroll with a 71–48 victory over Depew.[32] According to the morning announcements, ten players entered the scoring column, and all players received plenty of playing time. I gleaned that they

---

[28] (Jones, Boys' Cathedral High School vs. Hutch-Tech High School; The Hutch-Tech Tip Off Tournament, 1990)

[29] (Jones, Boys' Cathedral High School vs. Hutch-Tech High School; The Hutch-Tech Tip Off Tournament, 1990)

[30] (Jones, Niagara Falls High School vs Hutch-Tech; Hutch-Tech Tip Off Tournament, 1990)

[31] (Jones, Hutch-Tech High School vs Turner/Carroll High School; Non-Leauge, 1990)

[32] (Jones, Hutch-Tech High School vs. Depew High School; Non-League, 1990)

were gradually gaining *momentum*, although I didn't completely understand momentum in the sports context. Something was building that you could just feel.

The Depew game was followed by the Engineers' first home game of the season on December 16, 1990, against Lafayette High School in a non-league game. The Engineers overwhelmed the Violets 89–64 behind excellent team play and an aggressive defense, enabling them to score 32 points in the first quarter. The Engineers held the lead throughout the game.[33] All thirteen players saw plenty of action for the second straight game, and ten players got into the scoring column. They shot 60% from the field and 70% from the free-throw line. They were now 4–1 and rolling.

Curtis Brooks and company next went on the road and won their first Yale Cup league game. They dispatched South Park high School 106–84 on December 18, 1990, a victory sparked by an aggressive team defense that generated 32 second-quarter points.[34] As the days went by, the word defense came up regularly in the announcements.

The Engineer's record was now 5–1, and their winning streak seemed like it was how it was supposed to be. The Engineers were rising to new heights with every victory. If you listened closely to the announcements, certain patterns emerged. They were being led by their core nucleus of seniors Curtis Brooks, Pep Skillon, and Chuck Thompson. The three of them regularly led the charge regarding points, rebounds, and assists. I would later learn that these were the three critical statistical categories for individual players in basketball. There were also key team statistics which were indicators of how effective a given team was on offense and defense.

In the Turner/Carroll game, for example, the team was led by Pep Skillon, Chuck Thompson, Paul Saunders and Curtis Brooks, who each had 24, 23, 12, and 10 points, respectively. Pep Skillon and Chuck Thompson led the team in rebounding with 16 and 12, a recurring theme throughout the season. Curtis Brooks and Pep Skillon both had 14 and 5 assists, respectively. In the other games the statistical spread could have easily been in the reverse order, where someone else led in scoring, but they all contributed something. They all played distinct roles and the engine powering the team in all instances seemed to be No. 13, Curtis Brooks.

The assists were significant because they showed that the team shared the ball and the players unselfishly set each other up for scores. In many of the announcements, we heard about stellar defensive efforts by Paul Saunders or Quincy Lee, who had racked up a bunch of steals and/or blocks. Other players

---

[33] (Jones, Lafayette High School vs. Hutch-Tech High School; Non-League, 1990)

[34] (Jones, Hutch-Tech High School vs. South Park High School, 1990)

also contributed as needed. In the beginning their victories were due to balanced team efforts. No one player was doing it alone.

Coach Jones and the Engineers next traveled north of Buffalo for another mainstay on Hutch-Tech's schedule in those years, the Festival of Lights Tournament in Niagara Falls. Coach Jones' veteran squad opened the tournament with a rematch against Niagara Falls Senior High School, a winnable game as the first game was close. Unfortunately, they fell to Niagara Falls for the second time in a lopsided 83–63 defeat before winning a 'consolation game' against Bennett High School 83–70.[35]

Their four-game winning streak snapped. The lone bright spot was that Chuck Thompson had two excellent games with 49 points and 36 rebounds, which made him an excellent selection for the all-tournament team. The Engineers rode into the Christmas break ranked No. 5 in the *Buffalo News'* Cage Poll for Large Schools. The weekly poll, which was published every Tuesday, ranked both the *large* and the *small* schools, which were designated by the total enrollment of schools.[36]

* * *

As I said earlier, if you did not attend the basketball games for yourself, you were updated on the results the day after the game during the morning announcements. Summaries that the announcers read were also posted on the bulletin board near the coaches' offices every day. Those one-pagers were sometimes marked up with underlines and other scribbles by someone. They were generated using a dot matrix printer, and all the letters were capitalized. The font was something other than Times Roman, something used by early Apple or IBM computers.

While the body of the summaries were word-processed, scribbled words in red ink, saying things like "LOOK", were often on the top margin with two smiley faces inside the Os, probably to catch the attention of the players walking by, or maybe other members of the student body. Most of the summaries ended with, "COME AND SUPPORT YOUR TEAM." In addition to the summaries, the statistics sheets were posted so the players and the student body could see each player's points scored, rebounds, assists, shooting percentages and turnovers. The statistics were written into a grid-like chart with the same handwriting as the scribbles on the game summaries.

The good statistics had smiley faces around them, while the bad statistics had squiggly unhappy faces around them, in red ink. At the bottom of the statistics sheets were messages to the team saying things like, "KEEP ROLLING

[35] (Jones, The 1990 Festival of Lights Boys' Basketball Tournament Results, 1991)

[36] (Staff, The Buffalo News' Cage Poll, 1990)

ENGINEERS," after a win or, "POOR INTENSITY, NO KILLER INSTINCT, NO POISE, PRIDE or GUTS," after losses such as those to Niagara Falls. Whoever it was, the preparer of these materials was very passionate about the boys' basketball team.

* * *

As the 1990–91 Hutch-Tech Engineers marched through their non-league schedule, I was buckling down in the classroom as best I could and focusing on my schoolwork. In Global Studies, where I earned a 67% grade in the first quarter, I was now showing more focus. I was determined to get above the 70% threshold for the second quarter. This would allow me to participate in the basketball program to some degree.

"You don't want to just get by, son," my father told me on a phone call from Schenectady one night. "You want to excel!" They were words that I never forgot, but would not understand until much later.

Ironically, politics/current events and world history would be subjects that would fascinate me later in life. I just lacked the maturity and the focus to excel in my coursework. As opposed to thinking about going to college and my future, my thoughts were solely on my little high school world and becoming eligible to participate in the basketball program during the next quarter.

Chapter 8. The 1990–91 Yale Cup Schedule: A Run at History

"No one is going to go undefeated in the Yale Cup this year!" —**Arthur 'Art' Serotte, the Grover Cleveland High School Head Basketball and Football Coach in the 1980s and 1990s, January 1991**

Just after the new year in 1991, a summary of the results of the Festival of Lights Tournament, which took place over the Christmas break, was read over the morning announcements. The Hutch-Tech Engineers lost 83–67 in the opening round to Niagara Falls Senior High School. They then defeated Bennett High School 83–70 in the consolation game to finish in third place in the tournament. They were now ranked the No. 5 Large School in the *Buffalo News'* Cage Poll with an overall record of 6–2.

Early in 1991 they continued their Yale Cup league play on Friday, January 6, against No. 6-ranked Grover Cleveland High School. The morning announcement read like all the others before. It ended with the words, "COME AND SUPPORT YOUR TEAM," which was exactly how it was written on the summary on the bulletin board near the coaches' offices.

Come and support your team. The ending of the announcement resonated with me this time. I had not seen the Engineers play the previous month as most of their games were away. However, this upcoming game against Grover Cleveland was right there at Hutch-Tech, so I could easily go after classes on Friday. With their 6–2 record and their No. 5 ranking, they sounded quite competitive. I then decided that I would go to their first home game of 1991.

I thought about the Grover Cleveland game all week and it was in the back of my mind as the day approached. Coach Jones left one more reminder for the student body in the Friday morning announcements. After the final buzzer that day, I got my things together from my second-floor locker, and descended into the basement to the small, dated gymnasium carrying my blue backpack on my right shoulder.

With the wood shops and boiler system in the basement, the factory scent became very noticeable. I exited the stairwell and heard a faint buzz. Walking closer to the gym, I heard the game taking place. There were sounds of the crowd, the whistles from the referees, the buzzer from the scoreboard, and finally, the sound of the basketball bouncing on the hardwood floor. The buzz became increasingly louder as I approached the entrance. It made me a little nervous because I had never gone to any event with so many students in one place before.

After paying my $3 to get in, I entered the gymnasium to watch my very first high school basketball game. In my brief time at Hutch-Tech, I had never seen the gym filled with students before. To my left the cheerleaders were underneath the southernmost basket, cheering in their maroon and white uniforms. They wore sweater-like tops, short skirts and sneakers. Members of the band played while teachers and staff stood around the periphery of the court looking on. Some were in the stands. A large group had gathered to support their No. 6-ranked Engineers just as Coach Jones requested in the morning announcements.

The bleachers were packed on both sides with students from Hutch-Tech and Grover Cleveland. There was one scoreboard above the north entrance on the eastern side of the gym, and the scorer's table was set up in the middle of the bleachers on the western side, separating the teams and coaches. It was the same gym where we played intramurals. It had solid white backboards with non-breakaway rims extending from the walls, old paint, climbing ropes on the ceiling, cushions on the walls and the skylight above us. The gym was now miraculously transformed into a venue for a game, and it was rocking.

Wearing my Chicago Bulls jacket, I found a seat in the corner bleachers behind the Grover Cleveland team. Their colors were lime green and white, and they were coached by a mean-looking older white man named Arthur 'Art' Serotte (pronounced Sherotty), a legendary football coach in the school system. He had graying hair and was balding. His face was weathered and embattled, and he wore a green Grover Cleveland windbreaker with khakis and sneakers.

I noticed that Matt McDowell, from my class of 1994, was on the bench with Coach Jones and the Engineers. He was one of the managers, along with more senior students. Eboni Carson, Hillary Pearson, Monica Peterson and Turhan Wilbur had all been with the team in prior years. I noted that some of them assisted the team by supporting Coach Jones and the players directly on the bench, while others worked the scorer's table, tabulating the statistics and running the game clock. Those working the scorer's table coordinated directly with the referees at various points of the game.

On the other side of the scorer's table Coach Jones patrolled the sidelines in a beige, light brown or tan blazer, a shirt and tie, khakis, and now running sneakers. It was my first time seeing his game persona, and I had never seen anything like it before. He was very animated and into the game, calling plays and yelling at his players and the referees.

He frequently yelled, "BALL! BALL! BALL!" He screamed it at his own players, among other things. It was like a demand. Sometimes he was in a crouched position with his fists clenched while looking possessed by the devil. Other times he stormed back and forth. His face grimaced and scrunched up in some instances. You could feel the desperation and urgency as he yelled.

At first I thought he was singling out Paul Saunders, yelling, "PAUL, PAUL, PAUL," but later I realized that he was yelling, "BALL!" It meant rebounding or diving on the floor for a loose ball, particularly on defense. Scrape some skin off your elbow if you must, but get the damn ball! It was like Coach Jones wanted to rip off his blazer and play the game himself. Neither of my coaches at Campus West carried on like this. His players must have been used to it though. The players seemed to focus on the task at hand, while the players on the bench looked calm and unfazed by all of it.

Our team wore their white tops and maroon shorts with gold trim. Most of them wore white tee shirts underneath their V-neck tank tops, which had large block maroon numbers on them. Neither our school's nor the players' names were on either side. Most of the players wore black sneakers, except Pep Skillon, who wore a white pair. All the team members had yellow ribbons tied to their laces in tribute to the U.S. soldiers in the Middle East fighting in Operation Desert Storm.

I had only seen the team in pictures until now and it all looked so cool. The maroon and gold colors looked beautiful. During timeouts some of the players on the bench wore warmup shirts over their tank tops. When he brought them home, I saw my brother's cross country and track and field uniforms with the same colors. These basketball uniforms were different. They were special and right then and there, I knew that I wanted to wear one.

I eagerly watched the unfolding action on the court, much of which I did not completely understand beyond the players playing offense and defense, dribbling the ball, and putting it through the hoop. Our team was led by the five seniors with No. 13, Curtis Brooks, handling the ball at the beginning of every play. My eyes immediately focused on him. He yelled plays to his teammates as he calmly brought the ball up the court in a controlled manner.

Curtis had a low and fast dribble and was not going to let the orange leather basketball get stolen by anyone. He handled it like a prized possession. His head and eyes were always up, surveying the court, running the offense, and ready to make a play. Whatever he called out, the other four players knew what to do immediately. They looked highly organized on offense, making crisp movements and passes, which typically led to easy baskets or trips to the free-throw line. It was not a particularly flashy style of basketball—I could see that immediately. There were no careless passes, no excessive dribbling, no errant shots, and they were not playing 'above the rim'. Instead, it was a patient and methodical style of offense, and their baskets were usually made after multiple players touched the ball, as opposed to one guy shooting it immediately.

On defense, the Engineers played man-to-man and no zone. Each Engineer followed his man around closely, always verbally communicating with one another. They slid their feet, never crossing them, and their arms were constantly up and extended, denying their men the ball. The players who were not on the 'ball side' played off their men slightly in the lane, keeping their eyes on the action on both sides of the floor. Also, all of them systematically turned and put their bodies on the men they were guarding whenever Grover put up a shot. They likewise seemed to come up with every rebound on defense, and Grover seldom got a second shot.

Curtis Brooks and No. 40, Paul Saunders, played particularly aggressive and smart defense, using their size, long arms, quickness and fast-moving hands to create steals which led to fast breaks and easy baskets—the lifeblood of the 1990–91 Engineers. They were on a mission defensively. Their eyes were wide and intense, and even when the men they guarded did not have the ball, they were close by and anticipating the next steal. After any of the Engineers scored, there was no hot-dogging, showboating, or trash-talking; just sprinting back down the floor to get back on defense with that hungry look in their eyes.

Occasionally Coach Jones substituted, in his 5'8" backup point guard, junior No. 21, Michael Mann, when Curtis Brooks needed a breather, but it was always brief. Curtis was the undisputed leader of the team, and the intensity of the game on both sides of the floor visibly changed when he went out. No. 24, Dion Frasier, and No. 44, Chris Souter, occasionally were put in to spell the forwards, and I did not see any of the other players get into the contest that day.

The Engineers got off to a fast start, leading 26–19 at the end of the first quarter. If they did not score off Grover's turnovers, Curtis Brooks again methodically dribbled the ball up the floor and initiated their half-court offenses. The offensive sets he called usually ended in layups by the 6'5" No. 55, Chuck Thompson, and No. 32, Pep Skillon, both with hulk-like physiques. The other players made occasional jump shots and layups. Curtis Brooks provided most of the outside shooting, with No. 11 Quincy Lee, being effective from long-range.

Even though the Engineers raced out to their first-quarter lead, No. 6, Grover Cleveland, battled back using a combination of both size and quickness. The game produced the first up-close and live dunk I had ever seen. One of the Presidents' big men, who had to be at least 6'6", took the ball the length of the floor by himself from an Engineer turnover. Similar to an NBA player, he elevated off one foot in stride and authoritatively slammed the ball through the basket with two hands. While I shuddered at the play and was in awe of it, none of the Engineers were openly affected by it.

Instead, Curtis Brooks calmly received the inbound pass, dribbled the ball up the floor, and initiated the offense again. This was the battle for much of that second quarter, where Coach Jones' team sought to control the tempo of the game while Coach Serotte's team sought to get out and run in the open court for layups and dunks. At halftime the score was tied 42–42. During the intermission, the Hutch-Tech cheerleaders graced us with new routines before the players filed back onto the court.

As they say in the NBA, the second half was more nip and tuck. Grover Cleveland had a long and athletic team, but the Engineers had a level of athleticism, strength, and explosiveness as well, allowing them to hang with their opponents. It was controlled and structured. They were not afraid of the Presidents and you could both see and hear their bodies colliding. You could hear the pushing and the shoving both on the perimeter and closer to the basket. This was the varsity basketball Mr. Cook told us about at Campus West, though I never imagined this level of physicality.

As the Engineers hung with Grover Cleveland, one player seemed to really get off offensively, No. 32, Pep Skillon. While the Engineers played man-to-man defense, Grover seemed to play a zone. To counter it, the Engineers patiently *worked* the ball. They didn't take quick or uncontrolled shots. They patiently moved it from one side of the halfcourt to the other, looking for openings in the zone. Later I would learn that this was called *reversing* the ball.

Pep Skillon skillfully scored points using his own off-the-ball movement, slashing to the basket, or by snatching offensive rebounds. When he was fouled and went to the free-throw line, he converted his shots with perfect form. As a matter of fact, most of the Engineers converted their free throws that day as a team.

Late in the fourth quarter of this slugfest, Grover eventually pulled ahead causing me to think our team might lose the first game I attended. However, the Engineers' wills were not easily broken. They battled back and kept the game close down to the final stretch of the fourth quarter. With only minutes on the clock, the tension high, and the score tied, the ball was once again in the hands of No. 13, Curtis Brooks.

On a key play No. 13 confidently advanced the ball without initiating the team's offense. He calmly chose the right moment and took the game into his own hands. Just outside of the top of the three-point arc, with the closest defender giving him just enough room, without hesitation he gracefully picked up his dribble and rose up high into his jump shot, just like in the picture in Amahl's 1989–90 yearbook. He released a line-drive three-pointer with perfect form. It was on the opposite basket, the Johnson Park-side basket, so I saw it from the other end of the court. I saw the back of his No. 13 jersey.

For the briefest moment all the air went out of the gym as the ball descended towards the basket almost in slow motion. It sailed through the net cleanly, causing our gym to erupt and Coach Serotte to call a timeout. I leaped up, pumping my fist in the air. Coach Jones did too. Curtis Brooks had just carried the team and the whole gym on his shoulders to the promised land on that single play.

After that timeout the momentum permanently shifted in our team's favor, and they held on for a 93–90 victory behind the clutch free throw shooting and the inside play of Chuck Thompson, Pep Skillon, and Quincy Lee.[37] Pep Skillon, Chuck Thompson, and Curtis Brooks each scored 36, 23, and 20 points, respectively. Pep Skillon, Chuck Thompson, and Paul Saunders each grabbed 11, 11, and 8 rebounds, respectively. Dion Frasier came off the bench and added 6 points and 5 rebounds. Hutch-Tech's record was now 2–0 in the Yale Cup, and the entire school was electrified. Immediately after the game I watched as the teams shook hands, the players and then Coach Jones and Coach Serotte. They exchanged brief words before going their separate ways. I went home excited about what I had just seen.

* * *

The Grover Cleveland game was just the first of many victories in January of 1991. Over the coming weeks, there was more winning against other city schools whose names I recognized, unlike most of the Engineers' early season opponents. They followed up their Grover Cleveland win with victories over City Honors 68–53, Bennett High School 104–89, and then Burgard Vocational High School 104–92, extending their overall record to 10–2 and their Yale Cup record to 5–0.[38,39,40]

By mid-January the Engineers were still ranked No. 5 in the *Buffalo News'* Cage Poll for Large Schools, and they were on a roll. The race for the Yale Cup championship was far from over. For their next test, the Engineers traveled north on Elmwood Avenue to face McKinley Vocational High School. Being spearheaded by Paul Saunders, excellent team play and team defense enabled the Engineers to pull away late in the third quarter for a 93–76 victory.[41] They followed up that victory by defeating then No. 6-ranked Kensington High School 84–62.[42] Next, they downed Buffalo Traditional 92–85, the No. 1 Small School, running their Yale Cup record to 8–0.[43,44]

By that time the team's chemistry had solidified, and with every morning announcement, you heard the same trends. The class of 1991 was leading the charge, with other players pitching in where needed offensively and defensively. Like the non-league schedule the bulk of the scoring came from Curtis Brooks, Pep Skillon, and Chuck Thompson; the Engineers' *big three*. The bulk of rebounds

---

[37] (Staff, Hutch-Tech rallies to top Grover, 1991)
[38] (Jones, Hutch-Tech High School vs. City Honors High School; Yale Cup, 1991)
[39] (Jones, Bennett High School vs. Hutch-Tech High School; Yale Cup, 1991)
[40] (Jones, Burgard High School vs. Hutch-Tech High School; Yale Cup, 1991)
[41] (Jones, Hutch-Tech High School vs. McKinley High School; Yale Cup, 1991)
[42] (Jones, Kensington High School vs. Hutch-Tech High School, 1991)
[43] (Jones, Buffalo Traditional High School vs. Hutch-Tech High School, 1991)
[44] (Staff, The Buffalo News' Cage Poll, 1991)

came from Pep Skillon and Chuck Thompson. The bulk of the assists came from the team's engine, Curtis Brooks.

Against Burgard, for example, both Curtis Brooks and Pep Skillon logged triple-doubles with Brooks registering 26 points, 12 rebounds, and 10 assists and Skillon having 22 points, 11 rebounds, and 10 assists.[45] Chuck Thompson had 22 points and 18 rebounds.[46] During that stretch, Curtis Brooks put together a streak of four games where he logged the triple-doubles.

Triple-doubles were a statistic often associated with the Los Angeles Lakers' Ervin 'Magic' Johnson. Because of his ability to affect the game many considered him the greatest point guard of all time and the greatest player of all time. Watching Magic play in his prime, it is hard to argue against that. The significance of the triple-double statistic was that it showed how one player could affect the game in multiple statistical categories, not just one or two. Only the elite players could do this and do it consistently. Prior to Magic there was the great Oscar Robertson, also known as 'The Big O'.

No matter who led the team in scoring another critical piece of the Engineers' formula was their consistent and accurate free-throw shooting. I saw that firsthand in the Grover Cleveland game. The *Buffalo News* actually wrote a feature on 1990-91 Engineers' free throw shooting and the team's early morning competitions following their win over Buffalo Traditional. It was entitled, *Hutch-Tech's free throws sink Traditional, 92-85, in Yale Cup; Intrasquad contests pay off in 42-of-54 day at line.*[47] They also had a great team defense. It was spearheaded by players like Paul Saunders, Quincy Lee and Dion Frasier, who played an excellent game against Kensington's star guard that year, Taka Molson.

* * *

While the Engineers progressed through their league schedule, I worked on improving my grades. By the end of the second quarter, I had pulled each of my grades above the 70% minimum necessary to participate in our sports programs. In Global Studies, where I earned a 67% grade in the first quarter, I now had a 78% grade. In English, where I earned 76% grade in the first quarter, I now had a 90% grade. In Sequential Math Course 1, I earned a 73% grade in the first quarter, and I now had a 71% grade. In General Biology, my strongest course, I earned a 96% grade in the first quarter, but my grade slid down slightly to an 87% grade. My Spanish grade was similar, changing from an 80% to a 79% grade. In

---

[45] (Jones, Burgard High School vs. Hutch-Tech High School; Yale Cup, 1991)

[46] (Jones, Burgard High School vs. Hutch-Tech High School; Yale Cup, 1991)

[47] (Staff, Hutch-Tech's free throws sink Traditional, 92-85, in Yale Cup; Intrasquad contests pay off in 42-of-45 day at line, 1991)

Mechanical Drawing, my grade increased from an 80% to an 87%. In Introduction to Occupations, I maintained a 75% grade.

I was proud of myself to a small degree that I did not have any grades below the 70% threshold as I did in the first quarter. Looking back, though the expectation was to go to college, I do not remember the pressure to get 90% grades or better. When I say pressure, I mean punishment. I heard rumors in some of my classmate's and peers' homes of their parents mandating 90% or better grades in every class.

Now that I was eligible to participate in the basketball program, I took my evaluation sheets to all my teachers so that they could certify that I had made the 70%, then took them to Coach Jones. I was cleared to participate in the junior varsity practices, which took place early in the morning before classes started. The practices were led by Coach Jones himself.

Other guys there were mostly sophomores from the class of 1993. They included Jason Majchrowicz, Carlton Ford, Damon Kimbrew and Jason Hellerman. They all hoped to make the varsity team the next year. There were a couple of freshmen from my class, 1994, such as Terrance Collison, who I didn't know very well at the time; and possibly Martavious Johnson. I do not remember any other would-be basketball players from my class participating.

We met up in the gym first thing in the morning to go through all kinds of drills, including the 'Mikan Drill' and the 'Two-Ball Dribbling Drill', which were skill-related. We also practiced an assortment of defensive drills. I had never been exposed to the fundamentals of basketball before. The things Coach Jones had us doing were much more in-depth than anything I had done at Campus West.

Towards the end of practice Coach Jones split us up into separate teams of five and scrimmaged us, meaning that we played against each other in pseudo-game conditions. He stopped us with his whistle from time to time to instruct and give us guidance, just as I saw him do at the open house during my eighth-grade year at Campus West. I was happy to be there and religiously got up early in the morning to attend the practices.

"This Coach Jones seems to be taking quite a hold in your life. I'm not sure that I like that," Mom said one morning which I didn't know how to respond to, so I didn't. She eventually softened her position and told me one morning as I was leaving, "I admire your commitment and conviction to your participation with the basketball team." Mom and Dad were never afraid to tell us that they were proud of us, which were important words for any child. At that age, it was likewise important for me to have her blessing in this new endeavor that I was interested in.

She may not have said it in those words exactly, but she acknowledged that I found something that I loved and believed in—something that I was now committed to—an important part of a young person's development and transition to adulthood. As a teenage boy, just like at Campus West, I wanted to belong to something. I wanted to be a part of something, a brotherhood. I had, in fact, found something in which I was personally invested.

"Where were you this morning for practice?" Coach Jones asked me about my whereabouts early one Monday morning. There was one instance where I missed one of the practices and slept in. I think it was a Friday, and I did not think we would have practice for some reason.

"It was Friday, and I didn't think we had practice," I told him.

"We *always* have practice," he replied to me in his passionate and raspy voice, sternly looking at me through his glasses while grabbing my shirt in his clenched fist and gently shaking me with a hint of mischief on his face.

"I was thinking to myself, 'I'm surprised that Anwar isn't here,' when I came and sat in on the practice," Damion Alexander, a fellow member of my class, jokingly said one morning. He was a dark-skinned guy and had made a habit of wandering into the early morning junior varsity practices. He would find a comfortable spot on the bleachers and watch everything. He noticed that I was there every morning and found it odd when I was not.

We went on like that for about three to four weeks during the middle of the varsity team's run through league play. We were up every morning at the crack of dawn while the rest of our classmates gradually filed into our old H-shaped building. Towards the end of our practices, the varsity players gathered for a group free throw shooting exercise. And then, just like that, we stopped. It was late January or early February of 1991.

* * *

Deep into the team's run through the Yale Cup, it became commonplace to hear of another victory for the 1990–91 Hutch-Tech boys' basketball team over the morning announcements. In fact, it got to the point where it was expected. I do not know how it affected the rest of the school, but it gave me a sense of pride. Others were getting caught up in the winning, as the team started experiencing super star statuses. Even one of the news stations referred to them as 'The Mighty Hutch-Tech'. The girls were feeling it too. I vividly remember the beautiful Tomi Lyons from my class gushing over Paul Saunders and agonizing when he got a concussion in one of the games.

The 1990–91 team became my heroes, and it got to the point where I was bragging about them outside of school to Gabe. Not one to be outdone, Gabe rebuffed my pride in Hutch-Tech by saying that the point guard of the Cleveland Hill team, Quincy Morris, could beat Curtis Brooks. That was outrageous to me, and we argued over it. It is funny now, but it's a testament to how a team's success can uplift an entire school and spark debates between kids the players on the team don't even know. Curtis Brooks and Quincy Morris would probably have laughed if they knew two best friends were arguing over them.

* * *

Having crossed into the month of February with their 8–0 record in the Yale Cup, the Engineers stared down five more league games and the potential of going undefeated in league play. They ran off three more victories, decisively downing Seneca Vocational High School 81–58, Lafayette High School 117–93, and then Riverside High School 82–56.[48,49,50] They seemed unstoppable, like a runaway freight train barreling down the tracks, demolishing everything in its path.

On Friday, February 8th, close to 3 p.m. in the afternoon, I saw Paul Saunders practicing his free throws. He was alone in the gym in his button-down pattern shirt, jeans and boots. We had just finished swimming class and were cutting across the gym. He had both joy and focus on his face. The old rim rattled on some of his shots as the ball hit it and rolled around and into the basket for him. I can still hear that rattling sound and the echo of the ball hitting the floor of the empty box of a gym.

That afternoon the Engineers hosted Emerson Vocational High School, and they once again triumphed 67–59 to win their twelfth-straight game, clinching the Yale Cup title outright with a 12–0 record.[51] It was the second game I attended. I sat on the Elmwood Avenue side of the gym this time. Emerson's colors were red and white, with the same block numbers on their uniforms with no names on either side, just like Hutch-Tech.

I vividly remember Quincy Lee playing with a lot of intensity in that game and putting defensive pressure on an Emerson wing player right in front of me. The player had no choice but to call time out when he couldn't do anything else with the ball. Pep Skillon and Chuck Thompson routinely got to the free throw line and shot high percentages. Curtis Brooks again methodically controlled the tempo of the game. There was a looseness about Coach Jones and his team that day. The victory was inevitable, and all the players got in.

After the game the players climbed on a ladder and cut the nets down, just like in the college basketball world. I hung around and saw Quincy Lee laughing with some of his classmates in the bleachers, who congratulated him before heading to the locker room to be with his teammates. Now 12–0, the Engineers' final Yale

[48] (Jones, Hutch-Tech High School vs. Seneca High School; Yale Cup, 1991)

[49] (Jones, Hutch-Tech High School vs. Lafayette High School; Yale Cup, 1991)

[50] (Jones, Hutch-Tech High School vs. Riverside High School; Yale Cup, 1991)

[51] (Jones, Emerson High School vs. Hutch-Tech High School; Yale Cup, 1991)

Cup test would be at Performing Arts, also known as the Buffalo Academy for the Visual and Performing Arts.

On February 12, 1991, the Engineers completed their Yale Cup league season undefeated, 13–0, by downing Performing Arts 84–80 in a thrilling game.[52] Paul Saunders scored 19 points and hit a key layup in the final seconds to help secure the victory and the first undefeated Yale Cup season by any team in five years.[53] The only other time Hutch-Tech had gone undefeated was the 1967–68 season.[54]

Things came together just right for the Engineers that season and the resulting 13–0 record was a thing of beauty at a school that was at the bottom of the league just four years earlier. With the non-league and league play now completed, it was time for something called sectional play, according to the morning announcements. In sectional play the Engineers would battle it out with other teams from all over Western New York for ultimate bragging rights and the potential to ascend even higher. It was a magical ride for them and the rest of us at the school as well.

---

[52] (Jones, Hutch-Tech High School vs. Performing Arts High School; Yale Cup, 1991)
[53] (Jones, Hutch-Tech High School vs. Performing Arts High School; Yale Cup, 1991)
[54] (Jones, Hutch-Tech High School vs. Performing Arts High School; Yale Cup, 1991)

Chapter 9. The 1991 Class B Sectionals

"Where would you rather be than right here and right now?" **—Marv Levy, Head Coach, the Buffalo Bills, Super Bowl XXV, February 1991**

While the Hutch-Tech Engineers embarked on their 13–0 run through the Yale Cup, the entire Western New York region witnessed another magical run. The Buffalo Bills marched all the way through the American Football Conference (AFC) playoffs to Super Bowl XXV in Tampa, FL. After a decade of ineptitude and mediocrity, the front office built a nucleus of competitive players on both sides of the ball. It did not happen overnight. The team made gradual progress each year while also taking its lumps. Most notable were their 21–10 and 34–30 playoff losses to the Cincinnati Bengals and the Cleveland Browns at the end of the 1988 and 1989 seasons, respectively. It was the 1990 season that the Bills became a force to be reckoned with.

With a solid offensive line in front of him and a variety of targets to throw the ball, No. 12, Jim Kelly, destroyed opposing defenses out of the 'K-Gun' offensive formation in the Bills 'No Huddle' offense, which put up a lot of points, while tiring out the defense of the opposition. The defensive unit was led by No. 78, Bruce Smith, who had grown into one of the best defensive ends in the National Football League. The pressure he caused led to many takeaways by the Bills' opportunistic defense. It was not a dominant defense, but it complemented the Bills' quick strike 'hurry-up' or 'no-huddle' offense.

As a freshman, I heard about what the Bills were doing peripherally, just like with the Hutch-Tech basketball team. Gradually I heard that something was building. Many of their early wins were comeback victories, games where they were on the verge of losing. Somehow, they were able to turn the tables on their opponents and come out victorious in the closing minutes. The comeback I remember most was against the Los Angeles Raiders, which was sparked by the return of a blocked punt by No. 31, J.D. Williams, and the return of a fumble by No. 37, Nate Odoms for the 38–24 victory. They were on a roll and eventually won the AFC East Division which they'd done in previous years. Then they locked up the No. 1 seed in the AFC playoffs with a 13–3 record, which meant they would have the home-field advantage leading to the Super Bowl. Likewise, any opponent would have to come play in our cold Western New York winter conditions and contend with our raucous home crowd.

On Saturday, January 12, 1991, the Miami Dolphins returned to Rich Stadium on a snowy 31-degree Western New York day in the AFC divisional round. They put up a fight, but ultimately the Bills pulled out a victory of 44–34. In the AFC Championship Game the following week, on Sunday, January 20th, the Los Angeles Raiders returned minus their legendary running back, Bo Jackson, whose football career ended a week earlier in Cincinnati with a freak hip injury. It was an historic game and I was completely tuned in. I thought the Raiders would make a game of it, but the Bills won, going away 51–3 to advance to the team's first-ever Super Bowl. Western New York was electrified in a way that I had never seen before.

There are many things I could say about Super Bowl XXV, which took place on Sunday, January 27, 1991 in Tampa, FL, at the 'Old Sombrero' as Chris Berman of ESPN called it. There was so much hype surrounding the game. The Persian Gulf War was taking place in Iraq and my father was there as a part of a medical unit. Whitney Houston sang her rendition of *The Star-Spangled Banner* which went down in history. Super Bowl XXV was also one of the first football games I watched from start to finish. It was further special because Amahl and I watched the game with other men.

We attended the Tried Stone Baptist Church then, and some men decided to have a Super Bowl party. I think it was Reverend Jamison, a middle-aged man, and the young Reverend Dennis L. Gray, and some of his brothers, Donnell and Terry, whom we watched the game with. They had lots of food and it was a lot of fun. It was the first time Amahl and I had watched football and bonded with adult males outside of our family.

In my opinion, Super Bowl XXV will always be the greatest Super Bowl. The Bills matched up against Bill Parcells' New York Giants, a team mixed with grizzled veterans and young talent. The Bills had beaten them earlier that year at Giants Stadium, in the Meadowlands, New Jersey, 17–13. I think I was at the William-Emslie YMCA playing basketball that day and saw some of it on television. The play I saw might have been a Thurman Thomas touchdown run. Both starting quarterbacks went down that day, Jim Kelly for our Buffalo Bills and No. 11, Phil Sims, for the New York Giants. Kelly would eventually return that season, but not Sims.

The Giants advanced to the Super Bowl by upsetting the then kings of the NFL, the San Francisco 49ers, 15–13 at Candlestick Park in the Bay Area in a physical, hard-fought game where the big blue only scored five field goals—the opposite of the Bills' victory over the Raiders. The Giants played a different style of football than the Bills. While Buffalo liked throwing the ball and scoring many points, the Giants played a more physical game, running the ball to set up the pass and playing tough physical defense. These were all hallmarks of Coach Bill Parcells, who led the Giants to a Super Bowl title earlier in the mid-80s against the Denver Broncos.

The Giants had been to the big game before and knew what to do. After Super Bowl XXV, stories emerged that the younger Bills partied during the week and did not adequately prepare for their opponents, who many predicted they would blow out. Thus, even though the Bills arrived at the game with most of their team intact, and the Giants were starting backup quarterback No. 15, Jeff Hostetler, and backup running back No. 24, Otis Anderson, they had some advantages over the Bills.

The Giants also had two future hall-of-fame coaches on their sideline, Head Coach Bill Parcells and Defensive Coordinator Bill Belichick, who designed a special defense to slow down Jim Kelly and the offense that day. Instead of using the standard number of linemen, linebackers and defensive backs, the Giants used two *down* linemen and multiple defensive backs, ultimately slowing down Jim Kelly and the Bills offense. It was a brilliant tactical plan which frustrated the Bills and us fans.

While I did not understand all the intricacies of football at the time, I could see that the Bills were not running up the score as we were used to seeing them do. Meanwhile, the Giants stayed in the game by possessing the ball and seemingly pounding the Bills into submission, especially Bruce Smith and the defense. Only the heroic play of the Bills' running back No. 34, Thurman Thomas, kept them in the game.

The game ended with No. 11, Scott Norwood's historic 48-yard wide-right missed field goal. It was a play that dictated the futures of the kicker, the players and coaches on both sidelines. I looked at it on TV and thought that it might have gone through the uprights from the camera angle I saw, but it turned out that he missed it. And with that, all the air went out of our little party on Humboldt Parkway, the whole City of Buffalo, and all of Western New York. The Giants upset our Bills 20–19, and history was made for that game, setting the stage for the seasons to come. The Bills' magical 1990–91 season was over. Fortunately for me, and everyone at Hutch-Tech, there was another run at our school whose ending was still unwritten.

* * *

With their 13–0 Yale Cup record and now their No. 3 ranking in the *Buffalo News'* Cage Poll for the Large Schools, the 1990–91 Engineers earned the No. 1 seed in the Section VI Class B-1 playoff bracket.[55] There were other schools in the bracket I had heard about from the Yale Cup and some I was unfamiliar with.[56] The Engineers would open against No. 8-seeded Maryvale. The No. 2 seed in the

[55] (Harrington, February Madness starts for WNY basketball powers, 1991)

[56] (Harrington, Presidents forfeit playoff berth, 1991)

bracket was Olean, who opened against No. 7-seeded Iroquois. The No. 3-seeded team was Kenmore East, who drew No. 6-seeded Bennett. Finally, No. 4-seeded Kensington drew No. 5-seeded Clarence.

Grover Cleveland was one team absent from the bracket that could have given the Engineers a hard time. They had a 10–3 record in the Yale Cup and were ranked No. 9 in the same poll as the Engineers. They forfeited sectional play because they used four academically ineligible players for their last four games and finished with a below 0.500 record.[57] The Engineers narrowly defeated them 93–90 in early January in the Hutch-Tech gym, which was the first time I saw our team play. The Presidents had the athleticism to take Coach Jones' team down to the wire again and maybe even upset them, but now they were not a threat to anyone, and it was all because of academics.

Unlike the Yale Cup league games, which were all within the City of Buffalo, the sectional games were mostly held at suburban schools and, in some instances, college gymnasiums. Unlike in the smaller towns and suburbs, where students stereotypically piled onto buses to follow their teams, we had to find our own way to the games. I didn't know enough then to determine where each sectional game was and how to get there. Going to the games was not high on Amahl's list either, and he had a car. So, I heard about the outcomes on the morning announcements. The games were mostly in the evenings now, and I could have asked Mom or Amahl to take me, but that would've meant a late night for someone or leaving the games early.

On the morning announcements of February 25, 1991, we heard that the Engineers decisively dispatched Maryvale 77–61 in a game which took place at Erie Community College (ECC) South in Orchard Park.[58] It was the same formula that guided them through Yale Cup play. Good team defense spearheaded by Paul Saunders and Dion Frasier, and a good team field goal shooting percentage along with excellent team play allowed them to move out to a 20–12 first-quarter lead which they never relinquished.[59] It was the usual spread of statistics. Curtis Brooks scored 22 points and dished out 7 assists, followed by Chuck Thompson's 19 points, and Pep Skillon's and Quincy Lee's 13 and 11 points.[60] Pep Skillon, Chuck Thompson and Quincy Lee had 13, 11, and 7 rebounds each.[61] Paul Saunders dished out 6 assists of his own.[62]

---

[57] (Harrington, Presidents forfeit playoff berth, 1991)

[58] (Staff, Lackawanna struggles but wins, 1991)

[59] (Jones, Maryvale High School vs. Hutch-Tech High School; Class B-1 Sectionals, 1991)

[60] (Jones, Maryvale High School vs. Hutch-Tech High School; Class B-1 Sectionals, 1991)

[61] (Jones, Maryvale High School vs. Hutch-Tech High School; Class B-1 Sectionals, 1991)

[62] (Jones, Maryvale High School vs. Hutch-Tech High School; Class B-1 Sectionals, 1991)

Another suburban high school called Clarence eliminated Kensington 61–57, setting up a semifinal matchup with the Engineers.[63] Coach Jones' team subsequently made short work of Clarence, downing them 85–52 to advance to the Class B-1 final.[64] The recipe was the same. It involved tough team defense led by No. 40, Paul Saunders' 10 steals, and great teamwork on offense, spearheaded by Curtis Brooks' and Pep Skillon's 6 assists each.[65,66] Curtis finished with 18 points and was eight-for-eight from the free-throw line.[67] Pep, Paul, and Dion each had 12, 11, and 9 points, respectively.[68]

Because of my lack of familiarity with Section VI basketball at the time, I did not completely grasp what was taking place. I knew that the Engineers kept winning, and with every morning announcement, it just seemed that it was the way it was supposed to be. The Hutch-Tech basketball team was supposed to win all its games. It was something I was used to hearing since early January just before they marched through the Yale Cup. They were now marching through this Section VI Class B-1 playoff bracket with ease, and it seemed like it would just go on forever.

* * *

On the road to glory many championship teams encounter opponents who take them to the brink of elimination. They make them prove that they are who they say they are. This happens frequently in single-elimination playoff formats like the NCAA Tournament and the above-mentioned NFL playoffs. In some cases, the higher-seeded team may have slipped into a mindset of overconfidence and complacency. In other cases, the lower seed may be *tailor-made* to exploit the weaknesses of the favored team, leading to an upset.

Either of these instances creates matchups where each team must dig deep and fight for their lives through *slugfests,* where one team usually ends up escaping by the skin of its teeth. With the Engineers steamrolling their first two opponents, it would have been easy to assume that they would do the same thing to their opponent in the Class B-1 final round. Their opponents, the Kenmore East Bulldogs, had other plans though.

Waiting for Coach Jones and the Engineers in the Class B-1 final was No. 3 seeded Kenmore East, who had just defeated Olean 66–61 in the other semifinal.[69]

---

[63] (Harrington, High School Basketball: Class B-1 Quarterfinal, 1991)
[64] (Jones, Clarence High School vs. Hutch-Tech High School; Class B-1 Sectionals, 1991)
[65] (Jones, Clarence High School vs. Hutch-Tech High School; Class B-1 Sectionals, 1991)
[66] (Jones, Clarence High School vs. Hutch-Tech High School; Class B-1 Sectionals, 1991)
[67] (Jones, Clarence High School vs. Hutch-Tech High School; Class B-1 Sectionals, 1991)
[68] (Jones, Clarence High School vs. Hutch-Tech High School; Class B-1 Sectionals, 1991)
[69] (Staff, Riverside ousts top-seed Wilson, 1991)

Just like Hutch-Tech, Kenmore East fielded a senior-laden squad led by Ken Warren, who was on his way to play football for Syracuse University the next year. At 6'7" and 270 lbs., Warren was bigger than the Engineers' Chuck Thompson, something I could not wrap my mind around.

The game took place at Fredonia State College on Friday, February 29, 1991. Unfortunately, I did not go to the game for reasons described earlier. Hutch-Tech may have organized a bus to take students to the game, but I have no recollection of it. I read about it the next day in the *Buffalo News*. That Saturday morning, I walked to our neighborhood corner Convenient market and bought a newspaper, perhaps for a homework assignment. I turned to the sports page as I walked home in the snow and saw the headline entitled, *Hutch-Tech holds off Kenmore East upset bid.*[70] It was our Hutch-Tech boys' basketball team, but the title read like a professional sports story. I wasn't sure. Was this the same group of guys I saw daily walking through the hallways of our school?

According to the *Buffalo News'* Mike Harrington, the game was in fact, a good old-fashioned slugfest where the Engineers trailed by as many as 14 points in the first half, going down 28–14 mid-way through the second quarter. Most of the Engineers' trouble was with the above-mentioned center, Ken Warren, from Kenmore East. The Engineers never had the lead until Pep Skillon fed Chuck Thompson for a layup that put the Engineers up 57–55 with 2:27 left on the clock.[71] A free throw by Curtis Brooks with 1:09 left in regulation extended the lead to three, but East rallied off a jump shot by Gary Welgoss with forty-eight seconds to go, and his free throw with twenty-three seconds to go.[72] The Engineers worked for the last shot as Brooks struggled against Kenmore East's Ray Holder, who had him well-defended. Brooks was off balance when he released a shot, but was still able to bank it in.[73]

According to Harrington's write-up, Kenmore East had a chance to tie the game, but Adam Benzel's desperation seventeen-footer after a scramble for the ball clanked off the rim. Coach Jones had the team use a quicker tempo and tenacious defense spearheaded by Curtis Brooks and Paul Saunders that kickstarted an 11–4 run to open up the second half, where they pulled even with the Bulldogs at 39–39.[74] Neither team led by more than 4 points the rest of the way.[75] The Engineers were once again led by Curtis Brooks and Pep Skillon with 13 points apiece, while Chuck Thompson added 12, followed by Paul Saunders

---

[70] (Harrington, Hutch-Tech holds off Kenmore East upset bid, 1991)
[71] (Harrington, Hutch-Tech holds off Kenmore East upset bid, 1991)
[72] (Harrington, Hutch-Tech holds off Kenmore East upset bid, 1991)
[73] (Harrington, Hutch-Tech holds off Kenmore East upset bid, 1991)
[74] (Harrington, Hutch-Tech holds off Kenmore East upset bid, 1991)
[75] (Harrington, Hutch-Tech holds off Kenmore East upset bid, 1991)

and Dion Frasier, each with 10 points, and minor contributions from the other players.[76]

"It was pure gratification," said Brooks in the *Buffalo News'* postgame interview. "I knew that I would be the one to take it to the hoop. I was looking for the best shot that I could get. It was a tough one, but it went in."[77]

Again, I can only imagine what it would have been like to be at the game. I imagine it was quite electric, and all who were in attendance participated in the emotional ride with the Hutch-Tech and Kenmore East players and coaches. Walking down the snow-covered block of Hastings Avenue between Kay Street and Eggert Road, I pumped my fist in jubilation for their victory and for how they captured the Section VI Class B-1 Championship.

What would it have been like to go to that game? How much could I have learned by just watching from the stands and participating in the ride as a fan? I did not go because I did not know how to get to Fredonia. I felt like I would have gained more knowledge of the sectionals and the high school basketball world. Had I asked my mother early enough, she probably could have driven to Fredonia State College, which was in the south towns about forty-five minutes from Buffalo. Or if Hutch-Tech had organized a bus for us students to go, maybe I could have gotten there that way. My brother had not made plans to attend the game, nor had any of my immediate friends, so I didn't either. That was a missed opportunity!

* * *

In addition to hearing about their miraculous win over Kenmore East, we were told on the morning announcements that the 1990–91 Engineers' ride was not over yet, and there was the potential for it to continue much further. Winning the Class B-1 final, they advanced to the overall Class B final and be matched against the Class B-2 champion, Williamsville South, another suburban high. It was a quick turnaround as the overall Class B final would take place the next Tuesday night at ECC North.

According to Mike Harrington's article, the 1990–91 Hutch-Tech Engineers and Williamsville South Billies were mirror images of one another arriving at the matchup with nearly identical records of 21–2 and 18–5, respectively. The core group of players for both teams had been together for at least three years under the tutelage of coaches who had nurtured them consistently through the good and bad times. His article in the *Buffalo News* entitled, *Tech, South to meet in Class B Title*

[76] (Harrington, Hutch-Tech holds off Kenmore East upset bid, 1991)
[77] (Harrington, Hutch-Tech holds off Kenmore East upset bid, 1991)

Game, stated that the Williamsville South Billies had a similar road to their current place of success as Hutch-Tech.[78]

During the 1990–91 season, the Billies won more games than in the previous three years combined. Their turnaround was credited to several things. First, Coach Alan Monaco, who had coached at Turner/Carroll and Cardinal O'Hara. There was also the emergence of point guard Mike Mitchell, who averaged 27.3 points per game. And finally, the arrival of the 6'5" Lockport transfer junior, Andre Graves, who provided inside toughness and rebounding for the Billies.

Like the Engineers, the Billies had veteran players and *character* guys who held the team together—Co-Captain Scott Machemer and fellow senior, Todd DeStefano.[79] Character or 'glue' guys are guys who are not always the most visible, but whose temperaments and leadership keep their teams from breaking apart during the most challenging games. All championship teams have them, and those who do not usually do not make it far.

The No. 2-seeded Williamsville South Billies marched to the overall Class B final behind the play of their two-star juniors Mike Mitchell and Andre Graves. They defeated No. 7, Cheektowaga Central 79–76 in the quarterfinal round and No. 6-seeded, Fredonia 58–48 in the semifinals before meeting up with another perennial power, the No. 1-seeded, Lackawanna Steelers in the Class B-2 final.[80] Behind Mike Mitchell's 22 points and Scott Machemer's 17 points, the Billies stunned the Steelers with a 61– 56 win, setting a matchup with the Engineers in the Class B final.[81]

The Engineers and the Billies tipped off at 8:15 p.m. at ECC North on Tuesday, March 5, 1991 in a matchup that was never out of reach for either team. As written in the *Buffalo News'*, in front of a crowd of 1,800, both teams battled back and forth as Hutch-Tech raced to a 28–19 lead behind 13 first-half points by Pep Skillon, only to see it narrowed to 28–23 at halftime.[82] Williamsville South's No. 55, Andre Graves, exploded early in the second half scoring seven of his 17 points to tie the game 30–30.[83] In the battle of the point guards, Williamsville South's No. 12, Mike Mitchell, fought and clawed, giving the Engineers fits in transition, leading to ten second-half lead changes on his way to scoring a team-high of 19 points.[84]

With a narrow 53–50 lead, the Engineers went into their 'Four Corners' delay offense with 4:20 minutes to go in the fourth quarter to try to protect and expand

[78] (Harrington, Tech, South to meet in Class B title game, 1991)
[79] (Harrington, Tech, South to meet in Class B title game, 1991)
[80] (Harrington, Tech, South to meet in Class B title game, 1991)
[81] (Harrington, Tech, South to meet in Class B title game, 1991)
[82] (Harrington, Tech, South to meet in Class B title game, 1991)
[83] (Harrington, Tech, South to meet in Class B title game, 1991)
[84] (Harrington, Hutch-Tech tips South to capture Class B crown, 1991)

their lead.[85] Possession by possession, the Engineers steadily shaved time off the clock forcing the Billies to foul them. On its first possession going into their delay game, the Engineers shaved off seventy-nine seconds before Pep Skillon scored an offensive rebound pushing the lead to 55–50 with 3:01 minutes left in regulation.[86] The two other possessions lasted longer than thirty seconds each and helped the Engineers cap an 11–0 burst which gave them a 60–50 lead with fifty-nine seconds left.[87] Curtis Brooks ended Williamsville South's hopes by going seven-for-eight from the free throw line.[88]

At the final buzzer, the Engineers won the game 63–57 to win the overall Section VI Class B Championship.[89] Pep Skillon was the high scorer for the Engineers finishing with 21 points.[90] Curtis Brooks was next with 19 points, followed by 11 points from Chuck Thompson.[91] Paul Saunders contributed 7 points, 5 assists, and 7 steals to the victory.[92] It was the same formula they had worked to perfection the entire year. It consisted of senior leadership, stingy defense, patient and unselfish offense, and clutch free throw shooting down the stretch of games.

Mike Harrington once again wrote up a postgame article about the 1991 Class B final entitled, *Hutch-Tech tips South to capture Class B crown.*[93] In the article he described the key points of the game in addition to giving sound bites from the players and coaches. Despite the run, they went on through the Yale Cup during league play. It was the only picture of the 1990–91 Engineers in the *Buffalo News* that year. The picture captured both teams' point guards. Curtis Brooks was captured sprinting on defense in his black Nike Flights, his untucked No. 13 tank top with his tee shirt and maroon trunks. Next to him, Mike Mitchell was captured dribbling the ball, looking to do a crossover dribble in a dark-colored jersey with Williamsville South written in cursive letters sandwiching in the No. 12. He, too, wore a tee shirt underneath his tank top with black sneakers.

---

[85] (Harrington, Hutch-Tech tips South to capture Class B crown, 1991)
[86] (Harrington, Hutch-Tech tips South to capture Class B crown, 1991)
[87] (Harrington, Hutch-Tech tips South to capture Class B crown, 1991)
[88] (Harrington, Hutch-Tech tips South to capture Class B crown, 1991)
[89] (Harrington, Hutch-Tech tips South to capture Class B crown, 1991)
[90] (Jones, Williamsville South High School vs. Hutch-Tech High School; Class B Sectionals, 1991)
[91] (Jones, Williamsville South High School vs. Hutch-Tech High School; Class B Sectionals, 1991)
[92] (Jones, Williamsville South High School vs. Hutch-Tech High School; Class B Sectionals, 1991)
[93] (Harrington, Hutch-Tech tips South to capture Class B crown, 1991)

"We figured with that amount of time left on the clock, we would try to run time off of it," Coach Jones said after the game to the *Buffalo News*. "We do a lot of hard work in practice, and these kids execute what we try to teach them."[94]

"I was a little surprised when they went to it that early," Williamsville South's Coach Alan Monaco said afterward. He discussed the *delay* offense Coach Jones strategically used in the game's closing stages, a powerful tactic in an era where there was no shot clock violation at the high school level. "I thought that if we were patient and sent a couple of guys out on it, maybe they would turn the ball over. They play with a lot of discipline. I give them a lot of credit."[95]

"I was at the game between Williamsville South and Hutch-Tech. Andre Graves was matched against Chuck Thompson," said Mr. Kenneth Bernard Smith, Gabe's father, weeks after the overall Class B final. He wore one of his signature top hats, and we were driving around in his teal Cadillac. I think he was dropping me off at home or taking me to meet Gabe somewhere. Mr. Smith had a deep, scratchy voice, almost like a bear's grunt.

"I work with Andre's father at Sheraton ITT and have known him since he was little. Don't get me wrong, Chuck had a good game, but Andre had a better game!" Mr. Smith kept hitting on this point, reminding me of when Gabe insisted that Quincy Morris, the point guard at Cleveland Hill, was better than our point guard at Hutch-Tech, Curtis Brooks. I wondered what was up with the Smiths. It was like they always had to be right. Was there some postgame score to settle?

The Engineers had risen to the top of Western New York basketball and won the overall Class B Championship in Section VI, extending their winning streak to 17 straight games and ascending to No. 3 for Large Schools in the *Buffalo News'* Cage Polls on March 10, 1991. It seemed like forever since they had lost to Niagara Falls in the Festival of Lights Tournament, and it seemed like they couldn't lose to anyone else. The Hutch-Tech Engineers were poised, hot, and on a roll!

Now that they had won the Section VI Class B Championship, the Engineers had to face the Class B Champion from the Rochester area and its surrounding towns. They would have to travel an hour to face their next opponent at the Rochester War Memorial Stadium the following Saturday. Their opponent was yet to be determined at the time of the announcement. It did not seem to matter who they would play. Coach Jones and his team would just keep winning, and we would keep getting good news about their victories in the morning announcements. It would just go on and on.

---

[94] (Harrington, Hutch-Tech tips South to capture Class B crown, 1991)

[95] (Harrington, Hutch-Tech tips South to capture Class B crown, 1991)

Chapter 10. The 1991 Class B Far West Regional

"I scouted both Newark and Wilson. Those were the teams that we were going to have to play. In my mind, it didn't make any difference who we played!"
—Ken Jones, Head Coach, the Hutch-Tech boys' basketball team, 1988-1993, June 2014

While I thought the 1990–91 Engineers would go on winning forever, the reality was that their season would end eventually. The seasons for all sports teams do, and the only question is how. Will it be by coronation or elimination? There can only be one team to win its last game. Regardless of the sport, most high school athletic teams' seasons ended in their hometowns/municipalities or nearby. For a select few high school basketball teams in New York State, their seasons ended in a small town just north of Albany called Glens Falls. The New York State Public High School Athletic Association Tournament and the New York State Federation Tournament were held in the rural oasis just north of the state capital, Albany.

For student-athletes participating in interscholastic athletics, there may be no greater experience than advancing to the state tournament, where the best teams from every region of the state gather to decide the best team of the year. Even the players on the teams who do not win could at least say they experienced the excitement, the crowds, the college recruiters, the media coverage—all of it.

Glens Falls was a small town of roughly 15,000 people in the Adirondack Region of New York State. It sat in the woodlands just before Lake George, heading north on Interstate 87 from Albany. Residents of that part of New York State affectionately referred to that stretch of Interstate 87 between Albany and the Quebec border as 'The Northway'. It was near the northeastern New York State-Vermont border. I had heard of Glens Falls before, and it seemed like such a faraway place even though it was close to the Albany area where Dad lived. The World Wrestling Federation, which we watched regularly as kids in the 1980s, held matches there.

Winning the 1991 Section VI Class B Championship was a tremendous accomplishment for the Hutch-Tech basketball team. The team was not even sectional-eligible two years earlier. The Engineers' ride was not over. The potential was there for the ride to continue a little further, and the stakes were now even higher. They now had the opportunity to make the journey to Glens Falls, the equivalent of the NCAA Men's Division I Final Four Championship Weekend.

While Section VI champions emerged every year, not all of them made it past the Far West Regional. There they matched up against the best teams from the Rochester area of similar size and classification, the Section V champions. Some people called the regionals *super* sectionals designating a higher level of competition. If Coach Jones and the Engineers could win the Class B Far West Regional, they would join an elite company and further secure legendary status.

In the morning announcement on Tuesday, March 6, 1991, following the Engineers' 63–57 victory over Williamsville South, Coach Jones shared that their next game would be in the State Regionals at the Rochester War Memorial Stadium. It was scheduled to take place at 3 p.m. on Saturday, March 9th. Their opponent was yet to be determined. After the write-up of the Williamsville South victory, he wrote, "CONGRATULATIONS ENGINEERS—GOOD LUCK IN THE STATE TOURNEY!" It was posted near the coaches' offices.

The announcement also said, "Get your game and transportation ticket for the game in Rochester, Saturday at 3 p.m.," so it seemed some of the students once again would go, though I did not. The Engineers were in the State Tournament, and they would probably win again. They were on a 17-game winning streak, so why would they not continue to win?

* * *

We collectively heard about the results of the State Regional game on the morning announcements on Monday, March 11, 1991, as we had most of the season. The news was unexpected and startling this time, at least for me. The Engineers fell to a team called Newark in a lopsided 77–47 loss. Not only had they lost, but they lost by 30 points. I had not heard of them losing since their second defeat to Niagara Falls in December, and even then, it was not by 30 points. Furthermore, it was their last game, so there would be no more news of their victories or future games. The morning announcement, which was later posted on the bulletin board outside the coaches' offices, read as follows:

"The State's third-ranked Hutch-Tech basketball season came to an end Saturday when they lost to the number one ranked Class B team from Newark, NY, 77–47. The loss came after 17 straight victories, an undefeated Yale Cup Championship, a Section VI Class B-1 Championship, and a Section VI Class B Championship. It was a great season for the school and the team, which included five seniors: Curtis Brooks, Quincy Lee, Paul Saunders, Pep Skillon, Charles Thompson and nine underclassmen. A special thanks goes to all players and managers for their time and effort from Coach Jones.

"Coach Jones and the team members would like to thank the staff, faculty, students, cheerleaders, and band for their support. A special thanks goes to Mr. Karlin, Mr. Fried, and Mr. Saracki.

"CONGRATULATIONS ENGINEERS ON A GREAT SEASON"

3-13-91 K. Jones[96]

Underneath the write-up on the bulletin board someone wrote, "ALL PLAYERS HAVE TO VACATE THE "TEAM" LOCKER ROOM TODAY."

Again, I had personally become accustomed to hearing about the 1990–91 Engineers winning, and I was not prepared to hear that they had lost, especially by 30 points. The morning announcement was very solemn and morbid for me. Although it was brief, you could hear the disappointment of the writer. You could feel that a golden opportunity had been missed. It was a loss that would sting many people for years to come, long after the final buzzer of that 1991 Class B Far West Regional.

* * *

Despite the Far West Regional outcome that year, the 1990–91 Engineers were still royalty around the school. I know that I at least looked at them with reverence whenever I saw them around our H-shaped building, particularly the seniors Curtis Brooks, Pep Skillon, Chuck Thompson, Paul Saunders, and Quincy Lee. They did not know who I was, but I knew who they were.

"What's up, Pep?" I think I spoke to Pep Skillon once in the hallways to which he looked at me like I was a little crazy as he didn't know who I was.

Every year after the winter sports season concluded, there was an assembly in the auditorium where all the sports teams were recognized and celebrated. In addition to the boys' basketball team, the girls' basketball team, the bowling team, the boys' hockey team, and the boys' and girls' swimming teams were all recognized. I watched from the balcony of the auditorium as the teams gathered on stage as a group one by one, and their coaches made speeches about them and reflected on the season that had just concluded. Awards were given to players who had distinguished themselves in special ways.

Coach Jones, dressed in his signature blazer, shirt and tie, khakis, and running sneakers and looking professorial, gave an overview of the magical 1990–91

---

[96] (Jones, Hutch-Tech High School vs. Newark High School; Class B Far West Regionals, 1991)

season.[97] With the fourteen players and managers standing next to him on stage, he read the following summary from the podium in his raspy, scratchy, and grandfatherly voice:

"The Engineers enjoyed an excellent basketball season with twenty-two wins and only three losses. Although the Engineers failed to win their own Tip-Off Tournament or the Festival of Lights Tournament, this had been a championship season for the Hutch-Tech boys' basketball team in more ways than one.

"The Engineers had a perfect 13–0 record in their league to claim the Yale Cup Championship. Then the Engineers won their way to the Section VI, Class B-1 Championship by defeating Kenmore East in a thrilling comeback victory 60–58. We will remember the great defensive drive and the clutch field goal by Curtis Brooks in that game.

"They say championships are won with defense and team play, and this was exhibited by the Engineers in their 63–57 victory over Williamsville South to claim their third championship of the season, the Section VI Class B crown. This victory allowed the Hutch-Tech boys' basketball team their first entry in the New York State Public High School Athletic Association State Basketball Tournament. The Engineers, ranked 3rd in the State, traveled to Rochester, NY, to play the number 1 ranked team, Newark Central School. Unfortunately, the seventeen-game winning streak of the Engineers and their dream of a state championship came to a halt when Tech lost the game.

"The entire squad was awarded certificates. Curtis Brooks, Dion Frasier, Andre Higgins, Quincy Lee, Michael Mann, Paul Saunders, Jerrold Skillon, Christian Souter, and Charles Thompson were awarded varsity letters as players. Monica Peterson, Jonathan Koval, Matthew McDowell, Tuhran Wilbur, and Frank Williamson were awarded letters as managers.

"The following players were awarded coach's trophies in the following categories:

1. Best Intra-squad Free Throw Player- Curtis Brooks- 86.3%
2. Best Free Throw Shooting % in Games- Curtis Brooks- 78%
3. Best Rebounding Average/Game- Charles Thompson- 12.0
4. Best Field Goal % in Games- Charles Thompson- 59.3%
5. Best Assists Average/Game- Curtis Brooks- 6.6
6. Voted Best Defensive Player- Paul Saunders
7. Voted Best Practice Player- Michael Mann and Chris Souter
8. Most Valuable Player- Curtis Brooks

---

[97] (Jones, The 1990-91 Hutch-Tech Boys' Basketball Team Season Summary, 1991)

"We have five players who are candidates for the All-High Basketball Team. They are Curtis Brooks, Pep Skillon, Quincy Lee, Charles Thompson, and Paul Saunders. We will have a difficult task replacing the graduating seniors. Naturally, we wish all of them the best of success. Also, we would like to thank all the students and faculty for their cooperation and support throughout the season."

"CONGRATULATIONS ENGINEERS ON A GREAT SEASON!"

As Coach Jones read his speech, I looked at the players who stood watching in their button-down shirts, sweaters, hoodies, jeans or khakis, sneakers and shoes. Their facial expressions varied. Some were blank. Some were somber. Others were a mixture of stoic, jovial, and relaxed. It was all mentally setting in for them regarding what they had just completed and what was left on the table concerning the opportunity missed. For the class of 1991 seniors, a chapter was permanently closing, which may have also been on their minds.

That 1990-91 Hutch-Tech boys' basketball team would continue to live on in the memories of those who were there, for anyone who read the newspaper clippings, those sectional books, or had copies of the 1990-91 yearbook. From then on, I regularly looked at their pictures and the associated captions on pages 146 and 147 in my freshman yearbook.[98]

For the 1990-91 team, you could see the mixture of athleticism, discipline, experience, maturity, strength, and the seeds of Engineers teams to come. They were battle-tested, and you could see a cohesiveness about them as they wore their white tank tops with white tee shirts, maroon shorts, and mostly black sneakers with white ankle socks. I would dream of being just like them one day and going on a magical run like the one they had just embarked upon. They were like gods or titans to me, whichever you prefer.

Once the presentation was finished, the Engineers filed off the stage, never to be assembled or seen as a unit again. The five seniors would be gone the next year, and the returning players would come back with a crop of new players under them. Who would that new crop be? And would the 1991–92 team be able to measure up to the 1990–91 team? Whatever the case, my mind was set. All through the year up to that point and looking at them on stage, I knew that I wanted to be one of them. I wanted to be just like them. I wanted to be on a championship team and be a hero in the school, just like them.

---

[98] (School, Impressions: Stepping Into 91, 1991)

Chapter 11. Aspiring to Play on the Team, and the Rest of the 1990–91 School Year

"Are you hoopin?" —**Shaun Willis, Student, Hutch-Tech High School, the William-Emslie YMCA, the 1990-91 school year**

Once the 1990–91 Hutch-Tech boys' basketball teams' season ended, I knew I wanted to be on the 1991–92 team the next year. Tryouts were seven months away. One thing I knew was that by the time October rolled around, I needed the grades in my core courses to all be above 70%. I was not going to repeat that mistake I made in Global Studies any time soon. I also had to get my skill level up so that Coach Jones would deem me worthy of donning the maroon and gold just like Curtis Brooks and the 1990–91 team. But how would I do it?

As freshmen at Hutch-Tech, we did not take gym classes like the upperclassmen did. Instead, we had to take swimming classes our entire first year. This meant that the only real time we could play basketball at school was during intramurals when Coach Jones hosted them before and after the basketball season. Other opportunities to play were in the Interclass Tournament and outside of school.

During Coach Jones' tenure, he hosted a tournament where the classes would compete against each other. There were two rounds. In the opening round, boys from the freshman class played boys from the junior class, and boys from the sophomore class played boys from the senior class in two separate brackets. It was like the Men's NCAA Tournament Final Four. The winners advanced to play in the championship game, which usually ended up being the juniors and the seniors in those days because they were bigger, stronger, and more experienced than the underclasses.

In addition to myself, the freshmen boys who played on our team in the tournament were: Shaun Willis, Amar Hendrickson, Torri Lowe, Omari Ferguson, Andrew Arnold, Terrance Collison, Mike Saamol, Martevious Johnson, Gary Lane, Davin Matthewson, Jarrod Hiddleston, and Jason Wardlawer. There were no tryouts for the tournament, and it was strictly voluntary. We were also assigned a coach. For us, one of the upperclassmen from the boys' basketball team determined who would play and when.

I have a few vivid memories of that game. First, there was a crowd of our screaming classmates in the bleachers which made me a little nervous. I was not used to playing in front of large crowds. Dion Frasier from the varsity team was our coach, and he subbed us in and out of the game as he saw fit. He did not start me, and I spent a lot of time on the sidelines wondering when I would get into the game. In a way, it was like being back at Campus West.

Donald Garfield, Jermaine 'J-Bird' Skillon, Leon Steward, Henry Steward, and others made up the class of 1992 juniors' team. Donald Garfield was particularly amped up for that game. We had to play as either shirts or skins, and unfortunately, we were the skins which at the time made me uncomfortable as I was not confident about my body and image.

Specific plays that come to mind include Gary Lane hitting a three-pointer from forty-five degrees. I remember Torri Lowe pushing the ball up the floor with his speed and throwing a no-look pass to Michael Saamol. Mike was kind of chubby and could not get high enough in the air to catch the pass. When the ball sailed out of bounds, Torri turned around with a disgruntled look on his face and walked away, shaking his head with his fists balled up.

My most vivid memory of getting into the game was matching up against Jermaine 'J-Bird' Skillon. Unlike his brother, Pep, who had more of a hulkish and athletic build, J-Bird was round and stocky. For some reason, I thought I could match up with him and guard him. It turned out to be more difficult than I had anticipated. Play after play, the juniors brought the ball down, and J-Bird posted me up, overpowering my fourteen-year-old body and shoving me out of the way with ease. In those moments, I recalled that J-Bird played on the offensive line on the football team, and with good reason. I believe the juniors blew us out in that game and then beat the seniors. The class of 1992 had a lot of talent.

* * *

The rest of the year I played most of my basketball at the William-Emslie Young Men's Christian Association (YMCA) on Friday nights or Saturday mornings. Sometime during the transition from middle school to high school, Mom bought us a basket with a fiberglass backboard mounted on our garage. I think her coworker and friend from the United Way put it up for us. We spent hours back there playing on it, and kids from all over the neighborhood would come. It wasn't regulation-height, so after a while, it became a place where guys could come and live out their NBA fantasies in terms of dunking. One afternoon my Grandma Lena got fed up with all the guys there, and she threw everyone out. I eventually realized that I needed to play with other players on regulation-sized courts and baskets. I also got tired of guys dunking on our now-beleaguered basket. Thus, I ventured out to other places to play like the William-Emslie Y.

Mom dropped me off there, and sometimes Gabe would come with me. The William-Emslie Y was a brown brick structure that you could easily miss driving down William Street. It was a single-level structure and it was not until you entered the building that you saw that you realized there was a large gymnasium in the basement, like the gym at Campus West. I get goosebumps thinking about those first days going there. It was new and uncharted territory for me. At the time, I felt it held the keys to my becoming a better basketball player, and in some ways it did.

I think it sat across the street from a car wash and soul food take-out restaurant. Speaking of soul food, Amahl's friend Dorian Johnson's stepfather Gus, owned a steak sub shop near the corner of William and Jefferson Streets called 'Gusto's Steakhouse'. I would go there sometimes to get a nice greasy Philadelphia-style steak sub with beef, cheese, onions, and sauce on a French roll. I would never have ventured to the Jefferson-William corridor if not for the YMCA. Folks from my mother's generation said it used to be a bustling area in terms of black businesses prior to integration in the 1960s.

"If you want to be a good basketball player, you have to go where the basketball players are," Dad said in a conversation over the phone during my first year at Hutch-Tech. Dad's athletic background was mostly in baseball, with some judo mixed in later in his life. This piece of advice was spot on though I didn't completely understand it at the time. Back then, I looked to play wherever I could, and that place was now the William-Emslie YMCA, mostly on Saturday mornings, but also as often as I could get over there.

* * *

Sometimes Shaun Willis from Hutch-Tech showed up at the William-Emslie Y. I didn't know him personally, but I looked up to him the way I looked up to Ronald Jennings at Campus West. I thought he was the best basketball player in our class. It was more hero worship—something I would not break out of for a while.

I had heard about playing at the William-Emslie Y from Shaun coincidentally. He told me about it one day when we ran into each other on Bailey Avenue one Saturday afternoon. I was walking south on Bailey Avenue between East Ferry Street and Delevan Avenue. I might have been leaving the Bailey-Doat Boys Club and didn't feel like waiting for the next bus. I looked behind myself continually to check my surroundings and recognized him. He wore a jacket, blue sweatpants, sneakers, and his signature glasses. Shaun took long and confident strides, and we started talking once we recognized each other. We hadn't really spoken before then, even though we were classmates. I told him that I was looking for places to play basketball, and he told me about the William-Emslie YMCA.

If you weren't a member at the William-Emslie Y, there was a $2–$3 entry fee which you could gradually put towards a membership. I saved all my receipts, and I eventually purchased one. I brought a collection of them in one day and paid the balance, which was roughly $20. Afterward, they gave me a laminated card, which I showed to the front desk each time I went.

A whole cast of characters and regulars played at the William-Emslie Y. They were primarily teenage black kids from various neighborhoods. There was a mischievous dark-skinned kid, named James, with a pretty good handle. *Handle* was a slang term used to describe someone's ability to dribble the ball. A short stocky guy, named Gerald, liked to shoot the ball and dominate it. I usually set picks for him on offense when we teamed up, just like in the NBA. There was also a girl who the guys called 'Missy'. She was a *tomboy* and played basketball at an all-girls private school called Mount Saint Mary Academy. Tomboys were girls who liked to do things classically associated with boys, and who regularly played with them. Mom introduced the term to me.

Missy had a good game and was used to playing with the boys. She was a good ball handler and a good jump shooter. I did not understand why she and other girls wanted to get out and play with the boys. I also did not know how to play with girls in terms of physical contact. For example, was it okay to shove them around and foul them like the boys? It was one of many things that perplexed me at the time.

"Are you hoopin?" Shaun Willis asked me this often when he showed up at the Emslie Y. He would see me in the bleachers just watching the games. *Hoopin* was slang for hooping, which meant playing games of basketball. He was asking me, "Are you playing or just watching? Are you going to get into any of the games or just sit there?"

"Uhhhh, yeah," I replied to him. When I started going to the Emslie Y I did not understand the culture and rules of playground and street basketball. There was a whole vernacular with code words and rules—like when our elders played Spades. For a while, I just sat and watched the other players play. I did not get into any of the games because I did not know how. Whether or not you played at William-Emslie Y or one of the playgrounds, there was universal street basketball vocabulary and a code of conduct.

"I GOT WINNERS!" This announcement set you up to take on the winner of the game in progress. A variation of this was, "I GOT NEXT!" Once you made your announcement, if there were a bunch of guys already there watching or just walking in, you would get asked, "Hey, can I run with you?" or simply, "Can I run?" This meant, "Can I play on your team?" If you were the player asking to play on someone else's team, sometimes you would get an immediate, "Yes," but in other instances, the captain of that new team would stall you out so he could see what players would be available once the current game finished.

Chapter 11. Aspiring to Play on the Team, and the Rest of the 1990-91 School Year

Because I had not gotten out and played street basketball much, it took me a little while to understand the culture. I had to build the confidence to call winners myself and to ask the other kids if I could run with them. Unfortunately, I was shy and uncomfortable with guys, especially street guys, that I didn't know. My childhood was sheltered. So, there were knowledge deficits that I had to fill in as I went along.

"I've got so and so," or "Give me so and so," is what the captain of the challenging team said when announcing who was on his team in a quick and crude draft. The captain usually mentioned his players by name if he knew them, and if not, they were identified by an article of clothing they wore or a well-known person they looked like. It was strictly your physical attributes if you could not be identified that way. For me, it was usually, "I've got *Big* Man!" I was often called 'Big Man' because of my size. James, who I discussed earlier, gave me the nickname 'Hooper'. I don't know why, but some guys were just given nicknames.

"STAY HERE!" This was code for, "I just got fouled," and it was usually by a player driving the ball to the basket or trying to make a layup off an offensive rebound. We did not take many jump shots when playing street basketball. The preferred way to play was using your handle to 'go to the hole'. Going to the hole simply meant penetrating to the basket for a layup. When you got fouled playing at the Emslie Y or on the streets, you had to call your foul out. If not, the other team would take the ball down to their basket and continue playing. Those were the rules.

When we were not playing pickup games, we played games of Twenty-One. In Buffalo, depending on the circle you ran in, the game was also called Rochester. It was basically every man or woman for themselves. There could be two players or as many as 15 or more at one basket at one time. If you scored a two-pointer or a three-pointer, you went to the free-throw line and shot until you made five straight baskets. Then you had to take the ball at the top of the key and try to score again off the dribble, but by that time you probably had two or more guys guarding you.

Twenty-One was good in some ways for your individual game, but not necessarily your team game. Playing Twenty-One and pickup basketball were how many of us city kids learned to play without formal vehicles to learn the structure and fundamentals of organized basketball. For many of us, this was all we knew and unless there was someone in your circle to mentor you and show you more, this was all you got.

In addition to teaching me a lot about the game of basketball, the kids at the Y taught me lessons about fitting into black culture—appearances and what does and does not look cool. At least for a while, I wore two tank tops there when I played basketball. One was a teal color with a cartoon shark on the front of it. I had another one that was black with two crazed cartoon white men on a beach driving a vehicle that said 'Wave Warriors' on it. I also wore pairs of multicolored shorts which they probably thought were funny too.

One day we played Twenty-One, and some of the other kids closer to the basket looked at my shirt and snickered. I noticed some laughing, but did not know I was the brunt of the jokes. Who cared about fashion? We were just out playing basketball, right?

"They're laughing at your shirt," Gabe whispered to me. "You probably shouldn't wear that here anymore."

"Oh," I said, embarrassed, and I never wore them again, at least not to play basketball with those kids.

Between my freshman and sophomore years, most of my basketball was played at the William-Emslie Y in the way of pickup games and games of Twenty-One. There was little work on my actual fundamentals and building my basketball IQ. I constantly worked on my free throw shooting, but not other parts of my game, whatever those were. I was an empty vessel looking to be filled by someone, but receiving little guidance. One day though, I did receive some valuable advice.

"COUNT IT! COUNT IT! COUNT IT!" Hank Sullivan, one of the staff/counselors at the William-Emslie YMCA, hung around the courts and yelled this out as he would run up and down the court firing up half-court shots. He was an older brown-complexioned man, probably in his 50s. He was bowlegged, had a bit of paunch, and had a happy disposition. He always wore a blue and gold Empire State Games sweatsuit, just like Mr. Cook at Campus West. He really cared about the kids at that YMCA and regularly mentored us.

"I notice you work on your free throw shooting all of the time, and you're a pretty good free throw shooter," Hank told me one day. He continued, "You're not always going to be at the free throw line, so you should work on the other parts of your game!" I looked at him and nodded slowly. It was valuable advice, but again I did not know what else to work on in terms of formal drills. I also enjoyed the free throw shooting due to the peacefulness of it, among other things. It was also something I could perfect on my own, and I loved seeing the ball go through the hoop, whether it sailed smoothly through the net or rattled in. It also allowed me to imitate No. 23, Michael Jordan, whose routine and form I mimicked, probably like many kids.

As a youngster who sought wisdom, our conversations sometimes went into other areas. Hank talked to me once about his lower back being broken and how thankful he was to be able to move around again. He then told me that he sometimes went to church in his exercise apparel because, "God doesn't care how you come just as long as you come!" It impressed me. However, Mom did not buy it when I tried to explain it to her on a ride home.

Sometimes I would go over to the YMCA without Gabe. I did not know how to work on the individual facets of my game, but I played hard, working to rebound the ball and to go up strong, just like Ronald Jennings encouraged me to do at Campus West. I eventually earned the respect of some of the players there. I would go home on Friday nights and sleep well after leaving it all out there on the court. Sometimes my legs would cramp up late at night as I lay there reflecting and thinking about the great game of basketball. I also dreamt about making the boys' varsity basketball team at Hutch-Tech.

When the weather warmed up I would go over to Roosevelt Park and play pickup games with kids from the surrounding neighborhoods. I rarely ventured to Delaware Park where all the grown men played. I thought they played the game a little too rough, which I did not realize would accelerate my development. At that time, I thought basketball was a non-contact sport which I later found to be false.

* * *

In the spring of 1991, Coach Jones posted a flyer on the bulletin board outside the coaches' offices where he had posted the game summaries and statistics for the 1990–91 team. It was a red and white, laminated flyer with black print that read, "The Ken Jones Basketball Camp: A Season of Basketball in a Session!" A slogan that was all over the flyer was, "Basketball is our Game, and Yours Can be the Same!" The flyer had illustrations of basketball players all over it, shooting, dribbling, and playing defense.

There were pictures not only of Coach Jones, but other coaches whom I did not recognize, such as Gary Oehlbeck, Bruce Voorhees, and Tom McCarthy. An older coach named Tony Alvaro looked particularly mean and did not smile. They were all from schools I had never heard of, like Gates-Chili, DeSales of Geneva, and Guilderland. There was no internet back then where you could do a quick search of the schools and their locations. From the flyer, I deduced that Coach Jones' camp took place at the end of July and lasted one week. It was held in Clinton, NY, in the foothills of the Adirondack Mountains, at a school called Hamilton College. Campers learned the fundamentals of basketball there.

"Take all you can eat and eat all you take!" Meals were included in the tuition for the camp, and this was another slogan on the flyer. From the instant I saw it, I was sold. I also intuitively had the feeling that if I wanted to make the team next year, I ought to go for no other reason than to show Coach Jones my initiative.

There was only one thing. The cost of the camp was $343, and it was all the way out in the foothills of the Adirondack Mountains. When I got home, I asked Mom about it, and she said it would be okay for me to go. She said I should also ask my father for some assistance, which he agreed to. I pitched the idea to Gabe, and he said that he wanted to go too. At that point, it was important to me that we did things together in tandem. After all, we were best friends.

The only thing left for me to do was to pass all my final exams. Going to summer school would prevent me from going to camp. Based on my academic performance that year, my not going to summer school was not a foregone conclusion, as I had not figured out how to excel academically. I had not figured out that I had control over my academic performance and grades.

* * *

As my freshman year progressed into its second half, my grades stabilized. By the third quarter, I saw some of my averages go up in my core courses. My overall average remained mediocre, going from a second-quarter overall average of 81% to a third-quarter average of 82%. In English, my grade went from a 90% to an 89%. In Global Studies, the class that prevented me from participating in the basketball program at the end of the first quarter, I stayed at a grade of 78%. In Sequential Math Course 1, my grade jumped from 71% to an 84% between the second and third quarters. In General Biology, I stayed relatively consistent, going from a grade of 87% to 92%. In Spanish, I jumped from a grade of 79% to 88%.

"Capable of doing better work," were the comments under my grade for Introduction to Occupations, where I scored 78%. It was taught by Mr. DiCorzo, a young Italian teacher with a mustache and curly and slightly graying hair. I think that was also his first year at Hutch-Tech. I excelled in his Mechanical Drawing class, where I earned an 80% and an 87% in the first two quarters. Lastly, in Computer Programming, I scored a measly 65%. What stood out to me the most about that class was my lack of interest. It could have also been the presentation. The teacher was Ms. Robertson, an attractive and shapely black woman. Every day it seemed like she was at her wit's end with us by the time eighth period rolled around.

I did not understand why I had to learn about the programming language FORTRAN (Formula Translation). I remember having a discussion with my mother about whether I even needed to take the class seriously. She, of course, said, "Yes." Again, it was not until later in life that I realized that every bit of information had some value. Coincidentally in about another five years, our entire society would start to become computerized.

Our classes ended just after Memorial Day weekend, and then our final exams started in early June. Though I had experienced a great jump in Sequential Math Course 1, it would be the one class that decided whether I would be able to go to the Ken Jones Basketball Camp. In every other class, I left the exam feeling that I did enough to get a grade greater than 65% at least, but something about that Course 1 Math exam stayed in the back of my mind. Was it the fractions? Was it the angles? The circumferences and decimals?

Chapter 11. Aspiring to Play on the Team, and the Rest of the 1990-91 School Year

The suspense killed me, so one day, I went down to Hutch-Tech to do some detective work regarding my exams. Mrs. Ciminellia was in her classroom with some other students with piles of exams in front of her. Her grade book was also close by. I walked over to her timidly, holding my red Chicago Bulls cap, hoping for a favorable answer, though whatever had been done had already been settled.

"Hello, Mrs. Ciminellia," I said to her like a patient going to the doctor for test results, hoping the prognosis was good. "I was just wondering if you knew what I got on my final exam."

"What's your name?" Mrs. Ciminellia asked me my name, looking at me with a blank stare through her glasses.

"I'm Anwar Dunbar," I said, slightly smiling.

"Oh yes, I remember you," she said after pausing and then going through her exam stack. As she went through her stack, I noticed her curly black hair, one of her defining characteristics. In what felt like an eternity, she searched through one stack, then another, and then another. Eventually, she came to my exam, snatched it out of the pile, and looked up at me, causing my heart to jump.

"You got a 67%," she said, looking down and verifying the score in her grade book. "I had to go through and find some extra points for you, but your grade is 67%."

"Oh, okay, thank you, Mrs. Ciminellia. Have a nice summer!" I bowed and then hurried out of the classroom. In the hallway, I jumped for joy and walked with a little extra pep in my step, reveling over my 67%. It was one of the first near misses in my life, and there were other major ones in my future. The only consequence of this would have been going to summer school with my brother Amahl, who had to attend one of his classes.

Having passed all my classes, I could now attend the Ken Jones Basketball Camp, strengthening my chances of making the Hutch-Tech boys' basketball team the next year. It is amazing how my little teenage mind worked back then. I focused solely on making the basketball team so I could be like Curtis Brooks and the 1990–91 Engineers. I was not thinking about college or the next step in my life. But then again, how many teens do? I had my sites set only on the here and now and not on what was coming on the horizon. It was an horizon that looked far away, but was always moving closer and closer, and doing so with deceptive speed.

Chapter 12. The Summer of 1991

"The two downfalls of many smart men have classically been their favorite sports teams and beautiful women!" —**Colin Cowherd, Sports Talk Show Host, 2015 on the radio**

I did not know it heading into it, but a lot would happen in my life during the summer of 1991. There were changes on the horizon in my personal life and in the world. Several changes were coming to the basketball world as well.

"WHAT TIME IS IT?" No. 53, Cliff Levingston hollered out to his huddled Chicago Bulls teammates before they emerged onto the floor of the Chicago Stadium or the opponent's home floor.

"GAME TIME! AWHOOOOO!" Following Levingston's initial call, his Bulls teammates responded in unison. I don't know if the Bulls had been performing the ritual the entire season, but I first took notice of it during coverage of the 1991 NBA playoffs on NBC. The ritual was one of the many steps in the Bulls' evolution. There were roster updates and the new spiritual and defensive approaches introduced by Head Coach, Phil Jackson. The *Zen Master* recommended books for his players while also pulling in Native American and Asian spiritual rituals during practices.

The NBA broadcasts moving to NBC was another change that season. In my short time watching professional basketball, the broadcasts had been on CBS which had its own specific introduction and music. NBC had its own introduction and music by artist John Tesh, but I preferred the introduction on CBS. I had also gotten used to Dick Stockton and Hubie Brown commentating on the games, as opposed to Marv Albert and former Atlanta Hawks Coach Mike Fratello. The latter was nicknamed 'The Czar of the Telestrator'. Albert referred to him that way jokingly during games.

Back to Bulls' pregame preparation, whether it was in their home whites or their visiting reds, the newly acquired Levingston led this ritual instead of their team captains, Michael Jordan and Bill Cartwright, or their second-best player, Scottie Pippen. It seemed that while teams had their best players and captains, there were also spiritual/vocal leaders who helped prepare the team to go to battle. This same pep ritual was depicted years later in Frank Miller's classic film *300,* which is about the Spartans from Greece and their legendary battles against Persia.

Following years of disappointment, Michael Jordan and the Chicago Bulls reached new heights. After sweeping the Detroit Pistons in the 1991 Eastern Conference finals, they beat Magic Johnson and the Los Angeles Lakers in five games to win their first NBA World Championship in the 1991 NBA Finals. No. 23 in red, Michael Jordan, took home the NBA finals Most Valuable Player Award. The Bulls were my heroes back then, and after watching Detroit knock them off the previous two or three years, it was surreal to see Michael Jordan, Scottie Pippen, Horace Grant, and the other Bulls celebrating in the locker room and dousing themselves with champagne.

The Bulls won the second major basketball championship that year. Coach Mike Krzyzewski's Duke Blue Devils (pronounced She-Shef-Ski), led by a tall white kid with lots of shooting touch named Christian Laettner, won the NCAA Men's College Basketball National Championship. They upset the UNLV Runnin' Rebels, 79–77, in the national semifinal game. They then defeated the Kansas Jayhawks, 72–65, in the national final game.

"HMMM. They couldn't get a better shot than that?" My Uncle John was in town for that game as he typically was around that time of year, visiting from Birmingham, AL. Uncle Tony was there too, as they were usually joined at the hip on Uncle John's visits. Uncle John jokingly grumbled while peering at the TV screen through his glasses, sipping on his beer, questioning No. 32, Larry Johnson's Hail Mary three-pointer. The desperation shot clanked off the back iron of the Hoosier Dome basket as time expired.

"The game was fixed!" Gabe was crushed by UNLV's loss and insisted there was something more behind Duke's victory. He passionately rooted for UNLV and took their loss to Duke hard. Still learning about the game of basketball, I, too, was disappointed that the Runnin' Rebels lost, but I could sense as I watched the game unfold in Indianapolis that Duke was more ready to play that game. I'd heard about Jerry 'Tark the Shark' Tarkanian's UNLV team's dominance all year with players like No. 12, Anderson Hunt, No. 4, Larry Johnson and No. 32, Stacey Augmon.

"Anderson Hunt had *one* good game, and they named him the Most Outstanding Player." Anderson Hunt's name stayed in my mind from the previous year because Ronald Jennings, from Campus West, sarcastically mentioned him after the Runnin' Rebels blew out the Blue Devils the previous year in the 1990 national final game 103–73. Like many other anti-Duke spectators, I felt that the *black* team lost and the *white* team won. Despite Duke winning, it had been a good year for basketball.

* * *

Having survived Sequential Math Course 1 and the rest of my coursework, my primary focus heading into the summer of 1991 should have been making myself a better basketball player and getting ready for the Ken Jones Basketball Camp. October was fast approaching, as were the tryouts for the 1991–92 Hutch-Tech boys' basketball team. The road was clear, and all I had to do was prepare for my objective. Being an Engineer was within my grasp.

I think it is also worth noting that it was around that time that my basketball focus shifted away from the professional level and more so to the high school level. I still watched, but once Michael Jordan and the Bulls won their first title, something changed. They had vanquished their arch-enemies. There were still teams that sought to knock them off their new perch atop the NBA, but as a fan, nothing was like those battles with the Detroit Pistons on their way up–the anticipation, the physicality, and the drama, all of it.

One of the truths that I would come to understand about my life is that I was always different from the rest of the kids. I was a late bloomer, and things that happened for the other kids early in life often happened late for me. The same thing was true for my first kiss with a girl.

For the sake of privacy, I will refer to her as Maria Harrison. Maria lived down the street from us, close to Kay Street. Her family had lived on Hastings Avenue for several years before we moved there. I believe she attended the Buffalo Academy for the Visual and Performing Arts, because she could sing. Maria was beautiful, and everywhere she went in the city guys chased her. Picture a beautiful smile, golden brown skin, and a tall young woman with a voluptuous shape.

Maria's father, Mr. Wallace Harrison, was half black and half white, while her mother, Mrs. Janna Harrison, was half black and half Native American. The blending of ethnicities created three stunningly beautiful daughters. They were Maria, her sister Terra who was my age, and their baby sister Christi. Mr. Harrison surely must have slept with a shotgun at night to keep the boys away, as there were many interested young men. Gabe always interestingly thought their mother, Janna, was the most beautiful of them all.

Just as Amahl and I were close in age (two years apart), Maria and Terra were as well (one year apart), while Christi was at least five or six years younger than her sisters. Maria received most of the attention from boys as she was the oldest, while Terra, who went to City Honors, was a star in her own right. She lived in Maria's shadow, however, at least for the time being. It was like the way I lived in Amahl's shadow. That said, Terra would cast her own shadow one day.

I think it happened sometime during the summer of 1990. As the year went on, I found myself desiring Maria more and more. It was as though something had taken hold of me one day, and I had become just as enamored with her as the rest of the guys. One time when it was snowing outside, I balled up snowballs and threw them at her as she stood in her driveway trying to get inside of her house.

"STOP," she cried out as she waited for her mother to let her into her house. Another time I randomly hugged her, and she asked me, "What was that for?" There was no reason other than the fact that I had developed this intense crush on her and a physical desire for the opposite sex. I had previously only felt those feelings and urges toward Nideara Hawkins and Tamekia Toller at Campus West, when I was in middle school.

Then one night, seemingly out of nowhere, something magical happened. Maria took an interest in me, of all people. It was a random summer night when no one else was around. Amahl, Gabe, her sister Terra, and any of the other guys from the neighborhood were nowhere to be found. We were alone in their garage, and Maria asked me in her soft voice, "Do you like me?"

Not believing what was happening, I gave her a resounding, "Yes!" That night we hung out a little longer, and then she walked me down to my driveway as we held hands. In my driveway in the stillness of the night, we kissed each other goodnight. It was the first time I had ever kissed a girl, and it felt good to the point where I didn't want to stop.

"MARIA!" Her mother yelled down the street as she had so many times before, interrupting my newfound moments of bliss. Just further up the driveway, my own mother slept in her own bed. I did not want Maria to leave, but she had to go back to her house. I wanted to keep my arms wrapped around her and my lips pressed against hers. That night, she wore a black Tee-shirt, a long denim skirt, and flat slip-on shoes. I can still see her waving goodbye to me as she disappeared quickly down the street. I wondered if this was all really happening, but it was.

"You may enjoy her now, but just because she is there now does not mean that she *always* will be there," Dad said over the phone when I told him about my new teenage romance. There was a hint of past personal hardship and pessimism in his voice, and my young mind did not understand the depth of his words. I was launching into what felt like a new and exciting world with little to no experience.

* * *

I was not the only guy who was smitten with Maria Harrison. Many young men and some older men wanted to have her love and likely other things. Perhaps no one wanted her more than James Anthony Forrester, who we all just called Anthony. Anthony lived around the corner from us on Davidson Avenue near the corner of Kay Street. He went to Kensington High School not far from where we all lived, and I believe he was in the class of 1992, like my brother.

Anthony was a husky dark-skinned guy who looked kind of like the rapper Biz Markie. He had a goatee and typically wore his baseball cap turned backward. He always walked around the neighborhood with David Lees, Dan Rab, Carl McGown, Kevin Leeder, and a punky, skinny, trash-talking kid named Johnny, whose last name I do not know. Anthony was the leader of that crew, as he was always walking in front of the pack. He was always tossing a small football back and forth with Kevin Leeder, who delivered newspapers in our neighborhood along with his mother. He rode his bike while his mother drove her station wagon around the streets.

I called them the 'Davidson-Kay Boys' because they seemed like their own little gang. We sometimes played basketball with them around the neighborhood or at the St. Aloysius School on Cleveland Drive in Cheektowaga near Gabe's house. Everyone referred to it as 'St. Al's' for short. We were cordial with the Davidson-Kay Boys, but never completely merged crews.

Out of all of us, Anthony was probably caught up in Maria's allure the most. One day we were all in Maria's driveway and garage, and the two of us somehow got into an argument about who was better at basketball. It was all to impress Maria, so after barking at one another and the inevitable challenge from one to the other, everyone migrated to Dan Rab's backyard, where there was a basketball hoop on a pole, and the two of us squared off.

In front of Maria, her sisters Terra and Christi, Dan Rab and whoever else was there, me and Anthony played a fierce game of one-on-one basketball to try to impress Maria. At least, that was my motivation. You would have thought it was a boxing or wrestling match as intense as we were playing and trash-talking to one another. Both of us had something to prove.

The game turned out to be harder than I thought it would be. Anthony was two years older than me, and he weighed at least 50 pounds more than my thinner 14-year-old frame. My offensive game was also very raw and underdeveloped. I was not strong enough to back him down to get a layup off, so I either had to score with fifteen-foot jump shots or try to drive past him. Finally, I did not have a solid dribble move or a particularly quick first step, which further limited my options for scoring baskets.

Without a reliable mid-range game, each of my shots was a gamble when they left my fingertips. Some of my shots fell, while others got blocked. Some just clanked off the rim. Had I become adept at using the backboard (for bank shots), it might have helped, but I was not thinking along those lines at the time. The same went for him. I sent a couple of his shots back, and neither one of us got far ahead of the other scoring-wise. It all amounted to an ugly game of one-on-one between two gladiators battling it out for the heart of the maiden we both desired.

I think the score was 8–9 or 10–11 or something when Maria announced that they had to leave because her family had to go somewhere. I could not believe it. She was my reason for taking on the ogre in the first place. We both lost our intensity when she left. I don't remember who won those games. We could have easily both agreed to stop once she left, and I think we did. In hindsight, it's funny that I would try to use the great game of basketball to impress Maria by trying to beat Anthony. It's something I'll never forget, and it was just one of the silly things that happened during that summer. It was just the beginning of what would be one of the most memorable two or three-month stretches of my life.

Chapter 13. The Ken Jones Basketball Camp Year One

"After scoring a basket, a lot of guys want to run up the court and smile while waving at their girlfriend, mother, and grandmother. NO! You have to run back down the floor, sit down, and get into a defensive stance because your opponent is going to try to score, and you have to stop him!" **—Coach Bruce Voorhees, the Ken Jones Basketball Camp, July 1991**

In those early days of high school, I did not do things without my best friend Gabe. That did not change even though he went to Cleveland Hill High School in Cheektowaga while I attended Hutch-Tech High School in downtown Buffalo. In my mind, if I was going to go to basketball camp, he had to go too. I, thus, lived and died on the grades he got at the end of the year in addition to my own. I also hoped that his parents would let him go to basketball camp with me. It turned out that the stars lined up just right that summer, and he was able to go with me.

The camp was held towards the end of July. Leading up to it, I continued playing basketball at the William-Emslie YMCA and then sometimes at Roosevelt Park. I was not necessarily improving my fundamentals which I had little understanding of at the time. Instead, I played mostly pickup street basketball and games of Twenty-One. I was developing as best I knew how. It was the way a lot of kids in the inner-city developed.

Those days leading up to the camp were filled with lots of anticipation as I had never been to one before. I heard my Uncle Scottie discuss going to one at St. Bonaventure University in Olean, NY, when he was a teen. While there, one of the camp coaches taught him to, "EXPLODE to the basket!" He shared that story often with me, among others. Whoever taught him that was encouraging him to drive to the basket with lots of quickness and strength.

Amahl and I went to day camps at the Salvation Army and a summer sports camp at Canisius College. The goal was to give us exposure to multiple sports and keep us occupied during the summer months. I had never been to anything specializing solely in basketball, which is what I really wanted all along. This was the one sport that I was truly interested in. It was the one sport I dreamed about all the time. We were going three to four hours away to immerse ourselves in the game, and I was excited.

At Hutch-Tech, Coach Jones brought in some of his photo albums from previous camps so we could get a glimpse of what it would be like to attend. He called them scrapbooks. Looking through them, I saw that the previous year, Curtis Brooks, Pep Skillon, Chuck Thompson, Dion Frasier, and Chris Souter all attended. None of the other players on the 1990–91 team went that year, which I thought was a little strange. Why wouldn't the entire team go? I was not personally cool with anyone on the team, or those who were thinking about trying out, so I didn't know who else from Hutch-Tech was going that summer of 1991.

* * *

Registration for the Ken Jones Basketball Camp was from noon to 4 p.m., so we had to get an early start leaving Buffalo. Mr. Smith dropped Gabe off early that Sunday morning, probably between 9 and 10 a.m. On most Sunday mornings, we would be going to Sunday school and church service, and I was happy to get away from our weekly ritual whenever possible. What better reason to skip church than the great game of basketball?

It was mid-morning and our street was illuminated by the morning sun from the eastern sky. I looked out the front window of our home, awaiting Gabe's arrival. I could have easily been a kid waiting by the window, looking up at a snowy night sky, trying to spot Santa Claus and his reindeer late on Christmas Eve. Eventually, Mr. Smith's teal Cadillac pulled up into our driveway, and I ran to meet Gabe outside.

Gabe got out, holding his single duffle bag. Mr. Smith, wearing his signature top hat, short-sleeved button-down shirt, slacks, and shoes, peeled off some money, gave it to him and then left. They might have exchanged a quick hug and a few words, but it was brief. Mr. and Mrs. Smith could not have known how happy I was that they were allowing Gabe to come on this adventure with me. Gabe wore his gold and white Chicago Bulls sweatsuit. It was the one that amused my Uncle Tony and Uncle Scottie. Amahl said they thought Gabe looked like a *genie* it. He also wore a pair of Air Jordans. Gabe always had a pair of Air Jordans in those days. Gabe had a lot of Michael Jordan and Chicago Bulls paraphernalia; more than me.

Shortly afterward we loaded into my mother's white 1990 Subaru Legacy and headed for Interstate 90 to make the drive to Hamilton, NY. Mom's friend at the time, Roger, whom she had been seeing for a little while, helped us make the drive. They sat up front while Gabe and I sat in the back of the four-door sedan. As we departed towards Kay Street, I looked over at Maria Harrison's house. There was no visible activity there that I could see. Though I was embarking on what may have been the greatest adventure to date of my young life, I wondered when I would see her again.

The drive along I-90 from Western to Central New York State was very scenic. We passed by Rochester, Syracuse, and all the small towns along the way. Just outside of Rochester, I saw a sign for the town of Newark, the home of the team that defeated our 1990–91 Hutch-Tech boys' basketball team in the state regional game earlier that year. Upstate New York was beautiful. The landscape changed from flat farmland to forest and then into the foothills of the Adirondack Mountains after Syracuse. There were also swamps and marshes all along Interstate 90.

Somewhere around Rome or Utica, we got off the interstate at exit 32 and headed south on Route 233, a series of backroads and single-lane winding highways. The trip took us into very rural areas and small towns, which I did not know existed in New York State. I wondered if we were even going to the right place.

We crossed over Highway 5, the Seneca Turnpike, and then shortly afterward, we turned right onto Route 13, College Hill Road, where Hamilton College sat. The school was in the middle of nowhere and could not have been any bigger than Buffalo State College back home. Immediately upon entering the campus grounds, there were signs directing campers and their families to 'Scott Field House', the home of the camp that year.

Inside of Scott Field House, a massive sports complex, the camp staff registered the attendees who slowly trickled in. I still remember the smell of the field house. It was a plastic, rubbery smell, the smell of something brand new just out of its wrapping. It was nothing like the old gyms I was used to playing in with wooden floors that smelled like dust and sweat.

Speaking of which, the floor of the field house was not wooden but, instead, a synthetic rubber. This was probably easier on the athletes' joints. Looking around at the enormity of the facility and its high arching roof, I recognized it as the place where Coach Jones carried out his dribbling drills in the picture from his camp brochure.

We, as campers, received our own red and white Ken Jones Basketball Camp basketballs made by a company called Mohinder. We were further encouraged to write our names on our basketballs with magic markers, as there would be several hundred of them bouncing around that weekend. We also received powder blue Ken Jones Basketball Camp tee-shirts made by Champion, our itinerary, and keys for our dorm rooms. A camp rule was that you always had to dribble your basketball and could never carry it around the campus.

There were also vendors there at registration selling things like new sneakers and other apparel to the campers. Some kids picked up additional sneakers or even brought multiple pairs. I wore my one pair of low-top black Nike Flights. It did not occur to me to ask my parents for a second pair, as just getting to the camp was a big deal monetarily. It also did not occur to me that wearing low-top sneakers at the camp might not be the safest thing to do in terms of potential ankle injuries and sprains. I think Gabe wore his pair of Nike Air Jordans throughout the camp.

Once Gabe and I got our balls, we immediately went to the main court, which had college-style breakaway rims, which were amazing to me as I had never played in such a facility before. Immediately above the center of the court, there was a large college-style scoreboard hanging from the ceiling. Around the main court, there were other courts set up so that multiple games could be played at the same time. All of it had me in awe.

Mom's friend Roger was roughly 6'4" and lean. With a grin, he took a couple of dribbles, planted his feet, rose straight up, and flushed (dunked) one of our basketballs through the basket with ease. I could not dunk at that point and was in awe of what he had just done. As we continued shooting, two other African American kids walked over to the main court to join us. They grinned from ear to ear, and they were fair-skinned guys and tall like me.

"Hey, what's going on?" I said to the two other guys. "My name is Anwar, and this is Gabe."

"I'm Keenan," said one of the guys who was kind of on the skinny side. He wore his hair close with a 'shag', a small puff of hair on the back of his neck. "This is my cousin Justin. I'm from Poughkeepsie and Justin is visiting us for the summer from Florida." Justin was huskier than Keenan. They made the trip all the way up from the Hudson River Valley.

I think the four of us were all happy to see one another because of the rural location we were in, and we felt an instant camaraderie. The other African American kids at the camp in my age group were a skinny kid named Theron, who wore a high-top fade, and another skinny kid named Jamone, with big eyes and a small afro. We didn't really speak to Jamone that much. I didn't know where either of them was from, or I didn't ask them. The handful of us might've been the only black kids there.

Dion Frasier and Adonis Coble, two of the class of 1992 seniors who played on the 1990–91 team, showed up. I was not tight with either of them, but they knew that I was Amahl's younger brother. Dion jokingly referred to me several times around the halls of Hutch-Tech as 'Little Amahl' that year.

"What's up, Anwar?" Curtis Brooks was also there as a counselor. I recall him greeting me once, which was a big deal for me as I highly revered him. He did not have a particularly loud and imposing presence, but instead had more of a low-key persona, at least at the camp. Unfortunately, I did not know how to engage him and 'pick his brain', as they say, about what he and his teammates accomplished earlier that year. I could have learned a lot from him just by striking up a conversation. Socially, I just didn't know how to do it.

The only other kid from Hutch-Tech was Tim Bodek, a tall white kid who was into hip-hop music just like most black kids. He was in my class of 1994. He wore his hair long and curly in what was called back in the 1970s a 'Jew-Fro'. Gabe thought he was a little odd and wondered why he came by my room so much. Tim was 6'4" or 6'5" height-wise, with lots of potential. I imagine Coach Jones salivated over the prospect of being able to coach him up. No other kids from Buffalo came to the camp that year that I knew of.

Gabe made a friend named Brett, a short white kid with his hair faded on the sides. He was from the Capital Region, the Albany area where Dad lived. They joked about wearing boxers and not briefs under their gym shorts. Many campers were from the Rochester area, and some were from the Syracuse area. Others were from the downstate or the Adirondack Region. One of my biggest regrets was not networking and staying in touch with kids from the camp. It was the pre-internet, pre-cell phone, and pre-social media era, so it was more difficult to stay in contact with friends in other cities.

After checking into the camp, the different age groups were all put together to scrimmage so that we could be divided into teams. The age groups were divided into leagues. I was transitioning into my sophomore year of high school, so I played with the thirteen- to fifteen-year-old kids. The older kids were in the 'NBA' league, while my age group was in the 'NCAA' league. The kids under us were in the 'NAIA' league. The youngest kids were in the 'Scholastic' division.

The first night of the camp we received a lecture and a demonstration on man-to-man defense from Coach Bruce Voorhees. Coach Voorhees could not have been any taller than 5'7". He looked a little odd in his short John Stockton-like shorts (like Coach Jones) and his mop-top haircut. He had what I will describe as a distinct grin and a deep and hoarse voice. I recognized him immediately from the brochure.

"After scoring a basket, a lot of guys want to run up the court and smile while waving at their girlfriend, mother, and grandmother. NO! You have to run back down the floor, sit down and get into a defensive stance because your opponent is going to try to score, and you have to stop him," Coach Vorhees said, using this funny story to impart the importance of defense. Picturing in my mind the scenario he described, made me laugh.

I was looking to learn how to score the ball more effectively and regularly, and the early emphasis on defense at the camp surprised me. Also surprisingly, the instructors did not teach us anything about zone defenses, only man-to-man. We eventually spent time on shooting and offensive skills, but the underlying theme was defense. It was fascinating as most of the basketball played at the William-Emslie Y and on the courts in Buffalo, emphasized isolation-style basketball, going up strong to the hole and slashing to the basket.

That lecture followed dinner, which was true to the brochure's quote, "Take all you can eat and eat all you can take!" There was no shortage of burgers, hotdogs, fries, sodas, and desserts—pretty much anything young growing boys would want. This was a sample of college living, and it was great. They warned us not to drink too much soda as it would run right through us, causing us to dehydrate during competition.

* * *

Living in the dormitories was fun, aside from sharing bathrooms with a floor of guys I didn't know. We were three to four campers in a room with bunk beds. Each room had a desk and a view of the outside, which, for my room, was a campus roadway and a forest. Late at night, you could hear some of the counselors outside talking and socializing or even telling some of the campers to get to sleep. There was also the subtle hum of a generator and the sounds of creatures in the trees. Bedtime every night was 10 p.m.

Early that Monday morning in our dormitories, all slept peacefully as the summer sun slowly rose, ushering in a new day. That was, of course, until there was a distinct noise in the hallways. It was the distinct, raspy, and gritty voice of an older man. Consistent with our itineraries, the morning call was promptly at 6:30 a.m. It felt very much like depictions of boot camps I had seen on TV. The movie *Stripes,* starring Bill Murray and Harold Ramis, came to mind. In a notable scene, Sergeant Hulka blasted into their barracks early in the morning, waking them up obnoxiously and slamming a garbage can lid on the can. Coach Jones did not use a garbage can, though. Instead, he used a foghorn.

"GET UP! GET UP! COME ON, LET'S GO!" Coach Jones yelled through his megaphone and blew his foghorn while knocking on doors and coming into each of our rooms. He was dressed in his signature Ken Jones Basketball Camp polo shirt, shorts, and sneakers. He had undoubtedly already been up for a while himself. Maybe he had not gone to sleep at all. He was wired and ready for a full day of drills, games, and lectures while all of us teenagers were trying to make sense of what was going on. "COME ON, GET UP! GET UP! IT'S TIME TO GET UP! LET'S GO!"

Coach Jones was probably used to being up at that hour while most of us teenagers were normally up all hours of the night and sleeping late, especially during the summertime when there was no school to attend the next day. Most of the guys got up when they heard him coming. I jumped up immediately when he entered my room. If you stayed in bed like Gabe did one morning, you got the foghorn right in your ear. Allegedly, Coach Jones saw Gabe's dormant body still buried underneath his covers and gave him a high-decibel surprise. It is a story that still tickles me every time I hear it.

* * *

Morning calisthenics and basketball dribbling drills took place from 7:15 to 8 a.m. at Scott Field House, a five-minute walk from our dorms. Entering the vast fieldhouse, you could hear hundreds of basketballs bouncing up and down. Boys of all age groups, mostly from the suburbs of New York State and rural areas, shot baskets and talked. Things were eventually called to order by Coach Jones and his foghorn. He stood on a stage on the sidelines of the main court. We all sat on the field house court as he gave us his opening remarks for the day. He wore a mini-microphone and spoke to us through the speaker system of the field house.

"All four schools from the Rochester area advanced to the state tournament in their respective classes. All four schools!" His remarks ranged from the dominance of the Rochester area in the state high school playoffs to what it took to be a good basketball player, to, once again, the importance of defense. He told stories both about his experiences as a player and a coach and his love for the game. Once finished, the calisthenics began with a series of stretches and exercises, including jumping jacks, hurdler's stretches, and spread eagles–you name it, and we did it!

Once the stretches were finished, we'd do 'Foot Fires'. We would all crouch in a defensive position and move our feet as fast as we could in place. Altogether it sounded like hundreds of drummers drumming. Coach Jones held a basketball in his hands and moved it quickly to the right. In response we all quickly turned and clapped, and then snapped back in our forward orientation while still moving our feet. He did the same thing to the left, and we all snapped back and forth in that direction while still moving our feet. Whenever he pointed the ball at an angle towards the right or the left, we would all slide and shuffle our feet backward in that direction as a group. When he pointed the ball backward, we likewise shuffled towards him. These drills once again underscored the most important principle of the camp, DEFENSE!

Another staple of morning calisthenics was the dribbling drills. Coach Jones did them with us. One by one with our own basketballs, he led us through the sideways dribble, then the back-and-forth dribble, then the 'rolling' dribble, which was a fake crossover, and then a dribble with a hop step to the side. Sometimes, he'd do the Two Ball Dribbling Drill.

One by one, he dismissed the campers by age group to go to the cafeteria for breakfast. The youngest kids who were in the Scholastic and NAIA divisions went first. As the rest of us stayed to do more exercises, we watched all the kids enthusiastically dribble their balls out of the field house. It was like a flock of insects departing. Our NCAA division went next, and then the older kids in the NBA division joined everyone in the dining hall last.

Just as with lunch and dinner, anything you could possibly want at breakfast was there. There was cereal, eggs, bacon, sausage, hash browns, waffles and pancakes, anything. I loved it. It was important to get enough, but not to overeat as we had a full day of drills and games ahead of us.

Our teams were announced before going to breakfast on the first day full day. The previous night, when they scrimmaged us, the coaches assessed our skill and talent levels. They tried to create the most balanced teams possible so that there would be enough parity, and everyone would get a chance to play. We were assigned one coach for the first two days and then reassigned a second coach for the last couple of days and into the playoffs at the conclusion of camp.

I hoped that Gabe and I would be on the same team, but things did not work out that way, probably by design, and that was a good thing. Gabe raved about one of his coaches, Coach Manion, who wore a mustache and had thinning black hair. In addition to being a knowledgeable coach, he seemed to match Gabe's comical temperament, making them a perfect match. Most of what I heard about Gabe and his team were jokes and stories about other campers who got on his nerves, like a kid named Pete from Lyons, NY.

Ryan Sharon, Mike Bonafena (pronounced Bonafeena), Keenan Byner, Chris Busher, and Ian Huffman were my teammates. Looking at our team photo, there was a kid named Steve, who was from Switzerland, I think, and another kid with a buzz cut whose name I cannot recall. I was happy to have Keenan on my team because I knew him prior to the basketball camp. Every team in the NCAA division was named after a college team. My team was called the St. John's Redmen from the Big East Conference.

Both Chris Busher and I were the tallest kids on our team. Chris stands out to me because he was my height or a little taller, and his game was more developed than mine. He had a consistent fifteen-foot jump shot with good form, and he had a lot of confidence in it, which impressed me. In Buffalo the emphasis was mostly on beating your man off the dribble and driving strong to the basket. I didn't entirely grasp it at the time, but I was starting to see that there were different ways to play the game other than how we played it in inner-city Buffalo.

What I did not understand at the time was that part of getting the most out of the camp experience was being on teams with campers that you did not know. It was about being on a new team, meeting and learning from new players, and learning to blend with them. The whole point of the camp was to grow, and to become better basketball players, which should have transcended race. I had a lot of work to do.

Chapter 14. A Season of Basketball in a Session

"Be sure to keep moving when you don't have the ball. Your hard work ethic is very evident!" —**Coach Chris Ford, the Ken Jones Basketball Camp, July 1991**

I did not know it at the time, but the Ken Jones Basketball Camp was a true *teaching* camp. From Monday to Friday we were up at 6:30 a.m. Then we had to be at the Scott Field House by 7:15 a.m. for calisthenics and dribbling drills until about 8:00 a.m. From 8:00-8:45 a.m. we had breakfast in the dining hall. From 8:45- 8:55 a.m. we could go back to our dorm rooms for any post-meal activities. From 9:00- 10 a.m. we had stations and drills.

"Nice shot!" Keenan Byner reacted in amazement after I made a running hook shot, which I just sort of threw up and hoped for the best. We were at a station for individual offensive moves. Our coach for that station had just shown us the proper techniques for a *drop* step and *hook* shot. I think Keenan was guarding me as the rest of our teammates looked on. The ball banked off the backboard of the portable goal and ricocheted cleanly into the net for me. I also looked on, marveling at my shot immediately afterward. It was powerful for me to see the ball go through the basket.

The station drills took place in no certain order—dribbling, low post moves, proper shooting technique, rebounding, and proper defensive techniques. From 10:05-10:30 a.m. we had team practices with our coaches. From 10:35-11:50 a.m. we played league games. If we did not have league games, we were supposed to play one-on-one against each other or practice our free throw shooting. Lunch was at noon, and we usually had a lecture from 1:15-2:00 p.m.

From 2:00-3:00 p.m. we had more stations and drills. From 3:05-4:50 p.m. we had another league game or one of the other variations above. Dinner was at 5:00 p.m. Our third league game was either at 6:30 p.m. or 8:00 p.m. If your league game wasn't at 8 p.m., you had the option of watching the other games, going swimming, or going back to the dorm. At 9:30 p.m. we were supposed to shower and get ready for bed. At 10:00 p.m. it was lights out, so we could get up and do the whole thing all over again in the morning. Campers really could not break the rules and stay up late because the coaches and counselors were usually out in front of the dorms or walking through the halls to make sure everyone was asleep.

* * *

"You look, but you don't see. You listen, but you don't hear," Coach Tony Alvaro said, lecturing us in a workshop about defense with his fire and brimstone demeanor. He gave his lecture on the main court of Scott Field House, and it is still vivid in my mind years later. In his picture in the camp brochure, Coach Alvaro looked angry, and in person he looked the same way. He was an older, pudgy man with silver-gray hair and a round Italian nose. He wore a black shirt with black slacks, and he had a deep and commanding voice. He was what you would think of when you think of a stereotypical older, grizzled coach. He coached at DeSales of Geneva High School in the Rochester area.

"Throughout my talk, if I raise my hand, you are going to quickly stand up until I tell you to sit back down," Coach Alvaro said. His main messages involved the importance of discipline and players being coachable. Whenever he raised his hand, we all had to jump to our feet. It was a cool concept of teaching, though at the time, a little annoying. You didn't want to be called out by him though. The older coaches were big on discipline and having every single player gain insight from their teachings.

"I didn't pay my money and came all of this way to have some old guy tell me to get up and sit down," Gabe said another camper sarcastically joked in the back of our group while listening to Coach Alvaro's lecture.

The message was clear though. There was a mental aspect to the game of basketball. There was also an aspect that required discipline on the part of the players. In this instance it involved submitting to the leadership of your coach. For coaches like Coach Alvaro, who appeared to be an old school disciplinarian-type, there were consequences for not submitting.

* * *

Our St. John's team struggled early on. Not only were we composed of different skill levels and backgrounds, but we had to try to *gel* together quickly. Mike Bonafena was our primary ball handler. Chris Busher and I were the tallest guys on the team and thus handled most of the rebounding while the other players pretty much filled in the other parts. Ryan Sharon lent some outside shooting, while Keenan Byner lent versatility. The games went for two twenty-minute halves, and we used a numbering system for the first three quarters of the game. The coaches had the flexibility to play whomever they wanted for the last five minutes of the game.

While I was not the most polished player on the team, I considered myself one of our best players. I did not understand why the best players could not play all the time. Coach Alvaro later explained to me that the numbering system was put in place so that every camper, despite his skill level, would get enough playing time, which made sense in terms of fairness for everyone. After all, every camper paid the same $343 tuition.

Our games were played either in the Scott Field House or in the Alumni Gymnasium. The latter was a classic gymnasium with wooden floors, bleachers, non-breakaway rims, and natural light during the day. We played shirts and skins, and the games were a lot different than those that I played at the William-Emslie YMCA and Buffalo's playgrounds. The games were timed, we ran distinct offensive sets, and we had to get back on defense every time. We only ran a little bit of offense at Campus West, so the concept was still new to me, and my basketball IQ was on the low side.

"Anwar, I'm uncomfortable with you taking that shot right now! Stay a little closer or take it to the basket," Coach Lee, our first coach, pulled me aside on the next dead ball situation and told me after I shot a fifteen-footer just like my teammate Chris Busher. Unlike Chris' shots, which sailed through the net, mine clanged off the back of the rim or missed the basket altogether. Chris had excellent shooting mechanics and was able to *feather* his fifteen-footers in with ease, and I thought it would be cool to hoist some up myself. I hadn't done the work yet, and my offensive game was not as developed as his. I only knew how to hustle, to go up strong, and to rebound the ball.

"Anwar, we do not need a double team there unless I call it! You must stay with your own man!" Coach Lee called out to me from the sidelines after my man scored a basket. On one distinct defensive play I tried to double-team my teammate's man. Under Phil Jackson the Chicago Bulls used some *trapping* defenses like the New York Knicks under Rick Pitino. I thought it would be a cool thing to do. The only problem was that our coach had not installed anything like that, and I left my man wide open, who scored on an uncontested layup.

We lost most of our games early on. We felt like the incompetent California Bears, from the movie *The Bad News Bears,* from our division because we could not do anything right. The other teams seemed to score on us at will, and on offense it felt like we were inept. Our teammate, Steve from Europe, got so frustrated after one play that he slammed the ball down on the floor with both hands, drawing a technical foul.

"Hey, what do you think about what Steve did?" I did not like it and afterwards talked to Mike Bonafena on our way to the dining hall.

"Well, what are you going to do?" Mike replied after the game, shrugging his shoulders and remaining even-keeled.

The best team in our division was UNLV, which was led by point guard John Terminera, an Italian kid with braces. He had a solid dribble and a deadly accurate jump shot. They also had one of the other African American kids in the camp, Theron. UNLV quickly established itself as the best team in our division. At camp,

I learned that when you are playing the best team in your league, you often rise to a heightened state of competitiveness, and our team did just that.

The game took place in the old Alumni Gymnasium. We were skins, and they were shirts. We hung with them early on, but it did not take long for UNLV to assert itself as the better team. On one play that is forever etched in my memory, John Terminera casually advanced the ball, setting up his team's offense. Mike Bonafena challenged John by crouching down and slapping the floor with both hands in a defensive stance. It was something made famous by the guards who played for the Duke Blue Devils around that time. I looked for Mike to put the clamp down on John. John responded by effortlessly picking up his dribble and dropping in a fifteen-footer over Mike near the free-throw line.

"Hey, there's nothing you can do about that," Coach Lee said, shaking his head and shrugging his shoulders after the play, as we all looked stunned. Many of the campers were blessed with at least one or two moments of brilliance. I had one myself.

"OOOOOH," players on both teams erupted after I scored off a Michael Jordan-style reverse layup from underneath our basket. I launched into the air from the right side of the basket to the left. I didn't even see it go in. I don't know how I did it; I just did it instinctively. Maybe it was the William-Emslie YMCA momentarily coming out of me. That basket allowed me a few seconds of pride and exhilaration as I ran back up the court and got back on defense as everyone went nuts. It was one of our few highlights against UNLV that day.

"Nice shot! Nice shot! Nice shot!" In addition to my teammates, several UNLV players lauded me after the game as we shook hands and departed the gym. I particularly remember John Terminera and Theron telling me that. The small victory felt good for a little while. It was a brief flash of brilliance, but I was unable to consistently reproduce that moment throughout the camp.

"Hey, Anwar, come here!" One of the referees, nicknamed 'Cheese', called me over after the game. Cheese was a stocky older black man, and he had a buddy much like himself nicknamed 'Chief'. Maybe they were from the Rochester area, not sure. He turned out to be Theron's older brother. As they refereed, they saw my raw game and thought I would be receptive to their guidance, which I was.

"When you get the ball down low, you should just do a *drop* step!" Cheese took the ball and went to one of the low blocks on the free-throw lane. With me and Chief looking on, he took one dribble and slid his left foot into the lane before turning, pivoting, and throwing up a hook shot, which banked off the backboard into the basket. "It's an unstoppable move! Once you get the ball on the low block, you can pretty much score or go to the free-throw line any time you want to. You try it."

I slowly took the ball and tried reproducing what Cheese did as they watched me. I did it a couple of times not completely understanding the science behind the move. After a couple of times, they thought I had grasped it and gave me the nod to go on and meet up with my team. It was a true teaching camp. Even the referees took it upon themselves to show you something.

"Do you play for your high school team?" The pair also got their laughs off some of the campers. Gabe told me that Cheese and Chief snickered at him after one of his games. They asked him if he played on his school team after officiating one of his games and observing his play on the court. According to Gabe, the two kept straight faces when he answered their question, but he heard what sounded like subtle giggles as he turned around to walk away with his basketball.

Aside from UNLV, the other good team in our division was Georgia Tech. They were led by a modest, but skilled, blonde-haired, lean, 5'10" kid named Brian Nolan. They also had a 6'5" player named Cory Leglerand with short black hair, who I took the challenge of guarding when we played them. After those two teams, everyone else was average. Gabe was on the team with his new friend, Brett, and experienced moderate success as well.

* * *

On the second or third day of the camp, everyone's bodies started aching from the constant grind. The continuous running, jumping, starting, and stopping caused even a fourteen-year-old's body to start to wear down. For me, it was my feet to a small degree, and then my shins just below my knees got sore. For the other campers, it was other things like their knees.

Gabe started spending a lot of time in the trainer's room. The head trainer for the camp was a woman named Sharon, a short brunette woman in her twenties with her hair pulled back into a ponytail. She wore a polo shirt, shorts, and sneakers. Sharon was why Gabe spent more time in the training room, not his injuries.

He told me one day that when he was in the training room, Adonis Coble and Dion Frasier were getting some of their own aches and pains treated. He said he introduced himself and asked them if they knew me. They said they did, but that they knew me mostly as Amahl's younger sibling.

Gabe also said they referred to my brother as 'Amooh' and joked amongst themselves about him sitting on the bench on the Hutch-Tech cross-country team. One of them asked the other how someone could sit on the bench on the cross country team, and the other replied, "When you're as DOO-DOO as Amooh!" This was another one of Gabe's many funny and timeless camp stories.

An irony to Gabe's discussion with Adonis and Dion is that I did not say one word to either of them at the camp, and we were there for those six days. I watched them play their games and go through drills on the main court, but we never talked. They were veteran players who had been through the fire, guys who were familiar with Coach Jones' system. As much as I could have learned from the two seniors, I did not know how to go up to them and just start talking to them as I described with Curtis Brooks.

* * *

In multiple ways, Gabe left his mark on the Ken Jones Basketball Camp that year. As more of a follower at that point in my life, there was always the likelihood for me to get sucked into his capers. One morning at the camp, he did, in fact, suck me into one.

"Hey, Gabe, are you ready to go over?" After getting ready to go over to the field house for morning calisthenics and stretches, I went to his room to get him.

"I don't feel like going over to calisthenics this morning," he said. "We should just skip them."

It was vintage Gabe–forsaking structure, resisting the system, and setting off on his own path. Something told me not to skip them, but Gabe was persuasive, and after going back and forth for a little while, my fear of the consequences won out. We tried to sneak into the back where no one could see us. Unfortunately, a counselor caught us.

"Hey! Why are you guys late?" The counselor confronted us and was not happy. "Put your balls down and run two laps around the track!"

And so, because Gabe did not want to follow the rules and go to our morning exercises like everyone else, he and I were stuck running laps in front of everyone. At my prospective coach's camp, I felt ashamed and embarrassed. Gabe? It did not make much difference to him.

There was also the saltshaker incident in the dining hall. Gabe and his team sat at the table just next to the table where I was sitting. He somehow got the idea to sprinkle salt crystals on the back of my teammate Keenan's neck. I silently watched the caper unfold. Slowly and discretely, Gabe turned around with the saltshaker and gently shook crystals on the back of Keenan's neck. Each time, Keenan felt something, and he quickly turned around, but Gabe turned around too, avoiding getting caught. No one said anything, partially out of disbelief, but also because it was hilarious.

"HEY! STOP THAT RIGHT NOW!" One of the counselors caught Gabe red-handed after the third or fourth time. We all broke out in laughter.

There was also the time Gabe kicked Jamone Tanner's basketball out of the field house. It was late in the afternoon, and many of us were shooting around. We were down at the court at the far end of the field house, away from the main court. Several of the doors were open to let in the summer air. Off a missed shot, Jamone's basketball bounced down to our end of the court.

"HELP! HELP! HELP!" Jamone yelling, "Help," basically meant, "Can you get my ball and throw it back to me?"

Instead of simply picking Jamone's ball up, Gabe kicked it. When he did, it sailed outside. Before retrieving it outside, Jamone stood glaring emotionless with his bug eyes in disbelief, wondering why Gabe did what he did. Gabe stood with his arms open with a smirk saying, "My bad!" I watched in disbelief as well, but I was also amused by what had just happened.

There were so many fun times like that. Once, I remember walking into the TV area in our dorm, and a bunch of the guys were watching music videos. A song came on that I had never heard of called *3 A.M. Eternal* by a group called The KLF. Some of them were black, but had a European-pop style. It was not the hardcore hip hop that we listened to in Buffalo.

"You've never heard of The KLF?" Mike Bonafena asked me about the group, smiling from ear to ear as he got up and started dancing to the song in his socks. I watched briefly, shrugging my shoulders before returning to my room.

"You know you guys probably shouldn't be doing this," Brian Nobel said when he entered Gabe's room. One night Brett danced on top of a desk. According to Gabe, he almost slid out of the dorm room window a couple of stories, which would not have ended well.

"Shut up and get out of here!" The other guys in the room allegedly dismissed Brian, who was said to have just shrugged his shoulders and left.

There were a lot of stories like that, and those are just the few that I remember. Gabe also kept going on about Coach Gary Oehlbeck's daughter, a beautiful young blonde woman who had come to the camp with the rest of his family. It was a fun time for young teenagers like us united by the great game of basketball and who were away from home, especially a kid like me from the east side of Buffalo. It was one of the best times of my life.

* * *

Even at the camp, with all that we were learning and all the fun we had, part of my mind was on my girlfriend, Maria Harrison, back in Buffalo. One night, I called her from a pay phone in our dormitory. I used the phone card my father gave me to call him. He gave me permission to use it to call her. As the phone rang, nervousness overtook me, and my heart pounded inside my chest. All I wanted was to hear her voice on the other end. After a couple of rings, someone picked up. I really hoped it was not one of her parents.

"Hello?" A female's voice answered on the other end. It might have been her sister Terra.

"Hello, may I speak to Maria?" I said, excited on my end of the call. After setting the phone down for a moment, Maria came and picked it up.

"Hello?" she said.

"Hello, Maria? It's me, Anwar," I said. "I'm out here at camp and just wanted to call you and see how you were doing."

"Oh, I'm fine. We are fine," she said almost in a whisper.

"Okay, well, I just had to call you," I said. "I'm really looking forward to seeing you when I return on Friday."

"Oh, okay," she said.

"Okay, well, I'll let you get back to whatever it is you were doing," I said, ending the conversation, which did not go how I thought it would.

I cannot remember the particulars of the conversation, but I can tell you that it was short. She sounded distracted and not as excited to hear from me as I was to talk to her. Had something changed between us? If so, what was it and why? Something certainly felt different in our short conversation. I pondered it all briefly before refocusing my mind on what was left of basketball camp.

* * *

The playoffs started on Wednesday evening. The staff set it up so that the games we played culminated in a single-elimination playoff where a champion would be crowned. This playoff would have seedings in which the team with the best record had the top seed and drew the team with the worst record in the opening rounds, just like in postseason play in the NCAA Tournament and the NBA playoffs. There was a quarterfinal round, a semifinal round, and then a championship round.

Our team had the worst record in the NCAA division, and so we drew UNLV. As with most playoffs where the teams are familiar with one another, we played hard against them, keeping the game close well into the second half. Our new coach, whose name I believe was Chris Ford, knew how to inspire us and get the most out of the team. We fought all the way to the end before falling to them. That was my first-ever taste of a playoff-style competition where I got to play and be in an elimination situation. It was exhilarating and a lot of fun.

The teams that were eliminated early from postseason play participated in something called consolation games. None of the teams were competing for the championship in these games, and in a way, it seemed like a way to keep us occupied and still playing. That said, if you used them wisely, they were also opportunities to further practice and polish your game, so they were valuable in that way. Furthermore, no one wanted to lose their last game.

From the sidelines, I watched the rest of the tournament play out. In the final round, UNLV was upset by Brian Nolan and Cory Leglerand's Georgia Tech team. Their emotional and volatile Coach, Ivan Purdy, inherited the team and devised a strategy for slowing down John Terminera. Coach Purdy had a mustache and brown hair, wore glasses, and was short and pudgy. He looked like a college professor, like many of the other coaches. He wore short shorts, just like Coach Jones and Coach Vorhees, with his white socks pulled up. He further paced up and down the sidelines yelling like a man possessed. In fact, he became livid just like Coach Jones did during the 1990-91 basketball season. Having Cory Leglerand in the middle, who was the tallest kid in our division, did not hurt either, in terms of defeating UNLV. As I watched the game, I noticed that Brian Nolan had the ball in his hands most of the time on key possessions. He was poised, in control, and unflappable.

* * *

At the end of the camp, every player received evaluations from their second coaches. Our attitude, level of coachability, ball handling skills, shooting and rebounding, aggressiveness, hustle, and finally, team plays and speed were all evaluated. Each category was on a scale from one to four, and the coach circled each one. Fours were our strengths. Threes were considered our potential strengths; things that were evident with some more work, could become strengths. Twos were aspects of the game that were improving. Progress was shown in that area, and it should continue to be worked on. Finally, the ones were aspects that needed lots of work and more time.

On my evaluation, for all sixteen categories I received threes and fours. Attitude, coachability, offensive and defensive rebounding, aggressiveness and hustle, and team play were my threes and fours. Also evaluated were passing, dribbling, ball handling, defense on and away from the ball, movement without the ball, shooting, speed, and quickness for which I was given ones and twos. The coaches also had the option of writing additional feedback at the bottom of the evaluation. For me, Coach Ford wrote:

"Good camp, Anwar. Be sure to keep moving when you don't have the ball. Your hard work ethic is very evident. Work on your post moves and shooting. Best of luck! (scribbled)"

Coach Ford

Once the camp was finished, Mom came to pick up Gabe and me. We jumped back onto the New York State Thruway and headed west back to Buffalo for the rest of the summer of '91. Basketball camp was more fun than I expected, and I learned a lot about the game. Unfortunately, I did not try to keep in contact with any of the other players that I met there. Most importantly, after going to the camp, I believed that I had improved my chances of making the varsity basketball team in October.

With basketball camp over and a month left until the start of school, my priority, aside from resting my joints, should have been perfecting what I learned. That is what I should have done. My fourteen-year-old mind's priority, however, was to see my girlfriend, Maria, and to continue what we started in the first part of the summer. I thought about her periodically during the camp, but more so on that trip home.

When we made it back to Buffalo, we dropped Gabe off at his house on Burke Drive in Cheektowaga. We exchanged brief goodbyes, and then he got out of the car. He grabbed his belongings, and as we drove off, I watched him climb up the front porch of his white house. I think Mrs. Smith was there to greet him. I saw her open the front door open, then Gabe disappeared into his house with her as we sped away.

The engine of Mom's 1990 Subaru Legacy howled as she steadily shifted the gears as we drove back home. As we rode up Kensington Avenue to Kay Street, and then to Hastings, the only thing I could think about was seeing Maria again. I would give her kisses and hugs, tell her about the camp, and ask her what was happening with her. We would pick up right where we left off.

We turned right onto Hastings Avenue from Kay Street, and passed the Harrison's house. I turned and looked to see if Maria was outside, but she was not. Their station wagon was gone, and it looked like no one was home. We turned into our driveway, and then I got out and grabbed my belongings, just as Gabe had done ten minutes earlier. Mom went into the house while I lingered in the driveway. It was the same driveway where Maria gave me my first kiss.

I walked out to the opening of our driveway in my white Chicago Bulls jacket and looked left towards her house. There was a stillness to the street that late Friday afternoon, a stillness before the final act of the summer of 1991. I looked forward to our magic continuing.

Chapter 15. Almost Blowing It Yet Again

"There are many people out here in these streets messing up their lives. There are a lot of people who made bad decisions when they were your age, young bruh."
—Herb, Our Next-Door Neighbor, August 1991

After attending the Ken Jones Basketball Camp, I should have returned to Buffalo with the goal of making myself into the best basketball player I could be for tryouts in October. I am certain many other campers did that, but not me. To have done that would have taken an extreme desire, focus, and foresight that I just didn't have at fourteen years old. I had some of those attributes, but not the ability to block everything else out of my mind to create a singular focus. Little did I know at the time, but I was in danger of destroying my innocent basketball dreams.

My focus had changed and the change threatened to alter my trajectory. Most of my focus was now on seeing my girlfriend, Maria, whom I had not seen since before I went to camp. It felt like an eternity. Before going to camp, Maria and I saw each other somewhat regularly. However, when I returned, things were different, and I did not see her as much as I did before. It was not because I was not eager, but instead it was something on her end that I did not understand. She was now *busy* each time I tried to see her. Was it her parents? Was it true? Was she really that busy? The more she turned me away, the more frustrated I became.

I was born with a determined mind once I focused on something. Day after day, I would get up in the morning hoping to see her, only to go to bed defeated at night. Instead of taking my ball and going to the courts, I would plan most of my days around seeing her. Suddenly the goal of making the Hutch-Tech boys' basketball team in two to three months was an afterthought. Why could I not see her for just a little while? She just lived up the street, after all.

In addition to not understanding what was happening, it started hurting me emotionally. It started showing to the point where it became visible to all around me, especially my mother. There was also what felt like a lack of support from the two closest guys to me, Amahl and Gabe. This was probably because, in our little teenage world, whatever dealings they had with Maria themselves, they felt like they were experts on her, and they thought I was on a fool's errand in getting involved with her. None of it felt fair.

Things came to a head on my fifteenth birthday, of all days, on August 25, 1991. It was one of the first times I felt my world grind to a screeching halt. I thought that on my birthday, of all days, I would be able to see my girlfriend. Mom was taking me out to dinner at one of the buffets, probably around 4 p.m. All I wanted was to see Maria, and that would have made my day.

In the afternoon, I went to the mailbox and found a card. There was a baseball player on the front of it with a small message from her on the inside that I cannot remember. It did not make sense. Someone brought the card down and left it in our mailbox, maybe her. If it was her, why did she not stop and visit me for five minutes? It was my special day, and now it was ruined by Maria, or maybe even her parents. Again, it did not feel fair.

"I do not want you seeing Maria anymore," Mom said, personally taking control of the situation, as she had done so many times during those years. She saw what was going on and had had enough. She responded in the only way that she knew how, and that was to be protective. She set me aside and made her declaration shortly before going to dinner, and her words hit me like a sack of bricks. You could also say they cut into me like a knife because that is what I felt emotionally.

Why was this happening on my birthday of all days? I pondered it all in my now fifteen-year-old mind. It was another punch, one of the worst ways to spend one's birthday. It was something I would never forget. Now Mom was forbidding me from being with the girl that I felt like I loved. It was a time when the empowering wisdom and guidance of a man would have really helped. Some parents might have sat their child down and attempted to reason things out. At the time, though, I felt like my hand was being forced—something disempowering, humiliating and painful.

"YOU'RE NOT GOING TO SEE ME AGAIN FOR A LONG TIME!" I acted like I was going to get into the car and then ran to the edge of the driveway, yelled my declaration to my mother, and then darted towards Kay Street, passing Maria's house. It just happened, and I did not think about the fact that I would have to return to the house later that night. After all, that was where my food and shelter were. It was the emotion of the moment.

"GET OVER HERE!" Mom yelled back at me as I took off running. She tried to exert her power over me once again, but in my mind, I had to break free. I did not want anyone's control over me anymore. I did not care if they were right. I had to get away from her, from the situation, and from the street. I had to get away.

In my white Chicago Bulls Swingster jacket, tee shirt, shorts, and sneakers, I ran up Hastings and then turned left onto Kay Street. I ran towards Eggert Road and eventually started walking. I was tired and out of breath. By that point, I was also emotionally spent, and I did not have an appetite. The world seemed to move slowly, and all my senses were heightened.

I passed by an older girl named Tamika Lott and a friend of hers. Tamika was a very beautiful light-skinned female who went to Campus West with us and then Hutch-Tech as a part of my brother's class of 1992 for a little while. She recognized me and spoke. She walked with another girl from Amahl's class. It might have been

Shawndre Horner, and they both seemed to recognize me. On any other day, being recognized by two pretty girls from one of the senior classes would have been a really big deal. I wasn't feeling very social at the time, so I said something short in passing and blew them off, something I wish I had not done years later as Tamika Lott got steadily more gorgeous as the years progressed.

One thought raced through my mind. I had to find Gabe. Even though I did not feel supported by him throughout much of this ordeal, he was one of the few people who could help make sense of what was happening. He was my other half, my shadow and my twin. I would say he was like my soulmate, but not in the romantic sense. He just had a way of comforting things and smoothing them over.

As I ran down Kensington and crossed into Cheektowaga, I saw him walking with a gang of ten or more rough-looking guys who I did not recognize. I identified him by his height, his red Chicago Bulls Starter jacket, his Air Jordans, his thick calves, and his walk and unique stride. His haircut gave him away too. We were all still wearing high-top fades or slope haircuts. I really needed to talk to him, but would he break off from this group to sit and sit with me for a little bit?

"GABE!" I yelled with feelings of desperation in my own voice. The whole gang of guys stopped and turned around to see who I was, perhaps thinking I was a threat of some sort. They all stared momentarily. One of the guys turned and mumbled something to Gabe, perhaps asking him if I was a danger in any way, as they all sized me up.

Gabe recognized me and signaled to them that he would catch up with them later. He approached me slowly and came to talk to me. We started walking together by the 12-A Utica bus stop at the corner of Kensington Avenue and Huntley Road in Cheektowaga, not far from his home on Burke Drive. We walked behind Cleveland Hill Plaza and sat down on one of the stoops at one of the loading docks for the stores in the plaza. We must have passed by that location thousands of times, driving up and down Kensington Avenue with our parents. This late summer evening, it became a makeshift therapist's office.

"Gabe, my mother said I can't see Maria anymore. This is FUCKED UP, and it's not fair!" My eyes started watering. I closed them and gradually opened them as I told him what was happening. I was ready to hit something or someone out of frustration. Why was this happening? Why was this happening to me, of all people?

Gabe approached it as a friend telling me that it would be alright. He also reminded me of Maria's history and of her dating carousel or merry-go-round. He said that it was visibly taking a toll on me and that it was only natural for everyone else to be concerned. He told me that she and her family were not worth the stress and that I would be okay. They were soothing words, but the pain of it all was still there like a fresh wound receiving medicine for the first time. We talked for about an hour or so at the loading dock on Kensington.

"Are you going to be alright?" Our conversation organically arrived at its conclusion, with Gabe giving me one last verbal check on my health and well-being, and then it was time to go. The summer sun was setting, and it was getting dark. We shook hands, hugged, and then went our separate ways. As I walked, I turned around to see him slowly disappear into that late summer night.

I really did not want to part ways, as his words were therapeutic. I still felt alone, and I did not want to go home to face my mother. She was probably going to reprimand me in some way and pour the proverbial peroxide on my wounds. What was I going to say? What could I say? I lived in *her* house and didn't pay any bills. None of my thoughts were on my innocent basketball dreams, just the teen romance maelstrom that I had been engulfed in.

That walk back up Kensington, to Edison, and then to Hastings seemed to take forever. It would have been nice to see Tamika Lott again, but I did not. The air was short, and the world seemed to move slowly. I did not want to go home. I was not hungry, so I did not want to go out to dinner with my mother either. Even though she was doing what she was doing out of love and protection for me, I felt resentful towards her. Hell, I felt resentful towards everyone, Maria's parents and even Maria herself to some degree. Why was this happening?

As I turned right on Hastings towards home, I walked by the Harrison house. I turned and looked, but no one seemed to be home. They did not care about what I was going through anyway. I did not feel welcome there or in my home either. I wondered what I would say and do when I walked back into the house. On the inside, I had not come to terms with not being able to see Maria yet, and I felt as though no one was going to tell me how to run my life. In addition to my feelings for Maria, this was in large part about control and personal reflections.

As I walked to our house, I could hear the cars speeding up and down the Kensington expressway, but I heard something behind me. It sounded like the singing of a church hymn. Just then our neighbor Herb strolled out of his driveway with his Bible in hand with that signature bounce in his step. He was headed to an evening service at Faith Bible Tabernacle Church. It was right on the edge of the Langfield Projects, overlooking the Kensington expressway.

Herb was in his late 20s or early 30s at the time. He was a little shorter than me, he had a birdlike nose and his hair was cut short. He wore a white button-down shirt, black slacks, and black shoes. On most days Herb wore a tee shirt and sweatpants as he jogged around the neighborhood. He stayed upstairs with his father, Milton, who was older and was probably taking care of him. Herb was a *spiritual* man, and we regularly heard him singing church hymns in the shower. We could hear him from our driveway, which Gabe and I joked about. He was very friendly too, and always had a very buoyant personality, something you could both see and feel.

"HEYYYYY MAN!" He was always happy to see me for some reason. That night he greeted me with his signature salutation. He could not have known what was happening in my life that fateful birthday evening. He did not know my name, and every time he saw me, he referred to me simply as 'Man'.

"How is it going young bruh?" He had no idea how happy I was to see him. He gave me a reason not to go into the house. He gave me someone else to talk to and I followed him to wherever he was going. He was a Godsend.

"Can I walk and talk with you Herb?" I asked him, needing any support or wisdom that his godly spirit could give me.

"Sure, man, come on," he said. We walked up Hastings Avenue to Kay Street and then turned right towards the Langfield Projects. Herb had a certain *pep* in his step, as they say. He was high on life and strutted up the street holding his Bible.

"Herb, my mother is making me break up with my girlfriend," I lamented to him as we passed Phyllis and Martha Avenues. "I can't believe this. It's not fair!"

"Your mother is just trying to protect you, young bruh!" His natural excitement came down into a place of seriousness. "You are still young and have a lot of life left to live," he continued, assuring me that life would go on beyond the feelings I was experiencing in those moments. We stopped and talked on the bridge above the Kensington Expressway. The cars speeding underneath created a background noise as Herb spoke to me. Again, we never talked extensively before, but right there on that bridge, Herb told me a bunch of different things—you might say he ministered to me. There have been certain moments in my life when I have felt like God was talking to me through someone else, and this was one of those moments. It might have been the first such highlighted moment in my life.

I'll be okay. I'll be fine. Life will go on, I pondered to myself as I listened to him, slowly nodding my head. It was a form of mentoring and teaching that Mom had not, and maybe could not, give me in her motherly protection of me. Dad had his own unique way of viewing the world and never mentored me in this way before, either. My conversation with Herb was a light in one of the storms of life when things seemed to be at their darkest. It was a form of grounded guidance that Dad did not or could not give me with his rigid and draconian form of mentorship on my journey toward manhood.

"Your life will not stop with this one, young bruh," he continued. "You'll meet many more ladies in your lifetime, and you will not die over this one. There are a lot of people out here in these streets messing their lives up, young bruh, and there are a lot of people who made bad decisions when they were your age. I made many decisions that I would change if I were your age again," he continued as the happiness slowly drained from his face. It caused me to wonder what exactly this man of God had experienced in his younger years.

"Everything will be fine, young bruh. Just enjoy being young while you can," he concluded.

I will be okay. I will be okay, I continued pondering internally and nodding as the cars sped by underneath us as Herb's words continued to sooth me. It was exactly what I needed to hear in those moments from someone not immediately connected to the situation. We eventually shook hands, exchanged a short half-hug, and parted ways. Herb went to church, and I turned and went home. His words allowed me to go back home. To this day, I have never forgotten that discussion and what it did for me.

When I returned to the house, Mom had gone to bed. Eventually, I did too. It was a restless night, my first night being fifteen years old. It was a rough way to bring in the next year of my life. I tossed and turned in my room in the back of our house on that late summer Buffalo night. There were so many emotions in my head and on my heart, some of which I had never felt before, but would experience many more times in a future that seemed so distant.

I let the radio play all night at a low volume, and as the first rays of sunlight peeked through my window, I heard the baseline from the group New Edition's song, *Word to the Mutha,* come on Power 94 WBLK. It was about six o'clock in the morning. It was so surreal. Some of the innocence I carried with me for 15 years, which had been protected by the same house I slept so uncomfortably in that night, had been stripped away, never to return.

* * *

I eventually talked to my mother and begrudgingly conceded that she had only done what she had done out of protection for me—we were able to communicate openly that way. I verbally agreed that I would not see Maria anymore, but I did not mean it. I rebelliously decided that no one was going to tell me who I could and could not see. If Maria and I were going to stop talking, it was going to be on our terms and no one else's.

For that last part of the summer and into the early part of the school year, my mind was still focused on her and not the great game of basketball. I continued trying to see her, though unsuccessfully. I did not know what was happening on her end or why, just that I still was not seeing her much. I pretty much kept it from everyone on my end, so they were none the wiser. One time I leaked it out to Gabe and asked, "You and Maria, that is still going on?"

As we got closer to the start of the school year, Maria communicated with me one day about how she felt about things. I did not get the revelation on the bumper of their family station wagon the way many other guys did. We were on some swings at the park next to the St. Aloysius School on Cleveland Drive. As we sat, she started talking to me while looking kind of sad.

"When the school year starts, you are probably not going to see me that much," she said in her low and soft voice. It was childlike in a way. It was as though she was telling her parents about a rule she had broken or something she knew would disappoint them.

"It is okay, Maria, we will be able to see each other as much as we want," I replied. My fifteen-year-old mind did not understand that women sometimes say things indirectly (softly at first), and that as men, we must develop the ability to sift through what is being said to get to the truth. In this case, she was trying to let me down *easily*. She did not directly say that she was not interested in me anymore, that her parents were going to restrict her social time further once the school year started, or both. It was a soft way of saying that continuing to try to see her would be a waste of time.

"We do not have to stop being together just because the school year is starting. I still want to be with you, and I think that we should still be a couple," I continued. At that point, she did not really say much, so I thought things were cool. Nevertheless, things pretty much went on as they had been going, with me wanting to see her, but not really seeing her.

* * *

By the time September rolls around in Western New York, summer visibly starts transitioning into fall. The weather starts cooling. The leaves start changing color, and the skies get a little grayer. School starts, as does football season. Everything changes. Whatever the fling that I had with Maria Harrison over the summer, it had changed. And I was not ready for it to change.

When my sophomore year of high school began, most of my thoughts were still pretty much consumed by Maria; not my grades and not making the 1991–92 Hutch-Tech boys' varsity basketball team. Likewise, I expended a lot of mental energy thinking about how I would see her before or after school. After all, she did just live a couple of houses down from me.

I figured that if I left at the right time in the morning, I could catch her before she got on her bus. Performing Arts was one of the only high schools that still sent cheese buses around in the mornings for their students. I think City Honors did too. If I did not catch her in the morning, I thought maybe I could catch her in the afternoon on the way home from school. Both strategies were unsuccessful in September and October.

The only thing I knew was that I was still in love with her and wanted to be with her. A song that was getting lots of airplay at the time was *I Adore,* by the group, Color Me Badd. It was a love ballad where the chorus basically says, "I Adore Mi Amor," or, "I adore my love." Those lines typified what and how I felt about Maria. My mind had become delusional, and she was my *Sweet* Maria. She was all I thought about to the point where I started leaving notes at her house.

Many mornings I sat in Ms. Placene's English class thinking about Maria, what she was doing, and when I would see her again. My body was physically in class, but my mind was elsewhere. I could not see clearly, and I was coming awfully close to repeating my freshman year first quarter in terms of my grades. Here I was hoping to make the Hutch-Tech boys' varsity basketball team, and all I could think about was Maria. I was not thinking about improving my game and my chances of making the cut in late October and early November. I was not thinking about getting to tryouts with the best possible grades. I only thought about Maria.

"I think we should just be friends," Maria said one evening on the phone, finally putting me out of my misery. Her words stung a little bit, and yet the loss was not so significant because she had not been there for me anyway. It was quick, and it felt better to have ended that way as opposed to at the hands of someone else. Her folks probably did have something to do with it. It was good, though, as I was now free from the four-month trance I had fallen into at the beginning of that summer. It was something I had almost no control over at the time and could not break free of. My soul did feel noticeably lighter and freer afterward. Gabe described it as a tremendous *weight* lifted off my shoulders. I wanted desperately to maintain what we had, but I now felt free due to a liberation that was not my doing.

* * *

It was like snapping out of a coma or a trance. It was like a light switch turning off, like the switch that turned on when my initial strong attraction for her started less than a year earlier, seemingly out of nowhere. Now that I did not have love on my mind, I refocused on my mission from the beginning of the summer. In order to be eligible for the team, each player had to have at least a 70% average grade in every class, or at least our core classes. Had I applied myself and been 100% focused, I could have easily made the grades I needed. Because I was distracted however, I just barely made it across the eligibility threshold. I was not a bad student and could do the work. I was just not devoting 100% of my mental capacity to my schoolwork.

Now I could refocus on the greatest goal in my life, making the 1991–92 Hutch-Tech boys' varsity basketball team. I wasted a lot of time over the summer. Could I now rebound and achieve my goal of becoming a Hutch-Tech Engineer? Could I wear one of the maroon and gold uniforms that I watched from the sidelines in the previous year? The answers would unfold over the next several months.

Chapter 16. Sophomore Year, Fall Grades and Intramurals

"Do you want to be a captain, Dunbar?" **—Coach Ken Jones, the Hutch-Tech boys' basketball team 1988-93, September 1991**

With the Maria Harrison summer romance behind me, I could now do what I should have done all along, and that is to focus on school and basketball. They should have been my top two priorities after returning from the Ken Jones Basketball Camp that summer. Life happens and though I did not understand how to navigate the new waters I found myself in, it was a valuable lesson. It would be years before I would develop the *razor-sharp* focus necessary to accomplish meaningful goals. I am specifically talking about learning to block out distractions altogether when necessary and when possible. From that experience and many others since, I have learned that distractions never completely go away, and you must learn to manage them as best you can.

So many hours were lost that last month of the summer alone, hours that could have been used working on the basketball fundamentals I had learned at camp. So many hours were lost that could have been spent not only solidifying a roster spot for myself, but also increasing my chances of getting on the court were I to make the team. Coach Jones knew that I attended his camp and that I really wanted to be a part of his basketball program, but would that desire and effort be enough to land me a roster spot? Would I be ready for tryouts?

* * *

When I looked at myself in the bathroom mirror that fall, a slightly more mature young man looked back at me. I had a little bit more facial hair and a little less baby fat on my face. A mustache was also developing. Instead of the standard high-top fade, I had Amahl cut a forward slope or Gumby hairstyle for me. The style that year, clothing-wise, involved denim overalls with boots or sneakers. The style was to wear one strap of the overalls unclasped and hanging loosely. The shirt you wore underneath the overalls varied. Sweatshirts and hoodies were also still in style, like my favorite red UNLV hoodie, which I wore often. Nike gear, in general, was in style and I mostly wore a black pair of Nike Flights with everything. I had also grown to 6'2".

At Hutch-Tech High School, the 1991–92 school year would be a return to the old guard, at least on the administrative front. During my freshman year, the principal was Ms. Barbara Schnell, who was known most for her bright pink slippers. She resigned for some reason, and Mr. Joseph Gentile returned. In my mind, he was synonymous with Hutch-Tech. He was the face of our school. Reading through my brother's first two yearbooks at Hutch-Tech, Mr. Gentile was the defining persona of the school. He presided over Hutch-Tech, winning the 'National School of Excellence' distinction in Amahl's freshman year. Tech was his baby, and he had overseen the ascension of the school.

* * *

The record I remember listening to most in my sophomore year was *The Low End Theory,* by the rap group, A Tribe Called Quest. They consisted of Q-Tip, Phife Dawg, Jerobi and Ali Shaheed Muhammed. They were not gangsters like NWA and the Geto Boyz. Instead, they were a group of eclectic and rootsy lyrical MCs out of New York City, who rapped over old-school, jazzy, and R&B-type beats. All their album covers were graced with a beautiful woman, suggestively and provocatively painted with streaks of red and green with varying backgrounds. You could also see her real seductive eyes. Their first hits were, *I Left My Wallet in El Segundo*, and *Bonita Applebum* from their first album titled *The People's Instinctive Travels and the Paths of Rhythm.*

The track that really got me hooked on A Tribe Called Quest music was *Check the Rhyme* off *The Low End Theory*. Once I got the album, I also fell in love with *We've Got the Jazz*. The most well known track on the record was *The Scenario,* featuring The Leaders of the New School. These included Charlie Brown, Scooby-Doo and Busta-Rhymes who contributed the infamous 'Dungeon Dragon's final verse. Along with similar groups like De La Soul, Jungle Brothers and The Black Sheep, they collectively called themselves the Native Tongues Tribe. That year Ice-Cube continued to evolve after leaving NWA and released *Death Certificate* which contained hits like *Be True to the Game* and *Steady Mobbin.*

Later that year, another pioneering and legendary album emerged from the West Coast, called *The Chronic,* by Dr. Dre, one of Ice-Cube's former fellow bandmates in the rap group NWA. I did not own a copy of *The Chronic*, but it was played everywhere. On the record Dr. Dre sampled a lot of Parliament's old beats, the older *P-Funk* sound, which gave rise to the new *G-Funk* sound. With hits like *Nuthin' but a 'G' Thang*, it introduced young artists like Snoop Doggy Dog, who became a household name and a fixture in hip hop and pop cultures. The duo exploded on the scene on the title track for the movie soundtrack, D*eep Cover,* starring Lawrence Fishburne.

In terms of R&B, Ricky Bell, Michael Bivins, and Ronny Devoe of New Edition spun off as a trio and created a group called Bell, Biv, Devoe, or BBD for short. Their first single off that record was the title track *Poison*, which became a classic for years to come with its danceable beat and mixture of singing and rapping. The entire album was gold, and my brother played it continuously. It was not just the music, but also their style of dress and overall level of smoothness. There were so many creative R&B groups that emerged that year, like Jodeci, in addition to groups who were continuing their success, such as Guy. That was a great year for R&B and hip-hop music. There were just too many groups to name, and that includes the female acts as well.

* * *

As a sophomore, there was now a class below me, the class of 1995. It is worth discussing the class of 1995, because my basketball and life destinies would intertwine with theirs, particularly as it relates to the basketball team. Furthermore, the1995 class was a lot different than mine in several ways.

In my class of 1994, there were no dominant personalities or unique groups in the school like the other classes. In contrast, the class of 1995 was full of spirit. They were a more rambunctious group, full of colorful personalities. Some of them regularly got into trouble and did not appear happy to be at Hutch-Tech. You name it, and they did it. For example, one year a group of them walked around school wearing gangster headwraps or bandanas the way rappers like Tupac and Ice Cube wore in their videos. It was a stunt for which all of them got into trouble. Mr. Gentile made a mass midday announcement for any student with bandanas on their head to be sent to the office immediately.

They were also aggressive, loud, and had a lot of attitude. This class was not afraid to get in your face and speak their mind no matter who liked it or not, and no matter how off the wall or audacious it was. They were not afraid to tell you how great they thought they were. Nor were they afraid to tell you how much you sucked. They were an interesting group and a new breed. They were arguably the second coming of the class of 1993. It was fascinating to me that my class and I were sandwiched between them.

There were a lot of pretty girls in the class of 1995 too. As with all the classes, they know who they are. Each class had *diamonds* who all the guys wanted to talk to right away. Then there were always *diamonds in the rough*.

* * *

Even after my fling with Maria Harrison ended, I did not do enough in my classes to get on the Honor Roll. The core curriculum of classes for my second year at Hutch-Tech consisted of Global Studies with Mr. Gallucciano, General Chemistry with Mr. Kozek, Sequential Math Course 2 with Ms. Ungeran, and

English with Ms. Placene. My electives were Architectural Design with Mr. Augustine, Spanish 2 with Ms. Baker, and then finally, gym class.

I was happy to have gym class and not swimming class that year. Gym class at Hutch-Tech was not anything spectacular. Two classes crowded into our tiny gym. I believe my teacher was Ms. Garcenea. After taking attendance in a single file line, we had to run two laps and then they turned us loose. I usually ended up playing basketball with the guys in my class.

Architectural Design was like Mechanical Drawing the previous year with Mr. Dicorzo. It took place in the basement in one of the machine shops and was taught by Mr. Augustine, a studious-looking man with brown hair who wore glasses, button-down shirts, slacks and shoes. It consisted of drawing complex designs using fancy architectural kits like those we used the previous year. Course 2 Math was taught by Ms. Ungeran, a middle-aged white woman with curly brown hair and a birdlike appearance. She was a little bit eccentric personality-wise, but I did better in her class than I did in Course 1 Math. I did not focus well enough, by any means, to say that I mastered it in any way. I understood just enough to get by, but not excel.

I never developed a comfort level with Mrs. Ungeran as a teacher. She gave me detention one time because another student was talking to me during class. She also got on me because I asked my mother to help me out with some of the complex math concepts we were learning, and she was unfamiliar with them. Mrs. Ungeran also gave me pushback regarding helping me after school with questions I had. She insisted that I get the help I needed during classroom hours, which was fair, I guess. Some teachers wanted to leave punctually after school, it seemed.

Mr. Galluciano's Global Studies 2 class was fun. He was a short middle-aged Italian man with a round nose and glasses. Mr. Galluciano was really into history, and he coached both the boys' and girls' bowling teams. There was a full-body picture of Napoleon Bonaparte at the front of the classroom. He was supposed to tell me why Napoleon constantly kept his hand in his shirt, but I do not remember ever getting a clear explanation from him. During tests and in-class assignments, Mr. Galluciano would walk by and give us little fist bumps on our shoulders. One day I recall him making me take my hood off in class. I wore my red UNLV Runnin' Rebels hooded sweatshirt that year, and my teenage mind thought it was cool to have the hood up over my head during class.

In addition to my memories of daydreaming about Maria Harrison in her class early in the 1991–92 school year, I enjoyed Ms. Placene's English class. Ms. Placene was a mature white woman with graying blonde hair. She always wore glasses, skirts and low heels, showing off her muscular calves. She might have been a runner. Yes, as a teen, I looked at her legs sometimes.

She looked very secretary-like, and I recall her always chewing gum and talking very casually. She came across as an Ivy League-trained teacher, just like Dr. David

Sylveres at Campus West. I recall her reading a Nikki Giovanni poem to us, perhaps her *Kidnap Poem*. At one point, we also had to memorize a literary work and recite it to the class. I memorized a passage from *The Autobiography of Malcolm X*. It was his last run-in with West Indian Archie before fleeing Harlem. I practiced it and then acted it out in front of the class.

And then there was General Chemistry class. I was a Biotechnology major, and General Chemistry was a requirement for us. As much as I liked it, I did not take to it well enough to master it. While it was about mixing solutions, acids and bases, and the periodic table, there was also some math involved. It involved integrating those concepts with calculations which I did not completely put together in my mind. It was also my last class of the day. Mr. Paul Kozek seemed as normal as any of the teachers. He had a bushy dark mustache and wore button-down shirts and khakis most days.

Next door to Mr. Kozek's classroom was Mr. Beckettstein's classroom. They were in the rear corner of our H-shaped building on the Chippewa Street side. Mr. Duane Beckettstein was an eccentric elderly monster of a man with a scary look and a bass-filled voice that projected well outside of his classroom. He was stocky with curly hair and a lower lip that poked out. He always wore a sweater or sweatshirt with khakis and sneakers. At times, he yelled loud enough to be heard in the class next door. Sometimes Mr. Kozek, who was more mild-mannered, rolled his eyes in disgust.

The 1991–92 school year was my brother's senior year, and all non-Biotechnology and Chemical Technology students had to take General Chemistry as seniors. One day Mr. Beckettstein yelled, "DUNBAR!" I looked up, thinking that he might be referring to me, but it was my brother he was yelling at that day, something we laughed about years later.

* * *

One of the joys of the fall at Hutch-Tech was the morning boys' basketball intramurals. Like the previous year, Coach Jones organized intramurals where students picked teams and named them. The teams competed in league play and then a playoff at the end of the semester for the intramural championship. Coach Jones kept track of the standings and seeded the teams in a single-elimination playoff. It was just like at the Ken Jones Basketball Camp.

It all began with a morning announcement about a meeting for intramurals after school in the auditorium. Now that I was a sophomore, I could play with the juniors and seniors. I still remember that meeting in the auditorium. There weren't enough captains, so Coach Jones sought me out with an unexpected question.

"Would you like to be a Captain Dunbar?" Of all the boys in the auditorium, Coach Jones approached me and propositioned me in his low and raspy, grandfatherly voice, referring to me by my last name. Only a handful of guys had stepped up to be captains, and he needed more. Coach wore his signature polo shirt, his short John Stockton-length shorts, his striped socks, his Converse sneakers and a whistle around his neck. He looked like a professor with his sharp chin, sharp nose, balding hair on the top of his head, and curly black hair around the sides and the back.

"Uhhhh. Okay," I reluctantly agreed. I did not show up that day looking to be anyone's captain. I just wanted to play on a team and have a chance to show what I could do.

Being a captain never crossed my mind. I did not know the first thing about being a captain and did not want any part of leadership. Our team also needed a name. I selected the Georgia Tech Yellow Jackets from the Atlantic Coast Conference in the college basketball world.

Under Head Coach Bobby Cremins, Georgia Tech was a very successful college basketball program during that era, producing several NBA players, including Mark Price, Kenny Anderson, Dennis Scott and John Salley. I chose the name not because I was a fan of their team per se, but because it was one of the few college programs that I was familiar with. I gave some thought to NBA teams, but I opted for a college basketball team.

Coach Jones basically ran a draft where players submitted their names, and each team picked players. The first player I chose was one of the returning seniors from the '90–'91 basketball team, Adonis Coble. I didn't know Adonis that well or if he would have liked being on my team, but he was there so I picked him. Next, I picked Omari Ferguson, Terrance Collison, Torri Lowe, and David Lees, who lived around the corner from me on Davidson Avenue. The rest of the team consisted of guys from my class. I didn't intend to pick a team consisting of predominately the 1994 class. It just happened that way.

"Who picked me?" Adonis asked a general question to whoever heard him in his high-pitched, soft, and unthreatening voice. He walked into the auditorium slowly in his football practice gear and cleats and slowly looked through the rosters for his name. He had a pea-shaped head, a wiry build and he was slightly bow legged. I nervously told him that I had picked him—they were potentially the first words we had ever spoken to one another at Hutch-Tech.

He looked at me suspiciously momentarily and then looked at the rest of our newly formed roster. I will just say that he did not look impressed. He shrugged his shoulders and then left the auditorium with the same slow walk with which he entered. Someone afterward said, "You guys are going to go as far as 'Donnie' takes you!" *Donnie* was one of Adonis' other nicknames, in addition to 'AD'.

For a shy, unassuming, and socially unsure kid like myself, having Adonis on the team was cool, but a somewhat intimidating also. He had been on the Yale Cup and Class B Sectional Championship team the previous year. He was also in my brother's senior class, and he was popular. I gave him automatic respect and reverence. I did not know if he wanted to play on a team full of sophomores, but I was happy to have him.

We played relatively well as a group. Our starters were usually Adonis, Omari, Terrance, Torri and me. Adonis got most of the touches, which was to be expected, and he unselfishly shared the ball with teammates who were not as skilled as he was. He honestly could have abused the entire situation, bullied some of us, and taken all the shots, but he did not.

Torri usually brought the ball up the court for the team. No one on the team was a particularly great shooter other than Adonis, so I remember each of us scoring off layups. I made my living at the foul line. Since I practiced free throws often, I was able to knock them down with a great deal of consistency. David Lees complained about not getting enough playing time and not touching the ball enough. I had to talk him off the ledge at times, so to speak, in terms of his getting frustrated and threatening to quit.

Once the intramural regular season finished, we had the playoffs. We fell to one of the more senior-laden teams like Mike Mann's team, the Howard University Bison, or one of the other teams. Those teams had bigger guys up front like Jermaine 'J-Bird' Skillon, Wilbert 'Deuce' Green, Henry Steward, and Leon Steward. Either way, I thought playing on the team with Adonis earned me some cool points and was a confidence booster.

* * *

As with the previous year, there were separate intramurals for freshmen, which was where I first saw the players from the class of 1995 show what they could do. The freshmen once again played on Friday mornings. Out of curiosity, I stopped down to see them play, and I had never seen anything like it before. That is putting it mildly.

I immediately saw the personality of the class of 1995 as a group. They were a much different group than we were on the court. They were uber-talented, and they had a lot of attitude, confidence, and swagger. They were not afraid to let you know about it either. All throughout the gym, you could hear things like, "You can't check me," or, "I'm just too nice for you!" There was also, "You're DOO-DOO!" Some of them self-glossed themselves, calling out their own names while running up the court after scores. Baskets were being made, and smooth passes were being thrown, followed by looks that said, "I told you so," with slow and confident trots up the court.

Certain players stood out to me. There was a shorter dark-skinned kid named Reggie Hokes. I had seen him play at the William-Emslie YMCA on some Saturday mornings. He played like an NBA point guard and had a masterful handle of the basketball. He threw beautiful no-look passes, just like Magic Johnson. He did not appear to be talking much, just playing his game and sharing the ball. Just like at the YMCA, he wore a Tee-shirt and sweatpants.

There was a short light-skinned kid who had a nice jump shot. He knew it, too, as he ran up the court after making baskets, visibly reveling in his abilities. He had a smug and mischievous look on his face, not something intentional, but a natural expression. He had a high-pitched, whiny and squeaky voice. His name was Adrian Callahan.

There was another kid with a mature and lean physique who had lots of hops and who I was somewhat familiar with already. His name was Brian Hargrove. There was another light-skinned, skinny kid with lots of game named Tim Bowler. Then there was another skinny and whiny, trash-talking kid named Earl Holmes.

There was also Darrell Hendrickson, a clown of a kid who had skills, but did not make a big impression on me early on. Then there was a dark-skinned bow-legged kid with thick lips and a West Indian accent. His name was Kevin Glenford Adkins. His classmates jokingly called him 'Trinidad'. His game was unpolished and rough around the edges, but his hustle and tenacity made him very effective.

There were also two taller kids who were both already 6'4" to 6'5" as freshmen. One of them looked mean and nasty. He had a round-faced, was husky and wore a shag haircut. His name was Andre Clark. When he played, it was like he had a chip on his shoulder and readily talked trash to his opponents after scoring baskets. The other was a tall white kid who was awkward, clumsy, and uncoordinated. He had long black hair down to his shoulders, kind of like an MTV-rocker. His name was Randy Halan. He drew a lot of attention from the upperclassmen, who pointed at him and laughed during the freshman games.

"STOP TALKING AND JUST PLAY!" Coach Jones yelled at the 1995 class guys often during intramurals. He wanted them to just play the game, even though just playing the game did not seem to be what they were about. They had to stand out and make their presence known. These guys were so bold that they would provoke you and talk trash to you even if you did not do anything to warrant it, a behavior very different than any other class.

They were just freshmen, and I had bigger fish to fry. I had my own mission which was securing a spot on the '91–'92 Hutch-Tech boys' varsity basketball team. It was early October and soon Coach Jones would make his announcement about varsity tryouts. I had waited for these tryouts ever since the '90–'91 Engineers' season ended seven months earlier. Would I get to be one of them? Would I get to don the maroon and gold and be a Hutch-Tech Engineer? The time had come to either realize that dream or have it put off for another year.

* * *

"I was talking to someone, and they told me that basketball players run an average of two miles every game, so to get your conditioning up before tryouts, you might want to go out and do some running," Dad said one day on the phone in his deliberate and stern voice.

I wanted to give myself the best chance of making the Hutch-Tech boys' basketball team, so I made some effort to go out running. I didn't really enjoy long-distance running, but if it's what I had to do to make the team, I was going to try it. Running one mile around high school tracks was four times around. The key for me was ignoring the monotony and the pain and continuing to keep going. Gabe's school, Cleveland Hill High School, had such a track. One weekend, I developed a painful patch of dead skin on the ball of my right foot because of the long-distance running. I needed a special skin treatment from one of the drug stores to heal it. It was a salicylic acid treatment purchased from Rite-Aid. This prompted me to double my socks afterward for most athletic activities.

"WEIGHT TRAINING. WORK TO LEARN. LEARN TO WORK." Coach Jones also left unofficial recommendations for weight training for prospects on the bulletin board in the athletic department. This is where he left all his materials for the '90-'91 Engineers the previous year. Everything was typed in capital letters. Underneath the title, he wrote, "DEVELOP STRENGTH, ENDURANCE AND MUSCLE DEFINITION." The notice had directions for warmups, including skipping rope, stretching and lifting light weights. It had further directions including, "USE A WEIGHT YOU CAN HANDLE 10 TIMES," "DO THREE (3) SETS," "WORK OUT THREE (3) TIMES A WEEK OR EVERY OTHER DAY." Some of the exercises he recommended were the military press, bent rowing, upright rowing, and quadricep (thigh) lifts, among others. It ended with the quote, "WHERE THE WEAK GET STRONG AND THE STRONG GET STRONGER."

We didn't have an official dedicated weight room at Hutch-Tech, just a makeshift set of weights in the storage area underneath the basket in the big gym. I did the best I could on my own volition to do some weightlifting when I remembered to do it in gym class or on weekends. It was sparse though.

* * *

"There's a shooting workshop later this week, Anwar. George Lehman of the company Eastbay is giving it. Would you like to go?" Coach Jones approached me and asked me in his raspy and grandfatherly voice in mid-October if I wanted to attend some shooting event in the evening one night during the week. I did not know who George Lehman was, but I agreed to go after getting Mom's consent. That fall day after school, Coach Jones drove Kidada Williams, Adonis Coble and me in his gray Lincoln Town Car to Newfane High School, a school I had never heard of.

It was a thirty- to forty-minute drive to the northeastern outskirts of Buffalo to one of the rural areas; in the middle of nowhere, as they say. We arrived at an impressive-looking school with a full parking lot. When we walked into the vast Newfane gym, the bleachers were full of a predominantly white audience. On the court, there was a middle-aged, partially bald white man wearing a tee-shirt and shorts, throwing basketballs off a square net, catching them, and then making shot after shot. He was not jumping high and hanging in the air like Michael Jordan. His movements were effortless nonetheless, and identical every time he shot the ball. The results were too. SWOOSH. SWOOSH. SWOOSH. He didn't miss a single shot, and it was very impressive.

Eventually, he stopped his demonstration, turned on his wireless microphone, and addressed the crowd. He gave us a brief lecture about the acronym BEEF. He was not there to talk to us about burgers or steaks. Body balance, Eyes on the basket, Elbow in, and Follow through were the four elements of the *BEEF* he referred to. It was the exact same acronym we learned at the Ken Jones Basketball Camp for proper shooting mechanics.

"COACHES DON'T CUT PLAYERS. PLAYERS CUT PLAYERS!" He made this proclamation in a stern voice as his breath gradually slowed. He held the ball under one arm and then used his free arm to accentuate his points.

"Your job is to show up to tryouts ready to go in the fall! When the season ends in the spring, you have seven months to prepare for the next season! It is YOUR job to show up to tryouts ready to go and the coach picks the guys who are best prepared. If you're not ready, it's YOUR responsibility and NOT the coach's!"

Mr. Lehman's demonstration that night was profound, and I would gradually come to understand his words completely in the years to come. Each time I looked at the Eastbay catalog we received that night with his and others' products, I heard his voice and saw his shooting demonstration in my mind. For the next month, I wondered if I had prepared enough to earn a roster spot on this year's basketball team. It was a speech that I could've used in the spring and leading up to that eventful summer of 1991. It had been a long, winding and perilous road and not an ideal one.

But I was there now and available to try out for the team, along with everyone else who had made the grades and had the desire to play varsity basketball at Hutch-Tech. What would be the outcome for me and all the other hopefuls and prospects at the old H-shaped building standing on the corner of South Elmwood Avenue and Chippewa Street? Who would make the 1991–92 Hutch-Tech boys' basketball team? Who would sit and watch in the stands? That remained to be seen.

Chapter 17. Sophomore Year Tryouts: Assembling the 1991–92 Engineers

"COACHES DON'T CUT PLAYERS. PLAYERS CUT PLAYERS!" **—George Lehman of the Eastbay Company, Newfane High School, October 1991**

"Coach Jones would like to announce tryouts for the 1991–92 Hutch-Tech boys' varsity basketball team. An informational meeting will be announced by Coach Jones soon." The announcement made me sit up straight at my desk the morning I heard it. It was mid-to-late October 1991, and the time had come. It was time for tryouts, and I would either get to don the maroon and gold, or I would get cut. Being a player in Coach Jones' basketball program would be the greatest achievement of my young life and thoughts of it gave me chills.

"I'll be posting an invite list shortly, Dunbar," Coach Jones said when I giddily approached him about the tryouts after hearing the announcements.

I'll be posting an invite list. What is an invite list? I had never heard of an invite list before. It seemed that you had to be *invited* to try out for the Hutch-Tech boys' basketball team, and you could not just come out. In hindsight, it was sort of a first cut, and if you were not invited, you did not have a chance of making the team from day one.

At the informational meeting in the auditorium or the gym, Coach Jones distributed multi-page packets to all invited prospects.[99] They included a cover page with quadruplicate images of a player dunking a basketball. The box-like graphics looked like something off an old Atari game system. Between the top two players, the cover page read, "HUTCH-TECH BASKETBALL 1991–92." Below the lower two players were the words, "BE A PART OF THE WINNING TRADITION!" In the center of the cover page, Coach Jones pasted a newspaper clipping with manually underlined words from the *Buffalo News*, which read:

Hoop happenings 10-29-91 (scribbled by hand)

"Defending Section VI champions Hutch-Tech and Williamsville South and the State Federation finalist Turner/Carroll are among the entrants for the sixth annual Al Pastor Memorial Basketball Tournament.

---

[99] (Jones, Hutch-Tech Boys' Basketball Team 1991-92 Tryout Informational Materials, 1991)

"All first-round games are at Buffalo State's Houston Gym. On Dec. 3, Grover Cleveland meets Williamsville South at 6 p.m. with Hutch-Tech battling Turner/ Carroll at 8 p.m. In the other bracket, Emerson plays Buffalo Arts Dec. 5 at 6 p.m., with South Park meeting Timon at 8 p.m.

"Hutch-Tech and Williamsville South could meet in their bracket final in a rematch of last year's overall Class B final, won by Tech. Turner/Carroll got to the state Class C final last March in Glens Falls before losing to unbeaten Watervliet of Section II. Tournament sponsors include the Pepsi-Cola Buffalo Bottling Corporation and the city Division of Youth."

Turner/Carroll was a Federation finalist? I remembered Hutch-Tech and Williamsville South matching up in the Class B sectionals, but I did not understand what *federation* finalists were. That said, reading the clipping gave me butterflies. There was more inside the packet. The 1991–92 schedule was on the second page. The opening game was in our gym against Turner/Carroll on November 27, the day before Thanksgiving. The next game was also against Turner/Carroll, but this time it was in the opening round of the Al Pastor Memorial Tournament described in the above-mentioned clipping. That would be followed up with a game against either Williamsville South or Grover Cleveland.

Next was the Hutch-Tech Tip-Off Tournament. It would take place at Seneca High School, followed by a game at Emerson High School on December 12. On December 20, there was the Festival of Lights Tournament at a school in Niagara Falls called LaSalle Senior High School. The rest of the games, which started in early 1992, were against other schools in Buffalo. The final game was on February 11 against Riverside High School in our gym.

There were more pages in the packet. One sheet read, "TO BE THE BEST YOU HAVE TO PLAY THE BEST!" It had the graphics of the same player dunking the basketball copied several times on the page. Another page had a copy of a varsity letter 'T'. On the upper part of the T it said 'Yale Cup' horizontally and then 'CHAMPS' spelled out vertically. Below that, on the lower part of the T was a basketball with 90 to the right and 91 to the left. On another page with the same four digital players, there were statements that read, "THE WILL TO WIN IS NOT ENOUGH," and below that, "IF YOU ARE NOT WILLING TO PREPARE TO WIN!"

An article was photocopied on the next page entitled, *The Joy of Victory is Why Sports Exist*, written by Jeff Riggenbach from *USA Today*. It discussed how the desire to win is what makes sports fun and what kids learn from competition. On the next page, Coach Jones typed, "ONE PERSON CAN MAKE THE DIFFERENCE AND EVERY PERSON SHOULD TRY!"

The final two pages were titled in all capital letters 'PICKING THE TEAM', which consisted of an exhaustive description of how Coach Jones would pick the team and the *ideal* makeup of the team. Coach Jone meticulously listed the attributes of the kinds of boys he was looking for and, finally, the kinds of boys he did *not* want. It was like a job description. His ideal makeup for a varsity team was five seniors, five juniors, and two sophomores, a number he was close to with his beloved 1990–91 team. The characteristics of the boys that Coach Jones thus looked for included:

- Academic soundness
- Those who are coachable
- Those who could concentrate
- Those who hustle
- Those with aggressiveness
- Those with loyalty

The list of characteristics of boys that Coach Jones avoided was interestingly longer and included:

- Troublemakers
- Those who know it all
- Those who always have excuses when they make mistakes
- Those who blame others for their mistakes
- Those who never get a chance because the coach will not let them
- Those who are only interested in themselves and not the welfare of the team
- Those who quit on themselves
- Those who are habitual hypochondriacs
- Those who are losers
- Those who are unable to get along with the other players or the coach on and off the court

A couple of things stood out to me about Coach Jones' criteria for the boys he looked for. He clearly stated that being on the team the previous year was not a guarantee for making the current roster. Also, tryouts were a game of war where the hungry ones made the team. Furthermore, making the team was simply the threshold, and each player had to continue to work. Finally, he rated loyalty highly. That is, he would keep a kid less talented kid who was loyal over a more talented kid he deemed not loyal. It wasn't *all* about talent, it seemed.

There was a section called 'Cutting the Squad', where Coach Jones outlined his thought process for not bringing players back. Lastly there was a final section titled,

'EVALUATION/ASSESSMENT SHEETS'. In that section, Coach Jones wrote, "Prospective player evaluation/assessment forms must be completed by their teachers and turned into Coach Jones prior to the first practice session!" Prospects finally needed physicals from their doctors.

The last quote on the bottom of that page stated, "IF YOU'RE GOING TO BE A CHAMPION, YOU MUST BE WILLING TO PAY A BIGGER PRICE THAN YOUR OPPONENT WILL EVER PAY!" And then finally, it explicitly stated that "AN INVITE LIST WILL BE POSTED," followed by "YOURS IN GOOD SPORTS," signed by Coach Jones.

* * *

My loss of focus towards the end of the summer of 1991 almost came back to bite me. I barely made the 70% requirement in some of my classes. Being academically ineligible for basketball tryouts for a second straight year would have been both devastating and embarrassing for me. In hindsight it would have been interesting to see how I would have done with my mind completely clear and focused.

There were about 30–40 players on the initial invite list, and Coach Jones had to whittle it down to his ideal team. Dion Frasier, Michael Mann, Christain Souter, Jermaine 'J-Bird' Skillon, Adonis Coble, Jason Paris aka 'J-Paris' and Juno Patterson were the seniors returning from the 1990-91 team. The two juniors were Jermaine Fuller and Andre Higgins. That was nine players already. Jamar Moore, Jason Hellerman, Carlton Ford, Jason Majchrowicz, Damon Kimbrew, and Roderick Peoples were on the junior varsity team the previous year and were trying out for the varsity team. They were all juniors. Finally, there was Terrance Collison from my class who also played with that group.

Players who were not on the team at all the previous year were juniors Keith Hearon and Dominique Gallon. Jason Wardlawer and Mike Saamol were two big and husky guys from my sophomore class who aspired to make the team, and finally, there was me. I remembered Jason Wardlawer from swimming class the previous year, but did not talk to him much. He was hard to miss at 6'5" and 250 or more pounds. He was a dark-skinned kid with a high-top fade. In classes and the hallways, he looked studious in his glasses, sweaters, and loafers, but was actually loud and cocky at times. He kind of bounced from side to side when he walked and was the only guy to alternate between shorts and the old-school gray sweatpants that year at tryouts.

There were a lot of other guys at tryouts, too, like Marwan Stamford from my brother's class of 1992. Adonis jokingly at times called him, "MARVIN!" Marwan was convinced that Coach Jones did not like him due to an incident in Health Class years earlier. Some guys from the football team tried out as well, including running back Rashan Tyler. There were a lot of other guys who I did not know at all.

* * *

Tryouts took place in the form of double sessions meaning that we gathered in our little old gym twice a day. In the mornings, Coach Jones started tryouts at 6:45 a.m. There we went for about an hour until about 7:45 a.m. After school, we started at 3:15 to 3:30 p.m. and went until between 5:30-6:00 p.m. It was very much like boot camp, and it was unlike anything I had done at Campus West under Mr. Cook or Mr. Rozlowski.

To get to Hutch-Tech for practice at 6:45 a.m., I had to get up around 5:20 a.m. to get on the 12-A Utica bus around 5:45 a.m. Mom bought me an alarm clock so that I could get up and leave on my own. It was an ovular-shaped white Westclox digital clock. It had red numbers and a black background. When it went off, it made a repeating high-pitched whining sound. Some nights I would roll over frequently, looking at the clock, trying to beat the noise.

The 12-A bus took me to Utica Rail Station, where I took the train down to Theater Place Station. Adonis Coble got on that exact same bus early on. He lived on Leonard Street, one of the next streets over from Hastings Avenue off Davidson Avenue, where my Uncle Tony also lived at that time. He usually had his headset on and sat in the back of the bus wearing his heavy winter coat, hat, and boots. He gave me an upwards nod of acknowledgment when he saw me, but that was all. We did not really have a rapport beyond his being in the same class as my brother and being on my intramural team.

Getting up that early in the morning was a pain in the ass, but it was also fun leaving the house while it was still dark outside. The residents of Buffalo slept or prepared for their day while we were on the move with other workers who were starting their morning shifts. There was a certain peacefulness during those early frigid Buffalo morning hours. Coach Jones must have been up even earlier every day than we were, as he was always there before us.

* * *

Tryouts took on the persona of the Ken Jones Basketball Camp. They were less like traditional tryouts, where the prospects scrimmaged while the coaches took notes and assessed their skill levels. Our tryouts were more like practices, and they were my first full-length sessions with Coach Jones. Television shows like *The White Shadow* and programs like *Michael Jordan's Playground* depicted the former. When I envisioned tryouts, I pictured guys fighting tooth and nail to prove that they deserved roster spots. The strong survived, and the weak had to come back the next year. Ours were not like that at all, so I never knew how I was doing.

"We don't have a lot of time to get ready for Turner/Carroll!" Coach Jones said this early and often with both some anxiety and urgency in his voice. Tryouts, whether morning or afternoon, never started with us going directly into drills and play. Instead, Coach Jones talked in his commanding and raspy voice, giving us anecdotes, stories, or jokes about when he was a player. He also talked about preparing for competition or something else altogether. He also did similar exercises to Coach Tony Alvaro's from camp, to gauge our levels of participation and interest, such as his arm crossing drill, where he wanted us to clap every time he crossed his arms. He looked to see if prospects were paying attention and were willing to submit to his coaching.

"If our opponents practice ten months out of the year, we must practice eleven!" Tryouts were full-on productions, and Coach Jones was the ringleader. While some of us were still in disbelief that we were in the gym at 6:45 a.m. going through drills and running around, Coach was wide awake and full of energy. He wore his signature polo shirt, short tight John Stockton-like shorts, his striped socks, his Converse sneakers with a whistle around his neck. He looked like a professor with his sharp chin, sharp nose and thinning hair on the top of his head. His practice/teaching voice was much different than his one-on-one voice. It was still raspy, but with more of a Dick Vitale-like command, power, enthusiasm, and a little more bass.

"We were ranked third in the state at one point last year for the Class B schools. THIRD! I couldn't believe we were ranked third," Coach said exuberantly and repeatedly about the 1990–91 team. After a few minutes of open shooting, he blew his whistle, gathered us together, and gave us some opening remarks just like at camp. He paced in front of us in his signature stride with a slight bounce, giving us our lesson for the day, and then, just like that, he initiated our activities.

All of us were basically dressed like we were in gym class with no apparel yet, designating that any of us were a part of a team of any kind. Because of this, there was an assortment of tank tops, tee shirts, and calf-length and ankle socks. Some guys wore knee braces or wristbands and sneaker brands of all kinds in our little box of a gym. Some guys wore mouthpieces.

To start things off, Coach led us through stretches and warmups. They involved everything from arm circles to toe touches, to sitting in Indian position, to the runner's stretch, to bridges, to finally the 'Spread Eagle'. During the toe touches, we would all reach down to one side, come back up, clap twice, extend our opposite arm upwards, and then reach down to the other side, all in unison. For the Spread Eagle, we laid on our backs, raised our legs up perpendicularly in the air, and spread them apart so we could stretch the muscles in our inner thighs. Some of the guys mimicked farting noises or made sexual jokes during the Spread

Eagle. Guys that come to mind are the class of 1993 like Dominique Gallon and Roderick Peoples.

After the stretches, Coach Jones held a basketball and led us through Foot Fires, the same drill that we regularly did at his camp. It was without question the signature drill of the camp. If he snapped the ball to the left, we immediately turned that way quickly and clapped, and then snapped back to face him, all the while with our feet moving quickly in a crouched defensive position. If he snapped it to the right, we would turn that way and do the same thing.

"We NEVER REST ON DEFENSE! If YOU MUST REST, YOU REST ON OFFENSE!" He would lower the ball, allowing us to rest briefly while giving us commentary about defense. "OHHHH," he would enthusiastically say as his eyes bulged with a "GOTCHA" look, quickly hoisting the ball back up in the air without warning as we all went back into our defensive positions with our feet moving.

"STEP SLIDE! STEP SLIDE! STEP SLIDE! On defense, you never cross your feet! If your man takes off running, you run with him!" He acted things out and demonstrated things for us with a childlike enthusiasm and youthfulness. There was a sense of urgency with everything he covered, but he was super excited about defense. He eventually transitioned us into the 'Gorilla Drill'. If he held the ball diagonally to the right or left, we would all defensively shuffle back in that direction in unison like gorillas. If he pulled the ball back toward himself, we would shuffle toward him. This was all taking place at 6:45 in the morning.

"On defense, you ANTICIPATE! On offense, you REACT!" Coach Jones hammered this home repeatedly. Defense was holy to him. We also did the 'Shadow Drill' where one player literally defensively shadowed another player up and down the long sideline of the court, sometimes with the ball and sometimes without. Another variation of this was the 'Zig-Zag Drill' where players ran the length of the court literally zigzagging. The defensive player practiced staying with his man while turning his body and adjusting his feet.

It was not all about defense. Sometimes Coach Jones would do dribbling drills with us, such as the Two Ball Dribbling Drill; once again from his camp. It involved dribbling the balls with both hands, practicing crossing the balls over side to side, and then back and forth. Sometimes he would have us dribble the two balls with gloves on our hands and goggles that were taped around the eyes, preventing us from looking down. Trying to control the balls with gloves was difficult because the natural adhesive provided by the moisture of our fingertips was gone. Dribbling with those accessories was hard, but if done often enough the drill, in theory, made you a much better ball handler with one ball during games.

"A GOOD STRONG PLAYER IS BETTER THAN A GOOD WEAK PLAYER!" Of the many sayings Coach Jones gave us, this one stayed in my mind. We did not have a nice modern gym and weight room at Hutch-Tech, or a formal strength/conditioning program with a dedicated strength coach. Coach Jones, however, saw tremendous value in his players eventually bulking up muscle-wise. It all suggested that there was a level of physicality to this *non-contact* sport. Pep Skillon and Chuck Thompson provided the muscle for the 1990–91 team. Curtis Brooks also provided a level of physicality from the point guard position. These attributes collectively paid huge dividends for the team and were a critical part of the run they put together.

In addition to strength training Coach Jones also saw the need for players to increase their foot speed, which is why he brought down a box of skip ropes along with the bins of basketballs, gloves, goggles and other accessories. I have vivid memories of players like Adonis Coble jumping rope like a prizefighter in practice during the skills portion of practice. I jumped rope at times, as well. I never would have associated many of the things Coach had us doing with basketball tryouts.

Coach Jones also had a whole host of shooting drills. The most basic of these drills was the Mikan Drill, named after the legendary Minneapolis Lakers center No. 99, George Mikan. Players stood next to the basket, launching off one foot and laying the ball up with the opposite hand using the backboard. The drill could also be done using a *hook* shot or a *reverse* layup underneath the basket. It was not a Michael Jordan-style reverse layup. It was more of an underneath scoop shot. I have vivid memories of learning the drill on our old solid white backboards.

"No, Anwar, you do it like this!" Jason Paris saw my unfamiliarity with the drill and showed me how to do the reverse layup properly. He could have seen me as competition for his roster spot and let me dangle, but instead he helped me. I was grateful for that and still am today. We also had jump shooting drills from the elbows of the key, roughly fifteen feet from the basket.

We continued practicing with *weave* drills, the 'Three-Man Weave', and the 'Five-Man Weave', which I did not know even existed. There was no dribbling involved, so the ball was not supposed to touch the floor. Each time you made a pass, you ran behind the man to whom you passed the ball. Eventually, the man closest to the basket took the layup.

"MAKE THE LAYUP!" Coach Jones reminded us sternly of the end goal of the exercise, while looking on during the weave drills. It was a drill about passing, precision and focus. It was also about making the basket and scoring at the end. Missing the layup gave you the feeling that you and your teammates ran for nothing and that you let them down if you were the one who missed the layup.

* * *

In addition to skills-related drills and exercises, we learned offensive and defensive team strategies; plays that Coach Jones started implementing. This part of the tryouts was more like practice or a clinic than the skills-related phase, as it involved some standing around, watching and learning, especially for the new players. It was probably a review for his returning players. The few times I saw the 1990–91 Engineers play, I watched as Coach Jones' teams ran structured plays on offense to complement his staunch man-to-man team defense. I was now experiencing this structure from both sides of the ball firsthand.

"ON OUT-OF-BOUNDS PLAYS UNDER THE OPPONENT'S BASKET, I WANT THE PLAYER GUARDING THE INBOUND PASSER TO PREVENT THE BACKDOOR PASS! AGAINST KENMORE EAST, WE WERE REPEATEDLY BURNED BY INBOUND PASSES UNDER THEIR BASKET FOR SCORES!" There was always a lot of anguish and pain when Coach Jones said this, and he was very adamant about cutting off passes under the basket of the offense. He would literally blow his whistle and physically move the player guarding the inbound player with the ball in position to prevent the same mistakes that were made with Kenmore East in the 1990–91 game in the Section VI Class B-1 finals last March.

"SEE THE MAN, SEE THE BALL!" Coach Jones' defensive philosophy was straightforward, and it was epitomized by this fundamental principle which he stressed to us hundreds of times. In the basketball school of Coach Ken Jones, man-to-man defense was holy, and no zone defenses were allowed. Playing *man-to-man* had its own distinct rules and nuances. "Make sure you talk to each other on defense and call out picks when defending in half-court situations," was one rule. Another was to, "See your man and see the ball," which meant that when the ball was on the other side of the court, you would play off your man a little bit to play 'help side' defense by sagging into the lane. When the ball came back to your side, you guarded your man more closely. Coach Jones taught this aspect with a lot of urgency. Again, he would regularly stop play and forcibly move players to demonstrate his point, along with providing explanations for why.

Coach Jones was immersed in the *science* of basketball. I had minimally been exposed to motion offenses under Mr. Cook at Campus West. Mr. Rozlowski may have taught us a few things aside from getting out of Ronald Jennings' way, flashing near the basket, and rebounding the ball. I did not remember more than that. This was my first time being exposed to the actual science of the game, and once I started learning it, it intrigued me. It was very different from just going up strong, and going strong to the hole, like the strategies that were emphasized on the playgrounds and in the recreational gyms of Buffalo.

"YOU HAVE TO GO WHERE YOU DON'T WANT TO GO TO GET TO WHERE YOU WANT TO GO!" Coach Jones had offensive sets for facing man-to-man and zone defenses. His main offensive set was called '5-Motion' or '5-M' for short. This involved the players passing, cutting to the basket, and moving without the ball. Players learned to dribble-drive the ball, to post up, to screen away for a teammate, or to screen the ball. It was imperative for us to understand the principles of playing fundamental team offensive basketball to properly execute these aspects and, initially, much of this went over my head. The quote about going where you do not want to go is meant to take your defender away from the ball and flash towards the ball again to get yourself open at times, but it was also a metaphor for life; something that occurred to many of us years later.

There was '5-MT Low', an offensive set that involved the use of a double low post on the left side. The point guard would pass the ball to a wing player who popped out from behind the post player. The wing player could shoot the ball, dump the ball into the post, or pass it to the man flashing in the lane who had been screened on the other side.

The team learned more plays called '14' and '14-M', both starting from '1-4' alignments. The set started with four players arranged in a straight line across the free-throw line, extended as the point guard advanced the ball into the halfcourt. Once the initial pass was made, some variation of the motion offense would start. Lastly, there was '5-Around Swing', a more complex motion offense that involved a series of intricate passes and cuts to the basket.

At that time, I knew a little bit about the differences between man-to-man and zone defenses. At Campus West, I observed that in man-to-man defenses, one player followed another player. In zone defenses, the players are set up in distinct alignments. Wherever the ball moved, the zone shifted. Gradually, I learned that zone defenses were designed to prevent dribble penetration. They were, however, vulnerable to smart and patient teams who could dribble-drive, pass the ball back out to the perimeter, and shoot the ball effectively from long range.

Coach Jones' zone offenses were '4-Z', '4-ZM', '5-Z', '5-ZM', and '5-Z High-Low'. 'Z' and 'M' in this context stood for *zone* and *motion*. Each set used some mixture of ball reversals, looking for open jump shots on the perimeter, looking for cutters/flashers or post players in the holes in the zones. Each used a mixture of alignments and formations. The latter, 5-Z High Low, involved the use of a high post player and a low post player. It was all very fascinating and new for me.

5-Z was a '1-2-2' formation where the two corners flashed in the paint when the ball swung to the opposite side. 5-ZM used a similar alignment, except every player flashed into openings in the zone while the others replaced them to keep the floor balanced. 4-Z and 4-ZM were '2-1-2' alignments with similar principles. 5-Z High-Low was a '1-3-1' formation. The point guard and the two wing players were the primary shooters. I noticed that offensive players were more stationary in these sets, and the ball moved amongst them more methodically. A major key to 5-Z High-Low, in particular, was the high and low post players working closely in sync to put pressure on the interior of the defense with timely passes to the low post. Capitalizing on mid- and long-range shots was also critical. All five players had to react to the zones they faced and look for openings to penetrate or shoot.

As if that was not enough, Coach Jones also had sets for inbounding the ball from underneath the basket. They were designed to quickly get the ball inbounds to score or set up his offenses. The name of each play was a multiple of 10 and was assigned numbers like '10', '20', '30', and '40'. Coach Jones had similar plays for inbounding the ball from the side of the court. His sets for breaking full-court defensive presses were also assigned similar numbers. These plays were set up in different formations throughout the full-court and were designed to quickly advance the ball from one end of the court to the other.

"No Anwar! Stand over there!" Jason Paris corrected me once again, pointing out where I was supposed to be when Coach Jones reviewed his full-court '40' set and alignment. I was on Jason's team at that time. We were the skins during that particular practice. He showed real leadership in that instance once again by pointing a novice like me in the right direction.

"I'm a true student of the game!" Coach Jones said these words to us often. While he knew more about basketball than most, he admitted that he did not know everything and was always open to learning more. That said, he came to tryouts prepared with a thick white binder of compiled plays, drills, notes and a plan for aspects he wanted to cover. It was a very detail-oriented and thorough approach to coaching—a very collegial approach to basketball that I had never seen before.

Tryouts ended with wind sprints and another drill where we would run around the old gym jumping up and touching the rims with two hands. After everything we had done for the previous two hours, I was wiped out. I had to remind myself that this is what it meant to be on the varsity team. I sucked wind, and my limbs both burned and felt like they were about to fall off, just like three years earlier at Campus West. My clothes were also drenched with sweat, something I think both me and my brother got from both our parents as athletic activity of any kind caused this to happen for all of us, something I didn't necessarily see happen to other people.

As the weeks progressed, Coach Jones slowly cut the list of players down from about 40 to 25. I wondered if I would be one of the prospects not asked to come back. During the scrimmaging, where each player's overall skill level was on display, I did not feel like I had done anything to separate myself from anyone else. I noted some of the more senior or newer guys who were shooting the ball with confidence and playing loose. Had I done enough to earn a spot on the team? The question cycled through my mind increasingly as time went on. I did not feel particularly confident that I had made a positive impact on whether I would be kept or not.

* * *

Around the time of tryouts, Mom discovered a program through the United Way where she worked, which she thought would be good for me to be involved in. It was called 'Youth Leadership of Western New York'. I had an inside track for getting into the program because I had met the director, Mary Quinn, several times when I visited Mom at work after school.

"It will be a good experience for you, and it'll be good for your *resume*!" Mom kept emphasizing the resume piece, trying to sell me on the program. I couldn't care less about a resume and had no idea why it was important at the time. I only cared about making the basketball team, and anything else was secondary. I did not want any part of the program, but Mom insisted that I apply for it. I likewise applied for it and got accepted.

Youth Leadership was a valuable program if for no other reason than for exposure. It put me in contact with kids from other backgrounds, particularly kids from the suburbs. At that time, suburbs like Amherst, Lancaster and Hamburg were different worlds, and those who lived in them might as well have been aliens. There were also kids from other Buffalo Public Schools, including Buffalo Traditional, Kensington High School, City Honors, and the Buffalo Academy of Science and Mathematics. While the bulk of students of color were from the Buffalo Public Schools, some of the girls of color were from suburban and private schools as well.

Like the Ken Jones Basketball Camp, I did not take full advantage of the program at the time. My natural inclination was to congregate with the kids who looked most like me. If I could do it all over again, I would get to know the kids from the suburbs better, most of whom were white. At the time all I could see was color and race and that they were different. I would name the suburban kids, but I just do not remember them.

I thought some of the suburban girls were cute, but I did not know how to interact with them or even if it was cool to do so. Talking to white girls was not popular in my circle. A petite blonde girl with freckles named Jill comes to mind. Some of the guys I remember were Dan and a guy named Gavin. I only remember Gavin because he went to the Gow School, a private school I had never heard of before.

That first weekend of the Youth Leadership Program involved us going away on a *retreat*. Forty of us piled onto a bus and drove out to a woodsy area on the outskirts of Buffalo. We stayed from Friday night to Sunday. My only experiences going away from home without family were a similar youth conference in Syracuse during my eighth-grade year at Campus West, and the Ken Jones Basketball Camp over the summer. This was different, because it was with other kids who were not like me, and it was to learn leadership skills. Gabe also was not with me, which was most unusual.

What were leadership skills anyway? For me, it was a nebulous concept. We had a lot of workshops on things like communication skills and team building. I was not socially developed and confident in myself, but I managed as best as I could. For a good part of the weekend, I was confused and tuned out, and my thoughts were back on tryouts.

Eboni Chelsea and Kidada Williams were both there from Hutch-Tech. They were in the class of 1993. That weekend I got some good basketball news from Kidada, who played for the girls' basketball team coached by Mr. Boyleston. She shared that Coach Jones had made some optimistic remarks about me making the boys' team. I was happy to hear that, but at the same time, I did not want to get my hopes up, only to be disappointed.

After that initial weekend, we met at locations around the city only once a month for the rest of the year. We learned about different topics, including how our city government worked, the importance of local businesses, and the roles of charities and nonprofit groups—all very important things to learn about for future leaders. None of it really made sense to my fifteen-year-old mind, nor did it seem relevant. I could only think about basketball, girls, and social acceptance from my peers.

* * *

As far as I could see, Jermaine 'J-Bird' Skillon and Jason Paris were earning their spots on the team. They seemed to be making plays and confidently scoring the ball, gleefully running up the court afterward during the scrimmages. That is what I saw.

Surprisingly, neither one of them were among the final 18 players Coach Jones kept. I was among the many who could not believe it. Coach Jones cut both of the seniors. It seemed to be a radical decision, but I also was not around the program long enough to know exactly why Coach Jones did what he did. There were rumors that he only kept J-Bird on the team in previous years to keep his older brother Jerrold 'Pep' Skillon happy, who was part of the nucleus of the 1990–91 team.

"J-Paris was slipping," Andre Higgins casually said in a group of us one day. I was not sure what he meant and kept quiet. J-Paris' getting cut may have been a good thing for Andre, as they likely would have competed for one of the starting guard positions. The news must have been devastating for both seniors. They were on the team the previous year, which had experienced so much success, and they were probably ready to solidify their legacies.

"Anwar, why did Coach Jones cut Jason Paris?" Tomi Lyons, the half Asian and African American beauty from my class, asked me about what happened on a bus ride home on the 17-Kensington bus one day. It was a very big deal not just on the court, but off the court, and in the hallways of our school. J-Bird and J-

Paris were popular guys not only in their class of 1992, but also in the lower classes, including mine.

"I don't know," I replied to her. I thought about echoing what Andre Higgins said, but decided against it so that there would not be any repercussions for me. I was just trying to make the team myself and had no knowledge of the backstories involving Coach Jones and his players from previous years.

* * *

On most TV shows, at the end of tryouts, all the players were usually made to stand in a line while the coach called out names. The players whose names were not called were usually thanked and then asked to leave. In other depictions, lists were posted. Students walked up and looked for their names. If their name was there, they knew that they had made the team, but if not, then they knew that they did not make the team. This was not how it went for us at Hutch-Tech in the late fall of 1991.

After one of those final tryouts, Coach Jones had all of us sit on the bleachers on the eastern side of the gym. It was still a large group, much larger than his ideal makeup of a team, which was five seniors, five juniors, and two sophomores—something I thought was set in stone. I thought he was going to read the names of the players to be kept like on TV.

"I'm going to *keep* all of you, but I will not be able to *play* all of you," he said to us in a subdued tone. It was his grandfatherly voice. "You will all participate in the varsity practices, while some of you are also going to practice and play on the junior varsity team." It was very anticlimactic. Once he finished speaking and the guys slowly dispersed, I approached him for clarification. I was not convinced that I had made the team. With some irritation, he reiterated his announcement saying, "I am going to *keep* all of you, but I won't necessarily be able to *play* all of you!"

Oh, ok, so I did make the varsity squad, well, sort of. But I am on the junior varsity team as well. I pondered what had just happened to me. After a long and winding road, I had achieved my goal. It was not what I thought it would be in terms of excitement. It may not have been what any of us thought it would be.

The initial roster for the 1991–92 Hutch-Tech boys' varsity basketball team consisted of five seniors, ten juniors, and three sophomores. It was a much larger team than Coach Jones' ideal makeup for a team. Something compelled him to keep eighteen players. I did not know his reasoning and probably did not care at the time. All I know is that I was a part of the final group. The initial roster for the 1991-92 Hutch-Tech boys' basketball team is listed in the following table.

The Initial 1991–92 Hutch-Tech Boys' Basketball Team Roster[100]		
Seniors	**Juniors**	**Sophomores**
• No. 23 Adonis Coble, 6' • No. 24 Dion Frasier, 6'1" • No. 12 Michael Mann, 5'8" • No. 13 Juno Patterson, 5'9" • No. 44 Christain Souter, 6'2"	• No. 35 Carlton Ford, 5'7" • No. 30 Jermaine Fuller, 6'3" • No. 43 Dominique Gallon, 5'9" • No. 34/50 Keith Hearon, 6'5" • No. 32 Jason Hellerman, 6'2" • No. 15 Andre Higgins, 5'8" • No. 42 Damon Kimbrew, 6' • No. 21 Jason Majchrowicz, 5'9" • No. 14 Jamar Moore, 5'11" • No. 22 Roderick Peoples, 6'	• No. 52 Anwar Dunbar, 6'2" • No. 11 Terrance Collison, 6' • No. 55 Jason Wardlawer, 6'5"
• The Team Managers- Monica Peterson, Turhan Wilbur, Jonathan Koval, Taraji Mogul, Eboni Chelsea, Leroy Copeland		

It is worth noting that while they did not compete for their positions, the team managers seemed to be crucial to this program that Coach Jones had built. They kept the statistics during the games and scrimmages and carried our basketballs to and from practice and the games. They pretty much did anything else Coach Jones asked them to do, and then even got swept up in the humor and chaos of some of our players. They were very much a part of the team.

"It is a long season, and all of our emotions will be tested during the three-to-four-month journey that lies ahead of us." Coach Jones prophetically said this to us early on and then several times throughout the 1991–92 season. His words could not have been more accurate about the adventure that awaited us.

---

[100] (Jones, The 1991-92 Hutch-Tech Boys' Basketball Varsity Team Roster, 1991)

Chapter 18. The 1991–92 Engineers: A Brotherhood and a Family

"Whoever that other team is, they aren't from around here playing like that!"
—A Random Onlooker, Niagara Falls Senior High School, November 1991

The 1991–92 Hutch-Tech boys' basketball team had large shoes to fill in trying to reproduce the accomplishments of the 1990–91 team. Curtis Brooks and company embarked on a seventeen-game winning streak, winning both the 1991 Yale Cup and Section VI Class B Championships. They went all the way to the Far West Regional with a chance to advance to the Final Four in Glens Falls, but lost to a team called Newark from the Rochester area.

At one point the Engineers were ranked third in the state for the Class B schools. The 1990–91 Engineers were powered by Curtis Brooks, Pep Skillon, Chuck Thompson, and the hardworking cast of players that complemented them. The seniors on the team were starters for most of their high school basketball careers, and they were *seasoned* by their final year. The 1991–92 team had players stepping into the starting lineup for the first time and a host of new players who had never played varsity basketball before.

* * *

Coach Jones named Dion Frasier, Michael Mann, and Chris Souter as our team captains. They were the *deans* of the team. They had been with Coach Jones since their freshmen year in 1988-89. They entered the program in its infancy when it was not very good, and they were a part of its ascension over the previous three-year period.

At 5'8", Michael was going to be our starting point guard and the leader of the team. Though small in stature, he had angry eyes and a lion's voice. It shook you when he yelled or raised it. At 6'2", Chris was partially of Polish descent and had what I will call a Mediterranean olive-colored complexion with short black hair. He was one of the three white players on the team. Unlike the other black players on the team, the 6'1" Dion Frasier wore his hair close cut, not the customary high-top fade. He had full lips and ears that stuck out a little bit. All his features complemented his comedic persona.

Appearance-wise all three of the captains looked preppy. Visually, nothing said that they were spectacular basketball players. They were not particularly tall. They were not physically imposing. It was their participation in the 1990-91 winning team that made you sit up and take notice of their presence.

Adonis Coble and Juno Patterson were the other two seniors who had been on the junior varsity team two years before joining the varsity team when they were juniors. Adonis was a wiry 6' and had a nice jump shot. His release looked sort of like Bill Cartwright's with the Chicago Bulls, by the way he held the ball over his head; only it was smoother and less awkward. He had a slender frame and a high-pitched voice. While comical, he could have both an angry disposition and short patience sometimes. At 5'9", Juno Patterson had a Native American appearance and resembled an owl. He was quiet and didn't say much.

At 5'8", Andre Higgins was a returning junior guard. He was a dark-skinned kid with bowed legs, a mischievous look and a high-pitched squeaky voice. Jermaine Fuller was also slender standing at 6'3". He was light-skinned and a returning frontcourt player from the junior class. His voice was deep and sounded like Rocky Balboa or, should I say, actor Sylvester Stallone. At 6'5", I imagined the slim and innocent-looking Keith Hearon would get on the court at some point.

According to legend, the studious-looking Jamar Moore was moved up to the 1990–91 team the previous year and experienced the entire postseason ride. Coach Jones held the soft-spoken 5'11" junior in high regard. The 5'7" Carlton Ford, 5'9" Dominique Gallon, 6' Damon Kimbrew, 6'2" Jason Hellerman, 5'9" Jason 'Magic' Majchrowizc and 6' Roderick 'Spanky' Peoples, were the other juniors on the team.

Magic Majchrowizc and Jason Hellerman were the other two white kids on the team that year. Both were preppy, soft-spoken, and well-mannered. Magic had short brown hair and could have been from any suburban school. Jason Hellerman stood 6'2" tall. He had short curly brown hair and what I will call a middle-American look. He had large rock-solid calves, and a cannon-like jump shot. It resembled a shot put from track and field.

From the beginning, the 1991–92 team felt like a family. The seniors were the responsible, trustworthy older brothers. They joked, but did not poke at anyone maliciously. The juniors, who were the largest constituency of the team, were split into two groups according to their personalities. Keith Hearon, Carlton Ford, Damon Kimbrough, Jamar Moore, Jason Hellerman and Jason Majchrowizc were all the responsible 'Peter Brady-types'.

Andre Higgins, Jermaine Fuller, Roderick Peoples, and Dominique Gallon all fit into the 'Wayne Arnold-Eddie Haskell' mold. They loved mischief and did things like smack you on the back of the head, among others. They liked pranks like pulling down your shorts, a trick Andre loved doing with me. They were bright guys, as evidenced by their grades. Curiously, one of the riddles of Hutch-Tech was that there was no direct relationship between intelligence, character, and behavior.

"It smells like someone stepped on a frog," Coach Jones mumbled in his grandfatherly voice when a peculiar and unpleasant smell emerged when groups of us were huddled in practice. It was because one of the above-mentioned juniors farted and passed gas.

The three sophomores on the team were considered the little brothers. There was Terrance Collison, Jason Wardlawer and me. I believe Coach Jones kept the three of us on the team based on our collective potential. We were not the most skilled players in our class by any means. Jason Wardlawer was a dark-skinned youth with the most potential at 6'5" and weighed roughly 250 pounds. Terrance was 6'1", lean and quick. He could jump high, and he was highly effective close to the basket. If he developed his ball handling skills and outside shooting, he could have easily turned into a stellar guard. I was about 6'2" and 180–190 pounds. I was very raw skill-wise. All three of us were *projects.*

"We are the future of Hutch-Tech basketball," Terrance Collison said one day after practice. The three of us gathered at the top of the stairwell near the visitors' locker room. It was all so clear. The three of us would be part of the future of the Hutch-Tech boys' basketball team, and these were my new brothers. We put our hands in the center and did a little shout before going to the locker room. Our time would come, and we would ride off into the sunset just like Curtis Brooks and his classmates.

"You guys get changed and ready to head home," Coach Jones said, breaking up our little post-practice sophomore huddle that day.

I felt a kinship with Terrance Collison. He was my closest brother on the team. We were from the same class and had similar temperaments. He was brown-complexioned and easygoing, and he was socially confident and suave, while I was shy and timid. I noticed that Andre Higgins associated mostly with Jermaine Fuller, while Adonis Coble was very close with Roderick Peoples. There were similar friendships and alliances within our roster. None of this hurt the 1991–92 team, because of the nucleus of the team. Michael Mann, Chris Souter, and Dion Frasier provided cohesion to the team. Something you could not see, but could feel.

"SCOOBY DOOBY DOOOO!" Dion Frasier yelled out, "SCOOBY-DOO," from the famous cartoon dog, as two other players and I ran the Three-Man Weave Drill at practice. As with any family, there was quite a bit of healthy picking and playing around with one another. For some reason, I reminded him of the famous talking cartoon canine Scooby-Doo. After that practice, 'Scooby' became my nickname. I did not like it at first, but later I did not mind it.

"SHAGGY, SHAGGY, SHAGGY," Andre Higgins said repeatedly one day in his Scooby-Doo voice, looking at me and then at Jonathan Koval, who just looked at him and shook his head. They eventually roped in our manager Jonathan Koval, who wore glasses, had brown bushy hair, and somewhat of a grungy, hippie appearance. It was either Andre or Dion who decided that he looked like Scooby-Doo's best friend in the gang, Shaggy.

"GRAPE APE! GRAPE APE! GRAPE APE!" Just as I was Scooby-Doo, Dion Frasier nicknamed Jason Wardlawer the 'Grape Ape', after the giant purple cartoon ape. Dion deepened his voice to an obnoxious grunt when he said it. Sometimes he walked down the hall like a gorilla, hunched over with his arms hanging when passing Jason. It probably embarrassed Jason, but again it was done playfully. It was fun watching someone else get it. Jason actually had two nicknames. The second was perhaps funnier than the first, 'Big Shirley' from the TV show *What's Happening?* Michael Mann loved the Big Shirley reference as well.

Some of those guys made fun of Jamar Moore, calling him 'JAZZ-MAR'. Jamar was soft-spoken and quiet, which I think made some of the more talkative guys want to take shots at him even more. Jamar simply responded by shrugging his shoulders, smiling it off, and mumbling something at a low decibel level such as "Whatever," or "There's only one Jamar!"

On several occasions Dion Frasier said that Carlton Ford, a short dark-skinned kid, looked like the Buffalo Bills' cornerback No. 37, Nate Odoms, whom he did resemble. Damon Kimbrew was a lean, light-skinned kid who wore glasses and was very soft-spoken, and seemingly unassuming. He associated mostly with Carlton. Dominique Gallon wore glasses and looked a little preppy, but not nerdy. He was a kidder, just like Andre, Jermaine, and Roderick. He wore a forward slope haircut like a rapper.

"There is only one Jamar!" The day Jamar uttered those words, all of us were in the gym in our street clothes participating in the drill, 'Shoot Til You Make, Shoot Til You Miss'. It was one of my favorite drills. It might have been before a game or a team walkthrough where Coach Jones left all of us alone in the gym. Each player got his turn at the free throw line to try to put together the longest streak of free throws possible. Once he missed, another player got a chance to shoot. Each time there was a make, everyone clapped twice, and when there was a miss, everyone clapped once. Everyone laughed and had a good time with plenty of joking.

When it was my turn, I strung together thirty to forty makes before finally missing. I tried using the same motion each time, dribbling the ball twice with my knees slightly bent and my eyes focused on the basket. I spun the ball backward to put my fingers on the seams, just like Michael Jordan. I 'put my fingers in the basket' on each release, in terms of my shooting mechanics, giving the ball a nice trajectory towards the hoop. I could not believe that I kept making them. Some shots went straight through the net for me and made that snapping/popping sound which was augmented due to the acoustics of our gym. Others hit the rim and then bounced or rolled around into the hoop for me. There was something special about seeing the ball go through the hoop. My teammates trash talked and joked during the drill to try to break my concentration, but it was all in fun. My missed free throw was not a bad miss. It hit the rim, bounced, and rattled around a little bit before finally rolling out slowly and dropping onto the court. I was animated like a child at the free throw line watching it, and I laughed when it rolled out.

Jamar put together the longest streak that day making fifty or sixty or more, all while the guys joked and tried to distract him, yelling out, "JAZZ-MAR!" Jamar remained cool as a cucumber and focused until he finally missed. What I remember most about that day was the sense of camaraderie. There was joking and poking at one another, but all in the spirit of brotherhood.

The seniors took us under their wings for the most part and used more of a mentoring approach, while the juniors, particularly Andre Higgins and Jermaine Fuller, treated us with tough love. They frequently picked on Terrance about one thing or another, especially Jermaine Fuller. Whenever they tried getting under my skin, I tried ignoring them. Jason Wardlawer indulged Andre in his shoving matches and impromptu fistfights. He fought back, something I think Andre both admired and respected.

* * *

"Hey, Anwar, let me tell you something. Do not skip Gym class! Being on the boys' basketball team, the coaches are going to be watching you and if you do not take gym class, Coach Boyleston will tell Coach Jones and you'll get in trouble," Adonis Coble said in a soft brotherly tone to me shortly after the 1991–92 roster was set. After our practice that morning and with another one in the afternoon, I was going to come up with an excuse not to take gym class that day, that was until Adonis' stern warning.

I was always the type of kid to heed warnings and so I quickly ran upstairs and got my practice jersey and shorts out of my locker and changed up for gym class. Adonis was in my gym class that year. He wore his practice shirt during class, and I followed his example. I was always grateful to him for looking out for me that day. He could have just sat back and let me get in trouble, but he did not.

"♫WHY DO *NIGGAS* ALWAYS GOT TO SHOW THEIR TEETH?♫" On another day Adonis greeted me aggressively in his high-pitched voice with a lyric from Ice Cube's *Be True To The Game*. With the team now set, we used the football team's locker room. It was an old, dark and cramped space with very old rusting lockers and benches on both sides. I didn't know how all the football players fit in there at the same time. It sat behind the bulletin board near the stairwell.

I walked into the locker room laughing loudly after clowning around with someone in the hallway. Adonis was in the locker room before practice, talking with Juno Patterson or Roderick Peoples. My smile slowly disappeared from my face, not knowing if I was being scolded for something or if a conflict was imminent. I noticed that Adonis was partially smirking, and I realized he was joking. It was like the famous funny guy scene from the movie *Goodfellas*. I proceeded to get ready for practice and remembered to keep my voice low afterward, and he turned back to his discussion.

* * *

There was no more practicing in shirts and skins now that the team was set. Coach Jones passed out cotton reversible practice jerseys, the outside being maroon and the inside gray. The upperclassmen got the first pick of the shirts and they took the ones that had numbers on the inside. The rest of us were stuck with shirts that only had numbers on the maroon side. Coach Jones washed the shirts for us every night. After practice we would throw them in a pile in his office by the door. He brought them back for us the next morning smelling like fabric softener. Roderick Peoples obnoxiously vowed not to wash his shirt until he scored in a game. Or was it 10 points or more in a game? I cannot remember which, but for a while, his practice jersey stunk, and he didn't mind wearing it daily.

The seniors and most of the juniors no longer had to attend the morning practices, except for the team free throw shooting competitions. The Intra-Squad Free Throw Shooting Competitions were documented in the *Buffalo News* the previous year when the 1990–91 team made its run. Coach Jones organized it so that the varsity players would be paired up in rotating matchups each morning to see who could shoot the best percentages.

"MAKE THEM! CONCENTRATE! FOCUS! GAMES ARE WON AND LOST ON THE FREE THROW LINE!" Coach Jones said this while walking around the gym as we shot free throws. On any given morning, I would be paired with Adonis Coble, Andre Higgins, Jermaine Fuller, Jason Hellerman or one of my other teammates. After every competition, Coach Jones asked who won and then logged the percentages and results into his thick white binder.

Afternoon practices were like tryouts. Before Mr. Boyleston assembled the girls' team, we had the big gym for the entire afternoon. We started with stretches, followed by Foot Fires and the Gorilla Drill. Then we did individual defensive drills, followed by individual offensive skills drills, followed by team offensive drills such as the Three- and Five-Man Weaves and the 'Truck and Trailer Drill'. Then we took a water break and came back to go over offensive and defensive sets and scrimmage. The scrimmages weren't free-flowing, as Coach Jones regularly stopped the play to correct or teach us something.

Practice ended with some form of conditioning, usually running and touching the quarter court, half-court, three-quarter court and full-court lines; then running back to where we started. Andre Higgins, Michael Mann, and Terrance Collison always finished first, while guys like me and Jason Wardlawer always brought up the rear. On some days Coach Jones had us run around the gym, jumping up to touch the rims with our fingertips which was exhausting. My practice jersey was usually drenched with sweat afterward, and both my lungs and my muscles were exhausted, especially early in the season. We also ran the stairs in some instances in the steep stairways of the school.

On days when we shared the facilities with the girls' team, we started our practices in the small gym. We did stretches and what individual drills we could in that space, in addition to some half-court offensive sets. There were certain parts of that gym where you could not shoot the ball too high because the ceiling was uneven. When it became hot in there, Coach Jones opened the screen using a long stick and slid the windows up to let the cool winter air.

As the weeks went on, Coach Jones added to his offensive and defensive game plans. Defensively, he implemented full-court presses, sets which extended our team defense full-court with the goal of pressuring the opposition's ball handlers into turnovers to create easy transition baskets for our team. Once again, they were named after numbers. '100' or '75' meant that we would apply pressure to 100% or 75% of the court immediately after our opponents inbounded the ball. 'Fifty' meant that we would apply pressure around half-court.

Coach Jones also worked in our pregame warm up routine. It involved the team splitting into two equal lines on the same baseline on opposite sides of the gym. Each line had a primary ball handler at the front. On cue the primary ball handlers each led their lines out and around the perimeter of the court. When the lines passed each other, it was optional for some of the players to slap their hands. After two laps, the primary ball handlers converged onto one basket and then lobbed the ball off the backboard. Each successive player jumped up, tapped the ball off the backboard, and ran to the back of the line to do it again. After two cycles, the last man banked the ball off the backboard to make the layup.

Next, we did a few cycles of the 'Seven Pass Drill'. This drill involved three players on each side. Player No. 1 stood just outside of the top of the key and threw a two-handed over-the-head pass to player No. 2, who flashed out from the baseline to the wing. After throwing the ball, player No. 1, at the top of the key, ran to player No. 2, took a 'handoff' pass, and then dribbled to the corner and did a 'jump-stop'. He pivoted towards player No. 2, who had cut towards the low block. Player No. 1 then passed the ball to player No. 2, who would pivot and pass the ball to player No. 3, who stood at the elbow of the top of the key. Player No. 3 passed the ball to player No. 1 on the wing while player No. 2 ran up, out, and around player No. 3, rubbed off him, and then cut towards the basket as player No. 1 passed him the ball for a layup in stride. Player No. 3 followed player No. 2. In the next round, player No. 2 started as player No. 3 at the elbow of the top of the key, and player No. 1 started as player No. 2 as the flashing wing player, while player No. 1 was the next person in line to start the drill. If this all sounds a little complicated, it was, especially for a kid just learning organized basketball.

"YOU'RE PREPARING TO GO FULL SPEED!" Coach Jones shouted this repeatedly, emphasizing that the warmup routine was for a purpose and was to be taken seriously. We were not to just go through the motions. We were preparing for the competition.

Next we did a modified version of the Three-Man Weave, where we touched the three-point lines between passes. Afterwards we did some layups, followed by shooting drills from the elbows, followed by open shooting. Before the actual games started, our captains would assemble at half-court with the referees to discuss the rules with our opponent's captains.

We ended practice every day between 5:30 and 6 p.m. We filed out of the school into the cold Buffalo early evenings, going our separate ways home using the Metrobus and Metrorail systems. Terrance and I lived on the same side of town, so we walked down Chippewa Street together to the metro rail where we rode to either Utica Station or South Campus Station. Once there we boarded either the #12, #13, or #19 bus. Not having the razor-sharp focus academically yet, my evenings consisted of doing homework and studying, watching TV for a little while and maybe talking on the phone. Bedtime was 10-11:00 p.m., and I was back up at 5:20 a.m. the next morning to do the whole thing all over again.

* * *

"That's why you don't have any hair on the top of your head!" Someone who was not officially a part of our program, but who was a fixture in and around it was our custodian, Kordell. I don't know Kordell's last name, but he was a black man, maybe in his 30s or 40s. He had a beard and a small afro and usually wore a dark tee-shirt and jeans. He wore sweatshirts in the summer months. I think Coach Jones interacted with him regularly for access to the gym early in the morning and on weekends. They jokingly cracked on each other in front of us at times, and it seemed to be a bit of a well-rehearsed comedy routine. It amused all of us. Kordell usually passed through the gym with his push broom, and their exchanges typically intermittently lasted for minutes at time.

* * *

With the Turner/Carroll game approaching, Coach Jones scheduled a scrimmage at Lancaster Senior High School. Scrimmages were informal practices between two or more teams where actual game conditions were simulated. They were almost rehearsals with timed periods, referees, and the keeping of statistics. Coaches got a feel for their player rotations, how their teams jelled offensively and defensively, and what needed more work before the first game.

This particular scrimmage was on a Saturday morning in early or mid-November. We all met at Hutch-Tech and piled onto a yellow 'cheese' bus. My family have driven through Lancaster often times during my youth to go to picnics, but I did not know anyone there. It was visibly different than inner-city Buffalo. It was green, peaceful and suburban. I was impressed by the facilities at Lancaster Senior High School. The school itself was a mini-campus, and the athletic facilities were as different as night and day compared to Hutch-Tech. They had two or three regulation-sized basketball courts as opposed to our undersized main gym and the half gym, which we shared with the girls' team. It was literally like two different worlds.

Coach Jones put together a junior varsity roster. In addition to the varsity team, those team members who played on the junior varsity team were brought along to scrimmage against the Lancaster junior varsity team. Since we were not going to get playing time with the varsity team that day, Terrance Collison, Jason Wardlawer and myself all played with the junior varsity team.

Based on the teams fielded, it was an inner-city basketball team versus a suburban team. Aside from Jason Majchrowicz, our team was all black, and the Lancaster team was mostly white. They wore distinct practice shirts while we wore inexpensive gold mesh shirts with maroon numbers with no other writing on them.

Because he was still injured from the football season, Dion Frasier was not ready to scrimmage with the varsity team. Instead, he coached us that day. He wore a sweatshirt, jeans and boots. Because he was one of my teammates, I had a hard time conceptualizing that he was now our coach for the day and not Coach Jones himself.

One thing I will never forget is Dion drawing up an offensive play for us to run called 'Techtonian'. It was a simple pass-and-screen-away type of concept, a simple motion set. My basketball IQ was still in its infancy, and I did not understand how to play in a formal offensive set. On one play I was on the low block, or the wing, and someone threw me the ball. When I caught the ball, I immediately turned to make a move towards the basket. In the next instant, I was either smothered by our opponents, or the ball went off my foot. Dion expected the ball to go to the other side of the court at least once. He immediately comically threw his hands up in the air in disbelief. I saw him do it and knew that I had messed up. Because I had played mostly street basketball, I still had not fully grasped the concept of patiently reversing the ball to the other side of the court to get a better shot for our team.

Aside from the Ken Jones Basketball Camp, that scrimmage was one of the first times I had played with set offenses and defenses, referees, clocks, fouls, etc. Playing organized basketball was so much different than playing pickup basketball at the playground or the YMCA. Then there was conditioning. The gym at Hutch-Tech was only a fraction of the size of the Lancaster gyms, and I got *winded* running up and down the regulation-size court. In organized basketball, in a program like ours, you were expected to play on both sides of the floor. Even the ball felt different than what I was used to. It felt harder and lighter, like a rock.

Terrance had a good scrimmage and got to the free-throw line regularly. He instinctively knew to go for layups and draw contact from defenders. He played on the junior varsity team the previous year and knew what to expect. I looked on with envy, and I rooted for him as well. As the quarters went on, Dion put some of the freshmen into the scrimmage.

Once our scrimmage was over, we went to the main gym to watch the varsity teams play. Our varsity team wore their reversible maroon practice tops, while Lancaster wore their red and white practice shirts. As we approached the gym, we could hear the ball hitting the floor, and the echo of the whistles and the buzzer. We could also hear a coach aggressively working the sidelines. He was in the game just as much as the players on the basketball court.

"BALL! BALL! BALL!" A loud, gritty, and raspy voice yelled out commands to its players. You could also say it made *demands* of its players. Sure enough, Coach Jones angrily patrolled the sidelines, fists balled up, yelling at the top of his lungs, and sometimes spitting as he directed his team. This was his game sideline persona which was much different than his practice persona. It was the Coach Jones I saw at the Grover Cleveland game earlier that year. This day he wore a sweatshirt, jeans, and boots.

Like the previous year, "BALL" meant to rebound the ball or dive on the floor for loose balls—*fight* for the ball and come up with the damn thing. Part of the fun of playing on our team was watching Coach Jones get animated, yell, and work the sidelines. It often seemed he was right there in the game with the players because he would work up his own sweat.

For the 1991–92 team, one of the things he looked to see was who would rebound the ball. The previous year, Pep Skillon and Chuck Thompson reliably 'cleaned the boards'. They led Hutch-Tech in rebounding, and it was a major part of the 1990–91 team's success. But who would do it this year? Chris Souter would be able to do some of the rebounding, but Coach Jones also looked to see if Jermaine Fuller, who was a wiry 6'3", would also answer the call.

"OH MY GOD, JERMAINE!" Coach Jones whined and was beside himself on the sidelines. Jermaine had gotten beaten on a rebound on one specific play. I think he showed minimal effort in terms of going for an offensive rebound. Again, Coach Jones expected his players to fight for every ball. The only reason I remember this specific outburst by Coach is that he had the scrimmage videotaped, and I watched it several times afterward. Whoever taped that scrimmage also caught my profile and my Gumby haircut in the stands looking on. It turned out that one of the managers' other very important duties was videotaping the team's games and scrimmages. This allowed Coach Jones to review game footage and, in some instances, scrutinize every basket, foul, play execution, rebound and turnover to ultimately try to get the most out of his team. He allowed us to take his VHS tapes home sometimes so that we could watch them. We had to bring them back, of course.

"OUT! OUT! OUT!" On another sequence, Coach Jones yelled at Michael Mann who advanced the ball in transition and tried to get an easy score. He thought that he had a numbers advantage, and he did, but it was only slight. Michael drove to the basket and tried to make an underhanded and fancy no-look pass to Adonis to his left on the baseline. It could have worked, but it went out of bounds off Adonis' fingertips. A Lancaster defender could possibly have slipped his hand in there. Regardless, Adonis flailed his arms in the air in frustration and then whirled around with a grimace on his face, immediately removing his mouthpiece.

"MICHAAAAEL, OUT!" Coach Jones walked over to Michael on the court, drilling in the message for what seemed like the hundredth time emphasizing it with his whole body before quickly turning and walking back to the bench. Coach Jones' words sounded like a child's words with a certain whiny emphasis. He was essentially saying, "Michael, you know better! Do what I tell you! Pull the ball back out and set up the halfcourt offense."

Michael nodded slowly, walking back up the floor with his head down and his hands at his sides, sucking wind as if to say, "Yes, Coach, I'm sorry. Next time I'll pull the ball back out." Coach Jones seemed to be very structured in terms of our team's offense, and it was critical to try to get a *good* shot for the team. Another piece to this was that our leader had not participated in a fall sport and was playing his way into shape, something players like Adonis and Chris were not doing because they took part in cross country and football.

Later on Coach Jones wanted to see what some of the new players could do. Both Dominique Gallon and Keith Hearon made a great play in one instance. Dominique put on a dribbling display, putting the ball through his legs multiple times before penetrating the lane and dishing a no-look pass to Keith Hearon for a layup and an *and one*. Some of our guys were impressed with the pass and yelled, "OOOOOH," as Keith strutted confidently to the free throw line, high-fiving the other guys and then sinking the foul shot.

"We can't afford to run up and down the court with some of these teams we'll play! We don't have that kind of team this year! Some of them will have guys who can really jump up and 'unscrew the light bulbs!'" Coach Jones repeatedly told us these things early on and throughout that season. In his first statement, he meant that the 91–92 team would have to play its games in a smart way to have a chance to win them consistently, especially against more athletic teams.

The 'unscrewing the light bulbs' analogy meant that our team was not athletic enough to play undisciplined basketball like the more athletically gifted teams. I did not understand all the Xs and Os yet, but I understood this part. I think the other guys did too. Consistently executing and trusting the game plan, and sticking to our principles and strategies in game situations was going to be the hard part.

* * *

Coach Jones scheduled a second scrimmage game closer to our season opener. I think it was the week before the Turner/Carroll game. This one was at Niagara Falls Senior High School in Niagara Falls, NY. Niagara Falls handed the 1990–91 Engineers two of their three losses. One was in the Hutch-Tech Tip-Off Tournament, and the other was in the Festival of Lights Tournament. Niagara Falls Senior High School was located in a residential neighborhood in the City of Niagara Falls, not far from the falls and the Canadian border.

Unlike the Lancaster scrimmage, which was on a Saturday morning, this scrimmage was on a weeknight after school, and only the varsity team made the trip. We left somewhere between 4 and 5 p.m. after piling onto another cheese bus and headed north on I-190. Unlike Lancaster, which looked more like a suburban campus, Niagara Falls Senior High School was an older structure, just like some of the high schools in Buffalo. Their gym was bigger than ours, but it also looked antiquated and like a factory, with numerous pipes protruding from the walls and the ceiling. To its credit, it had glass backboards with breakaway rims.

We started off the scrimmage by doing our pregame warm up routine for twenty minutes as the game clock ran. Coach Jones started Michael Mann and Andre Higgins at the guard positions. The starting forwards were Adonis Coble and Chris Souter. Jermaine Fuller started at center. Niagara Falls started a tall 6'7" white kid with a beard and closely cut hair. They also started a smooth 6'3" shooting guard and a very quick point guard, both of which were black. These are the players that stood out to me the most. Their coach was a middle-aged studious-looking white man who was balding on the top of his head with brown hair on the sides.

The scrimmage was a mixture of things. Five to six quarters were played, lasting eight minutes each. Once again, Coach Jones was trying to figure out what the right mix would be in terms of his rotation of players. Our standard sets on offense were called, including 5-M, 5-MT low, and 5-Around Swing. Whenever Niagara Falls switched to a zone, Coach Jones adjusted his offenses. Again, he also wanted to see who was going to play defense and rebound the ball. At various times, he subbed in Juno Patterson, Keith Hearon, Roderick Peoples, Dominique Gallon, and Jamar Moore. Jason Hellerman, Jason Majchrowizc, Carlton Ford, and Damon Kimbrew also saw some playing time later in the scrimmage.

"Dunbar, go in!" Coach looked down at the bench at me partway through the scrimmage. I was surprised to go in, but I jumped up nonetheless, went over to the scorer's table, and checked in. Out there on the court, I was like a 'deer in headlights', as they say. I knew a little bit about our offenses, but still I did not have much game experience and felt unprepared.

On my one offensive possession, Adonis had the ball on the right wing. He drove, made a move, and then threw a two handed over the head pass towards me as I stood at the top of the key. I froze, and the ball sailed right over my head out of bounds without my trying to grab it. It was an embarrassing play or non-play.

"ANWAR, WHAT ARE YOU DOING?" Adonis yelled at me in his high-pitched voice. The truth is I did not know what I was doing. I ran back on defense, and Coach Jones took me off the floor shortly afterward. Fortunately, Coach Jones did not cut me for that. No one else said anything to me about it afterward, though I never forgot.

The obvious thing from both scrimmages was that our team had a lot of work to do. Even though the first jump ball had not been thrown up yet, the 1991–92 team looked quite different from Curtis Brooks' 1990–91 team, at least from my vantage point. This team did not have that aura of dominance, and the play of our veterans was not making the game look easy. In fact, it looked difficult, and it looked painful in some ways.

"Who is that other team? Where are they from? Whoever they are, they are not from around here playing like that!" One of our managers, Damion Alexander, overheard some Niagara Falls spectators commenting on our team during the scrimmage and later shared them with me. It made me laugh even though it was a joke at our expense. The other guys might not have felt the same way. It also said something about the level of basketball competition in Niagara Falls.

* * *

The week before the Turner/Carroll game, Coach Jones distributed our jerseys. At the end of one of our practices, we were left to shoot around while he went upstairs to the equipment room, which was directly across from the coaches' offices. Coach Jones set up a desk right there in the doorway with an inventory of all the jerseys, shorts and warmup shirts. We each had to bring deposits of $10 to $20, and he called us up in order of class. One by one he took our money and accounted for each set of uniforms. Equipment for the other sports could be seen directly behind Coach. It looked literally like the storage room of a factory, but in this instance, it was a collection space for the sports teams at Hutch-Tech.

Our school uniforms were made by the Champion Company. The Champion patch said, "Made in Rochester, NY," and was stitched on the lower front left corner of our tank tops, as was the size. The little Champion seal was also sewn in our shorts just below the beltline on the left side. Our jerseys were not made up of breathable mesh as was most common, but were instead a thick 100% nylon fabric. The home tops were V-necks, while our maroon visiting tops were curved like a U in the front. Warmup shirts were made of a breathable mesh material and were V-necks. The top half of the front and the sleeves were white with maroon, white and gold stripes at the bottom of the short sleeves and a similar V-shaped line dividing the white top of the shirt with the maroon bottom and back of the shirt. The Hutch-Tech seal was positioned over our hearts.

Each man got a white top, white trunks, and a maroon top. Because the team was so large, there were not enough maroon trunks to go around, so some players got only white trunks. There were not enough warmup shirts either, which is why Carlton Ford did not get one that year. As one of the sophomores, I am not sure how I received maroon trunks, but I did. In fact, I got one of everything. I chose the number 52. I am not sure why I chose 52, but it spoke to me at the time. Both tops were double extra-large, so they were baggy on me.

"No. The warmup pants are something Michael was organizing," Coach Jones mumbled to me when I asked him about purchasing tearaway warmup pants like the NBA players wore. Around the time we were handed our uniform sets, I also recall Michael Mann tossing out the idea for all of us getting some extra money together and buying warmup pants like the professional players. There must not have been a lot of enthusiasm for it as a group because I didn't hear anything else about it.

When I was given my uniform, I was proud and could not believe it. I was legitimately on the varsity team now, just like I had dreamed. Despite what happened over the summer of 1991, I had somehow made it here. When I got home, I put my uniform on in different variations. At first, I wore the white top with white trunks. Then I wore the white top with the maroon trunks the way the 1990-91 team did the year before. Then I put on the maroon top with the maroon trunks. And finally, I put the warmup shirt on. I still get goosebumps thinking about those uniforms.

With each variation, I went into Mom's room. She had a full-length mirror, and she was in the living room watching TV at the time. I looked at myself from the front and then from the back. *I am the number 52*, I pondered to myself in my own world. Those large block numbers were special. The only thing that did not match were my black and purple Nike Flights, the only sneakers I wore that year both on the court and off, but it did not matter to me. I had my jersey, and I was a part of the varsity team. I was one of the guys.

I did not expect to play much, as Coach Jones said. I would sit, watch, and learn, and the next year I would get out on the floor and play. I excitedly anticipated the day when I would be developed to the point where I could confidently play. I knew it would happen eventually. I had my uniform now and I was a part of the varsity team. That was enough for me.

Chapter 19. The 1991–92 Non-League Schedule: Stumbling Out of the Gate

"Coble has the hot hand, so keep feeding him!" **—Ken Jones, Head Coach, the Hutch-Tech boys' basketball team, 1988-93, November 1991**

In previous years, the highlights of the winter months were the Thanksgiving and Christmas holidays, respectively. Since I was now on the Hutch-Tech boys' basketball team, they became afterthoughts. I had other things to consider, such as our practices and games. Our very first game was in the Hutch-Tech gym. It was against Turner/Carroll High School on the day before Thanksgiving, and it was coming up fast. Coach Jones' beloved 1990-91 team beat Turner/Carroll 80–67 on their home floor the previous year, surprising everyone and electrifying our school.

"I DON'T CARE HOW TALL SANFORD IS! IF WE REBOUND THE BALL AND PLAY DEFENSE, WE CAN WIN THE GAME!" Coach Jones made this proclamation leading up to the Turner/Carroll game after hearing some of our players whisper amongst themselves about a player named Kevin Sanford, who was 6'7". He wanted his team to feel that it had a chance to win the game no matter who the competition was and how athletically gifted they were.

At the end of practice the day before the Turner/Carroll game, Coach Jones gathered us at center court to go over some scouting notes he had compiled. They were written on a couple of sheets of scrap paper. He read off the names of their players and what their tendencies were. He then discussed what kinds of offensive and defensive sets our opponents would likely run and how we would counter them.

"Their point guard, Damone James, is gone, but they have Sanford back. Their guards are young and they mostly play through their three big guys. Aside from Sanford, they have two more 6'7" guys named Greene and Ortiz," Coach Jones said in his low, raspy, and scratchy, grandfatherly voice, reading from his pieces of paper.

"They play primarily a man-to-man defense, so we're going to run our motion sets," he continued. I stood around the huddle, eagerly taking my first scouting report in. We had never done scouting reports at Campus West, so this was all new for me. With all the practicing we had done and the two scrimmages, our team seemed more than up for this first challenge at hand.

* * *

Our season opener took place on Wednesday, November 27, 1991. I was not expecting to play in the game unless it was a blowout. Still, I was a part of the Hutch-Tech boys' varsity basketball team now, and by association, I was a part of the buzz that the school felt leading up to that day. It was a feeling I had never experienced before. It was different from any new toys on Christmas or any excitement I had had about a girl. The morning of the Turner/Carroll game, I anxiously packed up my jersey in my gym bag and went off to school.

As I walked up to Hutch-Tech at the southern entrance, Jermaine Fuller walked up, too. I asked him if he had a hair pick because my hair was not looking the way that I wanted it to. He then looked at me like I was crazy, telling me all he had was a brush for his hair. He demonstrated that he had short hair, by rubbing his hand over the top of his head as we walked into the double doors. I shrugged my shoulders, feeling slightly embarrassed as I should have seen that.

Now being a part of the basketball program, I regularly heard stories about Jermaine being advanced academically in elementary school and graduating early. Even though he was a part of the class of 1993, he could have been one of my peers in the class of 1994. Coach Jones bragged about Jermaine sometimes in amazement regarding his intelligence. I saw him clown around a lot like the other guys in his class, in spite of being very smart. A lot of guys at Tech were like that, smart comedians.

There was a definite electricity around the school, and that entire day seemed to take forever. All eight periods and lunch ground by slowly one by one. Our old clocks added to the suspense. You could hear the minute hand click with every advance. With each passing period, the anticipation for the game intensified. I was not going to see significant playing time, but I would get to put on my uniform for all to see for the first time. I was going to run out for warmups as a part of the varsity team. If I was feeling anxious and I didn't know if I was going to play, I could only imagine how the starters felt.

The locker room that the boys' basketball team used was the same locker room the football team used. It was right around the corner from the coaches' offices. The visiting teams used the locker room that we used for intramurals and gym classes. I ran down to the locker room just after the final bell rang.

As I approached the locker room, I saw the Turner/Carroll coaches and players assembling at the visitor's locker room. Unlike the other private schools in Western New York, the Turner/Carroll team was mostly black and Latino. They were dressed in winter coats, jeans, and boots and most of them wore headphones. In their street clothes, they could have easily been from a Buffalo Public School. I observed what felt like ominous gazes from some of them when I walked by with my gym bag.

In our locker room, there was dead silence and focus as we all dressed for the game. I faintly heard the school band playing in the gym downstairs and the buzz from our student body. Once we were all dressed, Coach Jones came and gave us some final words, passed out chewing gum, and we exited the locker room into the hallway.

There was a lot on the line as the 1991–92 season tipped off. Our program had experienced tremendous success the previous year, and the expectation was that our team would at least come close to that. This was also the last time around for our seniors. The core of our team had been in the program for four years, and I could feel that I was now a part of something, a brotherhood and a lineage of sorts. I had achieved my goal, one that I had put in jeopardy over a fleeting teenage love over the summer.

"You guys ready?" Michael Mann, smiling, asked the group. His high-top fade was fresh with a few lines in the front. We split into two lines for our pregame warmups as we had done in practice and at the scrimmages. Andre Higgins and Michael Mann, each with a basketball, led their respective lines into the gymnasium. I went into Andre's line which was gathered by the stairwell outside the visitor's locker room. Michael Mann's group went down the other stairway near the girls' locker room.

As we went down the stairwell, the buzz got louder, and I heard another set of balls bouncing off the floor. When Andre got to the bottom of the stairwell, the buzz in the gym grew louder. On cue Andre gave a nod to Michael Mann before charging out of the stairwell, bouncing his basketball, and we followed him.

As soon as we emerged into the gym, it erupted. Like the previous year, the gym had transformed into an arena for competition with cheerleaders, students, faculty, and relatives everywhere. My focus was on properly executing our warmup routine, but I glanced briefly into the bleachers and saw some students holding up signs or posters with messages I could not make out.

We circled the gym twice and then closed in on our basket as we practiced numerous times. We did our pre-game warmup drills: the Seven-Pass Drill, the Three-Man Weave, our layup lines, our jump shooting drills, and then open shooting. Our complicated Seven-Pass Drill was beautiful when we all ran it together as a team. Out of curiosity I looked at Turner/Carroll warming up. Their jerseys were solid black, and they did, in fact, have three big guys who were each 6'6" to 6'7". *This is the team we are tasked with beating. This is the source of all the hype*, I pondered.

"Don't look at them! Focus on our warmups!" Jason 'Magic' Majchrowicz saw me and sensed what I was thinking based upon my facial expression and body language. This was kind of like middle school, but different. It was bigger, with more people, more excitement, and higher stakes. I could feel it. Everyone in that gym could too.

After about ten minutes of warmups, the buzzer sounded and both teams went to their respective benches for the introduction of the starting lineups. Our bench was on the Johnson Park side of the gym. Frank Williamson, who had graduated in one of the previous classes, announced the starting lineups. He was back doing it again for us. He was brown-skinned, wore glasses, and had a short 'Afro' with some fuzz on his chin. Standing behind a podium with a microphone and a speaker directly underneath our scoreboard, he announced the lineups like one of the professional public address announcers for the NBA games.

"Welcome to Hutchinson Central Technical High School for the season opener for YOUR Hutch-Tech Engineers, as they host the visiting Turner/Carroll Chargers," Frank bellowed. *Their nickname is the Chargers, like the NFL football team*, I thought to myself. Our five starters sat on the bench while the rest of us formed two lines the way the college and professional teams did. Frank announced the lineups alternating between us and Turner/Carroll.

"For Turner/Carroll, a five-seven guard, sophomore, number eleven, Delwin Rhines." Delwin Rhines was a short dark-skinned kid. I had seen him around town and recognized him. "For Hutch-Tech, a five-eight guard, junior, number fifteen, ANDREEEE HIGGINS!" The crowd erupted.

"For Turner/Carroll, a five-seven guard, sophomore, number twenty-one, Shondell DUPREEEEEE," Frankie continued. Shondell Dupree was a light-skinned suave-looking kid with a small mustache and short wavy hair. "For Hutch-Tech, a five-eight guard, senior, number twelve MICHAEL MANNNN!"

"For Turner/Carroll, a six-seven center, senior, number fifty-two, Jamal Greene," Frank said as one of Turner/Carroll's three towers trotted out onto the floor, running over to shake Coach Jones' hand before going to stand with Delwyn Rhines and Shondell Dupree. Jamal Green was a dark-skinned kid with a short, faded haircut. He wore a black tee-shirt underneath his Turner/Carroll jersey and black spandex under his shorts like the college and professional players. "For Hutch-Tech, a six-three center, junior, number thirty, JERMAAAINE FULLER!"

"For Turner/Carroll, a six-seven forward, senior, number thirty-two Alfredo Ortiz," Frankie announced as Turner/Carroll's second tower trotted out. Alfredo Ortiz had that reddish-brown complexion that many Puerto Ricans have. He had Asian eyes and an unassuming appearance. He also wore a black tee-shirt under his jersey. "For Hutch-Tech, a six-two forward, senior, number forty-four, CHRIS SOOOUTER!"

"For Turner/Carroll, a six-seven forward, senior, number forty-four, Kevin Sanford," Frankie said as the last of Turner/Carroll's big men ran over to shake Coach Jones' hand before joining his teammates at the opposite free throw line. Just like Shondell Dupree, he was a light-skinned, suave-looking guy with the sides of his head faded with short curly hair on top. He could've been an R&B singer in a group like Kenny 'Babyface' Edmonds. Though he was taller than anyone on our team, he did not look particularly intimidating. He did look kind of like a tall stallion ready to run in a race. He, too, wore a black tee-shirt and black spandex under his black No. 44 jersey. He probably wore it for Syracuse University's star Derrick Coleman.

"And for Hutch Tech, a six-one forward, senior, number twenty-three, ADONIS COOOBLE!" Frank introduced the last of the players and then the coaches, "Turner/Carroll is coached by Fajri Ansari, and Hutch-Tech is coached by Ken Jones." In many ways, Coach Ansari was the opposite of Coach Jones. He was a suave-looking young black man. He was also well dressed in a sports jacket ensemble. As the game unfolded, he did not carry on or get excited like Coach Jones. At least, if he did, I didn't notice from where I sat at the end of the bench.

Following the Pledge of Allegiance and the introduction of the starting lineups, we assembled into one last huddle on the court before returning to the bench for final instructions. Michael Mann shouted something I could not understand because of the noise from the crowd. At the end, we all put our hands in, and Michael led us with, "ONE, TWO, THREE," and we followed in unison with, "TECH!"

"Play man-to-man defense and run our motion offense to start the game off. We will adjust as the game unfolds," Coach Jones said. At the end of his instructions, we all put our hands into the center once again and yelled, "TECH!"

At the center court of our little gym, the ten starters gathered around the half-court circle to shake hands and take their positions. Jermaine Fuller and Jamal Greene both stepped into the center circle across from one another. The Turner/Carroll jerseys had Chargers written on the front in white cursive letters at an angle, while ours were blank. With anticipation and electricity in the air, the referee tossed the ball up as Jermaine and Jamal each tried tipping it to one of their teammates. The game and our 1991–92 season were underway. It was exciting and an apex in my young life. I was experiencing something that I was a thread or two away from missing out on due to the events from a summer that now seemed so distant.

We gained the first possession and started on the south basket by Turner/Carroll's bench. Michael Mann barked out, "5-MOTION! 5-MOTION!" The gym went silent for our offensive possessions. Michael wore a white tee-shirt under his jersey and a brace on one of his knees, with black Nikes. Adonis flashed open on the right wing. His man gave him some space and he caught the ball uncontested. Without hesitation he squared up and shot a fifteen-footer from forty-five degrees. The ball sailed right through the net. Just like that, we were up 2–0, and our gym exploded.

"ADONIS COBLE!" Frankie Williamson yelled in a thunderous voice which made the whole gym shake. Adonis trotted up the court with a seemingly angry expression on his face, his gold mouthpiece half hanging out of his mouth, giving one of his teammates a high five. It was a confident and cocky trot, as though he was supposed to make that basket. He wore a sweatband on his right forearm, braces on both of his knees and black Converse sneakers with both letters and insignia colored yellow. Dion Frasier wore a similar pair that year, but with large ankle braces to provide him with support from his football injuries.

Early on, the game was like a prize fight where one boxer came out attacking while the other boxer gathered himself and tried figuring out which way the match would go. We were the boxer attacking immediately, and Turner/Carroll sustained the initial barrage. As intimidating as they appeared to be physically, Turner/Carroll appeared both scared and, to some degree, disorganized. Their first couple of possessions resulted in missed baskets and turnovers.

"ADONIS COBLE!" Frank Williamson yelled again after Adonis hit another shot from the same spot. Each time he scored, he trotted back down the floor, confidently high-fiving his teammates. Each time Turner missed a shot or turned the ball over, our starters took it right back down the court, fed it back to Adonis for another fifteen-footer from the wing, and he kept hitting them.

This went on for five or six straight possessions before Jermaine caught the ball at the free-throw line and drove down the lane for one of his signature two-handed double clutch layups. It did not ricochet directly off the backboard, but instead *tap danced* on the back iron of the rim briefly before finally falling into the basket. He almost toppled over running back on defense. Frankie Williams announced into the microphone, "JERMAINE FULLER!" Jermaine did not wear a tee-shirt under his jersey, but he did wear a knee brace on one knee with his black Nikes. Andre took a shot from the free throw line which also danced on the back iron and dropped in. He quickly retreated back on defense in his white and black Nikes.

And that is how the first quarter went for us. The momentum was completely on our side. Part way through the first quarter, Coach Jones subbed in Juno Patterson for Michael Mann. Pumped up himself, Juno played suffocating defense on one of Turner/Carroll's guards before Coach Ansari called timeout to settle them down.

"ADONIS COBLE!" The quarter ended just as it began, with Adonis sinking a fifteen-footer from the wing and our crowd exploding. When the buzzer sounded at the end of the first quarter, Juno went over to Adonis, and the two of them danced off the court, embracing in jubilation towards our bench. We were up by 10 or 12 points, a place where it seemed we were supposed to be.

"Coble has the hot hand, so keep feeding him," Coach Jones said in our huddle. I remember it like it was yesterday. It seemed we would ride Adonis to victory, and he would be our star. The way that first quarter went, he almost seemed destined for that role. Again, it was like a prize fight. Turner/Carroll sustained our initial flurry of punches, but how would they respond throughout the game?

In the second quarter, the momentum completely shifted, and the flow that we had in that first quarter gradually evaporated as the Turner/Carroll Chargers found their rhythm and gradually exerted their dominance. They found it in their frontcourt. Just as our offense flowed through No. 23, Adonis, in the first quarter, theirs now flowed through No. 44, Kevin Sanford, who stepped up, asserted himself and showed us just what all the hype was about.

No. 44 touched the ball now early and often. He was very skilled at 6'7", and he scored off jump shots from the left baseline, post moves, and run-out dunks in transition off our turnovers, which were now piling up. Our senior floor general, No. 12, Michael Mann, started visibly fatiguing, leading to mistakes and careless passes.

In addition to his skill level, Sanford had a height advantage and he was mostly guarded by Adonis, who was only 6'1". On one play, Shondell Dupree dribbled the ball around the top of the key and heard Kevin on the low block calling for the ball. Adonis was 'pinned' at his side, helpless to stop what was coming. Dupree brought the ball around in front of our bench and fed Sanford in the low post with a two-handed bounce pass. In textbook fashion, Sanford caught the ball under control and, with two dribbles, initiated a drop step towards the baseline, spun around Adonis, and then *kissed* the ball off the backboard with his right hand for an easy 2 points.

"OOOOOH." It was such a pretty move that some of the spectators in the crowd responded in awe. Chris Souter may have tried to guard him as well, but it did not make much difference. It seemed a sleeping giant had awoken and was now wreaking havoc.

"COME ON TECH! COME ON NOW!" A female's voice enthusiastically supported our team from behind our bench as our crowd was silenced by Turner/Carroll's play. It was Chris Souter's mother. She was a shapely middle-aged woman with a similar complexion and facial features.

Eventually, Turner/Carroll overtook us, and after a while, it was not just Kevin Sanford generating offense for them. Jamal Greene scored off easy layups following penetration by their quick and crafty young guards. Alfredo Ortiz did not really hurt us down low. He hovered around the three-point line and hoisted up shots from beyond the arc, making some of them. Rhines and Dupree also capitalized on our turnovers, and we went into the locker room at halftime down 43–31.

In the locker room at halftime, Coach Jones tried to get Adonis and the other starters to continue to fight and regain that lost first-quarter momentum. After halftime, it was more of the same. Kevin Sanford scored at will while Delwin Rhines and Shondell Dupree continued penetrating the lane to find their big men for layups. The Chargers continued capitalizing on our turnovers, turning them into easy baskets. They overpowered us and slowly extended their lead.

"BALL! BALL! BALL!" Coach Jones yelled from our bench in his blazer, shirt and tie, khakis, and running sneakers just as he did the previous season, trying to get his team to fight harder, but Turner continued separating themselves. Furthermore, as the game continued, you also heard fewer of Frankie Williamson's announcing the players' names.

Going into the fourth quarter, Turner/Carroll extended their advantage to 20 points or more. Coach Jones realized our chances of coming back were slim at best and started clearing the bench. Into the game went players like Roderick Peoples, Jamar Moore, and Jason Hellerman. Before coming out of the game, Chris Souter launched one last three-pointer, which went in. He walked towards the bench in his black Reeboks, smiling and holding his warmup shirt. The final score was Turner/Carroll 80 and Hutch-Tech 60.[101] They had come into our gym and beat us by 20 points, not the start I or anybody else thought we would have.

Adonis finished with 21 points, most of which came in the first quarter. Chris Souter was next with 9 points, while Michael Mann had 7.[102] Juno had 6, while Jermaine had 5.[103] Roderick Peoples and Andre Higgins each had 4, while Jamar Moore finished with 2.[104] Turner/Carroll had a more balanced scoring output. Kevin Sanford finished with 26 points, Shondell Dupree was next with 16 points.[105] Jamal Greene scored 12 points, while Alfredo Ortiz scored 10 points.[106] Delwin Rhines scored 5 points, while two of their bench players, Thomas and Hall, each scored 6 and 5 points, respectively.[107]

It was not the way any of us expected to start our season, but the reality was that it was a pretty strong team that we had just played. The good thing was that with one game down, there were now things that could be tweaked. Adonis had a strong game, and it looked like he would be our number-one option on offense. The other positive thing was that we would get a second chance to beat

---

[101] (Staff, Turner/Carroll High School vs. Hutch-Tech High School; Non-League Box Score, 1991)
[102] (Staff, Turner/Carroll High School vs. Hutch-Tech High School; Non-League Box Score, 1991)
[103] (Staff, Turner/Carroll High School vs. Hutch-Tech High School; Non-League Box Score, 1991)
[104] (Staff, Turner/Carroll High School vs. Hutch-Tech High School; Non-League Box Score, 1991)
[105] (Staff, Turner/Carroll High School vs. Hutch-Tech High School; Non-League Box Score, 1991)
[106] (Staff, Turner/Carroll High School vs. Hutch-Tech High School; Non-League Box Score, 1991)
[107] (Staff, Turner/Carroll High School vs. Hutch-Tech High School; Non-League Box Score, 1991)

Turner/Carroll in the Al Pastor Memorial/ Pepsi Cola Tournament that very next week at Buffalo State College.

* * *

Prior to the games in the Al Pastor Memorial/Pepsi Cola Tournament, there was a banquet at the Buffalo-Niagara Convention Center for the participating teams. Coach Jones was adamant about all of us players wearing shirts and ties. I did not realize their importance, and it would be another twenty years before I would see the power and significance of wearing them. At that age, for the most part, it was about doing the bare minimum. Wearing a tee-shirt or sweatshirt to the banquet would have honestly been good enough for me.

I wore my favorite yellow button-down shirt with tiny black bubbles. I thought it was good enough, but just before heading to the convention center, Coach Jones just so happened to have a small box of ties in his office, and he made me put one on. He had me stand still while he put it on me like a father would do a son. It was a dark maroon crocheted tie, and it went with my shirt for the most part. Later, I saw that it was common for athletic teams to wear suits and ties to banquets, games, and when taking team pictures. Most of us just did not understand it at the time.

The convention center was not far from Hutch-Tech, so it was a short drive to Franklin Street near Niagara Square in Coach Jones' Lincoln Town Car. I had already ridden in his beige full-sized car several times that year and was becoming a bit of a fixture in it. The rest of the guys walked over in the cold early Buffalo evening. Inside the convention center, all the teams gathered in the banquet hall. Other teams in the tournament were Turner/Carroll, Williamsville South, whom our 1990–91 team defeated in the overall Class B final the previous year, and Grover Cleveland. Emerson and Performing Arts were playing in another bracket. I noticed Turner/Carroll across the room. They pretty much kept to themselves and did not remind us of the beating they had just given us.

Most of the teams occupied two tables throughout the banquet hall. The food was served to us as it was at most banquets. We were first given salads, and then a main course which was chicken or beef, mashed potatoes, and a vegetable. Our beverage, of course, was Pepsi-Cola. The serving staff were dressed in white shirts and black pants. There was an ambiance inside the Buffalo Convention Center as many gatherings were held there by numerous groups within the city. Every time I would go there since then, I would reflect on that tournament banquet in 1991.

"Don't use your grades to get your basketball. Instead, use your basketball to get your grades!" As we ate, speakers from Pepsi-Cola and the City of Buffalo spoke at the podium, most of whom were older white men in executive capacities. Some speeches involved the history of the Pepsi-Cola Corporation. Another speech was about Al Pastor himself, who ran the Western New York Division of Pepsi-Cola for several years. He also supported high school basketball in Western New York which is probably why they named the tournament after him. Our final speaker's words stuck with me the most, a gentleman whose name I cannot remember. *Don't use your grades to get your basketball, use your basketball to get your grades.* They did not sink in immediately, but they were profound and took root in my mind as the years progressed.

Once the banquet was over, each team took a group picture. Both Terrance Collison and I sat at the table with Coach Jones between us. One of our managers, Taraji Mogul, may have sat at our table too. The rest of the guys stood around us. Everyone smiled, and we looked like one big happy family. Coach Jones posted the picture on the bulletin board near the coaches' offices for a little while, and I enjoyed seeing it daily. I was a part of something bigger than myself now. I was a part of a brotherhood and a team. I was not playing much, but I was a part of the team.

* * *

Our second game was a rematch against the same Turner/Carroll Chargers who demolished us in our own gym the previous week, 80–60. We had one game against them to think about and to try to adjust our strategies. The other difference about this game is that it would be played on a regulation-sized court, unlike the one in our tiny gym. The standard dimensions for a high school basketball court are a length of eighty-four feet and a width of fifty feet. Our gym was much smaller, which was advantageous for the three *trees* they had in their frontcourt.

The Al Pastor Memorial Tournament games were held at the 'Houston Gym' at Buffalo State College, which was only steps from my elementary school, the Campus West/College Learning Laboratory. I was somewhat familiar with the gym since we used to go over there in grade school for our swimming classes. We passed through it, or by it, to get to the swimming locker rooms.

Our rematch was in the evening the week after Thanksgiving on Tuesday, December 3, 1991. Our game plan was pretty much the same. Turner/Carroll would probably play man-to-man defense, and we would run our motion offenses against them. The other and probably most important key would be our defense and rebounding. With our height disadvantage, it would be crucial that our guys 'box out' and rebound the ball consistently.

"We can't afford to run up and down the floor with many of these other teams! We can't play that style of basketball! We just don't have that kind of team this year!" Coach Jones reminded us of this numerous times leading up to the rematch with an almost painful angst in his voice. It was like he was pleading for something.

Our 1991–92 team was not particularly quick or tall, so we would have to win games by playing smart on offense and playing disciplined team defense.

After Coach Jones' pregame talk in the locker room, we all walked out into the gymnasium, which felt large and cavernous compared to ours. Like the previous Wednesday, the Turner/Carroll Chargers were once again down at their own basket warming up. On cue, Andre Higgins and Michael Mann took off again, with each of us following them in two lines. I once again got into Andre's line. Not only did the gym look bigger, but it *was* bigger. I got *gassed* as we circled it twice. Unlike our gym, this one had vast bleachers on each side, with glass backboards and college and pro-style breakaway rims. It was also very bright in terms of lighting.

We were once again the home team, wearing our white tops and maroon trunks, while Turner/Carroll wore all black. After the starting lineups were announced, Jermaine Fuller matched up once again against Jamal Greene for the tipoff, and the rematch was underway. Unlike the first game, we did not race out to an early lead against the Chargers. It was more of an even game in the first half, with each team trading baskets. Unlike the first game, where Adonis did most of the heavy lifting early, we were now getting more balanced scoring from everyone else. Jermaine Fuller was particularly asserting himself, getting to the basket and the free-throw line early. Chris Souter and Andre Higgins asserted themselves as well.

"SHOT DONNIE!" Michael Mann yelled in his strong, commanding voice from the bench as the ball left Adonis' fingertips from the left wing and then rattled into the basket. His words gave me hope and visions of our winning the game. No. 23, Adonis trotted slowly up the court confidently, chewing on his mouthpiece while locating his man once again with that signature look of contempt on his face. Though Turner/Carroll was looking out for him, Adonis still led us early on and he could sink numerous fifteen-foot jump shots from the wing, his *sweet spot.*

After witnessing the first game, I watched from the bench with anticipation hoping that we would give the Chargers a fight all the way through this time. For that first half, we did, in fact, give them a fight, and they did not sprint out ahead of us the way that they did in the second quarter of the first game. At halftime, we went into the locker room with a three-point lead, 26–23, behind the scoring and rebounding of Jermaine Fuller and Chris Souter.[108] Our frontcourt players defended their big men well, limiting them to 6 points in the second quarter. It was their guards, Delwin Rhines and Shondell Dupree, that kept them close with their penetration and timely shooting from the perimeter.

Unfortunately, there were two halves to the game, and the second half played out exactly the way it did in the first game. Turner/Carroll once again made some adjustments and then came out and bull-dozed us behind the play of Kevin

---

[108] (Jones, Turner/Carroll High School vs. Hutch-Tech High School; Al Pastor Tournament, 1991)

Sanford. He once again scored off dunks, jump shots, and post moves. Furthermore, as our team fatigued, Turner/Carroll got easier baskets off our turnovers. In only his second game, No. 12, Michael Mann again looked winded, which was tough because he initiated our offense. The Chargers stretched the lead back to 20 points just like the first game and beat us, going away 69–49.[109]

The only consolation was that we got more of a balanced scoring effort this time. Adonis wound up with 9 points after getting off to a quick start. Three players scored in double digits for us. Jermaine Fuller scored 12 points, Andre Higgins scored 11 points and Chris Souter scored 10.[110] Adonis, Chris, and Andre had 11, 10, and 6 rebounds, respectively.[111] Roderick Peoples, Jamar Moore and Dominique Gallon all played well coming off the bench. Turner/Carroll's leading scorers were Kevin Sanford with 21 points and Shondell Dupree with 14 points.[112] Jamal Greene was next with 10 points, followed by Alfredo Ortiz's 9 points.[113]

Fortunately, we would not play the Turner/Carroll Chargers anymore that season. We were not finished in the Al Pastor Tournament, though. Our next chance for our first victory would be against Grover Cleveland. They lost to Williamsville South 71–60.[114] Williamsville South was led by their dynamic duo of Andre Graves and Mike Mitchell, who led them with 33 and 22 points.[115] Grover Cleveland's 6'6" big man, Jamie Clark, had his picture taken by the *Buffalo News* during the game, fighting for a rebound against Williamsville South's 6'5" Rob Esmond.[116]

While one half of the rematch of the 1991 Section VI Class B final was filled, we played the Grover Cleveland Presidents at Houston Gym at 7:00 p.m. on Friday, December 6, 1991. They were coached by Arthur 'Art' Serrotte, a veteran coach in the Buffalo Public School system, who also coached the Presidents' football team. Some of the star players for Grover Cleveland were guys named Carl Swindle, Joe Sappio, Jamie Clark, Antoine Sims, and Jerome Ware. The

---

[109] (Jones, Turner/Carroll High School vs. Hutch-Tech High School; Al Pastor Tournament, 1991)
[110] (Jones, Turner/Carroll High School vs. Hutch-Tech High School; Al Pastor Tournament, 1991)
[111] (Jones, Turner/Carroll High School vs. Hutch-Tech High School; Al Pastor Tournament, 1991)
[112] (Staff, Turner/Carroll High School vs. Hutch-Tech High School; Non-League Box Score, 1991)
[113] (Staff, Turner/Carroll High School vs. Hutch-Tech High School; Non-League Box Score, 1991)
[114] (Staff, Billies face Chargers in tourney final, 1991)
[115] (Staff, Billies face Chargers in tourney final, 1991)
[116] (Staff, Billies face Chargers in tourney final, 1991)

Presidents' colors were lime green and white. They were the home team and wore white tops and green trunks while we wore our all maroon visiting uniforms.

It was the consolation game of our bracket, a game with little fanfare and buzz. We methodically ran our offensive sets and eventually built a large margin going into the fourth quarter. We got our first win of the season, defeating the Presidents 77–62.[117] It was not a glamorous win, but it was a win nonetheless.

"DUNBAR GO IN!" Coach Jones put me in the game late in the fourth quarter. With his arms folded, he slowly walked backward towards the end of the bench with his eyes still on what was happening on the court. "Hurry up! Come on and make sure you know who you have," he demanded as I eagerly hurried off the bench, taking off my warmup shirt.

I ran to the scorer's table, got buzzed in, and ran to the free throw shooting lane where free throws were being shot. The Buffalo State court felt like a football field compared to our tiny gym. My body was ice cold, and I was hoping that I could get a basket. All I wanted was 2 points, but Grover Cleveland's starting point guard, Joe Sappio, had not been taken out of the game and was still playing at full speed. He stole the ball from me when I caught a pass from Carlton Ford close to the foul line of our basket. I hoped for another opportunity in the closing seconds of the game, but that was my best opportunity to score.

After our game was finished, we changed and went to the new Buffalo State Sports Arena to watch the start of the championship game between Turner/Carroll and Williamsville South. It was the team that had just defeated us twice and the team Curtis Brooks and the 1990–91 Engineers defeated in the Class B sectionals nine months earlier. I remember the opening tip of that game. Mike Mitchell, the point guard for Williamsville South, had the ball tipped to him and dribbled it up the court, putting Williamsville South into their half-court offense. South wore its home whites, and Turner/Carroll once again wore their all-black uniforms. We watched for a little while before leaving the arena shortly before halftime.

Turner/Carroll won that game 75–62, led by Kevin Sanford's 25 points.[118] Their other double-digit scorers were Delwin Rhines and Shondell Dupree with 15 and 12 points, respectively.[119] Williamsville South was led by Mike Mitchell and Andre Graves who had 26 and 21 points.[120] I remembered Andre Graves from my discussion with Gabe's father, Mr. Smith, shortly after the overall Section VI Class B finals in March.

---

[117] (Jones, Hutch-Tech High School vs Grover Cleveland High School; Al Pastor Tournament, 1991)

[118] (Staff, Fitzgibbons nets 54 for Nichols, 1991)

[119] (Staff, Fitzgibbons nets 54 for Nichols, 1991)

[120] (Staff, Fitzgibbons nets 54 for Nichols, 1991)

"Don't be front-runners! So many teams in our league fall further behind once they get down, but you must keep fighting!" Coach Jones often told the 1991–92 team this, probably out of necessity. At the time, I thought the context was strictly for the actual games, though it may have applied to the season in general and, from a broader perspective, life itself. In essence it meant, do not fall apart when faced with adversity. Continue to fight and persevere.

Although I was one of the least experienced members of the 1991–92 team, I knew something felt different and that Curtis Brooks and the 1990–91 Engineers did not start off with two twenty-point losses and a win in a consolation game. The 1991–92 team was a younger and more inexperienced group, and Coach Jones would have to use as much of his magic as he could muster to keep things together. Still, our roster had a veteran senior core that had faced adversity before. We were only three games into the season, so there was a lot of time for things to turn around for us.

Chapter 20. The 1991–92 Non-League Schedule: Injuries and More Losses

"This first part of the season was just the gravy! We are about to start the meat and potatoes of the season after the New Year!" **—Ken Jones, Head Coach, the Hutch-Tech boys' basketball team,1988-93, December 1991**

"I will retire from the Los Angeles Lakers and professional basketball due to the HIV virus I have attained." One of the most stark and sobering moments in both basketball and sports history was Magic Johnson's announcement that he had acquired the Human Immunodeficiency Virus (HIV), which led to Acquired Immune Deficiency Syndrome (AIDS) in most cases. The virus and the disease were the medical scourge of that era. It was November 7, 1991, and Johnson made his announcement prior to the start of the 1991–92 NBA season. It was around the time that Coach Jones had finalized the boys' varsity basketball roster.

Just six months earlier, I cheered for Michael Jordan and the Chicago Bulls after they defeated Magic Johnson and the Lakers in five games to win their first 1990-91 NBA World Championship. I taped some of the games and watched the classic duels between No. 23 and No. 32 and their teammates. Everyone thought that Magic, who was thirty-one years old, would go on and continue to lead the Lakers until he could not play anymore, and no one foresaw this end to his brilliant career. He was one of the NBA's all-time greats, arguably the greatest point guard ever and the best passer ever. It was an example of what I had started experiencing in life and in the great game of basketball. I came to the realization that things could and would change at any moment and unexpectedly.

* * *

"Duke is playing Canisius on one of the local stations!" Gabe called me on the phone to give me the news of a game on local TV. He was very, very excited. I had not heard him this excited in a while. It was Saturday, December 7, 1991.

Duke and Canisius? I pondered the two schools in my mind. I was at home, not doing anything when his phone call compelled me to rush to our living room TV and turn it on.

I turned to either our ABC or CBS affiliate, probably CBS. Sure enough, Coach Mike Krzyzewski's defending National Champion Duke Blue Devils were playing downtown at the Buffalo Memorial Auditorium, or 'The Aud'. It was the same arena that Mr. Smith took Gabe and me to when we were in the eighth grade to see Michael Jordan and the Chicago Bulls play the Miami Heat. It was also the home to our professional hockey team, the Buffalo Sabres. I did not watch hockey. The only other time I had been to the arena was when Mom's friend, Dennis, took us to a set of professional wrestling matches there.

Earlier that year, in the 1991 Men's Final Four, Duke broke many of our hearts by upsetting the UNLV Runnin' Rebels. Afterward, they defeated the Kansas Jayhawks to win their first-ever National Championship at the Hoosier Dome in Indianapolis. We were in the era of Duke basketball. It was early in the prime of their college basketball empire.

They returned all five starters and aspired to repeat for the 1991–92 season. They started No. 11, Bobby Hurley, and No. 12, Thomas Hill, in the backcourt. No. 23, Brian Davis, and No. 33, Grant Hill, started in the forward positions. Finally, No. 32, Christian Laettner, started at the center position. At 6'11", Laettner played the center position, but had the versatility of a guard-forward in terms of skill. He was ahead of his time as a skilled player. Twenty years later, he would be called a 'stretch four or five' due to his ability to face the basket offensively and to shoot the ball from long range with deadly accuracy.

Later, I learned that many coaches in the major college basketball conferences scheduled games in their seniors' home cities. I heard murmurs around that time and from then on, that Christian was from a town south of the city called Angola. He attended the Nichols School in Buffalo right next to Delaware Park. He played in the Buffalo Memorial Auditorium numerous times before going off to Durham to play at Duke. This was definitely a homecoming for him.[121,122]

By the time I turned the game on, it was in the second half, and Duke was on top by a large margin. They played in the Atlantic Coast Conference, one of the top and historic conferences in men's college basketball, which regularly sent players to the NBA. Michael Jordan was probably the most famous player during that time. For Duke, the game against Canisius was very much an exhibition game. They had multiple players who were 6'10", in addition to having considerable experience, size, and quickness in all positions. They were used to playing against equally skilled teams like the University of North Carolina, the University of Virginia, Georgia Tech and the University of Maryland, among others.

That night Duke wore their visiting royal blue jerseys, and Canisius wore their home whites with blue and gold trim. The tallest Canisius player was a white guy with a mustache, No. 33, Ed Book, who I believe, stood 7'. He matched up with Christian Laettner, and I did not notice any of their other players. When the game

---

121 (Gaughn, 1991)

122 (Northrup, 1991)

was out of reach, he was able to take the ball down the lane for a one-handed dunk which got the crowd riled up, but Duke won that game decisively 96–60.[123,124]

Even though Coach Marty Marbach's Golden Griffins played at the Koessler Center located at the corner of Delevan Avenue and Main Street, I did not go and see them play much. It was not because I did not want to see them play. Instead, it was ignorance and not understanding the importance of studying your craft and the next level up. There also did not seem to be a strong connection to the Canisius program, at least not at Hutch-Tech.

I feel like I could have benefitted from an older male figure who might have pulled my coat or provided encouragement about my basketball involvement. Mom, interestingly, had a male friend, named Rob, who she dated for a short period of time. He was a Metrobus driver. He told us stories about having after-school confrontations with students from schools like Buffalo Alternative, Riverside, and South Park on his buses. Those schools were from different worlds than Hutch-Tech, and I was amazed by his stories.

Rob encouraged me to watch the college games more than the professional games, which was valuable advice that I did not completely understand at the time. Why not focus on Michael Jordan flying through the air and dunking on opponents while his tongue hung out of his mouth? What was more spectacular than that? His reasoning was that college basketball was the next level up. It was the level that someone like me would play after playing at Hutch-Tech. Unfortunately, he was only around temporarily, so his message did not take root in a meaningful way. I remembered it though.

Their matchup with Canisius was a *tune-up* game for the Duke Blue Devils. The following Saturday, December 18, 1991, the Blue Devils traveled to Ann Abor, MI, to play the University of Michigan Wolverines. They were coached by Steve Fisher and won the national championship in Seattle two years earlier on a magical *Cinderella* run. Like nearby Syracuse University to the east, the University of Michigan was only hours away from Buffalo heading west.

In the college basketball world, a Cinderella team is a team that no one expects to go far in the NCAA Tournament, but advances deep into the latter rounds. Sometimes they go all the way to win the championship, just like the 1988–89 Michigan Wolverines, shocking everyone in the process. Others make deep tournament runs before losing somewhere short of the championship. Like many college teams, the program was unable to repeat the magic of Seattle in the previous two seasons. The school had a storied football program with a basketball program that made some runs over the years.

---

123 (Gaughan, 1991)

124 (Sullivan, 1991)

I tuned into the game either late in the first half or early in the second half by chance. Duke once again wore their royal blue visiting uniforms, and Michigan wore their home white jerseys with maize (gold or yellow) and blue trim. The player that stood out to me most was the Wolverines' freshman, No. 4, Chris Webber. He was 6'9" and uber-talented. He had agility, grace and strength to go along with his height.

Surprisingly, he was having his way inside with Christian Laettner, who could not stop him defensively. He seemed physically stronger than Laettner, posting him up, catching lob passes in the lane, and authoritatively dunking the ball with two hands. The Wolverines had another freshman that I noticed that day, the 6'9" No. 5, Jalen Rose. He unapologetically 'jawed' at the older Blue Devils, who gave it right back to them. It amazed me that he was not afraid of Duke.

The Wolverines had other notable players, but Webber and Rose made the biggest impressions on me as a basketball novice. The game was a thing of beauty and a coming-out party for the Wolverines, who narrowly lost the game 88–85 in overtime.[125] A Michigan junior guard, named Rob Pelinka, No. 3, took and missed a last-second three-pointer, which would have tied the game and sent it into a second overtime. When the game ended, I couldn't believe what I had just seen, just like the rest of the country, but it was spectacular.

* * *

With the Hutch-Tech season opener and first tournament out of the way, our record was 1–2. The next competition would come in our very own Hutch-Tech Tip-Off Tournament, which took place on December 10th and 12th of 1991. Coach Jones organized the tournament himself. The tournament was held at one of the other Yale Cup schools with large regulation-sized courts. This particular year the tournament took place at Seneca Vocational High School. The other two teams in the tournament were Lackawanna High School from just south of downtown Buffalo and a school from across the border in Canada, Regina-Pacis of Toronto, Ontario.

For the opening round of the tournament, we matched against Regina-Pacis, while Seneca matched against Lackawanna. Unfortunately, I had a Youth Leadership of Western New York event that day. Coach Jones understood my missing the game. It was probably because I was not going to log any major minutes, and I religiously attended practice. I may have taken it harder than he did, and he knew that I wanted to be there with my teammates. I took it as an opportunity to play politics a little bit.

---

[125] (Press, 1991)

"Hey, Dominique, you can take my maroon shorts for the opening game because I won't be there," I said to Dominique Gallon after practice the day before the game. I was trying to be a good teammate, but I was also trying to gain an ally from his rambunctious class of 1993.

"Oh, good looking out!" Dominique Gallon was both surprised, but thankful at the gesture. He was one of the juniors who had given me and my group a hard time, and I wanted to earn his respect somehow. Lending him my shorts was a bit of a peace offering.

Our tournament opener against Regina-Pacis took place on Tuesday, December 10, 1991, at 3 p.m. While I was at the Youth Leadership event, I thought about what was happening across town at Seneca High School. Immediately after getting home, I called Terrance Collison. We lost the game on a buzzer-beater by Regina Pacis' star player, Marion Archer. Apparently, he launched up a three-pointer from mid-court to give his team the 51–48 victory.[126] He finished with 16 points.[127] Adonis Coble and Andre Higgins led our team with 14 points and 12 points, respectively.[128] Our record was now 1–3. The game was Dion Frasier's first game back after his football injury, and he scored 8 points.[129]

In the other bracket, Lackawanna knocked off Seneca 62–59.[130] They were led by Warren Miles' 15 points. Ray Rodriguez and Roberto Rivera each had 11 points, and Seneca was led by Joe Brown's 19 points.[131]

The Hutch-Tech Tip Off Tournament was the second tournament where both Yale Cup teams played in the consolation game. We drew the Seneca Indians this time. It would be the first of two meetings with them that season, as we would see them again in Yale Cup play the next month. It wound up being a close game and hard-fought contest, more so than the consolation game in the Al Pastor/Pepsi Cola Tournament. No one wants to finish in fourth place.

"D-FRASSSSS..." Andre Higgins yelled from the bench in his high-pitched voice as No. 24, Dion Frasier trotted up the court, cheesing in his comical way. On that play he caught the ball on the left wing of their west basket and launched a fifteen-foot jump shot, which cleanly sailed through the net. Dion had beautiful mechanics in terms of his jump shot.

Roderick Peoples, Keith Hearon, Dominique Gallon, Jason Hellerman, Jamar Moore, and Jason Majchrowicz all got into the game, so it was a good out for our

---

[126] (Staff, Buzzer-beater sends Hutch-Tech to defeat, 1991)

[127] (Staff, Buzzer-beater sends Hutch-Tech to defeat, 1991)

[128] (Jones, Regina Pacis High School vs. Hutch-Tech High School; Hutch-Tech Tip Off Tournament, 1991)

[129] (Jones, Regina Pacis High School vs. Hutch-Tech High School; Hutch-Tech Tip Off Tournament, 1991)

[130] (Staff, Buzzer-beater sends Hutch-Tech to defeat, 1991)

[131] (Staff, Buzzer-beater sends Hutch-Tech to defeat, 1991)

juniors. The game went into overtime and we narrowly squeezed out a 67–63 victory.[132] Jermaine Fuller had a game-high 21 points, while Andre Higgins had 5 assists and 7 steals.[133] Chris Souter scored 5 of his 14 points in the overtime period and grabbed 14 rebounds on his way to the All-Tournament Team.[134] In his second game back, Dion scored 7 points.[135] Joe Brown and Anthony Dandridge led Seneca with 24 and 17 points.[136] Our overall record was now 2–3.

Dion Frasier's ankle injury was the first significant injury of the season, and he was fortunate to return from it. During the first Seneca game, we suffered the second major injury of the season. Jamar Moore landed on top of the foot of one of Seneca's players and broke his right ankle, ending his season. I do not remember seeing it happen or him coming off the floor hobbling, but he was done and did not participate in any further practices or games that season.

* * *

The Engineers opened the Yale Cup league play on Tuesday, December 17, 1991 against Emerson High School. I had heard of it, but had never been to Emerson High School, the sole culinary arts school in the Buffalo Public School System. It was located off Sycamore Street, headed towards Cheektowaga. Just like the Hutch-Tech Tip Off Tournament, we all caught the bus across town to the game.

Emerson had a regulation-sized basketball court just like Seneca, though their facilities in total were not modern in any way. I was still learning about the world of high school basketball, so I did not understand that we were starting our league play and were officially setting out to repeat as Yale Cup Champions. There wasn't a lot of buzz going into that game from our veteran players nor in Coach Jones' scouting report the previous day.

We beat the Emerson Eagles 56–41 going away.[137] It wasn't a pretty win like the 1990–91 teams' wins, but it was a win, nonetheless. The game was tied 23–23 at halftime, but the Engineer's hustle and defense held the Eagles to only 18

---

[132] (Jones, Seneca High School vs. Hutch-Tech High School; Hutch-Tech Tip Off Tournament, 1991)

[133] (Jones, Seneca High School vs. Hutch-Tech High School; Hutch-Tech Tip Off Tournament, 1991)

[134] (Jones, Seneca High School vs. Hutch-Tech High School; Hutch-Tech Tip Off Tournament, 1991)

[135] (Jones, Seneca High School vs. Hutch-Tech High School; Hutch-Tech Tip Off Tournament, 1991)

[136] (Jones, Seneca High School vs. Hutch-Tech High School; Hutch-Tech Tip Off Tournament, 1991)

[137] (Jones, Hutch-Tech High School vs Emerson High School; Yale Cup, 1991)

second-half points and allowed just six field goals.[138] Adonis and Chris scored 20 and 12 points each, grabbed 8 and 10 rebounds and 4 and 5 assists respectively.[139] Andre had 7 points, 7 rebounds and 2 assists.[140] Roderick contributed 4 points, 4 rebounds, and 3 steals off the bench.[141] We were now 1–0 in the Yale Cup and 3–3 overall, a 0.500 record.

* * *

"Most of their scoring comes from their guards Bradberry and Ellis. They play a fast and physical, defensive style of basketball. They also play lots of zone defenses, so we will look to run 4-Z, 4-ZM, 5-Z, and 5-Z High-Low," Coach Jones said to us in his raspy voice as he read notes from his scrap paper. It was the practice the day before our next game, and we were all once again gathered around him in the center court of the gym.

Though we had played the first Yale Cup game, our non-league schedule was wrapping up in the Festival of Lights/Public Athletic League (PAL) Tournament. It was going to be held at LaSalle Senior High School in Niagara Falls. I had never heard of LaSalle, and did not recognize any of the names Coach Jones mentioned. I was still learning his system, so I didn't comprehend much of what was being said.

"We're not going to beat LaSalle!" Jason Hellerman stated his prediction immediately after practice. It was moments after Coach Jones gave us the scouting report in the hallway near the coaches' offices. He wore his street clothes with his backpack hung over his shoulder. I wondered what kind of teammate he was and why he would say such a thing. We had a fighting chance to beat any team we played, right? Hell, we played two good games against Turner/Carroll. If we could hang with a team with three 6'7" guys, could we not hang with this LaSalle team?

The day of the LaSalle game was Friday, December 21, 1991. It was an evening game with an 8 p.m. tipoff, so we all gathered back at Hutch-Tech at 6 p.m. and piled onto a cheese bus so that we could make the ride up to Niagara Falls. Jason Hellerman did not ride with us because he was going to the game with his family. Coach Jones was not happy about that and, for the sake of camaraderie, wanted us to all ride together. I had not been to Niagara Falls much other than occasional visits to the actual falls and the national park, so this tournament was like going to a different world for me. In a way, it was like going to the suburbs.

---

[138] (Jones, Hutch-Tech High School vs Emerson High School; Yale Cup, 1991)
[139] (Jones, Hutch-Tech High School vs Emerson High School; Yale Cup, 1991)
[140] (Jones, Hutch-Tech High School vs Emerson High School; Yale Cup, 1991)
[141] (Jones, Hutch-Tech High School vs Emerson High School; Yale Cup, 1991)

The drive seemed to take forever. After going over the two bridges on the Interstate 190 expressway and passing through Grand Island, we exited on Niagara Falls Boulevard and then turned left onto Military Road. Eventually we entered an old area of the city with closed factories before emerging into a parking lot full of cars and buses. We had arrived at LaSalle Senior High School. Coach Jones got out first. Then I saw curly-haired Jason approach the bus in his winter coat with his backpack.

We entered LaSalle's gym to watch what was either a junior varsity game or one of the girls' games finish up. The gym felt like a giant wooden palace. Everything was brown and gold, and it had a homey feel to it. The bleachers were metallic and painted brown. I looked around in awe as we gathered high up in the bleachers in one of the corners. There were brown and gold banners everywhere, in addition to the flags of schools I did not recognize. They included Grand Island, Lewiston-Porter and Niagara-Wheatfield. I recognized Kenmore East and West. I remembered that James McClewer, from Campus West, went on to attend Kenmore West.

We all received programs and light blue Festival of Lights Tournament tee-shirts. I read my program as we sat up in the stands. The other teams in our bracket were the LaSalle Explorers, the host school, and the Niagara Falls Power Cats, both from the Niagara Frontier League. Finally, there were the Bennett Tigers from our league. I immediately sought out the Hutch-Tech Engineers where I quickly found my own name. I marveled at the fact that I was on the team and in the program brochure. I was a Hutch-Tech Engineer, and I was on the varsity team. Despite the tumultuous road I had taken, I was here and a part of the team.

I looked at the other three teams. Bennett was coached by Larry Veronica. Their tallest player was a 6'3" kid named Terrance Warren. Niagara Falls was coached by Dan Venuto, and their tallest player was a 6'8" guy named David Hunt. LaSalle was coached by Pat Monti. Their tallest player was a 6'5" kid named Todd Guetta. After our first two games against Turner/Carroll, height was the quality that stood out the most in terms of who the good players were, so I did not pay much attention to our opponent's other players.

Both Terrance Collison and I became restless in the stands and wandered out into the lobby just to poke around a little bit. We were two first-year players exploring a new world. While out there, we met two cute black girls from LaSalle's girls' basketball team. I think their names were Tamika and Keisha. They both wore warmup shirts with jeans and sneakers. Terrance was comfortable talking to them. I noticed that he was generally comfortable talking to girls, and he even attracted them when we were out and around in the City of Buffalo. I envied him for it. I just played along there in the lobby, and was happy to meet two new girls, though I did not know exactly what to say to them.

"We are going to beat your boys' team!" One of us jokingly blurted out those exact words to them. They slowly looked at each other and then back at us, smiling without saying anything. We exchanged a few more pleasantries, but no phone numbers were exchanged, something I regretted. Shortly afterward we returned to the gym with the rest of our teammates. I thought about them later, wishing that I had made a move.

Eventually, it was time for us to get ready for our game. Coach Jones disappeared and then reappeared, signaling for us to follow him. We went to the girls' varsity locker room behind the bleachers on the opposite side of the court from where we were sitting. We were the home team for this contest and wore our white tops and maroon trunks. Once in uniform, Coach Jones gave us a few words and handed out chewing gum. As per usual, we were going to play our man-to-man defense and run our offensive sets based upon the defense our opponents played. We would *react* as Coach Jones always stressed. We split into our two lines and ran out into the cavernous gym, starting our pregame warmup routine.

LaSalle was already down on the end of the court going through their warmup routine when we emerged from the locker room. Just as I gleaned from the program, they were not tall like the Turner/Carroll Chargers and, frankly, did not look particularly intimidating or skilled. Their tallest player was a skinny white kid with curly brown hair who looked a little out of place on his own team. LaSalle's team was mostly black, with three white players, just like our team. They had a large roster like ours, suggesting they were also rebuilding and transitioning just like us.

After the pre-game buzzer sounded the starting lineups were announced. Michael Mann, Andre Higgins, Adonis Coble, Chris Souter and Jermaine Fuller all started the game for us. It was the same lineup used in our opener against the Turner/Carroll Chargers and Coach Jones hadn't felt the need to change it. It was not an explosive starting five, and our team was still trying to figure out its chemistry and rhythm.

LaSalle started a sleek and tall guard named Carlos Bradberry. He stood at 6'3" and wore No. 50. He was brown-skinned, wore a closely faded haircut, and had a distinct large, curved, pointy nose. He looked kind of like a Latino kid from New York City. He was big enough to be a college basketball player. In the other guard position, they started a small, rugged-looking guard named Shino Ellis, who stood at 5'8" and wore No. 30. One of their starting forwards looked like someone out of the movie *The Road Warrior*. His name was Curtis Ralands. He stood at 6'1" and wore No. 44. He was bald-headed and wore goggles like the Los Angeles Lakers' James Worthy or Kareem Abdul-Jabbar.

The starting center for LaSalle was the tall skinny white kid I noticed during the warmups. Todd Guetta was his name, and he stood at 6'5" and wore No. 42. The other starting forward, I believe, was Chris Frank, who stood at a wiry 6' and wore No. 11. Except for Guetta, all the other starters were black, most likely inner-city youth. They were coached by Pat Monti, who had brown curly hair and a brown bushy mustache. He did not look like a coach per se. He generally wore a checkered or striped button-down shirt, or a sweater with jeans or khakis. He could have been an English or a history teacher at any school. The team wore their brown tank tops and gold shorts for the game.

From the opening tip, our two teams seemed to be playing at two different speeds. We tried controlling and possessing the ball to get good shots, as Coach Jones preached to us. He wanted the starters to *work* the ball and slow the game down. If executed properly, it was a sound game plan and strategy.

LaSalle looked to create turnovers, and they wanted to get out and push the ball at every opportunity. They played a 1-3-1 zone with Carlos Bradberry out front, and Shino Ellis and Chris Frank on the wings. Todd Guetta was in the middle, and Curtis Ralands was in the back, patrolling the baseline and corners when the ball swung to a particular side of the court. Their arms were up and extended, and they frantically followed the ball every time it changed hands or swung from one side of the court or the other.

LaSalle successfully applied pressure and disrupted our offense. Coach Jones was beside himself on pretty much every offensive possession in the first half of the game. Despite Mike and Andre's best efforts, LaSalle consistently knocked the ball loose and deflected passes up in the air. Once they recovered the loose balls, they were literally off to the races to score easy baskets at the other end.

On the rare instances when they had to run half-court sets, LaSalle ran what looked like a motion offense of their own where they passed the ball to the wing and cut away, eventually leading to layups mostly by Carlos Bradberry. They did not really have a post-up game inside, and they were not an outside shooting team either. Instead, they were a slash to the basket- and an offensive rebounding-type of a team.

"BALL! BALL! BALL!" Coach Jones yelled from our bench in his blazer, shirt and tie, khakis, and running sneakers, just as he did the previous season, trying to get his team to fight to stay in the game. LaSalle's onslaught was just too great. Coach Pat Monti was either relaxed or did not get as animated as Coach Jones, because I do not remember any antics from him during the game. His team had a full grasp of the contest, so he really did not need to exert himself.

"Carlos Bradberry! Carlos Bradberry! Carlos Bradberry!" On play after play, the announcer spoke Carlos Bradberry's name nonchalantly as the Explorers' all-purpose scoring guard relentlessly gashed us with a barrage of layups. Some of them were from their motion offense, while others were off turnovers created by their 1-3-1 zone, which we could not get good shots against. They were tenacious rebounders, too, and did not allow us any second shots. It was all happening so fast. I could not see any of the talking or interaction between the players because of the speed of the game, but this Carlos Bradberry did seem to be a bit angry, cocky, and vocal towards our players. He made a show of things each time he scored.

"♫WE WILL, WE WILL, WE WILL BEAT YOU! ♫" LaSalle's cheerleaders chanted a modified version of Queen's *We Will Rock You* under their basket. Amid the chaos of the game, I made out the chorus of the classic rock track. The cheer typified the way the Explores attacked us, their tenacity and their swagger. It was as though they were supposed to be doing what they were doing to us. Curiously, the cheerleaders had a black toddler down in the front who could not have been more than three years old. She cheered with the older girls and jumped up and down whenever the Explorers scored.

"Come on Todd..." The only bad thing I heard come from LaSalle's bench was, "Come on, Todd," which a bunch of their players uttered. Their center, Todd Guetta, walked slowly to the bench with his head down as their coach grimaced and looked to be in agony. Guetta had committed a bad foul or some other error. Otherwise, it was smooth sailing for them. Whatever the misstep was, I think we would have gladly traded places with them that night.

From the bench, that whole first half was a blur, and LaSalle led comfortably 37–22 at halftime though their advantage was not insurmountable.[142] A 15-point lead is not that big a deal, but it was the way that LaSalle was doing it that made it seem like a larger deficit than it was. Coach Jones' main goal going into the third quarter was just to keep our morale up, and to try to get our guys to make the game respectable. In the second half, LaSalle continued playing at its own speed and aggressiveness and went on to win the game 72–42 to advance to the championship game. We went to our third-straight consolation game in that young season.[143]

Coach Jones put us sophomores and other bench players in at the end of the game. Just as in the Al Pastor Tournament, I hoped to get a basket, but even the LaSalle reserve players were playing to win. Their baby-faced freshman guard, No. 12, Jody Crymes, defended me and stole the ball the exact same way one of Grover Cleveland's players did in the consolation game of the Al Pastor Tournament. I think it was No. 35, Carlton Ford, who once again looked for me. Jody Crymes was lightning-quick and a tremendous ball handler as a freshman. I got to participate in a few possessions before the final buzzer sounded, but I didn't get in the scoring column as I hoped.

---

[142] (Staff, LaSalle Senior High School vs. Hutch-Tech High School; Festival of Lights Tournament, 1991)

[143] (Staff, LaSalle Senior High School vs. Hutch-Tech High School; Festival of Lights Tournament, 1991)

Jermaine Fuller led the Engineers in that game with 11 points.[144] The next highest scorer was Adonis Coble, with 8 points.[145] Carlos Bradberry finished the game with 29 points for LaSalle, and their next highest scorers were Keith Young and Chris Frank, with 10 and 9 points, respectively.[146]

It was a long and quiet ride back to Buffalo that cold Western New York Friday night. I do not know what everyone else was thinking, because no one was talking. I reflected on how our season was shaping out. Early on it seemed to be very different from the 1990–91 team's season. I wondered to myself why we were not performing like them. Could a team go from the top to the bottom that quickly?

One by one, we were dropped off in our neighborhoods around Buffalo. For some reason, Michael Mann was very quiet and did not get off the bus. The next day Coach Jones informed us that he had fractured his right wrist in the LaSalle game. He took a spill and landed awkwardly on it during the game on a particular play. I did not notice it in the flurry of LaSalle's relentless attack. It was unclear how much time he would miss, but it was another big loss for the team.

The next day at 3 p.m. we played the Bennett Tigers in the consolation game. With Michael Mann down, Coach Jones adjusted the starting lineup. Andre Higgins would now play the point guard position, and Adonis Coble slid into the backcourt to play shooting guard. Dion Frasier moved into the starting lineup at the small forward position, and Chris Souter and Jermaine Fuller would continue to play the power forward and center positions.

Consolation games tough because both teams are battling not to finish last, and both teams know that they are not battling for the tournament championship. I did not pay close attention to Bennett's players in that game. Their roster was mostly black, just like ours, and they were not particularly tall. They were the home team and wore their white jerseys with orange letters with blue and orange trim. We wore our maroon-colored visitors jerseys.

Coach Larry Veronica's Tigers looked like they did not want to be there, and we went on to beat them 60–52 to finish in third place once again.[147] Adonis, Dion, Jermaine, and Chris each had 15, 15, 11, and 11 points in the victory.[148] LaSalle

---

[144] (Staff, LaSalle Senior High School vs. Hutch-Tech High School; Festival of Lights Tournament, 1991)

[145] (Staff, LaSalle Senior High School vs. Hutch-Tech High School; Festival of Lights Tournament, 1991)

[146] (Staff, LaSalle Senior High School vs. Hutch-Tech High School; Festival of Lights Tournament, 1991)

[147] (Jones, Hutch-Tech High School vs. Bennett High School; Festival of Lights Tournament, 1991)

[148] (Jones, Hutch-Tech High School vs. Bennett High School; Festival of Lights Tournament, 1991)

likewise defeated Niagara Falls later that night 72–54 to take home the tournament championship.[149]

"Don't get discouraged over the first part of the season," Coach Jones pleaded with our struggling team in LaSalle's locker room after the Bennett game. He tried giving hope to a group that expected to play better than it had played. Our core players could either salvage the season or they could slide even further into disappointment. "This first part of the season was just the *gravy*! We're about to start the *meat and potatoes* of the season!"

Our record was now 3–4 overall and 1–0 in Yale Cup play. Our league schedule would continue after the New Year. Dion Frasier returned, but we had two other key players go down due to injuries, Michael Mann and Jamar Moore. The season was not going the way any of us had envisioned, but there was much more basketball left to be played.

"Don't be front-runners!" Once again, this was one of Coach Jones' signature quotes to us that 1991–92 season in practices, games, and just in general. For the 1991–92 Engineers, the adversities he discussed that we would experience over our fourth-month journey were now hitting us with full force. It was a mediocre and disappointing start to the season, but it was not over. It was now up to the players to either fall apart, or to galvanize and stay focused. Which would it be? Only time would tell.

---

[149] (Staff, LaSalle extends Falls mastery, 1991)

Chapter 21. The 1991–92 League Schedule: Peaks and Valleys

"That whole 1991–92 season was strange. I was less than 100% most of the time health-wise." **—Dion Frasier, Captain and Player, the Hutch-Tech boys' basketball team, 1988–92, January 2015**

Coach Jones described our upcoming Yale Cup league schedule as the *meat and potatoes* of the season. In other words, if we could go on and have a good showing in league play, none of what happened in our mediocre and disappointing non-league schedule would matter. The goal now was to put those early losses behind us and focus on the twelve-game gauntlet that lay ahead. We were off to a good start, defeating the Emerson Eagles, making us 1–0 in the Yale Cup. How would we do against the rest of the league?

Our roster had undergone some more changes prior to the first Yale Cup game in 1991. Dion Frasier had become healthier, but we lost Jamar Moore to a broken ankle and Michael Mann to a broken wrist. Junior Jason 'Magic' Majchrowicz was now also lost. Magic was literally skin and bones in terms of his build. He broke his left collar bone playing pickup basketball over the Christmas holiday. He said he fell on it. If you look back at our team photo, you can see him standing in the back row right next to me in street clothes. Jamar Moore was in that picture too, in street clothes. Michael Mann knelt in a sweatshirt, jeans, and sneakers with a cast on his wrist.

"Yeah, Mr. Schreiberstein wrote me up in English class, THAT RACIST MOTHERFUCKER!" I still remember Dominique Gallon's angry words in the hallways of Hutch-Tech shortly after Coach Jones cut him. Mr. Schreiberstein, a middle-aged, brown-haired white English teacher with glasses, looked harmless enough from a distance. I do not know the details of what happened. I suspect that it involved some mischief. As I said before, the class of 1993 had a lot of class clowns and larger-than-life personalities.

Whatever Mr. Schreiberstein accused Dominique of, it impacted the rest of our season. Dominique had a quick 'first step' off the dribble, and he could create shots for himself and the rest of the team like Curtis Brooks did in previous years. Most elite point guards had this skill in their basketball toolboxes. Dominique was the only one on our team with that skill which was why Coach Jones initially kept him. Michael Mann, who was now hurt, was more of a game manager. Andre Higgins was more of a shooter than a penetrator. Losing Dominique Gallon thus took away an important dimension from our developing offense, one which had not been used yet. Nevertheless, our team carried on.

"Your *ATTITUDE* determines your *ALTITUDE*!" While this may be the first time this quote appears in this story, Coach Jones told it to us daily, and he did it from day one. It is the quote I remember him saying the most. Like most of his quotes, it applied far beyond the basketball court, but it was critical for our team and players who had experienced so much adversity. Perhaps the second quote he told us, which was also memorable for me, was "Success breeds confidence, and confidence breeds success!" In addition to not being front-runners, both sayings were important for our team considering the unimpressive start that we had.

* * *

The Burgard Bulldogs gave us our first helping of meat and potatoes on January 3, 1992. Going into the other Yale Cup schools that year was exciting for me, as I had only seen them from the outside. I had ridden past Burgard Vocational High School numerous times, which is located on Kensington Avenue between Grider and Fillmore Avenues, parallel to the 33 Kensington Expressway. I heard that students at Burgard learned how to work on cars and airplanes. They were learning blue-collar trades, whatever that meant.

The Burgard gymnasium was in the back of the school, away from Kensington Avenue. We had to go downstairs to the visitor's locker room to change. After being given our pre-game speech, we returned to the gym and started our pregame warmups on their regulation-sized court. While the court was bigger than ours, their facilities were older and antiquated, with dark lighting. The school had solid white backboards like ours, with no breakaway rims, and bleachers on one side of the gym.

When we began our pregame warmups, the Bulldogs had already started theirs. Their colors were red, white, and blue and their uniforms were similar in design to ours. Their school names were on the front of their tank tops. There were two faces that I recognized immediately—No. 11, Jeremiah Wilkes, and No. 55, Sharif Beecher. They were the tag team that ended my final season at Campus West. Jeremiah was already a playground legend and their starting point guard. Shareef, at 6'7", was maturing as a sophomore and started as center for the Bulldogs.

There was no introduction of the starting lineups at Burgard. After warmups, the teams simply gathered at center court, where Jermaine Fuller and Sharif Beecher matched up for the tipoff. Immediately, the game went in the opposite direction that Coach Jones wanted it to go.

Burgard sought to use their superior quickness, along with Shareef Beecher's height, to create turnovers and easy transition baskets. They played a 3-2 zone which we countered with our zone offenses. It put lots of pressure on Andre and

Adonis, who were not yet used to playing with each other in the backcourt. Our guys tried but could not patiently work the ball around to create the good shots necessary to punish their zone defense. Burgard went up by as many as 20 points in the first half and led 54–38 at halftime.[150]

"You guys are playing a good game. You just need to play some defense!" A tall and skinny dark-skinned man wandered into our locker room and gave us his opinion of the first half. Our starters sat stewing over the first sixteen minutes of the game, taking it all in. This man had a high-pitched voice, a pea-shaped head and wore a high-top fade. He was dressed casually in a jacket, jeans and shoes. He turned out to be one of Adonis Coble's older brothers.

Adonis did not say anything. He just sat on one of the benches with his gold mouthpiece in his hand, breathing slowly and seething angrily. Andre, Dion and Jermaine sat quietly. Chris breathed heavily and slowly and looked disheveled. The rest of the team sat silently, waiting for Coach Jones to come in and give his halftime speech. He was probably upstairs analyzing the halftime statistics.

"We cannot afford to run up and down the court with this kind of team! They have quite a few guys who can 'unscrew the light bulbs!'" This was Coach Jones' main message for this game and, in hindsight, most of that season. He wore his signature blazer, shirt and tie, khakis, and running sneakers. The rest of his message consisted of playing better defense, rebounding the ball, and getting better shots on offense. These were the fundamental pillars of his game plans and his overall basketball philosophy for winning games.

In the second half the Engineers team fought back, eventually closing the margin to 7 points. It was a combination of the execution of our game plan and Burgard's inability to hold the lead. They did not seem to have as much structure as we did offensively. That was as close as we were able to get, however, before they pulled away for good. They never trailed in the game.

Burgard scores 87–75 victory to snap Hutch-Tech win streak; Engineers had won 16 straight in Yale Cup series, the headline read in the *Buffalo News* Sports section the day after the game.[151] Burgard was powered by freshman guard, Jeremiah Wilkes and Jermaine Ziegler, who both scored 18 points for the Bulldogs.[152] Sharif Beecher was surprisingly scoreless in that game.[153] We were led by Adonis Coble, Dion

[150] (Staff, Burgard scores 87-75 victory to snap Hutch-Tech win streak: Engineers had won 16 straight in Yale Cup series, 1992)

[151] (Staff, Burgard scores 87-75 victory to snap Hutch-Tech win streak: Engineers had won 16 straight in Yale Cup series, 1992)

[152] (Staff, Burgard scores 87-75 victory to snap Hutch-Tech win streak: Engineers had won 16 straight in Yale Cup series, 1992)

[153] (Staff, Burgard scores 87-75 victory to snap Hutch-Tech win streak: Engineers had won 16 straight in Yale Cup series, 1992)

Frasier, and Jermaine Fuller, who had 19, 15 and 15 points each.[154] Our record was now 1–1 in league play.

"Jeremiah did not hurt us all that badly," I said after practice the next week. I only remembered Jeremiah taking some three-point shots, many hitting the front of the rim. He scored quite a bit, in transition, which I did not notice as much. Sometimes games are that way. You tend to remember specific plays from them and must watch the film afterward to see everything in its entirety.

"Yeah, Jeremiah didn't hurt us *too* bad, Anwar," Roderick Peoples sarcastically snapped at me, staring me down from behind his glasses. Like Jeremiah, Roderick was also from the Langfield Projects, so he had a high level of respect for Burgard's freshman phenom. "He *only* scored 18 points on us!" I saw Roderick's point, and after that exchange, I kept most of my comments to myself from then on.

* * *

Unlike the 1990–91 season, our 1991–92 Yale Cup schedule was a seesaw or a yoyo which went up and down. Most wins were hard-fought and ugly. There were few easy victories, and those were ugly too. There were no win streaks for us, only a frustrating revolving door of wins followed by losses. The league schedule was literally a grind for all fourteen teams that year in terms of each game.

Things momentarily returned to normal when we hosted South Park. Once the starting lineups were announced, the next thirty-two minutes were up-and-down in tempo. South Park's Coach, Ken Pope, was one of the few black coaches in the Yale Cup. He wore a mustache, a small Afro, a sweater, khakis and sneakers. He yelled and made demands of his players like Coach Jones, who worked the sidelines in his signature attire. We escaped with a close 69–62 win over the red, black, and white Sparks.[155] Our leading scorers were again Adonis, Dion, Jermaine, Andre and Chris, each with 16, 11, 13, and 13 points, respectively.[156] Our Yale Cup record was now 2–1.

The next game for the Engineers was against the Buffalo Traditional Bulls at their gym on the corner of East Ferry Street and Masten Avenue on Wednesday, January 8. It was my first time being in Buffalo Traditional. Though I had heard of it numerous times. It reminded me of Campus West in that it was a small and more intimate building. The gym was bigger than ours, with what I believe was a regulation-size court with bleachers on one side to seat the fans. It also had glass

---

[154] (Staff, Burgard scores 87-75 victory to snap Hutch-Tech win streak: Engineers had won 16 straight in Yale Cup series, 1992)

[155] (Jones, South Park High School vs. Hutch-Tech High School; Yale Cup, 1992)

[156] (Jones, South Park High School vs. Hutch-Tech High School; Yale Cup, 1992)

backboards with breakaway rims. It was completely enclosed, and there were no windows to the outside.

When we started our pregame warmups, I noticed that the Bulls had one tall player, a dark-skinned kid who was 6'8" and towered over his teammates. I did not recognize any of their other players. They wore their home whites, and their colors were dark blue and gold. Watching his team warmup was an older white man named Joe Cardinal, who was bald on the top of his head with gray hair around the sides. He had a bushy mustache that gave him a professorial look. He wore a dress shirt with a tie, slacks, and shoes and he looked mean. Another older black man was beside him with a mustache wearing a sweater, slacks and shoes.

Just like at the Emerson and Burgard games, there was no introduction of the starting lineups, just the pregame warmups. After the opening tip between Jermaine Fuller and their 6'8" center, the game was an evenly matched contest as I watched from the bench. Neither team got too far ahead of the other. The Bulls played a 2-3 zone on defense. Coach Jones had Andre Higgins run the 4-Z zone offense, where four of our players formed a box on the perimeter with Jermaine Fuller flashing in the middle to get shots for himself. He could also potentially *collapse* the defense to create open shots for someone else. In some instances, Coach Jones called 5-Z High-Low, where Jermaine, Dion or Keith teamed up in the high and low posts.

Like clockwork Jermaine caught the ball near the top of the key, turned, and made a move towards the basket, making the shot or getting fouled. He was an excellent free-throw shooter with beautiful mechanics, so fouling him was like giving him 2 points. Sometimes he would quickly dish the ball to Andre, Adonis, or Chris on the wings or in one of the corners for jump shots.

"SHOT DONNIE! BOOM!" Michael Mann cheered on Adonis from the bench as he sunk a jump shot from the left wing, which seemed to be his favorite spot from which to shoot. He quickly turned and pointed at the player who assisted him before getting back on defense.

Buffalo Traditional fans made themselves a part of the game. Some of the girls in the raucous crowd yelled out all kind of cheers, like the famous taunt from the classic movie *Wildcats,* starring Goldie Hawn and Wesley Snipes, "♫U-G-L-Y, YOU AIN'T GOT NO ALIBI, YOU UGLY!♫" One girl taunted Jermaine about being biracial and blurted out that he was a "WHITE BOY," when he was shooting his free throws. It wasn't enough to disrupt his perfect shooting mechanics and he sank both free throws.

"NOOOOO," they also mocked Coach Jones as he agonized over the officiating, a turnover, or some other missed opportunity. While we tried to *work* the ball for good shots just like we did with Burgard, Buffalo Traditional wanted to get out and run, and there were spurts of that. With our disciplined play we kept the game close, and at halftime we trailed with 36–29.[157]

In the second half of the game there was more for Coach Jones to agonize over because Buffalo Traditional played their style of basketball and blew the game wide open. It happened gradually in a series of plays. Interestingly, the Bulls did not seem to run plays on offense or use any kind of noticeable structure. They scored off easy transition baskets from our turnovers, missed shots, or our defensive breakdowns.

In other instances, their player who wore No. 24, sank random errant three-pointers. He hoisted them up even when he was not open, which their coach seemed to be okay with. One of the few white kids on their team, No. 43, also hit a three-pointer or two. He kind of flicked his shots up with both hands without much lift while leaning forward into his short leaps.

Their No. 4, who was no taller than 5'11", was continuously open for layups. Each time he scored, he smiled and pointed at whoever assisted his baskets. On another play, their 6'8" center, No. 30, 'cherry-picked' for his baskets. He was all alone at their basket following one of our turnovers. He cocked the ball behind his head and dunked it authoritatively with two hands before slowly and confidently trotting up the court.

The result of the Buffalo Traditional second-half flurry was a 72–57 loss for us.[158] As captured in the *Buffalo News* box scores, the Bulls were balanced scoring-wise and led by Ronald Green, Marlow Winston, Andre Montgomery, James Callens and Jeff Novarra. They all scored in double figures with 18, 14, 14, 12, and 10 points.[159] The leading scorers for Hutch-Tech were Adonis Coble, Jermaine Fuller, and Keith Hearon with 16, 14, and 11 points.[160] Dion Frasier did not play due to injury.[161] We were now 2–2 in league play.

Next for us was a rematch against the Bennett Tigers at their gym. We dispatched them less than a month earlier in the consolation game of the Festival of Lights/PAL Tournament, 60–52. It was Friday, January 10, and it was a gray and wintery Western New York day. Bennett was another Buffalo school I had seen countless times from the outside, but had never been inside before.

Coach Larry Veronica's Tigers no doubt had the game circled and were looking for revenge. We ran out onto the court first and started our pregame warmups. Bennett fans erupted when their team emerged moments later. They ran around

---

157 (Staff, Hutch-Tech High School vs. Buffalo Traditional High School; Yale Cup Box Score, 1992)

158 (Jones, Hutch-Tech High School vs. Buffalo Traditional High School; Yale Cup, 1992)

159 (Staff, Hutch-Tech High School vs. Buffalo Traditional High School; Yale Cup Box Score, 1992)

160 (Jones, Hutch-Tech High School vs. Buffalo Traditional High School; Yale Cup, 1992)

161 (Jones, Hutch-Tech High School vs. Buffalo Traditional High School; Yale Cup, 1992)

the court in a single line at what looked like a leisurely pace. Instead of the disinterested team we faced in Niagara Falls, the Tigers appeared to have a chip on their shoulders as they stared us down in their home whites with blue trimmed orange numbers.

There were no starting lineups introduced. After warmups and the meeting between the captains and the referees, Jermaine Fuller matched up against their center for the tipoff. From the outset the game took the form of most of the Yale Cup games I watched from the bench. Bennett fought hard against our patient and controlled style with tenacious rebounding, open court play, and lots of adrenaline as they tried to break the contest open. We stayed within striking distance, behind the strong inside play of Jermaine Fuller in the first half. With the battle of conflicting styles, it was a close game at halftime, where they only led us 30–25.[162]

"We can't afford to run up and down the floor with teams like this!" Coach Jones pleaded with his starters at halftime, who quietly looked on while the rest of us stood around taking it in. It was like the Burgard game. Andre Higgins looked winded and a little confused. Adonis Coble sat angrily, breathing slowly and quietly, and Chris Souter also sat breathing slowly.

"Bennett has a lot of guys who can really jump up and unscrew the light bulbs!' We don't have the team this year to play that style of basketball! Keep working the ball to get good shots, play defense, and rebound the ball," Coach Jones concluded as we put our hands in the center as Michael Mann led us with a, "One, Two, Three," followed by a group, "TECH!"

"BALL! BALL! BALL!" In the second half Bennett shifted into fifth gear as Coach Jones stormed the sidelines miserably watching, huffing and puffing, his fists balled up as the game slowly slipped away. I do not know if it was Bennett's intensity going up or our team just breaking, but the Tigers generated turnovers and quickly took the ball down to the other end of the floor for easy scores, driving Coach Jones nuts. None of his timeouts could stop it.

This was what Coach Jones meant by not being front-runners, something he stressed numerous times, though I was unfamiliar. There were games we would easily be in, but there were others where we would have to hold off opponents and even battle back from deficits. The 1991–92 team struggled to hold off surges like the ones Bennett was on, or it could have been due to our inexperience at the point guard position.

Andre Higgins did not start the year at point guard and was now there by default. At times he looked helpless to control the flow of the game. The frustration of these growing pains was most visible on Adonis Coble's face, who appeared more and more irritated and dejected each time the ball was turned over.

---

[162] (Jones, Hutch-Tech High School vs. Buffalo Traditional High School; Yale Cup, 1992)

With his mouthpiece partially hanging out of his mouth, he would turn and dash up the floor in disbelief each time.

Several Bennett baskets were punctuated by the dunks of a leanly built, 6'3" kid with intense eyes and short dreadlocks on the top of his head, named Solomon Jackson. He did not impact our first game with them, but he was making his presence known in this one. He finished off several of our turnovers with authoritative and ferocious two-handed slam dunks, one of which sent Roderick Peoples to the floor after he attempted to draw a charge that the referees did not honor. Their crowd erupted after that dunk and even heckled Roderick, calling him Dennis Rodman after the Detroit Pistons' star defensive forward.

Bennett ran us out of their gym and won that game, going away 66–49, led by Solomon Jackson's 16 points and 12 rebounds.[163] Our only scorer in double figures was Jermaine Fuller with 14 points, which says a lot about how the game went for our team.[164] We were now 5–7 overall and 2–3 in the Yale Cup.

"You guys are quiet. I know y'all just lost, but you have more games to play. What is your best player's name? Is it Adidas Coble?" I vividly remember Terrance's stepfather messing up Adonis' name. He was a dark-skinned bearded man. I didn't play in the game, but I was a part of the team, and we both felt somber after the loss. The entire team would share in the loss back in the hallways of Hutch-Tech. After blowout losses to Burgard, Buffalo Traditional, and Bennett, it was clear that this season was quite different from the previous year. With every loss, repeating as Yale Cup champions seemed more and more unlikely, and you could feel something slipping away.

The Performing Arts Cavaliers came into our gym on January 15, 1992. This game was significant for several reasons. It was my ex-flame, Maria Harrison's school. Would she be in attendance? It was also the game where we took our team pictures for the year. Prior to warmups, we all gathered at center court while someone from the yearbook committee photographed us.

When we ran out for pregame warmups, the Cavaliers were already going through their routine. Their uniforms were exactly like ours, except their colors were black and gold. They had two guys who were 6'5" and 6'6", one who I had seen around Buffalo. One of them, a kid named Mike Huiett, was their best player, and the rest of their team looked average. Just like Hutch-Tech and the Buffalo Traditional team, their team was mostly black with a couple of white kids. They were coached by Dave Thomas, a middle-aged, balding, clean-shaven, older white man who wore a sweater and khakis.

---

163 (Staff, JFK hands Holland first defeat: East Aurora survives Eden rally; Yale Cup, 1992)

164 (Staff, Hutch-Tech High School vs. Bennett High School; Yale Cup Box Score, 1992)

Despite some of their players being tall, the Cavaliers did not look well-coached. The ball did not go down low to Mike Huiett on most plays as one would have expected. Just like the other Yale Cup big men we faced, he was not dominant like Turner/Carroll's Kevin Sanford. It looked like they were kind of winging it with no offensive sets and random shots being thrown up. They almost did not look ready to play. We played our methodical game, running our patient zone offenses against their 2-3 zone defense, and slowly built a lead. It was an ugly game, and we sometimes seemed to be in a lull ourselves. No. 32, Jason Hellerman, had some success offensively, catching the ball on the wing and making his jump shots.

"COME ON MAN!" Michael Mann yelled out to No. 15, Andre Higgins, from the bench as his first free throw clanked off the back iron of the basket. I watched that footage several times afterward, which is why I remember it. Still in his street clothes with a cast on his right wrist, Michael Mann continued rooting his teammates on with his head in the game.

"BALL! BALL! BALL!" Coach Jones patrolled the sidelines in his signature game attire, motivating the team to protect the lead. "OUT! OUT! OUT!" On other plays, he demanded Andre, or whoever initiated the offense, to bring the ball back out to set up our offense. Again, he was not a coach who would passively sit and watch the game. It was fun to watch.

"DUNBAR GO IN!" In the third or the fourth quarter, with us up by 15 to 20 points, Coach Jones slowly walked backward toward the end of the bench, keeping his eyes on the game with his arms folded. He quickly whipped around, his eyes wide and animated, giving his order. I jumped off the bench, took off my warmup shirt, and ran towards the scorer's table.

"GO ON! HURRY UP AND ASK WHO YOU'VE GOT! MAKE SURE YOU KNOW WHO YOU'VE GOT!" Coach Jones continued his demands in his scratchy voice. Even subbing me into the game was a production. I went in for Chris Souter. After getting buzzed in, I went to the free throw lane, specifically to the right low block. I crouched down and extended my bent arms up just as we were taught. I felt nervous and cold in my jersey. One of our guys was shooting and it was in front of our bench. Maybe it was Juno Patterson.

The next time down the floor, we ran our basic 5Z-M set, and I ran the baseline flashing on either side of the basket with my arms extended, hoping to get the ball. It was similar to what I did when I scored my first basket at Campus West two years earlier. No. 22, Roderick Peoples, was in the game and caught the ball on the right wing close to the free throw line. He looked at me and hesitated. I stood there with my hands up close to the basket and my eyes wide open. At the last second, Roderick made up his mind and zipped the ball to me using a two-handed chest pass. I quickly caught it, pivoted with two hands, and laid the ball off the backboard. It ricocheted into the basket cleanly for me.

"SCOOBY!" Michael Mann and the other teammates yelled out as I spun around and backpedaled down the court in disbelief about what had just happened. Our crowd exploded too. I had just scored my very first basket for the varsity team, and it was awesome! It was assisted by Roderick 'Spanky' Peoples of all teammates. My heart raced, and I wanted to stay in the game longer, but Coach Jones pulled me out before I could get another one. I sat on the bench, breathing heavily, holding my warmup shirt, feeling like a million bucks!

We went on to beat the Cavaliers 79–64, and we were all excited about it.[165] Our leading scorers were Andre, Jermaine, Adonis, and Jason, who each had 15, 14, 12, and 12 points, respectively.[166] Chris Souter almost scored a triple-double, logging 10 points, 11 rebounds, and 9 assists.[167] Our record was now 3–3 in Yale Cup play.

"ANWAR SCORED HIS FIRST BASKET. COME ON, EVERYONE, ONE, TWO, THREE…AAAAAOOOOOH!" In the locker room, after Coach Jones finished his post-game speech, Michael Mann led a celebration for my first basket. My teammates raised their hands and then lowered them, yelling out a cheer in unison. I stood there enjoying the experience and feeling like I was part of a family. I went home that night and told my mother and brother about my feat. I even got a copy of the *Buffalo News* the next morning and cut out the box score showing my 2 points mixed in with everyone else."[168] I wrote a little narrative about my basket along with the newspaper clipping and put it in a safe place. I was like a kid on Christmas day. Finally, I did of course, take the VHS recording of that game home, and I watched my basket repeatedly before I had to return it to Coach Jones.

* * *

Our next opponent was the Grover Cleveland Presidents, who we beat in the consolation game of the Al Pastor/Pepsi Cola Tournament one month earlier. On Wednesday, January 15th, we traveled across town to their gym for a rematch. Now the stakes were higher. The Presidents wore white tops and lime green shorts as they had in our first matchup. The court was regulation-size. It was an antiquated facility just like Hutch-Tech. It had the solid white backboards found in most Yale Cup Schools and dim lighting. It also had an old salty, industrial odor. There were bleachers on one side of the court and a good number of their students turned out for the game. I looked at some of the girls in the bleachers (when I was not focused on the game), of course. There were many pretty ones.

---

[165] (Jones, Performing Arts High School vs. Hutch-Tech High School, 1992)
[166] (Jones, Performing Arts High School vs. Hutch-Tech High School, 1992)
[167] (Jones, Performing Arts High School vs. Hutch-Tech High School, 1992)
[168] (Jones, Performing Arts High School vs. Hutch-Tech High School, 1992)

Just like the Bennet Tigers, the Presidents had revenge on their minds. Just like Burgard and Traditional, they wanted to get out in the open court, push the ball, and run using their guards, senior No. 31, Joe Sappio and freshman No. 22, Antoine Sims. At times they asserted their muscle using the front court consisting of senior No. 21, Carl Swindle, and juniors No. 14, Tyrone Campbell, and the 6'6" No. 12, Jamie Clark.

Andre Higgins and Adonis Coble magically started gelling as a backcourt. They took care of the ball and consistently put us in our 4-Z zone offense to counter Grover's 3-2 zone defense. Patiently moving the ball around the perimeter, they made timely entry passes to both Jermaine and Keith, who either scored directly off high-percentage layups or by getting to the free-throw line. Open shots were created for Andre, Adonis, Chris, and Dion when the Presidents collapsed inside. In the fourth quarter, we pulled away and won the game 61–56. Again, it was not a spectacular win but a hard-fought one secured through discipline, grit, and patience.

Our offense was balanced with Adonis, Chris, Dion, Jermaine, and Andre, each scoring 15, 12, 10, 10, and 9 points, respectively.[169] Keith added 5 points in the fourth quarter to help keep the lead and ensure the win.[170] Chris held Grover's Kenyon Edwards to 11 points while gathering 10 rebounds, 4 assists, 1 steal and 2 blocked shots.[171] Jermaine also had 10 rebounds and 4 assists, while Dion had 9 rebounds and 3 assists.[172] Our league record was now 4–3.

"That victory was considered an upset!" Coach Jones said this several times after the Grover Cleveland game. We had now beaten them twice. The Presidents and McKinley and Riverside were tied for first place in the Yale Cup, so it certainly could have been considered an upset.[173]

Hutch-Tech's next game was yet another rematch against Coach Joe Knozzo's Seneca Indians in our gym on Friday, January 17, 1992. The first half was close, with each team trading baskets. It was a game of jump shots as both teams exchanged them like prizefighters exchanging jabs. We had a hard time pulling away due to costly mistakes, turnovers and miscues.

At one point, Adonis walked off the court, removed his mouthpiece, and threw it into the bleachers near our bench in frustration. It was no laughing matter, but I chuckled, seeing him openly show his frustration that way. Coach Jones spent much time that year keeping Adonis in a positive state of mind, just as he had to

[169] (Jones, Hutch-Tech High School vs. Grover Cleveland High School; Yale Cup, 1992)
[170] (Jones, Hutch-Tech High School vs. Grover Cleveland High School; Yale Cup, 1992)
[171] (Jones, Hutch-Tech High School vs. Grover Cleveland High School; Yale Cup, 1992)
[172] (Jones, Hutch-Tech High School vs. Grover Cleveland High School; Yale Cup, 1992)
[173] (Staff, Riverside Edges McKinley to take over first, 1992)

do now. The team yearbook pictures were taken at the Performing Arts game, but even then, one shot was of Coach Jones consoling Adonis as he left the floor.

Adonis' flying mouthpiece was not the only unusual thing to happen during that game. At halftime, Seneca trailed us by only 2 points, 39–37, and the game could have easily slipped away.[174] Coach Jones was deep into his halftime speech, giving our guys adjustments. You could only hear his strong, raspy voice and the distant sound of the gymnasium downstairs. Coach looked angry and worked up in his blazer, shirt and tie, khakis, and running sneakers.

"We have to play better defense and rebound the ball," he said in his crouched position, his arms tense and hands grabbing air. "We've got to get better shots on offense and—"

"♫Do you remember the time we fell in love? Do you remember the time when we first met? Do you remember the time…♫" A high pitched, whiny voice sang out, stopping Coach Jones dead in his tracks as he demonstrated something for us. Frozen in position, he turned slowly to see who was gracing us in song.

Andre Higgins sat on the floor with his legs extended straight out and crossed. He seemed to be in a bit of a daze while singing Michael Jackson's latest hit single, *Do You Remember the Time?* The rest of us were all stunned. He was a part of the class of 1993, and those guys would do almost anything at any time.

"SHUT UP!" Michael Mann yelled at Andre in his lion-like voice, silencing him and allowing Coach Jones to resume his halftime analysis and instructions. The adjustments worked, and we secured the 81–72 victory.[175] We were led in scoring by Dion, Chris, Jermaine, Adonis and Keith, who each had 20, 17, 13, 12, and 12 points, respectively.[176] Chris and Jermaine each had 11 rebounds and 4 assists, and Dion and Adonis each had 8 rebounds and 4 assists.[177] Our record was now 5–3.

Our next game was a matchup with the Lafayette Violets on Tuesday, January 21st, in their gym. I knew of Lafayette High School, but had never been there. Sitting in one of Buffalo's more pristine and historic west side neighborhoods, it was an old Gothic-looking building. Lafayette had one of the older and more antiquated gyms in the Yale Cup. Their court was longer than the court at Hutch-Tech, but it had one of those overhead tracks that made corner three-point shots impossible.

It was an ugly game where our guys could not settle into a rhythm and eventually played from behind. We only scored two field goals in the second half and fell behind by 14 points. Lafayette sensed the momentum and cockily did things like clap their hands when Chris Souter shot his free throws. The refs did

---

174 (Staff, Seneca High School vs. Hutch-Tech High School; Yale Cup Box Score, 1992)

175 (Jones, Seneca High School vs. Hutch-Tech High School; Yale Cup, 1992)

176 (Jones, Seneca High School vs. Hutch-Tech High School; Yale Cup, 1992)

177 (Jones, Seneca High School vs. Hutch-Tech High School; Yale Cup, 1992)

nothing about it and just watched the antics. We closed the gap to 6 points twice during the second half before the Violets put the game out of reach and beat us 69–54.[178] Jermaine, Adonis, Dion and Chris each scored 12, 11, 10, and 10 points.[179] Juno Patterson played a strong game coming off the bench and dished out 7 assists.[180] Our record was now 5–4.

Next we hosted the City Honors Centaurs on Friday, January 24th. City Honors was our academic rival, and it felt good to beat them in anything. Coach Francescone brought his young team into our little old gym, hoping to get a win following a decisive loss at the hands of the 1990–91 Engineers the previous year. I watched their team during warmups. Their colors were burgundy and gray, and their jerseys had the school's name on the front. The 6'5" Larry Gilbert played center. He was a tall, skinny kid who wore goggles, a high-top fade, and the No. 33. He had a distinct look, and I remembered playing 21 with him at Turner/Carroll one day in the spring.

I did not recognize the other guys. Their point guard was a dark-skinned kid with big eyes named Shaun Nelms, who wore No. 23, and the other players who logged significant time for them were Zaid Kaudeyr, who wore No. 25, and James Carlos Gant, who wore No. 32. Other players on the team were Montez Carter and Edreys Wajed. They were young. The nucleus of their team were sophomores just like me, Terrance Collison and Jason Wardlaw. They were getting hands-on training experience, unlike us. If our sophomore class matured as we were projected, we would have a monster matchup during our senior season.

In the meantime, the young Centaurs were overmatched by our veteran core. Behind good team defense and teamwork spearheaded by Andre, Adonis and Chris controlled the game and the Engineers went into halftime up 35–22.[181] In the second half, our starters blew the game open to the point where we were up by at least 20 points.

Coach Jones cleared the bench more generously than he had all season. No. 11, Terrance Collison, No. 55, Jason Wardlawer, No. 35, Carlton Ford, No. 42, Damon Kimbrew, and I got into the game. I hoped to get back into the scoring column, but it was not meant to be that day. I might have gotten one or two looks at the basket which I could not convert. The rest of the guys asserted themselves, trying hard to get into the scoring column. Damon Kimbrew drove the ball hard to the basket and scored 4 points. Terrance scored on a couple of layups himself, getting 4 points. Carlton Ford scored and got himself to the free-throw line for an old-fashioned three-point play.

---

[178] (Jones, Hutch-Tech High School vs. Lafayette High School, 1992)

[179] (Jones, Hutch-Tech High School vs. Lafayette High School, 1992)

[180] (Jones, Hutch-Tech High School vs. Lafayette High School, 1992)

[181] (Jones, City Honors High School vs. Hutch-Tech High School, 1992)

"SHIRLEY!" Michael Mann and Dion Frasier yelled out as Jason Wardlawer's baseline jump shot sailed through the net in front of our bench. When he made his basket, the gym erupted, maybe more so than it did for me. Jason jumped up in the air as much as his 6'5", 250-pound frame would allow him to and punched his fist in the air. It was fun watching him have his moment. We went on to beat the young City Honors Centaurs 77–49.[182]

Eleven players got into the scoring column for us that day, led by Keith Hearon's 19 points.[183] He added 6 rebounds, 2 steals and 2 blocked shots.[184] Chris Souter scored 13 points and had 7 rebounds and 4 assists.[185] Our next highest scorers were Adonis Coble and Andre Higgins with 9 points apiece and Dion Frasier with 8 points.[186]

As a first-year player, the '91–'92 season was shaping out as an epic journey. It was both a gut-wrenching and an unpredictable ride, with a few gratifying moments for everyone. We made it through most of our league schedule with a record of 6–4. Our record was now a mediocre 9–8, just over 0.500. There were three league games left in a season that literally swung from one extreme to the other, depending on the day and the game. It was not yet clear what kind of team we had or where we would be in the next few weeks.

---

[182] (Jones, City Honors High School vs. Hutch-Tech High School, 1992)
[183] (Jones, City Honors High School vs. Hutch-Tech High School, 1992)
[184] (Jones, City Honors High School vs. Hutch-Tech High School, 1992)
[185] (Jones, City Honors High School vs. Hutch-Tech High School, 1992)
[186] (Jones, City Honors High School vs. Hutch-Tech High School, 1992)

Chapter 22. Playing on the Junior Varsity and Varsity Teams: My Continuing Basketball Education

"Do you see how he is posting up on the low block and calling for the ball, Anwar? That is what I want you to do!" —**Andy Brown, Assistant Coach, the Hutch-Tech boys' basketball team, February 1992**

As he openly stated at the end of our varsity tryouts, Coach Jones could not play all of us. Truthfully, players like me were not ready for regular varsity minutes. Several of us, likewise, did not play much. We were thus relegated to playing at the end of our varsity games when they were out of reach for either side, learning the game from the bench and Coach Jones' system in practice every day.

I was a *project* and had a lot to learn—I was the proverbial empty vessel or a rough slab of clay that needed to be molded and shaped. Consistent with my performance at the Ken Jones Basketball Camp, I knew how to hustle, play hard, and defend, but the great game of basketball entailed much more than hustling, playing hard and defending. There were skills and fundamentals I needed to hone and sharpen to truly be competitive on the floor and contribute to the team. Some things I could learn and implement during the season, but other things could only be perfected in the offseason with rigorous practice and playing.

* * *

"They had to learn how to win!" Coach Jones made this declaration about Curtis Brooks and the '90-'91 team when I asked him about them, which I did quite often. Apparently, they weren't always the team that went 13-0 in the Yale Cup and won the overall Class B sectional the previous year. I saw from my brother's yearbooks that they weren't very good in their first year but transitioned into the team I saw playing when I was a freshman. *They had to learn how to win.* It sounded simple, but there was a lot involved in that magical word. The class of 1992 seniors and two juniors were also on that team. Did they learn the same lessons? What did it take to win?

"Brooks wasn't the best ball handler I've ever had…" Another surprising series of discussions I had with Coach Jones involved the engine that powered his '90-'91 city and sectional championship team, No. 13, Curtis Brooks. Coach Jones casually shared that one of his players from a school in the Rochester area called

McQuaid years ago, was his best ball handler. He coached in the Rochester area before coming to Buffalo. I don't think he said this to diminish Brooks' legacy in any way. He could tell that I highly looked up to him and wanted to give me some perspective on the topic. Interestingly, he also said that Curtis Brooks wasn't always the most *vocal* point guard, so there seemed to be value in point guards being verbally assertive, not just one of the best players. None of the 1991 seniors returned that season. Several of them had started playing college basketball. There were, in fact, a few instances where I watched Curtis Brooks play for Fredonia State College on the Empire Sports Network. He displayed the shooting ability Coach Jones said the Fredonia head coach was highly interested in during their discussions the previous year when Brooks was being recruited.

Aside from the drills mentioned earlier, another one stands out vividly in my mind. It was called 'War' or 'Battle'. Coach Jones had three or four players gather in the free throw lane while our teammates formed a circle around them and the basket. It was kind of like a mosh pit. Coach Jones would throw the ball up at the basket while each of the players in the key would have to battle for it and then try to score with it. The drill was over when one player scored, but it was difficult to do so as the drill emphasized tough and physical defense, hallmarks of Coach Jones' system. The drill got all the players excited and really sparked a sense of camaraderie, just like Shoot Till You Make, Shoot Till You Miss. I remember us doing that drill only a few times throughout the year.

"YOU'VE GOT FRANKIE HARRIS SYNDROME!" If someone passed the ball too much and was too unselfish, Coach Jones made a joke in an animated way about something called 'Frankie Harris Syndrome'. From my brother's yearbooks, I knew that Frankie Harris, who looked like a nice enough guy, was on the team with the class of 1992 seniors. He was in the class of 1990. Apparently, he was so unselfish that he would give up open layups to assist his teammates' scores. That seemed to be the meaning of Coach Jones' joke.

"Grandma Jones would roll over in her grave if she knew you guys shot free throws like this!" In some practices, Coach Jones told jokes about Grandma Jones. It was usually done to highlight something we were doing wrong or something someone had done wrong in years past, only told in a humorous way. It was typically in his grandfatherly voice, and he was not necessarily scolding anyone. I thought the Grandma Jones jokes were funny.

"DON'T SHOOT THE BALL ON THE WAY DOWN!" Coach Jones yelled this out while grimacing one day when watching Damon Kimbrew shoot a jump shot at the end of an ordered break. He had a specific play following our opponents' scored baskets where we had a designated inbound passer. The other four players ran a designed fast break, which involved running specific *lanes*, setting screens, and potential open jump shots for identified players. If it did not result in an immediate basket, the point guard could set up one of our offenses. During the practice play, it was Damon Kimbrew who shot the ball on the right corner of the side basket. He seemed to release the ball on his way down from the apex of his jump shot. I did not pick up on it, but Coach Jones obviously did.

"No, Anwar. Don't dribble the ball, just pass it." In one practice, Coach Jones had us simulate a tipoff at center court where he once again had a scripted fast break designed if our center was likely to win the tip. In basketball it is understood that the ball can travel faster via passing than anyone can dribble it, so the man who gained first possession of the ball was to turn and quickly pass it to a teammate for an easy layup in stride. For some reason, I wanted to dribble the ball first, prompting Coach Jones and my teammates to correct me. I did not understand it right away, an indication of my low basketball IQ. That day the seniors were not there or were released early. It was Keith Hearon, Roderick Peoples, Carlton Ford, Damon Kimbrew or Jason 'Magic' Majchrowizc, before he broke his collarbone and me.

"Don't fall away on your shot!" I think Dion Frasier said this to me one day when he coached a junior varsity game or in practice. I was a Chicago Bulls fan and saw Michael Jordan and even players like Patrick Ewing shoot fallaway (or fadeaway) jump shots. I thought it was okay and adopted the move to decrease the chances of my shot getting blocked. I did not have the most lift on my shots, so I was always thinking of ways to get them off successfully. If you made the fadeaway jump shots most of the time like Michael Jordan did, that was great. The shot did, however, leave you out of position to compete for the rebound if you missed.

"DON'T BRING THE BALL BACK DOWN!" Coach Jones stressed this to me one time during practice. He eventually stressed it to others too. There were times when I would bring the ball down below my shoulders on offensive rebounds to dribble it for a better position or just out of habit. The only problem was that the guards and other players would either strip it or tie it up for a jump ball, so I had to learn to keep the rebounds high and make another move immediately.

"Don't worry about that. That was good defense!" Adonis Coble said these encouraging words to me one day during practice. I guarded Jason Hellerman as we scrimmaged. He caught the ball on the wing and got off his cannon-like jump shot. I got a piece of the ball as he brought it up. I thought I used enough force to knock it loose, but he maintained possession and made the basket. He was a very accurate shooter. Despite my offensive shortcomings, I was a solid defender and a rebounder, which Coach Jones weighed heavily. I had that going for me.

"He's starting to fill out a little bit more," Coach Jones said at practice one day when lecturing us about the principle of "A good strong player is better than a good weak player!" I was surprised when he singled me out as opposed to someone like Roderick Peoples, who was our strongest player. I honestly did not know that

I was filling out muscle-wise. Just like many of my teammates, the importance of strengthening ourselves did not immediately sink in, and we did not have a defined weight program to help us bulk up.

"WE'VE GOT TO GET OUT OF THIS START AND STOP FOOTBALL WAY OF PLAYING THE GAME!" Speaking of Roderick, I distinctly recall Coach Jones blurting this out one day in practice. As described, Roderick was our most *physical* player. He came over from the football field, and he played basketball in a football way. It involved lots of contact and a starting and stopping fashion, as opposed to the fluidity inherent in basketball. Coach Jones wanted to smooth it all out. A bunch of us had a lot of things to learn that year.

"Who just shot that?" During a scrimmage or a drill, I hoisted up a shot from behind the three-point arc one day, and it rattled in for me. After a bunch of murmurings from Coach Jones and my teammates, I hesitantly raised my hand and acknowledged that I shot it. Coach murmured something to the effect of, "We don't want Dunbar shooting too many of those right now." His words caused me to not think about shooting three-pointers, at least for a little while.

What I was lacking the most on the offensive end was an identity. I had not developed a *go-to move,* whether it was a jump shot, a dribble move, or a post move. I did not know that I had to or that I should develop one. I was a good free-throw shooter. I also did not know how or where to push myself. A metric for a lot of the guys was dunking the ball, which I never pressured myself to do. Even with my horribly bad flat feet, it is something I could have achieved if I had worked on my lower body strength and pushed myself.

I just did not know how to push myself further and harder in a ruthless kind of way. In any case, these were just some of my own learning points that season. All of us who did not play much at the varsity level, learned a lot by watching and participating in practices that year.

"Patience is a virtue, they tell me." Of all the drills and fundamentals Coach Jones taught us, as stated earlier, there was a life and character-building component to his basketball program. Among the chaos of getting seventeen or eighteen kids on the same page, there were quotes like this one to keep us hopeful, reeled in, and even-keeled. Another powerful quote was, "We are creatures of habit, I was told."

There were also times during the season when Coach Jones gave me that grandfatherly wink in practices. It was times like that when he was more than a coach. Despite how some of the guys felt, he genuinely cared about his players beyond the great game of basketball. For some of us, he filled a fatherly/grandfatherly role. That was huge for players who didn't have it at home.

* * *

Chapter 22. Playing on the Junior Varsity and Varsity Teams: My Continuing Basketball Education

As our varsity schedule progressed, some of us new players logged in double duty. We practiced with the junior varsity team in the mornings before school and then with the varsity team after school. It was a significant commitment for thirteen- to fifteen-year-old boys and a lot of work. It required a lot of desire, discipline and focus. All three of the sophomores on the varsity team participated in the double sessions—Terrance Collison, Jason Wardlawer and myself. It was Coach Jones' way of developing us since we were not playing much on the varsity team.

Interestingly some of the juniors still participated on the junior varsity team. With my limited knowledge at the time, I knew that juniors did not normally play on junior varsity teams, as they were only supposed to be for freshmen and sophomores. I thought it was simply a rite of passage. I figured I would log major minutes on the varsity team and forge my own legacy the next year as a junior. A crop of underclassmen also played with us on the junior varsity team.

The junior varsity team was coached by Andy Brown, a young white man in his late twenties or early thirties. He was around 5'8", clean-faced and had brown hair with innocent eyes. He could have been from any small town. He was not a faculty member at Hutch-Tech; just a volunteer or protégé working with Coach Jones. I did not know what Coach Brown did at his full-time job, but he was there coaching us in the mornings and at our games that year. He was in the 1991–92 boys' basketball team's picture kneeling next to Coach Jones, and he was very much considered a part of the program.

Legend had it that the previous junior varsity coach was a young black man named 'Tate'. Coach Jones did not bring him back because of some falling out or philosophical differences. The players who played under Tate usually chuckled when they talked about him. I heard stories about him from Terrance Collison, Carlton Ford and Damon Kimbrew.

At those morning practices, Coach Brown usually wore a tee-shirt, shorts, and sneakers. He looked more like one of us; his shirts were baggier and his shorts were longer than Coach Jones'. His practices felt a lot different than those run by Coach Jones too, who was a seasoned veteran. Instead of having a powerful, thunderous, and gritty voice like Coach Jones, his was softer and more polite. As such, the respect level and seriousness of the practices were different.

Coach Jones usually sat in and watched our practices from the bleachers. Coach Brown adamantly tried getting me to *post up* on the low block with my back to the basket like Patrick Ewing or Hakeem Olajuwon. Of my memories of him, this is the most vivid. It made sense since, at 6'2", I was one of the taller guys on the team and playing the four and five positions.

In the highest levels of basketball, posting up was not something only done by big men. Michael Jordan, who was a tall guard, consistently posted up smaller guards. Magic Johnson did also. It was a powerful way to score the ball, but as a four or a five, you relied on the wing players to share the ball with you. Posting up also made you stationary, and there were many other ways to play offense and score. Another move involved cutting to the basket without the ball, facing the basket and shooting it, or slashing to the basket off the dribble. It took quite a bit of hammering by Coach Brown before posting up with my back to the basket finally stuck in my brain.

It turned out that basketball was a fun but complex game with multiple dimensions. A lot went into it besides simply putting the ball in the hoop more than your opponent. Though I watched lots of NBA basketball, had gone to the Ken Jones Basketball Camp, and played my share of street basketball, I still had a relatively low basketball IQ. My fundamentals and overall understanding of the game needed lots of work, and in general, I needed to put things together in terms of fundamentals and skills—knowing what to do and when, and mentally showing up for every game and practice.

There was one other sophomore on the junior varsity team with us that year, Jarrod Hiddleston. Jarrod was a skinny, light-skinned kid with short, curly hair. His parents were from Guatemala which he mentioned often, at least his father was. Martavious Johnson came out for a few practices and maybe one game. He had both the ability and quickness, but I do not think he wanted to play enough to continue to participate in the program long-term. Some of the freshmen from the class of 1995 also participated. Among them were Adrian Callahan, Earl Holmes, Kevin Adkins, Scott Bell, and another kid named David Brown, a light-skinned kid with sleepy eyes and a high-top fade.

As observed in intramurals, some of the guys from the class of 1995 were not very humble, probably because they were ahead of the curve talent-wise. They had lots of attitude, swagger, and immaturity early on. Some of them did not just show up to participate and learn. It was as though they had to leave their own unique mark on things, and they succeeded. Adrian Callahan, for example, gave Coach Brown a hard time, seemingly for no reason.

"Look, if you do not want to be here, then just GET OUT!" One morning Coach Brown reached the end of his patience with Adrian, and things boiled over. For some reason, Adrian did not want to receive his coaching. Numerous times when given instruction, he gave Coach Brown aggressive stares with his mouth open like he wanted to fight him. Perhaps he did not feel like he should have been playing on the junior varsity team. Perhaps he felt like he should have been getting instruction from the master himself. Either way, it was very noticeable, and you could feel something building up. Coach Jones and Coach Brown probably talked about it as it was happening, and they agreed not to have Adrian return.

Chapter 22. Playing on the Junior Varsity and Varsity Teams: My Continuing Basketball Education

"I'M GOING TO GET MY OLDER BROTHER ON YOU!" In his high-pitched and screechy voice, Adrian yelled as he darted out of the gym and back up to the locker room.

"YEAH, GO AND GET YOUR BROTHER!" Coach Brown yelled his reply at Adrian, not backing down and watching him run away. The rest of us looked on, surprised about what had happened, while others were amused. Practice just sort of resumed afterwards though some tension was still in the air.

The next morning, Adrian surprisingly returned to practice as though nothing happened. I looked on wondering how Coach Jones and Coach Brown would respond. Would they just take him back? Had everything been patched up since the meltdown the previous morning?

Coach Jones, in fact, saw him, intercepted him, and took him off to the side to talk privately. We all looked over in that direction. Coach Jones' voice lowered to a whisper, and Adrian gave him a clear level of respect, slowly receiving what he was being told. Whatever was said, He did not resist. He nodded, left and he did not play in the program again his freshman year. I was relieved that there would not be any more confrontations, or so I thought.

Adrian was not alone in terms of making a dubious early mark on the Hutch-Tech boys' basketball program. Like others in Adrian's class, Earl Holmes was also quite the talker. As a freshman, he was a skinny, light-skinned, pesky kid with an insular attitude and a smart mouth. One day Earl voiced a lack of respect for Michael Mann, one of our captains who was held in high regard by Coach Jones and his teammates.

Even though Michael fractured his wrist and sat out a great deal of his senior season, he regularly attended our junior varsity practices and games on those cold Saturday mornings when he could have stayed home in his warm bed. He loved the program though, and he thought it was important to support and encourage the younger guys. He was the last guy to get into a confrontation with anyone, but this one time Earl targeted and verbally attacked our senior captain.

"Michael, you are DOO-DOO! You're GARBAGE, and you do not have any game!" Earl let off a flurry of insults against our undeserving senior leader. I do not remember Michael ever provoking Earl into that tirade. It may have been an indicator of how some of the class of 1995 guys saw things. They may have thought that they were better than everyone else and would soon be taking over. Perhaps they saw it as a divide-and-conquer type of thing for themselves, as opposed to adding to the legacy of the program.

Michael's facial expression and body language showed that he was hurt by Earl's attack. He did not know what to say. Being a passive and nice guy myself, I did not know how to stick up for Michael at that time, and I wanted Earl to stop.

Who would do such a thing? And why? Just like Adrian, though, Earl eventually got his pieces of humble pie. One piece came from Coach Jones himself.

"GIVE ME PLAYERS WHO *WANT* TO PLAY VERSUS THOSE WHO *THINK* THEY WANT TO PLAY!" This quote from Coach Jones involved wanting to see the desires of players. Getting into the games was an opportunity and a privilege, and if the players did not recognize it initially, Coach Jones made sure they did. If they never appreciated it, he did not want them.

"I was not talented enough to get much playing time in high school, but whenever the coach called on me, I would jump up off the bench and be ready to play in an instant!" This story involved one of Coach Jones' core teachings to his players, and that was to be ready and appreciative of going into the game. He arguably beat this story into us. He always reenacted it, jumping off the bench and running to the imaginary scorer's table with his childlike enthusiasm. That story was an extension of his parable about wanting players who *wanted* to play versus players who *thought* they wanted to play.

"HOLMES GO IN," Coach Jones said during a game when Coach Brown was not there. At some point in the game, he looked down the bench and focused on Earl. Earl got off the bench in a very nonchalant way, walking slowly and smugly toward the scorer's table.

"SIT DOWN HOLMES," Coach Jones said disgusted, seeing his lack of urgency. A little later in the game, it happened again. Coach Jones yelled down to the end of the bench, "HOLMES GO IN!" Earl once again took his time getting off the bench, perhaps aware that Coach was trying to teach him a lesson and wanting to show that he could not be broken.

"SIT DOOOWN HOLMES," Coach Jones said, waving Earl away with his hand.

This went on about three to four more times until Earl finally broke down and cried. I am certain each of us was surprised to see the display. Afterward, Coach Jones lectured us about it. It was not over, however, for controversies involving Earl. His second piece of humble pie came from another player who made that 1991–92 season a memorable one.

"SHUT UP! You talk too much, and your game is not even all of that!" Adonis Coble confronted Earl one day in the gym in his high-pitched voice. Adonis was not one to hold his tongue either. I do not recall how it started, but when he finished, there was a silence where everyone just looked on, wondering what was going to happen next. Adonis looked at Earl, daring him to say something else. While Earl clearly had little respect for Michael Mann, he respected Adonis. He looked at Adonis with a half-smile, not knowing how to respond. I laughed inside and was happy someone stepped up and declared martial law even if just temporarily.

Chapter 22. Playing on the Junior Varsity and Varsity Teams: My Continuing Basketball Education

* * *

While I was watching the 1990–91 Hutch-Tech boys' basketball team's historic march to glory during my freshman year, Gabe was working his way up the Cleveland Hill basketball program, which had both formal modified and junior varsity programs. He played under Coach Glen Graham, whose name came up regularly in discussions about our respective basketball programs. One Saturday morning I asked Gabe if I could come sit in on one of their practices. After getting the okay from Coach Graham, I went with him one morning and sat in.

Cleveland Hill High School sat in a quiet suburban neighborhood off Harlem Road in Cheektowaga. Unlike Buffalo Public Schools, Cleve Hill was like a palace. They had multiple gymnasiums in the building, in addition to having their own football field and track in the back of the school. Even as a suburban school, Cleveland Hill had a high number of black students enrolled. Thus, Gabe was not alone in terms of race, and he had his own little crew out there, most of whom played football and basketball.

They were called the Cleveland Hill Eagles, and their colors were blue and gold. I had been in their main gym numerous times on visits to the school with Gabe, and it dwarfed ours. The court was regulation-size with glass backboards and breakaway rims which were regularly dunked on by some of their players. A 6'3" forward named Roland Shelton comes to mind, who we talked about regularly when comparing our two basketball programs.

Roland was not a particularly loud guy, but the strong and silent type. He had large, powerful thighs and a Gumby haircut, which was popular in the early '90s for young black men. He readily dunked the ball with authority in pickup games at places like St. Aloysius Catholic School on Cleveland Drive when groups of us gathered to play there. I also remember playing with Derrick Gray who had graduated by then, but who was still one of the pillars of that crew.

That Saturday practice I attended with Gabe was on a cold Western New York morning. Mr. Smith dropped us off in the rear of the school where we walked into the gym complex. Some of the other players had started trickling in and I waited in the gym for them to all come out. They all wore blue and gold practice tank tops.

Gabe introduced me to Coach Graham, who was a studious-looking, dark-skinned man with glasses and short hair. He wore a sweatshirt and sweatpants that morning with a whistle around his neck. Gabe later told me that Coach Graham went to Cleveland Hill back in his youth years earlier. I found a place in the bleachers and just looked on.

"EXECUTE! EXECUTE!" The Eagles went through their stretches, warmups, and drills, which were led by a skinny Italian kid named Jeff Sabatino, who barked out commands when he wanted them to do something. It was interesting seeing a program different from my own. Their modified team was ethnically mixed. In addition to the kid leading the warmups, there was also a tall skinny kid with goggles who reminded me of the Los Angeles Lakers' Kurt Rambis. His name was Dan Becker. There were other African American kids on the team in addition to Gabe, including Adrian Jones, Damion Richardson, and Jason Gray, the younger brother of the aforementioned Derrick Gray. I had heard so much about these guys that I felt like I knew them.

"HOP BASELINE! HOP BASELINE!" Coach Graham was a yeller like Coach Jones, and he seemed to emphasize team defense. He did not hesitate to call out his players, especially Gabe who did not always take practice seriously, and was not afraid to give it back to his coach. Just as in our practices, they had offensive and defensive drills and eventually scrimmaged against each other. I got a little fidgety up in the stands at times, wanting to go down, rip off my street clothes, and compete with them, but it was not my team or my school.

Their practice was very impressive, and I wondered how our players would match up against theirs. Aside from a non-league or pre-season tournament game, we probably would never play the Eagles. After practice, Gabe introduced me to some of his teammates. With Adrian and Jason, there was a natural camaraderie that we, as black students, shared in predominantly white environments. Just as I had heard about them, Gabe had probably told them about me.

That practice was the only time I saw my best friend practice or play in the Cleveland Hill blue and gold. He joked about getting physical in practice with players like Dan Becker. He would sometimes lower his shoulder and ram into his defenseless teammate when going up for a rebound or a shot. As with most things involving Gabe, it seemed like one big joke. It was an altogether different vibe than what I was experiencing at Hutch-Tech. In our sophomore year, while I earned a spot on the Hutch-Tech varsity basketball team, Gabe earned a roster spot on Cleveland Hill's junior varsity team with the same teammates that I saw him practice with. On the trajectory he was on, he would play on his varsity team as a junior and a senior. We both would.

* * *

My first junior varsity game was in the Hutch-Tech gym against Turner/Carroll. It was the Saturday morning after our varsity team's second loss to the Chargers in the Pepsi Cola/Al Pastor Memorial Tournament in early December of 1991. Our junior varsity games started at 10:00 a.m., so we had to get to school around 9:00 a.m. to get changed and warmed up. There were no formal pre-game warm up drills for the junior varsity games, just stretching and shooting around. There were no fans, no introductions to the starting lineups, and no buzz in our gym.

Chapter 22. Playing on the Junior Varsity and Varsity Teams: My Continuing Basketball Education

The energy and the aura were completely different than that of our varsity games. We did have two referees and one or two of the managers to work the scoreboard.

For that first game, we fielded a team consisting of some of the juniors who were not getting much playing time with the varsity team. I am thinking of Carlton Ford, Damon Kimbrew, and Jason 'Magic' Majchrowicz. In addition to Terrance Collison, Jason Wardlawer and me. Jarrod Hiddleston from the 1994 class was there, and the band of freshmen from the class of 1995 was also coming to the practices. Varsity team members wore our white tops and maroon shorts, while the freshman and sophomores who were not on the varsity team wore white tops and white shorts.

Turner/Carroll wore their visiting all-black uniforms with red and white numbers and letters. There was one face I recognized immediately on their team, one that I was happy to see, Ronald Jennings from Campus West. Being opponents now, we exchanged a quick greeting at the beginning of the game, but nothing more. He looked about the same and had not grown much height-wise. I did not start in that game and watched the tipoff from the bench. Ronald played point guard as he advanced the ball up the floor and put the Chargers into their offenses. He still wore No. 21 in honor of the Atlanta Hawks' Dominique Wilkins.

I got into the game sporadically and did not know what I was doing. I somewhat knew the offense we were running, but did not quite know *how* to play in it. What I did know to do was to 'cut to the backdoor' and 'flash' to the basket. Magic was fun to play with and was a 'pass-first' player. He hit me with a no-look pass on one play as I flashed to the basket, allowing me to score off a layup. On two other instances, I got to the free throw line and went one for two on each trip, finishing the game with 4 points and a couple of rebounds. We lost that game by 10 or 12 points. Ronald and I shook hands afterward. We had brief words and that was the last time I saw him for a long time, probably years. He was still one of my heroes.

My second junior varsity game was against St. Joseph's Collegiate Institute on Kenmore Avenue in North Buffalo. 'St. Joe's' as they were known for short, was a prestigious private school and a basketball powerhouse in Western New York. That Saturday morning was a typical wintery December Saturday in Buffalo with cloudy gray skies, frigid temperatures, and snowy and slushy streets.

St. Joe's basketball court was regulation-sized, with glass backboards and breakaway rims. Unlike the Turner/Carroll junior varsity game at Tech, the game was well-attended for a Saturday morning. Looking up in the stands, most of the spectators were white. Some were younger, but many were adults and seniors, perhaps grandparents of some of the kids we played against.

Coach Brown started me with Terrance Collison, Carlton Ford, Damon Kimbrew and Jason Majchrowicz. Playing against St. Joe's, I once again realized that playing organized sports was much different than playing pickup street games. The games were timed, set plays and strategies were being used, and referees called everything from reaching, to going over the back on rebounds, to offensive fouls. Conditioning was also key during organized basketball games, because you had to hustle back on defense and go for every rebound.

"REF THAT WAS A CARRY!" Someone in the crowd yelled out, immediately following one of my high dribbles. I caught the ball on the wing and reverted to my street game. I tried to beat my man off the dribble, and I tried to put the ball through my legs, and it just got away from me, but the referee let it go, fortunately. The ball felt light like a feather, but also solid like a rock, and I had difficulty controlling it.

We ran our motion offenses against St. Joe's that day. I did not understand how to integrate myself into the set and struggled to find my place. One of my few baskets came from an assist from Magic, who caught me cutting to the basket and flashing open.

"Do not do that! Just play ball!" Magic, who had an even-keeled personality, tried to keep me grounded after my score. I pumped my fist in the air and gave a look to the kid I had scored on. I was struggling and happy to finally get into the scoring column. I also got to the free-throw line several times, going one-for-two most of the time. The juniors were aggressive in that game and went strong to the basket.

"DUNBAR!" Coach Jones was in attendance and yelled out to me several times, standing up on the top row of the bleachers. He wore a sweatshirt, jeans, and boots. Coach Brown was coaching us that day, but Coach Jones exerted his influence from the stands. Looking up at him, he acted out, squeezing the ball in a crouched position with two hands in front of his chest, his eyes wide and bulging, with a menacing expression on his face. I was giving what I thought was a good effort, but he looked angry with me.

"Yes, I understand," I communicated to him through a nonverbal nod, sucking wind with my hands at my side. It was like the Lancaster scrimmage when he scolded Michael Mann for not bringing the ball back out and setting up the offense. Like the first-year starters on our varsity team, I was learning how to compete.

Some of the freshmen got in to play throughout the game. I think the young St. Joe's Marauders eventually pulled away from us and won that game. I did my best in my second junior varsity game. However, I still felt like I did not quite know what I was doing.

* * *

In addition to the games against Turner/Carroll and St. Joes, we had three more junior varsity games against Yale Cup opponents. They were: South Park, Lafayette and Buffalo Traditional. The games were played on Saturday mornings at 10 a.m. Coach Brown led us to the bench at South Park again. In the bleachers, Coach Jones was in the background, stirring and getting into the game himself, just like at St. Joe's. The bleachers were much closer to the benches than at our gym, so Coach Jones was closer too.

"DUNBAR!" I started off slow and after one play in the first half, he yelled out to me. I looked up at him in the stands, trying to catch my breath. "REBOUND THE BALL!" He made his demand once again in that crouched position using his two hands clutching an imaginary basketball in front of his chest. He had that same menacing look on his face, which made me hustle more when I saw it.

"IF DUNBAR ISN'T GOING TO PLAY, THEN GET HIM OUT OF THERE!" Coach Jones yelled those words to Coach Brown loud enough for everyone to hear them. He was not happy with my performance. He got my attention, and I immediately went from second to fifth gear. We lost that game to South Park, but I finished with about 8 points off layups and free throws and grabbed a bunch of rebounds. The Lafayette game was similar, where I was out there figuring things out and ended up with a handful of points and rebounds.

My best junior varsity game was our last contest against Buffalo Traditional. In that game, Terrance and I seemed to be in sync as we ran our 5-MT Low offense against Traditional's man-to-man defense. I grasped what Coach Brown wanted me to do regarding posting up on the low block. Most of the time when I would get into position and call for the ball on the low block, Terrance would catch it on the wing, look for me, and then unselfishly dump it into me so that I could make a move towards the basket.

On several plays after catching the ball, I initiated contact with some defenders, either scoring or getting to the free-throw line, where I converted most of my free throws. I was in a rhythm from the free throw line that day, taking my two dribbles and then following the acronym 'BEEF' we learned at camp (<u>B</u>ody balance, <u>E</u>yes on the basket, <u>E</u>lbow in, and <u>F</u>ollow through). Many of those shots sailed right through the net, while others rattled around the rim and then dropped in. I think I went eight-for-ten or something like that. Terrance also got into a rhythm.

We wound up winning that game. I scored 16 points, while Terrance scored 12 points. That Monday morning, Coach Jones wrote up a game summary for the announcements where Terrance and I were featured, and our scoring outputs were highlighted. It felt instantly good, but also a little hollow because it was not in one of the varsity games. Next year this rite of passage would be over, and the time would come to make our mark on the varsity team, where we would play until we graduated. That was the way it was going to go.

Chapter 23. The 1991–92 League Schedule: The Final Three Games

"Other Coaches told Jonesy that they knew his teams would be in it in the end because of the way they took care of the ball and played defense!" **—Kathleen Garcenea, Coach, multiple Hutch-Tech sports, the 1990s, June 2012**

By early February 1992, with the Yale Cup league schedule nearly complete, the Buffalo Bills advanced to the Super Bowl for the second-straight year. Super Bowl XXVI was held at the Hubert H. Humphrey Metrodome in Minneapolis, MN. There would be no partying in tropical weather this year by the Bills leading up to the game. The Bills had one Super Bowl trip under their belts and were in a prime position to redeem themselves. They finished the regular season with a 13–3 record, just like the previous year. Then they made it to the Super Bowl again by defeating the Kansas City Chiefs 37–14 and the Denver Broncos 10–7, both at home at Rich Stadium in Orchard Park, NY.

The Bills' opponent was the Washington Redskins. They were from the NFC East Division, like the New York Giants, who defeated the Bills the previous year. Interestingly, the Giants did not make the playoffs. The great Bill Parcells, who led the Giants to their only two Super Bowl victories at the time, retired. He had enough of the grind and decided to spend his time doing other things. He resurfaced further up the coast years later playing with the New England Patriots.

Joe Gibbs' Washington Redskins were a well-oiled machine that was clicking in all three phases of the game; offense, defense, and special teams. While the Buffalo Bills squeaked into Super Bowl XXVI, the Washington Redskins steamrolled both of their opponents. They defeated the Atlanta Falcons 24–7 and then the Detroit Lions 41–10 at home at RFK Stadium. I wondered how the Bills would do against the burgundy and gold, as this was not the New York Giants offense that would try to possess the ball and pound out yards in a low-scoring game. Like the Giants in the previous year, the Redskins had the right mix of experience and talent in both the ranks of the players and the coaching staff. Head Coach, Joe Gibbs, was making his third Super Bowl appearance with Mark Rypien as the quarterback. It is interesting to note that Rypien was not the starter in their previous two Super Bowl victories.

The Super Bowl started off controversially because the starting running back, and I believe league MVP No. 34, Thurman Thomas, lost his helmet and was unavailable for the first series of the game. The Bills likewise started off slow. The

Redskins, on the other hand, did not start off slow and moved the ball down the field at will behind the crisp passing of No. 7, Mark Rypien. He threw to his legendary wide receivers No. 81, Art Monk, No. 84, Gary Clark, and No. 83, Rickey Sanders, with bullets that hit them right on their numbers.

When the Redskins were not moving the ball in the air, they moved it on the ground as their legendary offensive line known as 'The Hogs' plowed their way through No. 78, Bruce Smith, and the Bills' front seven, creating nice running lanes for running back No. 21, Ernest Byner. On defense they slowed Jim Kelly and the offense down enough to create a comfortable lead that would never be threatened. At halftime the score was 17–0, and by the game's end, the Redskins won 37–24.

My brother and I watched the game with friends from our church that wintery Western New York Sunday evening. I understood the game much better that year, and I was not as emotionally vested in it as I was with Super Bowl XXV. It was a tough loss for the Bills and the city. They had gotten back to the big game and hoped to exorcise the demons of the previous year, only to be defeated again. Like what we were experiencing at Hutch-Tech, repeating the previous year's successes was not a given.

The Bills lost the Super Bowl two years in a row. However, change was all around us in sports and the world in general. Nothing seemed to ever stay the same. The year 1992 would present a three-way presidential race between President George H.W. Bush, Governor William 'Bill' Jefferson Clinton, and H. Ross Perot. It would have ramifications for everyone going forward. Would President Bush repeat? More importantly for us, the Hutch-Tech boys' basketball team did not seem to be on track to repeat as Yale Cup Champions. Could we, and would we, repeat as Section VI Class B Champions?

* * *

"Your *ATTITUDE* determines your *ALTITUDE*!" Coach Jones told our struggling team this daily in addition to a host of other quotes to compliment his vast knowledge of basketball. "As much as I want you all to become good basketball players, I want you to become even better people," was something else he regularly told us. Many of us looked on when he said it, some comprehending it and others not so much. I interpreted it as while the wins and losses mattered, how we did it mattered even more. Furthermore, Coach Jones also cared about developing quality and high-character human beings and men. Our basketball program was about winning games; it was about other things too.

* * *

"Brother Peoples is conspicuous by his absence," Coach Jones said to us a couple of times that season when Roderick was absent from practice, seemingly unannounced. It was not excessive to the point that Coach Jones cut him, but it was enough for him to periodically share these cryptic words with us at the start of our practices. Aside from Terrance Collison, I did not know enough about my teammates' lives to understand why they might have to miss even one of our mandated practices every now and then.

Late in the Yale Cup schedule that year, something transpired that forced Roderick to have to miss participating in the basketball program for a short stint. The Buffalo Public Schools were closed the last week in January. I believe we took standardized tests at Hutch-Tech that week, or there were parent-teacher conferences. However, that did not mean it was a week off for the boys' basketball team. Each day we returned to Hutch-Tech for practices in the mid-morning, and we were out of the gym by noon or shortly afterward. It might have been a week off for the other Yale Cup teams, but Coach Jones would fully use the time.

That week Coach Jones allowed some of the junior varsity players to come in and practice with the varsity team. After one of the practices, some guys played pickup games while the rest of us either dispersed, watched from the sidelines, or just shot baskets independently. I sat on the sidelines watching the guys play one day. Coach Jones might have gone upstairs. He usually hung out in the gym watching the players play or else walked around the gym with the wide push broom to clear any lint and debris off the court to give us all better traction, something he did before, during, or after practices.

Roderick 'Spanky' Peoples and Jerrod Hiddleston, from my class of 1994, wound up on opposite teams that day. I do not recall how the trash-talking started, but it did, and whatever Jarrod said to Roderick, who already had a short temper, it caused it to run hotter. You could visibly see Roderick playing more physically out there and getting agitated. He grunted and played more aggressively—he was still more of a football player than a basketball player. I did not think much of it as I looked on. He visibly shoved Jarrod around quite a bit close to the basket. It was easy as Jarrod was about half his size in build.

Once the game finished, most of the guys went upstairs. I hung out down in the gym, shooting free throws and doing the Mikan Drill or some other skill-building drill. That is when Kevin Adkins approached me, looking like he had seen a ghost.

"YO," he said in his somber, deep West Indian voice. "Roderick just body slammed Jarrod in the locker room." Kevin was a dark-skinned youth who was almost six feet and bow-legged. He had a slow and methodical walk, kind of like a deer, and his steps were very staccato.

"What?" I picked up the ball, smiling, almost laughing, and in disbelief. "Stop playing around Kevin."

"Yeah, I'm not playing. They were talking trash to one another, and Roderick picked him up and slammed him on the concrete," Kevin said, not laughing.

Most everyone had dispersed when I returned to the locker room, so I could not ask anyone else. I was stunned to hear what Kevin said, but on the other hand, I was not surprised because Roderick had a mean and impulsive side. He was a part of the class of 1993, after all, and at that time, I could see the tensions running high during that pickup game.

"I've suspended Brother Peoples for the next couple of practices and the Kensington game," Coach Jones said, making his somber announcement to the team in his low grandfatherly voice as we all sat looking on in the bleachers. "He did something to Jarrod Hiddleston from the junior varsity team. Hiddleston's father called and asked me about it, and I decided that the best thing would be to discipline Peoples." *Brother* Peoples was a nickname Coach Jones gave Roderick.

Jarrod must have gone home and told his father. Or his folks might have noticed him struggling to get around and asked him what was wrong. They must have been livid when they heard what had happened. After all, who would have expected such a thing to happen to their son at Hutch-Tech, of all the schools in Buffalo? I recall seeing Jarrod's parents a couple of times. His dad was a brown-skinned studious-looking Guatemalan man with a strong accent. His mother was a lovely brown-skinned, pleasant-looking woman.

Around that time, we also lost our backup point guard, Juno Patterson. I did not know what happened to him, only that he was not around much. Then one day during practice, he was at one end of the gym in street clothes with his backpack, talking to Coach Jones. They shook hands and Coach Jones patted him on the back. He left the gym never to wear the maroon and gold again. Our team had now suffered six hits to the initial roster, two of which we would be getting back.

Roderick's suspension was short-lived, and Michael Mann had been medically cleared to return to the team. The cast on his right wrist was gone, and he was now back out on the court with us in the afternoons getting back into shape and getting ready to play. Andre Higgins giggled in his high-pitched voice like a little kid, and he had lots of fun as he jokingly made Michael work during drills, like the Shadow Drill. Michael had to follow him around and play defense. It was like a kid on a playground. It was perfect timing, as we needed all our experienced players back for the final stretch of Yale Cup play that lay ahead of us.

* * *

The Hutch-Tech varsity league record was now 6–4, and three Yale Cup games lay ahead of us. None of the three teams were *cupcakes*. All three were athletic, racehorse-style teams with guys who could run, jump up, and "unscrew the light bulbs," as Coach Jones would say. Our first attempt at getting a seventh win was against the Kensington High School Knights in their gym. The school was next to the Kensington Expressway and beside the Langfield Projects, not far from my house on Hastings Avenue.

The Kensington game took place on Tuesday, February 4, 1992. Because we did not have buses to take us across town to our games, Coach Jones and maybe another faculty member, drove the players who logged in the most minutes to the games, while the rest of us used public transportation after leaving our last class early.

I was slightly late arriving at the game. When I got off the 12-A Utica bus, I hurried down Suffolk Avenue into the building, and up to the gym in the back of the school. Play had already started. We wore our maroon-colored visitors jerseys, while Kensington wore their home whites with green letters and gold and green trim. After changing into my locker room uniform, I ran out into the gym and onto the bench.

Dion Frasier tried to inbound the ball to Andre Higgins or Chris Souter. I still remember one of Kensington's long, athletic players deflecting the ball as Dion tried to inbound it. It shot up in the air all the way to the ceiling, where it hit one of the lights and made a crashing noise. I could feel the game's intensity just watching those couple of seconds. Both teams were fighting for their lives, and only one would win.

The game was literally a slugfest. While Coach Jones worked our sidelines, Coach Bob Mitchell worked his, grimacing and hollering at his players on the court, trying to get his team to execute his game plan. Coach Mitchell was an older black man with a small Afro, a mustache, and he was dressed in a suit. He wanted his Kensington Knights to create turnovers against our small and less physically gifted team, so their athletes could get out and run.

Kensington played a 2-3 zone against us. Coach Jones, as usual, wanted his team to be patient on offense and to *work* the ball for good shots, which they did. The ball was patiently moved around the perimeter for open jump shots and then passed into the *teeth* of the defense for timely layups or trips to the free-throw line. In the first half, Adonis Coble, Dion Frasier and Jermaine Fuller carried our offense. From the bench I recognized Sam Tucker from the Kensington roster. He was in the Youth Leadership of Western New York Program with me.

The game was tight at halftime, with Hutch-Tech leading 34–33. Coach Jones gave a spirited talk to our players who looked on, realizing they were in a real brawl and that the game was winnable. The way he coached and taught the great game of basketball, all games were winnable if the game plan was executed properly.

"Work the ball. Be patient on offense. We cannot afford to run up and down the floor with these guys," Coach Jones said in his raspy voice. "Continue to play disciplined defense and box out! Now bring it in here," he continued as we all reached our hands in, counted down, and yelled out our school name, led by Michael Mann. "ONE, TWO, THREE, TECH!"

The second half of the game mirrored the first.[187] Kensington's athletic ability eventually took its toll as two of our key frontcourt starters, Chris Souter and Jermaine Fuller, got into foul trouble, causing Coach Jones to buy time with juniors Keith Hearon and Jason Hellerman. The game continued to grind away, and at the end of regulation, it was knotted up 61–61, forcing overtime.[188]

In the overtime period, the game remained close until Hutch-Tech took a four-point lead late in the period. It evaporated, and Kensington's tall and wiry No. 33, Kilroy Jackson, found himself on the free throw line with his team down 66–64 with no time left on the clock. He could tie the game, or we would escape with the victory. Kilroy sank the first shot, shaving our margin to a one-point lead, 66–65.

The last shot seemed to take forever and had long-lasting consequences for both teams. Kilroy Jackson had excellent shooting mechanics, and even though it looked like he released the ball from his hands like his first shot, he put too much force on it. It hit the back iron of the rim and clanked back out, giving us the 66–65 hard-fought victory.

We had our seventh league win, but more importantly, we were now eligible for sectional play for the third-straight year.[189] Just as I remember Dion Frasier's pass ricocheting off the ceiling, I remember one of the Kensington players, Ricardo Waldrop, walking out of their locker room crying. Kensington had two more games left and finished 6–7 in league play.

Just like most of the wins for the 1991–92 team, the Kensington win was ugly, but our guys found a way to get it done, the mark of a winning team. We were led by Adonis who scored 20 points, followed by Dion and Jermaine, who both scored 16 points, respectively.[190] Chris and Andre played masterful defense on Kensington's top player, Radaun Hill.[191] Kensington was led by Terrance Shears' 16 points and Sam Tucker's 13 points.[192]

We were sectional eligible. The significance of what had just happened did not dawn on me immediately as I walked home after the game. League play was not

---

[187] (Staff, Hutch-Tech High School vs. Kensington High School; Yale Cup Box Score, 1992)
[188] (Staff, Hutch-Tech High School vs. Kensington High School; Yale Cup Box Score, 1992)
[189] (Staff, Hutch-Tech High School vs. Kensington High School; Yale Cup Box Score, 1992)
[190] (Jones, Hutch-Tech High School vs. Kensington High School; Yale Cup, 1992)
[191] (Jones, Hutch-Tech High School vs. Kensington High School; Yale Cup, 1992)
[192] (Staff, Hutch-Tech High School vs. Kensington High School; Yale Cup Box Score, 1992)

finished yet. Two more home games remained on our schedule. The first was against McKinley Vocational High School, and the second was against Riverside High School. Both teams were at the top of the league standings, but they were also winnable games.

The McKinley game took place on Friday, February 7, 1992. Just like the Turner/Carroll game two months earlier, when we ran out for our pregame warmups, McKinley was already on the floor going through their routine. Their colors were black and orange with no name on the front or back of their jerseys like most of the Yale Cup teams. They had one player who towered above the rest at 6'9". He was tall and skinny. The rest of their players looked average.

Where are the rest of their players? I pondered McKinley's roster size when looking down at the end of the court. They seemed to have just a handful of players which was odd to me. There seemed to be roughly six or seven players at most at their basket.

There was a certain looseness surrounding this game. For the Engineers much of it had to do with qualifying for sectional play. To our credit, our team had figured out how to play cohesively after a season full of peaks and valleys. The 1990–91 team was powered primarily by Curtis Brooks, Pep Skillon and Chuck Thompson. The 1991–92 team was more balanced in that any player could lead the team in scoring in any game. After the first Turner/Carroll game, when Adonis Coble led with 21 points, I thought he would be the featured offense guy, but multiple players led us during our up-and-down season.

Once warmups were finished, Dion, Mike, and Chris met at center court with McKinley's captains and the referees. Afterwards, the starting lineups were introduced. Despite Michael Mann being in good health, Coach Jones stuck with the starting lineup he used for most of our Yale Cup league play. McKinley's 6'9" player was No. 55, Dwayne Jackson. Starting with him were players No. 10, Lamar Snow, No. 21, Chelston Martin, No. 15, Nakia Johnson, and a fifth player I cannot recall. Shortly after the starting lineups were introduced, Dwayne Jackson matched up against Jermaine Fuller for the tipoff, and our second-to-last Yale Cup league game was underway.

"5 MT-LOW! 5MT-LOW!" Andre Higgins methodically advanced the ball and yelled out our offenses in his high-pitched voice. In the first half, McKinley used the basket on the Chippewa Street side of the gym, while we used the basket on the Johnson Park side of the court. They played a man-to-man defense against us, and the first half of the game was an even matchup, with most of our scoring coming from Jermaine and Adonis.

Jermaine particularly asserted himself against the Macks early on, consistently and aggressively finding ways to get to the basket and the free-throw line. After catching the ball at the top of the key, on the wing, or on the baseline, he instinctively put the ball on the floor and drove to the basket, challenging the taller

Jackson with his signature two-handed double clutch layups. When open, Adonis scored on the wing using his always-reliable jump shot. I looked for Jackson to use his height to alter our players' shots, but he did not. Instead, he seemed to pick and choose his spots, perhaps trying to avoid foul trouble.

"COME ON TECH! COME ON NOW!" Chris Souter's Mom was once again in attendance and cheering us on behind our bench. She had been there all season and supported Chris to the end. "COME ON TECH! COME ON NOW!"

While most of our scoring came from two players, McKinley got production from their whole team. They played textbook Yale Cup basketball, as most of their baskets came on fast breaks where they capitalized off our missed baskets, mistakes, and miscues. Just as in every other league game against more athletic teams, it was a clash of styles, and by halftime, McKinley led 33–32.[193] I don't remember hearing much from McKinley's Coach Fabian, a bearded Hispanic man. His team led by one point, but he didn't have to do much aside from letting his horses run, which they did effectively. At halftime, Coach Jones was mostly pleased with our players and instructed the starters to continue doing what they were doing. His one gripe was taking better care of the ball.

The second half was more of the same, a clash of styles. Our slow and patient style tried to tame the Macks, who wanted to get out and run, which they did effectively. Watching them play in the open court was a thing of beauty. They now used the basket right in front of our bench, so I got an up-close look at McKinley's transition attack. No. 10, Lamar Snow, effortlessly pushed the ball, dishing it to his teammates at times or scoring the ball himself. The player I remember hurting us the most was No. 21, Chelston Martin, a fair-skinned guy who I later learned was called 'Fats' by his classmates. He was husky and comical. If you saw him on the street, you would not think he could play with the grace and fluidity that he did.

Chelston Martin was surprisingly agile and handled the ball like Magic Johnson in the open court. On fast break after fast break, he threw no-look passes to the side at times and sometimes to players behind him, making the game look both easy and fun. Sometimes he even used the spin-dribble in the open court when dishing out his assists. The ease at which the Macks scored the ball frustrated the hell out of Coach Jones, who scowled with his fists balled up, huffing and puffing as they ran up and down the floor. Still, going into the fourth quarter, Adonis, Jermaine, and the rest of our guys stayed within striking distance.

With about thirty or so seconds left in the game, we were down by 2 points, 69–67, with everyone on the edge of their seats. According to the *Buffalo News*, Dwayne Jackson won the game for the Macks by hitting a free throw in the closing seconds of the game. His key play happened seconds before that. Coach Jones

---

[193] (Staff, McKinley High School vs. Hutch-Tech High School; Yale Cup Box Score, 1992)

called a timeout and designed a play to go to the basket to get 2 points. Dion Frasier caught the ball on the left wing and tried to penetrate to the basket. He got cut off near the baseline and then passed the ball to Chris Souter, a reliable jump shooter who caught the ball at the top of the free throw circle, just inside the three-point arc.

With little time, No. 44 instinctively shot up a seventeen-footer which most of us thought had a good chance of going through the hoop. That was until Dwayne Jackson leaped up and extended his 6'9" frame with an arm straight up in the air. He tipped Chris' shot before it could descend towards the basket. It all seemed to happen in slow motion.

It was a simple but brilliant play that took the air right out of our little old gym. Jackson subsequently did just what Kevin McHale said to do in the Boston Celtics' basketball fundamentals videotape Mom had gotten for me, *Winning Basketball.* He did not aggressively swat the ball out of bounds to give us another possession, but instead, he gently and gracefully deflected it in the air and caught it himself. It took me a moment to fathom what had just happened.

Chris Souter subsequently fouled Dwayne Jackson, sending him to the free-throw line for a one-and-one. With six seconds left, he hit the first shot extending the Macks' lead to three, 70–67.[194] After missing the second shot, Coach Jones called a quick time-out to try to draw something up. The best we could get was a quick shot from long-range, a 'Hail Mary' shot that did not have much chance of going in, and McKinley escaped with the 70–67 victory.

"That was a good game you guys played out there," Coach told our silent and dejected locker room, full of players who had just given it their all. "Sometimes you fight hard and just come up a little bit short. We have one more game and we must keep fighting!"

Our leading scorer for that game was Jermaine Fuller with 19 points, followed by Adonis Coble's 13 points and Andre Higgins's 11 points, respectively.[195] Chris Souter, who guarded Dwayne Jackson for most of the game, contributed 9 rebounds and 7 assists.[196] Keith Hearon had a good game off of the bench, scoring 7 points.[197] The Macks were powered by a balanced attack led by Dwayne Jackson and Chelston Martin, each with 20 points, followed by Lamar Snow's 16 points and Nakia Johnson's 10 points.[198] Our Yale Cup record was now 7–5.

The Hutch-Tech Yale Cup finale took place in our gym on Tuesday, February 11, 1992, against Riverside. The game was significant for several reasons. Just as

---

194 (Staff, St. Joe's extends win streak: Yale Cup, 1992)
195 (Jones, McKinley High School vs. Hutch-Tech High School; Yale Cup, 1992)
196 (Jones, McKinley High School vs. Hutch-Tech High School; Yale Cup, 1992)
197 (Jones, McKinley High School vs. Hutch-Tech High School; Yale Cup, 1992)
198 (Staff, McKinley High School vs. Hutch-Tech High School; Yale Cup Box Score, 1992)

we opened our season against Turner/Carroll in November in our tiny box of a gym, this would be the last game in it for the 1991-92 season.

Winning the game would make the Engineers 8–5 and give us a higher seed in the sectionals. We would finish our regular season knowing that we had beaten one of the top teams in the league. For the Riverside Frontiersman, the stakes were much higher. A win would make them the outright 1991-92 Yale Cup Champions. A loss to us could put them in a three-way tie for the league title with McKinley and Buffalo Traditional. They were highly motivated and wanted to avenge their 82–56 drubbing at the hands of Curtis Brooks and the 1990–91 Engineers the previous year.[199]

It was four days since our heartbreaking loss to McKinley, and we had one more shot at a strong finish for our regular season. After a pre-game pep talk by Coach Jones, the 1991–92 team formed two lines for the last time in our little old gymnasium and then ran out onto the court to the applause of our fans. It was the perfect bookend for our non-league and league schedules.

As with most of our home games, our visitors were already warming up on the court. Unlike McKinley, Riverside looked more imposing in their purple jerseys with the gold trim. They wore the Los Angeles Lakers' colors from the NBA, and their jerseys were beautiful to look at, just like our solid maroon-colored jerseys for road games. Like most of the Yale Cup teams, their school's name was not on the front of their tank tops.

Instead of one big guy, Riverside had two big guys. They also had what looked like a short Puerto Rican kid on their roster. When the starting lineups were introduced, they started with a skinny, fair-skinned guard. No. 21, Billy Nelson who was a senior and had a baby face. No. 13, Shawndel Planter, who had more of what I would call a stern scowl, was his backup off the bench. No. 23, Ed Harris, was their shooting guard. Their starting forwards were No. 30, Ben Rice, and No. 33, Emmanuel Parker. At the center position, they started a 6'7" dark-skinned kid, No. 50, Walter Gravely. Their other tree was No. 34, Andre Wilson, who came off the bench.

The Frontiers were coached by a short man named Bill Russell. He could not have been any taller than 5'7". He had a professorial look with his glasses, bald top, gray beard, and long, curly gray hair on the sides and the back of his head. I think he wore it in a mullet. He did not wear a sports coat like Coach Jones, but instead a sweater or button-down shirt, with jeans and sneakers.

After the meeting at the center of the court, Jermaine Fuller matched up against No. 50, Walter Gravely for the tipoff, and our 1992 game with Riverside was underway. The contest went back and forth in the first half, just like the McKinley game in some ways. The Frontiers did have some structure and patience on

---

199 (Jones, Hutch-Tech High School vs. Riverside High School; Yale Cup, 1991)

offense. They ran some offensive sets and did not come down and just fire the ball up. They had a balanced attack and got scoring from all their players.

In the first half, Riverside used the basket right in front of our bench. Their guards, No. 21, Billy Nelson, and No. 13, Shawndel Planter, aggressively slashed to the basket, creating shots for their teammates. Sometimes they hit shots on the wing, while other times they hit them from the top of the key. No. 30, Ben Rice, had the green light to shoot the ball whenever he wanted to and made what seemed like everything. No. 23, Ed Harris, had a nice jump shot and connected from all over the court as well.

On one play following one of our missed baskets or turnovers, Walter Gravely received an outlet pass and slam dunked the ball in stride with two hands and lots of power. The dunk made the whole wall shake. Interestingly, their offense did not seem to run through Gravely the way Turner/Carroll's ran through Kevin Sanford. He pretty much scored here and there whenever he got the opportunity.

True to form, our scoring was balanced as well. In the first half, Adonis got openings consistently around the free-throw line, and he repeatedly knocked down his jump shots. Like our season opener against Turner/Carroll, he played free and loose. He fearlessly shot the ball with confidence, almost knowing everything was going to hit the bottom of the net, and I was getting inspired watching him. He carried us in that first half, and the other guys pitched in where they could. Despite our fight, though, Riverside led at halftime 47–36.[200]

"They are comfortably walking the ball up the floor. We are going to play our '75' full-court press!" At halftime Coach Jones made a key defensive adjustment, realizing that Riverside had an easy time advancing the ball and getting into its offensive sets where it could exploit its size advantage from the inside.

The adjustment worked. While Riverside dominated the first half, our new pressure bothered them. To our collective delight, they struggled in the second half, now turning the ball over. On numerous plays, both Nelson and Planter looked confused as Andre, Adonis, and the others engaged them in the backcourt with their arms up and flailing. It was like how LaSalle attacked us almost two months earlier.

Riverside's guards continued carelessly throwing the ball away, creating easy transition baskets and fresh possessions for us. We took our first lead of the game off a reverse layup by Dion Frasier, which put us up 60–59 late in the game.[201] The lead changed seven more times before we went up off Jermaine Fuller's layup with 2:17 to go.[202]

---

[200] (Staff, Riverside High School vs. Hutch-Tech High School; Yale Cup Box Score, 1992)

[201] (Harrington, Parker layup ices title for Riverside, 1992)

[202] (Harrington, Parker layup ices title for Riverside, 1992)

The game was decided by free throw shooting and defense, two pillars of Coach Jones' basketball gospel. Two free throws by Riverside's Ed Harris tied the game 68–68 with twenty-nine seconds left.[203] On the next possession, a referee's whistle stopped the play as Dion Frasier was fouled while shooting the ball with ten seconds left. He went to the free-throw line right in front of our bench.[204] We could now steal the game if Dion converted both shots. He was a four-year veteran and a clutch free-throw shooter. He asked for a towel from the bench to dry himself off, and there was no doubt in our minds that he would sink both shots.

The gym went silent for Dion's free throws. All you heard was the massive thud of the basketball slamming against the hardwood of the tiny gymnasium and its echo. The first shot surprisingly hit the back iron of the rim and clanked out. We all held our breaths for the second shot. It visibly left his fingertips awkwardly and clanked off the cylinder like the first shot.

No. 50, Walter Gravely, quickly snatched his fourteenth rebound of the game.[205] He turned and fed Ed Harris, who then found a wide-open Emanuel Parker for an uncontested layup, putting the Frontiersman up 70–68 with little time left on the clock.[206] We inbounded the ball for another Hail Mary shot, like in the McKinley game, that sailed high in the air but landed nowhere near our basket. Riverside's players on the floor and the bench celebrated what had just happened.

Stunned, we slowly got up to shake the hands of the Frontiersman, the outright 1991-92 Yale Cup Champions, and the No. 6 Small School in the *Buffalo News* Cage Poll.[207] As I walked towards the south exit of the Johnson Park side of the gym, I saw them celebrating their championship and their 11–2 record. Buffalo Traditional and McKinley were tied for second place with records of 10–3. A crowd of purple and gold assembled around basket where Dion had just missed the free throws. Walter Gravely and Andre Wilson towered above everyone else. Watching them celebrate in our gym was weird, but they earned it. I noticed the Puerto Rican kid from their team; he stood out because of his complexion in the sea of dark-complected players and students. I processed all of it as I headed to the locker room with my teammates.

Our locker room was silent as the commotion outside gradually died down. Despite the loss, our guys played a good game. Like the home season opener against Turner/Carroll, Adonis Coble led us with 18 points. Dion Frasier scored 15 points. Chris Souter scored 12 points, and finally, Andre Higgins scored 10

[203] (Harrington, Parker layup ices title for Riverside, 1992)
[204] (Harrington, Parker layup ices title for Riverside, 1992)
[205] (Harrington, Parker layup ices title for Riverside, 1992)
[206] (Harrington, Parker layup ices title for Riverside, 1992)
[207] (Staff, JFK hands Holland first defeat: East Aurora survives Eden rally; Yale Cup, 1992)

points.[208] Chris Souter also grabbed 11 rebounds and contributed 7 assists.[209] Coach Jones eventually entered the locker room to deliver his postgame thoughts and words. We all turned as he entered and situated himself in the middle of his team, which was stunned after its second consecutive close loss.

"We fought hard today, but sometimes you just come up a little bit short. It just happens that way sometimes, guys," Coach Jones told us. He had come down from his in-game persona to his grandfatherly persona, consoling his sons and grandsons. His voice was still raspy, but now in its own interpretation of gentleness. There was no *moral* victory for this Riverside loss, and our locker room was dead quiet, full of dejected players after another heartbreaker. "Don't hang your heads. You fought hard, and we still have more to play for," Coach continued.

"There is another season," Chris Souter said quietly, looking drained in his bass-filled voice, coming down physically and emotionally from the battle he had just fought.

"That is right. There is another season," Coach Jones suddenly lit up and fanned the hope Chris had just spoken into existence. "We will have practice later this week and potentially a scrimmage while we wait to hear about who our opening-round opponent will be in the sectionals. Now, bring it in here," he said, putting his hand in the center of the room and prompting us to join him.

"ONE, TWO, THREE," Michael Mann, our team leader, called out.

"TECH!" We all called out in unison.

The other season Coach Jones and Chris Souter referred to was the sectionals, postseason play for the area's best varsity high school basketball teams. Despite our last two disappointing losses, the Kensington win qualified us for the Section VI Class B-1 playoffs, where the 1991–92 team would live to fight for another day. It was the other season and the last leg of our four-month journey. Our next loss, if we were to lose, would be the last for the 1991–92 season, but we were still alive and dreaming.

---

[208] (Jones, Riverside High School vs. Hutch-Tech High School; Yale Cup, 1992)

[209] (Jones, Riverside High School vs. Hutch-Tech High School; Yale Cup, 1992)

Chapter 24. The 1992 Sectionals: A New Season

"This seven-team field is the smallest—and the weakest—in the tournament. Sleeper: Defending champion Hutch-Tech has the lowest seed, but is getting healthy after a season-long struggle with injuries" **—Mike Harrington, Sports Reporter, the *Buffalo News*, February 1992**

"You have to be good to be lucky and lucky to be good!" Coach Jones told us this regularly during that season. It was often in the context of individual skills and team strategies. As with everything he told us, while it had application to the game of basketball, it also applied to life itself. He was trying to tell us that being good and getting lucky go hand in hand. That is, once you become proficient in your craft, good things tend to happen.

* * *

We finished league play with a 7–6 record, barely qualifying for sectional play. It was a very different finish than the 1990–91 Engineers' miraculous undefeated, 13–0 Yale Cup record. Some of our losses were by large margins to teams like Bennett, Burgard, and Buffalo Traditional. A few of them were by thin margins, such as the last two heartbreakers against McKinley and Riverside, the 1991-92 Yale Cup Champion. Despite our up-and-down season, the Engineers were still competitive, and still alive.

In addition to their high skill level and experience, Curtis Brooks and the 1990–91 Engineers were in good health most of the year. They also made a few lucky bounces here and there, as do most championship teams. The 1991–92 Engineers had many players who had not been in the fire before, in addition to its share of injuries and unlucky bounces. Subsequently, our team fought through the hard times and qualified for sectional play for the third-straight year.

Sectional play for us did not start until Saturday, February 29, 1992. We had two and a half weeks to prepare. The *Buffalo News* announced the Section VI Boys' Basketball Playoffs on February 19, 1992. Our opening-round opponent was the Niagara Falls Power Cats.[210] They had beaten us in our second scrimmage back in November, but our team had grown and evolved since then.

---

[210] (Harrington, Section VI basketball teams beginning journey for the state tourney, 1992)

Before the sectionals started, Coach Jones and Riverside's Coach, Bill Russell, scheduled a scrimmage at Riverside's gym. It felt odd that we would see the Frontiersman again so soon. They came into our gym and beat us in a nail-biter. This was just a scrimmage though, a way for both teams to tune up, stay in rhythm, and get ready for the final phase of the season, where everyone's next loss would be their last.

It was my first time ever setting foot in my mother's alma mater, which sat on Tonawanda Street, literally a few blocks from the Niagara River. It was an unremarkable, old-looking building. The gym was much bigger than ours at Hutch-Tech, and they had a regulation-sized basketball court with solid white backboards and non-breakaway rims. There was a cartoon of a white Frontiersman on one of the walls. It was basically a western explorer or a fur trapper from the Daniel Boon era wearing a raccoon hat and a fur or leather suit and carrying a rifle. And there were banners of all the other Yale Cup teams with their respective colors.

We wore our maroon and gold practice shirts, and the Frontiersman wore their purple and gold practice shirts. It was an even matchup for the most part. Riverside played their same man-to-man defense, and Coach Jones countered with our standard motion plays, 5-Motion, 5 Around, and 5-MT-Low.

The atmosphere that day was relatively loose, and our teams traded baskets like in the final Yale Cup game of that season, and the play was both intense and physical. Adonis made shots, as did Dion, Chris, Jermaine, and Andre. Keith Hearon went in and made some plays too, as did Roderick Peoples. Riverside had scoring from Ed Harris, Ben Rice, Emanuel Parker, and their guards, Billy Nelson and Shawndel Planter. I do not recall the 6'6" Walter Gravely hurting us that day, like he did in the final game.

Carlton Ford, Damon Kimbrew, Terrance Collison, Jason Wardlawer, and I all started getting playing time around the fourth quarter. One of the things I remember most about that scrimmage was going up against Ben Rice. I did not notice it during the game when we played them, but he was a very scrappy and, in some ways, a dirty player. He would shove you and try to punk you off when the referees were not looking, kind of like one of the Bad Boy Detroit Pistons.

Jason Hellerman fell on the ground on one play, and Ben Rice purposely trampled him, almost stepping on his face. I could not believe what I was seeing, and he got away with it. It is something Roderick Peoples would not have taken. Then again, Ben probably knew not to test him in the first place. As I grew older, I realized that guys know who and who not to test.

I eventually had my turn to tangle with Riverside's scrappy sharpshooter. When lining up for an out-of-bounds play or when rebounding the ball during free throws, Rice pushed and shoved me a couple of times, for no apparent reason. He may have knocked me down also, which mentally put me out of my game, especially since the referee did not call the contact.

"GET UP DUNBAR! GET TOUGH! KEEP PLAYING!" Coach Jones challenged me from the sidelines, not showing any sympathy. Though basketball was supposed to be a *non-contact* sport, it was, in fact, a *contact* sport. Good sportsmanship was expected, but there were dirty players who would test you mentally and try to slip things by the referees. Ben Rice taught me a valuable lesson that day. It is something I probably would have picked up had I played more at Delaware Park with the older men and more experienced players.

"COME ON MAN, HE HELD ME! HE PUSHED ME! HE SHOVED ME!" I complained in my fifteen-year-old, whiny, high-pitched voice after Coach Jones got on me.

"COME ON, MAN, ME PUSHED AND SHOVED ME," Roderick Peoples jokingly mocked my whining. Roderick, whom one could argue was our *enforcer*, had pulled the same antics at times in practices. I despised him in those moments, but he was right. Coach Jones, who also was not shy about pushing and shoving his opponents when playing the game himself, was right too. In any case, both teams got their tune-ups that day in addition to some semblance of game conditions. Some valuable lessons were also taught and learned about competition, at least for me.

* * *

Just prior to the opening round of the sectionals, Mike Harrington who covered boys' high school basketball for the *Buffalo News*, wrote a preview of the playoffs entitled, *Section VI basketball teams beginning journey for the state tourney*.[211] He went through each of the four brackets, Classes A, B, C, and D, discussing who the favored teams were versus the *dark horses* and the underdogs. He talked about Glens Falls being the destination for all the teams competing. Coach Jones did not discuss Glens Falls with us; he only talked about our next opponent.

"This seven-team bracket is the smallest and the weakest in the tournament (compared to the A, C, and D classes). No.1, Grand Island won eight of its last ten games and is a strong favorite. No. 2, Niagara Falls has figures to challenge. Sleeper defending champion Hutch-Tech has the lowest seed, but is getting healthy after a season-long struggle with injuries," Harrington wrote.[212] I wondered why there were only seven teams in our bracket. It turned out that the same McKinley team who beat us in one of our final two Yale Cup losses withdrew from the Class

---

[211] (Harrington, Section VI basketball teams beginning journey for the state tourney, 1992)

[212] (Harrington, Section VI basketball teams beginning journey for the state tourney, 1992)

B-1 bracket due to academic ineligibility.[213] This explained why their roster was so thin in terms of depth when they played us.

The sectionals kicked off on Wednesday, February 25, 1992. While we prepared for the game, I was curious about Gabe's Cleveland Hill Eagles. I had heard so much about them by him, but I had not seen them play all year. I was strongly considering going to see them play in their Class C opening game.

"Yes, Cleveland Hill will be playing, but *you* will be too busy preparing for battle yourself!" Coach Jones did not want me to think about other teams and games when I inquired about the other playoff brackets. Even though I probably was not going to play much, I guess he just wanted all of us focused and in bed at a good hour that night. Sure enough, the Eagles were seeded No. 10 in their bracket, and they were opening against a school called Silver Creek, who was seeded No. 7. The winner would face the winner of the No. 15, Cassadaga Valley vs. No. 2, Riverside game the Friday night before our game.

* * *

"Their leading scorer is a senior named Bradley. He can shoot and put the ball on the floor. Coble will guard him for the most part. They get scoring from another kid, a freshman named Thomas. They have a 6'8" kid named Hunt who does not score much for them." Coach Jones once again gave us the pregame scouting report. We all gathered around him at center court, listening closely. "They mostly play a 2-3 zone, so we are going to use our zone offenses against it, probably 5-Z High Low," he continued. It was going to be interesting to see how we would match up with the Niagara Falls Senior High School Power Cats this second time.

The morning of the opening round game against Niagara Falls, we met at Hutch-Tech around 10 a.m. It was a frigid February morning in Buffalo with the sun peeking through the clouds. Downtown Buffalo was peaceful as the activity of the city slowly ramped up to its weekend activity level. Around 10:30 a.m., Coach Jones took a head count, and we all piled onto our cheese bus to make the fourth trip north to Niagara Falls for the season. I looked out of the window at the Niagara River, the Peace Bridge, and the rest of the scenery, contemplating the game.

It would be my first sectional game. I had never been to one as a spectator, which surely sounds odd, but it was true. As a sophomore, I had two more years left to play. For seniors Adonis, Dion, Chris, and Michael, this could be their last game as Hutch-Tech Engineers. They had been in the program for three or four

---

213 (Harrington, Section VI basketball teams beginning journey for the state tourney, 1992)

years, spent much time together, and was a part of the program as it matured into a contender. In thirty-two minutes, it could all be over for them.

Within thirty minutes we arrived at LaSalle Senior High School, where we played in the Festival of Lights Tournament in mid-December. We got off the bus, went inside, and once again sat in the bleachers. The gym was chilly that morning. Unlike in December, ours was the first game on the roster. Some of us wandered back out to the lobby. There were no girls to see this time like the ones Terrance and I met in December, unfortunately.

"Man, I cannot stand that motherfucker!" Adonis looked at a picture of LaSalle's star guard, No. 50, Carlos Bradberry, and voiced his contempt for him. After beating us, the Explorers kept winning and were still undefeated. Their players had individual Polaroid pictures taken and put inside a display case outside of their gym, celebrating their season. In each picture, players held a basketball and posed for the camera like superstars. The only thing I remembered about that game was us getting blown out 72–42 and Michael Mann breaking his wrist. I realized then that Carlos must have been jawing at Adonis and he had not forgotten it.

Around 11 a.m., Coach Jones gave us the signal and we went to the locker room to change into our uniforms. We all stretched together and regrouped. It was now almost 11:20 a.m., and the sun was lighting the brown and gold gym. After Coach Jones' pre-game words, we once again walked into LaSalle's brown wooden palace and split up into two lines. We went to one end of the court and then initiated our pregame warmups. The Niagara Falls Power Cats eventually emerged from their locker room. Their colors were red and gray. Their uniforms said Power Cats on the front with a cat's head on the sides of their trunks, just like the NBA's Chicago Bulls.

Part of the way through our warmups, Michael Mann, Dion Frasier, and Chris Souter gathered at center court with the referees and the other team captains. Shortly afterward, our warmups concluded, and the starting lineups were introduced. Coach Jones went with the same starting lineup he selected to finish our league play. Consistent with Coach Jones' scouting report, Niagara Falls started seniors, Jermaine Bradley and David Hunt, sophomore, Darris Thomas, and two other players I do not remember. Coach Dan Venuto was a slim, middle-aged white man. He had brown hair and was balding like Coach Jones. He wore a sports coat, khakis, and shoes.

The game tipped off promptly at 12 noon, and the 1991–92 Class B-1 sectionals were underway. The game was evenly matched, with both teams fighting for their lives. We played our man-to-man defense, and Niagara Falls played a 2-3 zone defense, which we countered with our 5Z High-Low zone offense, a 1-3-1 alignment with a point guard, two wing players, and high and low post players. Dion Frasier played the high post, while Jermaine Fuller played the low post.

Adonis Coble and Chris Souter played on the wings, with Andre Higgins at the point.

"5Z HIGH-LOW!" Andre Higgins called out our offensive set in his high-pitched voice from the top of the key as each of the other four players methodically ran to their positions. It was beautiful watching them run the offense, and they ran it with perfection. They patiently passed the ball around the perimeter and, at the right time, dumped it into the heart of the zone. In some instances, they reversed the ball to the other side of the court for open shots as the zone shifted.

Once receiving the entry pass at the high post, Dion hit Adonis or Chris for open jump shots on the left or right wings. He also found Jermaine for layups, which he either converted or was fouled, sending him to the free-throw line. The Power Cats' 6'8" center, No. 30, David Hunt did not seem to bother our offense much. Overall, our starters looked loose, relaxed, and confident, the opposite of where they were at the beginning of the season.

Andre Higgins made an impressive basket of his own opposite the bench where we were sitting. With the Engineers having a numerical advantage on a fast break, Andre picked up his dribble at the free-throw line halfway through a spin move. He spun off his man and pivoted back for a jump shot which sailed right through the net. It was a beautiful move executed off pure instinct.

Niagara Falls was powered by their talented senior No. 23, Jermaine Bradley, who kept them in the game. Adonis guarded him and was careful not to get into foul trouble. Jermaine was very confident with the ball on offense and created his own shots, seemingly scoring at will. The Power Cats also had good minutes from their sophomore, Darris Thomas. It was shaping out to be a physical and ugly game, consistent with our season. We entered the locker room at halftime with a slim 26–25 lead.[214]

Coach Jones urged our guys to keep fighting, to continue to rebound the ball, and to be patient on offense. He urged Andre and Adonis, who took turns guarding Jermaine Bradley, to be smart, to move their feet, and to box out. He further encouraged Chris Souter, who guarded David Hunt, to continue to be physical with the Power Cats' 6'8" center, who had been relatively quiet. Like most of the Yale Cup big men, he was not impacting the game like Turner/Carroll's Kevin Sanford at the beginning of the season.

In the second half, the play became more physical. The scores of both teams stayed close with neither moving ahead by much. Every brilliant shot that Jermaine Bradley made was countered by a patient and methodical possession on the other end by our players, ending with layups, jump shots from the wing, or free throws.

[214] (Staff, Hutch-Tech High Schools vs. Niagara Falls High School; Class B-1 Sectionals, 1992)

The Engineers were now using the basket right in front of our bench, so the team gave them enormous moral support whenever they scored. Coach Jones' gospel of free throw shooting paid off as our team converted ten of twelve free throws in the fourth quarter.[215] The Power Cats were visibly wearing down, probably not expecting the game to be so close.[216] Jermaine Bradley looked particularly exhausted though he did not stop fighting.

The final game play came as we led the Power Cats 56–53 with only seconds to go. After a time-out, a play was drawn up that put the ball in Jermaine Bradley's hands. After catching it, he used a crossover dribble to create space for himself from forty-five degrees on the left side of the three-point arc. Either Andre or Adonis guarded him. His dribble move gave him a wide-open look at the basket. He was not squared up on the arc, but instead hovered near the sideline.

He picked up his dribble as the seconds ticked down. He rose up and fired his shot at his apex. It would have tied the game and sent it into overtime. His mechanics were damn near perfect when he released it, and it had a beautiful arc and backspin as it approached the goal. We all held our breaths as the ball left his hands. It all seemed to happen in slow motion, just like Curtis Brooks' go-ahead three-pointer against Grover Cleveland at Hutch-Tech a year earlier. The ball descended into the cylinder, bounced around, and then ricocheted out as the final buzzer sounded.

Our guys had done it! We survived and advanced to the semifinal round with a 56–53 victory over the Niagara Falls Power Cats, and our bench was a mix of joy and relief.[217] Adonis scored 14 points, followed by Dion's 12 points and Chris' 11 points.[218] Both Jermaine and Chris led our team with 12 rebounds and Adonis had 11.[219] Chris played excellent defense on their center, David Hunt, who scored 7 points.[220] Jermaine Bradley led the Power Cats with 27 points, their only double-figure scorer that day.[221]

---

[215] (Jones, Hutch-Tech High School vs. Niagara Falls High School; Class B-1 Sectionals, 1992)

[216] (Jones, Hutch-Tech High School vs. Niagara Falls High School; Class B-1 Sectionals, 1992)

[217] (Jones, Hutch-Tech High School vs. Niagara Falls High School; Class B-1 Sectionals, 1992)

[218] (Jones, Hutch-Tech High School vs. Niagara Falls High School; Class B-1 Sectionals, 1992)

[219] (Jones, Hutch-Tech High School vs. Niagara Falls High School; Class B-1 Sectionals, 1992)

[220] (Jones, Hutch-Tech High School vs. Niagara Falls High School; Class B-1 Sectionals, 1992)

[221] (Staff, Hutch-Tech vs. Niagara Falls; Class B-1 Sectionals Box Score, 1992)

After shaking hands with the Power Cats, who were in disbelief at the outcome, we jubilantly hurried into the locker room. Coach Jones was ecstatic that we pulled off the win. There was a buzz among the players, especially the seniors. It was a group that managed to stay together despite the adversity it had experienced throughout the season, especially Michael Mann.

"That was a great win, you guys," Coach said, smiling, looking like a proud father. He used his grandfatherly voice now. "We stuck together, played good defense, and we took them out of what they wanted to do. If we continue to play defense, rebound the ball, and persevere, we will be in all these games! Enjoy this victory now. Our next game will be on Tuesday night, and we will see who our opponent is going to be. Now bring it in here!" Coach Jones concluded by reaching his hand into the center.

"ONE, TWO, THREE," Michael Mann counted out as we all gathered around and put our hands in the center of the pile.

"TECH!" We all happily yelled out in unison.

As I changed out of my uniform, I listened to the banter taking place. The mood was light and playful as we all soaked in the victory; those who had gotten playing time and those of us who had not. One distinct voice caught my attention with great interest, as it always did.

"Hey, Dion. Hey, Dion," Adonis said in his high-pitched voice, this time not angry but with a mischievous smile on his face. "I was waiting for them to call traveling on you on that one play. If they did, I was going to hit you," Adonis joked. He had expressed anger most of the season, and it was the emotion I expected from him most of the time. His words shocked me, but when I looked at him, I realized that he was just playing around.

That 1991–92 team was so much fun to be a part of, and that moment between Adonis and Dion captured what it was like to be on that roster. While there were so many moments that year where we felt like the Bad News Bears, where nothing was going our way, things seemed to somehow work out for us in the end. It was like a family.

"Yeah, I was just glad that they didn't," Dion said, laughing back at Adonis as he changed out of his tank top.

We piled on the bus and headed back to Buffalo. The next day there was a picture from our game in the *Buffalo News*. In the picture, Niagara Falls' Darris Thomas was pulling down a rebound or going up for a shot in the paint. He was surrounded by No. 24, Dion Frasier, who appeared to be watching in awe, while No. 12, Michael Mann, seemed to be tangled up with him, and No. 44, Chris Souter, attempted to block the shot.[222] No. 30, Jermaine Fuller watched with his hands up. A Niagara Falls player was on the ground, probably David Hunt. In the

---

[222] (Staff, Riverside, Traditional post narrow wins, 1992)

distance, Niagara Falls' Coach Venuto sat watching the action. It was a picture that caught the essence of the game.

In terms of what had just happened, it gradually sunk in. This is what it was like to win a sectional game. This is what it was like to survive and advance with the steaks growing with each round. It was exciting! Curtis Brooks and the 1990–91 Engineers did it four times the previous year. It was a great victory for our team, but it was short-lived.

On Monday, we learned that our semifinal-round opponent would be No. 3-seeded Clarence, which had knocked off No. 6-seeded Depew in their opening-round matchup 69–68.[223] Our matchup would be on Tuesday night at 7 p.m. at Lockport High School. In our league, Grover Cleveland knocked off Bennett 68–44, setting up a showdown with No. 1-seeded Grand Island, who was idle in the opening round.[224]

* * *

"They have two big guys. One is 6'4", and the other is 6'5". Other than that, they are not very tall. They will post them up and then try to get outside shots for their guards. Chris and Jermaine are going to match up against their two big guys on defense," Coach Jones said, reading off his scratch paper in his grandfatherly voice at the center court of the little old gym. It was the day before our semifinal matchup with Clarence. "They play zone, so we will run our zone offenses against them," he continued as we all looked on silently.

The 1992 Class B-1 semifinal games took place the next day at Lockport High School. Ours was the first game at 6 p.m. I had heard of Lockport and knew that it was a small city not too far from Buffalo, but I had never been there. Between 4:00 and 4:30 p.m., as the Buffalo winter night started to set in, we boarded a cheese bus once again and took Interstate 190 north. This time we took Interstate 290 east towards Tonawanda and then Interstate 990 north towards Lockport. The expressway circled around a couple of times before ending at Millersport Highway.

We stayed on Millersport Highway and eventually exited at Route 78-Transit Road at a point further north than Clarence. It seemed to go on forever as we passed through farmlands and forests. At some point we crossed from Erie County into Niagara County. We traveled through a couple of plazas and eventually turned onto Lincoln Avenue, where the high school was located. Like most suburban schools in Western New York, Lockport High School was on a long, secluded residential road, and the school was more of a campus setting than a high school.

---

223 (Staff, Riverside, Traditional post narrow wins, 1992)

224 (Staff, Riverside, Traditional post narrow wins, 1992)

In back of the school building there was a large sports complex with baseball and football fields. It was nothing like the schools in Buffalo. Coming off the bus, Coach Jones led us into the building. There we found another lobby full of trophy cases just like at LaSalle Senior High School. Banners and pictures lined the walls leading to a cavernous gymnasium, which was decorated with the colors blue, yellow, and white, the colors of the Lockport Lions. More banners were all around the gym for each of the member schools in their league. I immediately recognized LaSalle and Niagara Falls Senior High Schools.

Being the lower seed, we wore our visiting maroon uniforms, and at 5:00 p.m., we went into the locker room to change. While there was jubilation following our victory over the Niagara Falls Power Cats, the mood in the locker room now was again subdued, as this game could be the last one for our seniors. Coach Jones passed out chewing gum and gave us our pregame speech. We walked out of the locker room and performed our pregame warmup routine. We were the first team to come out and started at the basket across from our bench.

As we were executing our routine, Clarence emerged from their locker room and ran their laps around the court. They ran in a single file like many of the other teams we faced. Their home uniforms were white with red numbers and letters with black and red border trim. They all wore warmup pants just like the NBA teams, and all their players were white.

Their two tallest players stood out just as Coach Jones had described them the previous afternoon. Would these guys dunk on us in the open court the way Kevin Sanford and Walter Gravely did? None of their other players appeared to have remarkable talent; they looked like your average suburban kids. Even though they were seeded higher than us, our records were similar. We were 10–10 overall and 7–6 in our league, while they were 9–10 overall and 7–5 in their league. This reflected an even field in which we were the lowest seed by only a small margin.

By the time we were in our pregame warmups, the gym had filled up with mostly fans from Clarence. As such, it now felt like a hostile environment as there was no one in the bleachers who looked like us. The vibe in the gym was in their favor, and an inexperienced team could have easily been overwhelmed.

The starting lineups were introduced the same way as at Hutch-Tech. A makeshift tunnel formed at the bench where each starter ran out to shake the opposing coach's hand, to where they gathered at a free throw circle for the final huddle. Coach Jones' starting lineup consisted of Andre Higgins, Adonis Coble, Dion Frasier, Chris Souter, and Jermaine Fuller. It was the lineup that had gotten us there.

Coach Charles Vesper was a younger man than Coach Jones, probably in his early 40s. He had black hair and a black mustache and was formally dressed. He started Rob Gill, who was 6'4", and Casey Filarecki, who was 6'5". Rob Gill, who wore No. 40, looked like a scientist with a broad European nose, a square jaw, and short, chaotic curly brown hair. Their other big man, No. 42, Casey Filarecki, looked like a tough guy. He had short black hair and broad shoulders. I cannot tell you exactly who else they started with their two big men, other than their point guard, No. 22, Ryan Vaughn. He was a 6' senior with black bushy hair and a goatee who looked like he could have been in a rock band.

Once the starting lineups were announced, the game was underway. Clarence came out fast, getting much of its scoring from their two big guys. Both had dunks early on. Rob Gill made a two-handed dunk where he launched off both feet. On another possession Casey Filarecki put the ball on the floor and launched off one foot for a one-handed slam dunk. Both dunks made their crowd go nuts. Other than those two plays, Clarence ran offensive sets like we did and played a structured game. We started slow. Adonis did not seem to be feeling well, as he looked both tired and sick.

"Do not get intimidated by a couple of dunks," Coach Jones told our starters after Clarence's initial run during a time-out. "Continue to play disciplined defense and *work* the ball on offense!"

Sure enough, Andre Higgins patiently advanced the ball, putting us into our motion offenses. Our 5-Z High-Low set was once again run to perfection, with the ball being patiently passed around the perimeter. At the right moment it was passed into the center of the zone, collapsing it to create layups for either Jermaine Fuller or Keith Hearon, who had a lot of playing minutes in the first half. If Clarence had the opportunity to defend the basket aggressively, they swung the ball outside to allow for jump shots from the wings or the corners.

With the scoring from Andre Higgins, Dion Frasier, Chris Souter, and Keith Hearon off the bench, we hung close with the Red Devils late in the first half. Towards the end of the second quarter, Clarence went into their own delay offense, which was kind of like a half-court three-man weave. Their fans clapped and cheered loudly as they ran it. At halftime, we were in striking distance and only down 30–26.[225]

"We are right there with them. Continue *working* the ball on offense and defending," Coach Jones said at halftime. The game was close, and the contest could go either way. "Continue playing disciplined defense and box out!"

The second half of the game was tight, with Clarence getting production from its big guys and us working the ball and getting patient, high-percentage shots on the perimeter or in the interior of their 2-3 zone. The game was blown open in the fourth quarter, when Coach Jones smelled blood and turned up the defensive pressure, which sparked us to go on a 29–19 run.[226] The Clarence players on the

---

[225] (Staff, Hutch-Tech vs. Clarence; Class B-1 Sectionals Box Score, 1992)

[226] (Jones, Hutch-Tech High School vs. Clarence High School; Class B-1 Sectionals, 1992)

other hand seemed to fatigue. Casey Filarecki left the game for a long stretch due to fouling trouble, and their guards struggled to keep things together without him.

Late in the game, Andre Higgins caught fire. He stepped into the limelight and knocked down two clutch three-pointers which kept us out in front for the remainder of the game.[227] It was amazing! He hadn't had a game like that all season, and now it was suddenly his moment. For both shots, his perfectly arched balls descended towards the basket in what felt like slow motion. Each time the balls sailed perfectly through the net. It was one of those moments where you felt the victory was near, but that the game could also be lost.

Andre found his confidence and seized his moment, taking and nailing those two three-pointers.[228] When he was fouled, he also confidently feathered in his foul shots. Watching it all unfold from the bench was magical, and it seemed like it was meant to be. We never looked back and went on to win the game 65–57, propelling us to the Class B-1 final the coming Saturday.[229]

Several things contributed to that victory. In the fourth quarter, our team went thirteen of nineteen from the free-throw line.[230] Andre went eight-for-eight from the line in addition to his two heroic three-pointers.[231] He scored 22 points, followed by Dion's 13 points and Chris' 12 points.[232] Michael, Andre and Chris spearheaded our team defense, while Jermaine and Adonis led us in rebounding with 10 and 8, respectively.[233] Adonis also had 5 assists, and Keith Hearon logged significant minutes off the bench as well.[234] It was the formula that the 1991–92 Engineers used all season. There was no 'alpha dog' asserting himself. Instead, it was a balanced scoring attack where players stepped up as needed.

The locker room was electric after that win. It was great being on the varsity team and experiencing a sectional run in my first year. It gave me something to

---

[227] (Jones, Hutch-Tech High School vs. Clarence High School; Class B-1 Sectionals, 1992)

[228] (Jones, Hutch-Tech High School vs. Clarence High School; Class B-1 Sectionals, 1992)

[229] (Jones, Hutch-Tech High School vs. Clarence High School; Class B-1 Sectionals, 1992)

[230] (Jones, Hutch-Tech High School vs. Clarence High School; Class B-1 Sectionals, 1992)

[231] (Jones, Hutch-Tech High School vs. Clarence High School; Class B-1 Sectionals, 1992)

[232] (Jones, Hutch-Tech High School vs. Clarence High School; Class B-1 Sectionals, 1992)

[233] (Jones, Hutch-Tech High School vs. Clarence High School; Class B-1 Sectionals, 1992)

[234] (Jones, Hutch-Tech High School vs. Clarence High School; Class B-1 Sectionals, 1992)

shoot for in my next two years and something to build upon. It was also cool to see Andre step up in the moment. Our team had experienced much adversity that year, and it was coming together at just the right time. We found ways to survive and advance, and we were in a position to repeat as Class B-1 Champions.

After changing into our street clothes, we went back to the gym and sat in the stands to see who our opponent in the Class B-1 final would be. I had seen the Grover Cleveland Presidents play before, but this was my first time seeing the Grand Island Vikings play. Their colors were blue and white. They were led by a 5'10" senior point guard, Grant Kozlowski, a 6'2" hulk, quarterback Anthony Scott, who wore goggles, the 6'4" Chris Tassy and finally, 6'8" center, Bob Bojarski, who looked like a skinny version of Ivan Drago from *Rocky IV*.

The first half of the game was ugly as Grover Cleveland tried to get out and run while Grand Island patiently advanced the ball up the court and looked to exploit their height advantage in the middle. Like us, the Vikings were more disciplined than the Presidents. I remember a specific play, Grover's Carl Swindle taking the ball to the hoop recklessly and falling on the floor.

"You see what their center is doing, Anwar?" Our assistant Coach, Andy Brown, asked me about something on the court. "He is posting up and calling for the ball. That is what I have been trying to get you to do!" Sure enough, Bob Bojarski posted up on the low block with textbook form. That was the first time that *posting up* stuck into my brain, and I never forgot it after that.

We left at halftime with Grand Island leading 34–23.[235] According to the *Buffalo News*, using their quickness in the second half, Grover Cleveland battled back, taking the lead 59–58 off of a three-pointer by freshman Antoine Sims.[236] Grand Island responded by going into a half-court trap and ending the game on a 12–1 run to win it, going away 70–60 and advancing to play Hutch-Tech.[237] Their leading scorers were Anthony Scott and Bob Bojarski with 22 and 16 points, respectively.[238]

It was amazing. After all the challenges our 1991–92 team had gone through, we were now in a position to repeat the postseason successes of the 1990–91 team. This was what it felt like to be a part of a championship postseason run. It seemed normal for our Hutch-Tech boys' basketball team and program now, and it felt good. We were so close to repeating and potentially going further than the 1990–91 team.

---

[235] (Staff, Explorers, Spartans battle for Class A title, 1992)
[236] (Staff, Explorers, Spartans battle for Class A title, 1992)
[237] (Staff, Explorers, Spartans battle for Class A title, 1992)
[238] (Staff, Explorers, Spartans battle for Class A title, 1992)

Chapter 25. The 1992 Class B-1 Final: A Chance to Repeat

"We ran a rhythm-style offense. If one player shot the ball too early without multiple players touching it, it would throw everyone else off!" —**Adonis Coble, Player, the Hutch-Tech boys' basketball team, 1990-92, June 2014**

We had three days to prepare for the Grand Island Vikings. Two things stood out to me from those three days. The first was a letter that Coach Jones received from a resident of the Village of Clarence. Coach Jones sat the team down on the Elmwood Avenue side of the gym, the same side where he announced that he would keep all of us three months earlier. He read us the letter, which was dated March 4, 1992, and was on letterhead from the Clarence Church of Christ. It was from one of their clergymen. Coach Jones read it to us with no microphone and simply projected using his normal voice. He wore his signature polo shirt, short shorts, colored socks, and sneakers. It read as follows:

Dear Ken

"Thanks for the information regarding your basketball camp. I will pass it on to friends. Unfortunately, the cost will prevent my son from attending…but maybe another year.

"Congratulations on your victory last night over Clarence. It seems to me that the disciplined style almost always defeats the undisciplined style. Your defensive pressure was turned up a notch in the second half. You kept bringing fresh people into the game while Clarence stayed with the same tired players. Your kids kept their heads while Clarence lost theirs. Coaching was the key to that victory, and I congratulate you. I regret that my son will have to play under the Clarence system. I will use my influence to help him learn to play a total game. It is a pleasure to see you coach your team.

"Best wishes on your game Saturday night. You can beat those guys by playing your style…and I hope you do."

High Regards
Mike Bowers

He posted the letter on the bulletin board near the locker rooms afterward. That letter was one of the highest compliments for Coach Jones. A fan from the team that we had just beaten praised the way he ran his program and his team. He thought very highly of Coach Jones' *disciplined* style. I did not understand the meaning of the letter when he read it to us. It was highly significant, though, especially with everything that transpired during his tenure as the boys' basketball coach over the years, which I had little knowledge of at the time.

Coach Jones did not take us through grueling practices at this stage in the season. He probably did not want to burn his horses out. Our practices were now more so walk-throughs where we went through light drills and tweaked some of our base strategies. One day, towards the end of practice, we reviewed our half-court offensive sets. The first team was in, and Andre Higgins felt the aftereffects of his 22-point game against Clarence. He had a noticeable bounce in his step, and he was almost glowing.

On one play, Andre caught the basketball at the top of the key, a few steps outside of the three-point arc. Without hesitation, he fired up a beautiful three-pointer which sailed cleanly through the net, making that popping/snapping sound. Andre had excellent shooting mechanics, and after that shot, he was floating even more.

"Wow. Higgins is on a roll," Coach Jones mumbled to himself, holding his whistle with his arms folded. He said it loud enough for me to hear him from the bleachers.

"DRAAAAYYY," I yelled out in almost a wail, celebrating Andre's groove.

"HEY," Adonis Coble immediately turned and yelled over to me with a stern look on his face in his high-pitched voice. I turned to him, smiling as he commanded, "SHUT UP!"

I was taken aback by Adonis's words, but did not take them personally. I was a little bit amused. There was a bit of a rivalry between Adonis and Andre that year, and Adonis' patience seemed to be wearing thinner than it had been all year, interestingly on the eve of another sectional title. That said, I was still a rookie, and Adonis might have known something that I did not know. On a run like ours it was crucial for everyone to remain levelheaded and focused.

In any case, our team was on a roll, and there was no reason to think that it would not continue against the Grand Island Vikings on Saturday at the University at Buffalo (UB). Their only real advantage was that they had a 6'8" guy. With our style of play and our senior leadership, there was no reason why we couldn't beat them? The 1991–92 team's sectional run was one of the most exciting experiences of my fifteen-year-old life. With another win, I would be a part of a sectional championship team, just like the group Curtis Brooks led the year before. I was not getting any minutes on the team, but I was a part of it. I was along for the magical ride.

* * *

Our matchup with Grand Island was scheduled for a 6 p.m. tip-off at Alumni Arena at the University at Buffalo on Saturday, March 7, 1992. Coach Jones had us meet at Hutch-Tech in the gym at 4:00 p.m. The mood of that day was calm and subdued. We wanted to extend our third season as far as we could go, and we had already gone further than many had expected based on the up-and-down season we had. The 1991–92 Engineers were still around and strong, and it was largely due to Ken Jones' coaching. Seniors Michael Mann, Dion Frasier, and Chris Souter were also critical for the team's success, as they kept our team together through all our difficulties.

I wore a black sweatshirt that day, along with a pair of faded black jeans that I accidentally bleached a year or two earlier. Prior to departing for UB, I was alone with one of our managers, Taraji Mogul, in the coaches' offices. She was an attractive, petite, brown-skinned junior. At that moment, I suddenly felt the need to flirt with her though I did not know what I was doing. She thought my advance was funny and jokingly called me a 'young buck' before we left the office and reconvened in the gym with the rest of the team, where the guys were shooting around.

We piled into our cheese bus around 4:30 p.m. as the Western New York winter night descended. The game was being played at the UB North Campus in Amherst. We took the I-290 across Tonawanda to the Millersport Highway exit, the route spanning from the UB South Campus on Main Street to the North Campus in Amherst. I had never been to the North Campus although it was relatively close to where I lived. When we arrived, I saw that it was like its own little city.

The bus let us out in front of the Alumni Arena, a massive multi-purpose sports complex made mostly of red brick. It was more modern and massive than anything I had seen before. When we walked into the lobby, there was a definite buzz in the air that you could feel. Fans from the Yale Cup schools and all the surrounding towns and suburbs were there. Many of them were white and they traveled from faraway places like Lancaster and West Seneca, and Fredonia and Dunkirk in the Southern Tier. These were people I otherwise would never have seen or interacted with at that point in my life, aside from opportunities like the Youth Leadership Program of Western New York.

Coach Jones alerted the Section VI representatives of our arrival, after which we received our credentials and were admitted into the arena. We all received complimentary green and white programs entitled, *Section VI Basketball: Boys' Championship Playoffs 1991–92*.[239] The books contained breakdowns of the different leagues comprising Section VI. It further contained the records and standings in those leagues for the season and the sectional classes in which each team played. It listed the teams that qualified for the semifinal rounds in each section. In the

---

[239] (Committee S. V., 1992)

back of the book, it listed the record holders for scoring and the sectional champions of years past. Every coach of every team was also listed in the book, Coach Jones included.

On the cover of that book was what appeared to be a picture of one of LaSalle's players from the previous year jumping in the air and throwing a no-look pass to one of his teammates. A player from Lancaster attempted to draw an offensive foul. He was dark-skinned and wore a high-top fade. The picture captured the perennial clash of city vs. suburban basketball.

The book was also full of the sponsors and local businesses that supported this Section VI basketball. It was my first time realizing just how big Western New York high school basketball was and how much money was needed to fund the league. It transcended Coach Jones and our little old gym on South Elmwood Avenue. It transcended our entire area.

As Coach Jones led us through the concourse, you could hear the sounds of a game going on inside the arena. Instead of the usual traditional buzzer that was in every high school gymnasium that we had played in that season, there was the sound of an air horn that echoed all the way out into the lobby. You could also hear the cheering of the crowd and the public announcer, but not the sound of the basketball itself or the referees' whistles because of the vastness of the arena. People were all over the concourse talking, going to the restrooms, and getting food. Anything you wanted was sold at the concession stands, including burgers, hot dogs, French fries, and sodas–you name it, and they had it.

All along the walls of the Alumni Arena concourse, there were black and white pictures of the greatest athletes to play at the school, including our Athletic Director, Willie Evans, who played football for the Bulls years ago. There were some black players, but most of them were white. Some of those players went on to play for the Buffalo Bills or started traditional careers.

We eventually walked through a short tunnel leading from the concourse into the arena. I had never seen anything like it before except maybe when Mr. Smith took Gabe and me to see the Chicago Bulls play the Miami Heat at the Buffalo Memorial Auditorium, which was a much older structure. This time I was going to change into my uniform, sit courtside, and potentially get into the game. As I looked around the arena, I saw observed fans in the stands above us, below us, and then down to the edges of the court. Across the court, it was the exact same thing, and I was in awe.

Above the center of the court, there was a large cube-shaped scoreboard, just like in the NBA. No bleachers were extended behind either of the baskets, creating a massive empty space. As opposed to the baskets hanging from the ceiling, the baskets were mounted to the floor with extensions, again just like in the NBA. The center court circle had the staggered letters UB in blue and white. This was where the UB men's and women's basketball teams played their collegiate games for the school, which had recently turned Division-1, and it was a beautiful arena.

We found a space on the bleachers to sit as a team. By the time we arrived, the Class C and D finals had already concluded. In the Class D Final, Franklinville defeated Ripley 66–48.[240] I knew nothing about the two teams because they were both from the Southern Tier, close to the Pennsylvania border, outside of our league boundaries. In the Class C final, Riverside narrowly defeated Buffalo Traditional in a Yale Cup rematch 51–49 behind late free throws by Ben Rice.[241] They both beaten us and finished at the top of the Yale Cup. I could only wish that I had seen that game.

On the court, the Class B-2 final between the Fredonia Hillbillies and the Williamsville South Billies was in its latter stages. It was in the first of two overtime periods. Fredonia was the visiting team dressed in solid black jerseys with orange letters and numbers, and Williamsville South was the home team dressed in white jerseys with red and blue letters. If we could defeat the Grand Island Vikings, we would face one of these teams in the overall Class B final. Perhaps there would be a rematch of the 1991 final where we would match up against Williamsville South. What were the chances?

The score was close in the closing minutes, and it was a battle of youth versus experience. I recognized one of the players on the floor, Williamsville South's center, No. 55, Andre Graves, though I had never met him. Gabe's father, Mr. Smith, boasted the year before that even though Chuck Thompson played a good game, Andre Graves was the better of the two centers in their 1991 overall Class B matchup. Andre was on the bench with his right shoe off, wearing an ankle brace like the one Dion Frasier wore all year; suggesting that he had hurt his ankle. He looked on helplessly as his team battled for its life against the younger Hillbillies.

His fellow senior, point guard No. 12, Mike Mitchell, did all he could to keep Williamsville South alive against the Hillbillies, who relentlessly attacked the basket, taking advantage of Andre Graves' absence. One kid on Fredonia's team, No. 24, Mike Heary, kept attacking the basket and getting fouled. With poise he continued to feather in his free throws, pushing his Hillbillies ahead by 3 to 5 points. He was a tall, skinny kid at 6'4" with black hair and bow legs. He had *guard* skills and looking at my sectional book, he was a sophomore just like myself, Terrance Collison, and Jason Wardlawer. He had trained and developed so that he was good enough to be on the floor for his varsity team, helping to decide its fate.

Mike Mitchell likewise advanced the ball and hoisted up three-pointers off the dribble, making them, either tying the game or pulling Williamsville South within 2 points. Williamsville South was just barely holding on while Fredonia was trying

---

240 (Harrington, Defense propels Franklinville to familiar top of the class, 66-48, 1992)

241 (Harrington, Rice's late free throw ices win for Frontiers, 1992)

to pull away, and Mike Mitchell was the only thing keeping his Billies alive. The more the clock wound down, the more the suspense built, causing everyone in the crowd to wonder if South could avoid the upset.

Because of my closeness with the Smith family, I rooted for our potential opponent, Williamsville South. After more clutch free throws by Mike Heary put Fredonia up 66–63, Mike Mitchell went down hard on a drive to the basket with twenty-three seconds left in the second overtime session and had to leave the game. The game was delayed twenty minutes, and Mitchell was taken away in an ambulance. Without him Williamsville South had nothing left. Fredonia won the nail-biter 68–66, advancing to the overall Section VI Class B final, and awaited the winner of our game.[242] Afterward, Fredonia and their fans celebrated on the court. There would be no rematch of the 1991 Section VI Class B final, unfortunately.

With the Class B-2 final finished, we descended to the court level and made our way to the locker room. The UB locker rooms were unlike the ones at Hutch-Tech. They were large, cavernous, and modern, just like the Alumni Arena as a whole. Just like the exterior of the arena, the interior was made of large gray bricks. The mood was once again subdued as we all changed in silence, and no one seemed excited or revved up. Once we got dressed in our visiting maroon uniforms, Coach Jones gave us some pre-game words, and we walked out into the hallway back towards the arena.

Michael Mann led the march and started clapping his hands over his head, trying to get our team pumped up for the task at hand. No one else joined him, so I did, and the two of us clapped as we emerged from the tunnel alongside one set of bleachers. On the side of the bleachers, our tri-captains, Michael Mann, Chris Souter, and Dion Frasier, led us through calisthenics and stretches as they had done all year. Commotion from the arena boomed and blasted all around us. The three captains were our senior leaders and the emotional core of the team. Whenever Adonis Coble became frustrated because Andre Higgins or one of the juniors acted out, or there was some other issue, it was their leadership that kept us together. They had been with Coach Jones since they were freshmen, and this could very well be their last game as Engineers.

With the Class B-2 final finished, we formed two lines on one end of the court and went into our pre-game warmup routine. I looked up in the stands and saw Mom there supporting us. I was glad she was there, though I didn't believe I was going to play much. Unlike most of our Yale Cup games, which were right after school, this game was in the evening on a weekend, so she could easily come.

On cue, both lines took off running. The UB court felt different. It was not a solid wood floor, but instead a synthetic surface like the one in Scott Field House at Hamilton College. It was as large as the crowd watching us. The baskets felt

---

242 (Usiak, Hillbillies tip Billies in double OT, 1992)

different as well. The rims were unforgiving to my unrefined jump shot, and they also seemed a little higher than what I was used to. Finally, they made a rattling noise when the balls hit them and did not readily give or allow for a shooter's roll, at least not for me. Shooters had to be very accurate on those rims.

The Grand Island Vikings emerged in a single file line from their locker room and started to warmup. Their colors were red, white, and blue. Their 6'8" center, No. 54, Bob Bojarski, towered above the rest of the team. They all looked bigger than they did on Tuesday night, especially their hulky forward Anthony Scott, who wore No. 34 and goggles. At 6'2", their two-sport star was a man-child. They also had another forward, 6'4" Chris Tassy, who wore No. 50. He looked biracial and was both long and lengthy. The other kids on their team looked average.

Grand Island's Head Coach, Jon Roth, was a middle-aged man with a clean, round face and slightly thinning brown hair. He started the above-mentioned Anthony Scott, Chris Tassy, and Bob Bojarski in the frontcourt. In the backcourt, he started a 6'1" kid with glasses, No. 32, Jay Moran. At point guard he started a senior with a buzz cut, No. 10, Grant Koslowski, who stood 5'11."

Coach Jones went with the starting lineup that had gotten us there; No. 15, Andre Higgins at point guard, No. 23, Adonis Coble at shooting guard, No. 44, Chris Souter, No. 24, Dion Frasier at the forward positions and No. 30, Jermaine Fuller at the center position. Ours was not a physically imposing lineup, but a patient and mature group that had taken its lumps, and which found ways to survive over the previous three to four months.

"All right, come on guys, let's go! We're thirty-two minutes away from repeating as Class B-1 Champions," said Michael Mann, the spiritual leader of the team, putting his hands into the middle of our huddle and speaking in his lion-like voice. "ONE, TWO, THREE," he counted off, to which we all yelled, "TECH!"

"We're going to start out with 5-M on offense to see what they are going to do," Coach Jones said, down on one knee as we all gathered around our starters. "Be patient with the ball and work for good shots on every possession. We are going to pick up half-court and play man-to-man defense and see what happens from there."

With that we all took our seats on the chairs that were set out for us, and our starters went out to win Coach Jones his second straight Section VI Class B-1 title. Once the referee threw the ball up in the air, Jermaine Fuller matched up against Bob Bojarski at the tipoff to try to secure the first possession, and the game was underway. As the game started, I pondered that I, too, could be a sectional champion at the end of these thirty-two minutes of regulation. After my tumultuous summer of 1991, who would have envisioned this?

If I could describe the first half of that Grand Island game for our team, I would say we were sluggish. We came out slow, like the games against Niagara

Falls and Clarence, but this time things were different. Andre and Adonis looked out of sync in the backcourt. Andre, our hero from the Clarence game, did not look like he had whatever it was that he had late in the semifinal game. He seemed to be pressing a little bit offensively. Adonis once again looked like he was not himself physically. Both shot low percentages from the perimeter.

Our scoring came from Dion, Chris and Jermaine, who matched up against Bob Bojarski, who was five inches taller than him. While I had difficulties during warmups, the baskets at Alumni Arena also seemed a little smaller and less generous for our starters than those in the gyms we had previously played in. It was a different game and overall, our guys had a hard time that night just putting the ball in the basket.

Grand Island had scoring from all around. Their attack was spearheaded by 5'10" senior point guard, No. 10, Grant Koslowski. They also got production from Anthony Scott, who used his muscular build to *bully* his way to the basket for layups. No. 50, Chris Tassy, who had a nice shooting touch, hit wide-open fifteen-footers regularly. They also had production from No. 54, Bob Bojarski, who gave them a decisive inside height advantage. The slugfest continued into the second quarter and at halftime Grand Island was up only by 6 points, 25–19.[243]

"Be patient with the ball, and the shots will start falling. Keep working hard on defense and rebounding the ball. Limit their second shots. We are not that far away," Coach Jones said, trying to spark our team in the locker room. The Vikings were not significantly better than us. If we could just get some offense going, we could easily take control of the game. The window to do it was there, and our players just had to step through it. In sixteen more minutes, our program would repeat as the Class B-1 Champions, or the Grand Island Vikings would emerge as the victors.

Despite Grand Island's slim halftime lead, our guys stormed back in the third quarter and hit their first five shots from the field through patient play and running the offense. They *worked* the ball just as Coach Jones had encouraged. Still and unfortunately, that run was short-lived, and we were unable to pull it all together to the point where we could overtake the Vikings. When we got close, they figured out ways to push themselves back out front again. Meanwhile, seconds and then minutes steadily ticked off the clock.

It seemed at times that Andre Higgins was pressing to recreate his magic from the Clarence game. Several times in the second half, he brought the ball down and shot up fifteen-footers early in the offense before the other four guys touched it. He was not making them this time, though. As a result, Grand Island expended little energy on defense during those possessions. The Vikings subsequently rebounded the ball and quickly went back the other way for more possessions.

243 (Usiak, Grand Island wins championship; plays Fredonia next, 1992)

Some of Andre's early shots visibly frustrated other players on the floor, most notably Adonis. He shot Andre several glances with his gold mouthpiece halfway hanging out of his mouth while displaying deflated body language while running back on defense.

Coming off the bench, Michael Mann did his best to spark our team, hustling as much as he could for any loose ball and trying to make *effort* plays. Running after a loose ball on a play early in the fourth quarter, he twisted his right knee the wrong way and could not go back into the game. He sat down at the end of the bench where Terrance Collison, Jason Wardlawer and I sat with his right leg extended. He breathed heavily, looking on helplessly as the battle continued. Our team continued to fight, especially Dion Frasier, who snatched an offensive rebound from the rim and laid it back up, ending one of our many scoring droughts. Coach Jones pumped his fist on that score as the baskets were not easily coming for us.

A basket off a rebound by Grant Koslowski gave the Vikings the 43–38 lead going into the fourth quarter.[244] It was the last time we were within striking distance. Coach Jon Roth's Vikings took a 56–46 lead on a pair of free throws by Koslowski with 2:42 left, and they iced it when he hit the front end of a one-and-one to make it 61–52.[245] I looked down at the end of our bench and saw Michael Mann's eyes turning red, followed by tears running down his face. He realized that he had put on his maroon and gold uniform for the last time and that his four-year run as an Engineer would soon be over.

"MIKE! MIKE!" Grand Island's Anthony Scott called over to Michael on a dead ball situation from the court. "Are you okay?"

Michael Mann slowly and silently nodded, coming to grips with what was happening on the floor. I did not know the two knew each other, and I was impressed that this Anthony Scott had enough compassion to ask one of my teammates how they were doing while the game was still in play. That interaction is something that I have never forgotten.

As the time steadily wound down and it was evident that we were not coming back, Coach Jones pulled his starters and started clearing the bench. Chris Souter, Dion Frasier, and Adonis Coble, our class of 1992 seniors came out of the game one by one. He then pulled out Andre Higgins and Jermaine Fuller. He put in Jason Hellerman, Carlton Ford, and Damon Kimbrew for a couple of minutes before finally looking down at the end of the bench at us sophomores.

He finally sent in Terrance Collison, Jason Wardlawer and myself. In unison, we all took off our warmup shirts and hurried into the game for the last thirty to forty-five seconds. We got into the game for just a couple of possessions. I was hoping to get in and get my second basket of the season, as the other guys were

---

244 (Usiak, Grand Island wins championship; plays Fredonia next, 1992)

245 (Usiak, Grand Island wins championship; plays Fredonia next, 1992)

hoping to get on the board as well. I got winded running up and down the college-sized court those few times. My entire body was cold, but my lungs burned as well from the sudden increase in activity.

Unlike Coach Jones, Grand Island's Coach Jon Roth had not cleared his bench, and some of his starters were still on the floor going full speed. On one of the last plays of the game, we were lined up on the free throw line. Grand Island was shooting, and both Jason Wardlawer and I were on the low blocks. The ball bounced out of the cylinder over to my side of the basket. I looked up at the ball, intending to jump up and secure it, but Chris Tassy competed for the rebound, causing the ball to ricochet out of bounds. On the next inbound play, the final buzzer sounded, and the game was over.

Grand Island defeated us to win the 1992 Section VI Class B-1 final 63–52.[246] They advanced to play Fredonia in the overall Class B final, and the winner would advance to the Class B Far West Regional. Neither team from the 1991 overall Class B final repeated.

Grand Island's high scorers were Grant Koslowski with 18 points, followed by Anthony Scott's 16 points (12 in the second half).[247] According to the *Buffalo News*, Koslowski attended his grandfather's funeral earlier that day and probably played an emotionally inspired game as a result. Dion Frasier led us with 13 points and 10 rebounds.[248] Chris Souter was our second-leading scorer with 10 points, 6 rebounds and 6 assists.[249] They were the only Engineers to score in double figures, which indicated how our team struggled that night. Adonis Coble was our next-highest scorer with 9 points and 7 rebounds.[250] Jermaine Fuller finished with 8 points and 10 rebounds.[251] Andre Higgins played another stellar defensive game though scoring only 4 points.[252] Jason Hellerman scored 3 points.

We did not receive awards for being the runners-up for the Class B-1 title. After shaking hands with the Vikings, though, I hung out long enough to watch them receive their awards and trophies. I was in my own thoughts, processing what had

---

246 (Usiak, Grand Island wins championship; plays Fredonia next, 1992)

247 (Usiak, Grand Island wins championship; plays Fredonia next, 1992)

248 (Jones, Hutch-Tech High School vs. Grand Island High School; Class B-1 Sectionals, 1992)

249 (Jones, Hutch-Tech High School vs. Grand Island High School; Class B-1 Sectionals, 1992)

250 (Jones, Hutch-Tech High School vs. Grand Island High School; Class B-1 Sectionals, 1992)

251 (Jones, Hutch-Tech High School vs. Grand Island High School; Class B-1 Sectionals, 1992)

252 (Jones, Hutch-Tech High School vs. Grand Island High School; Class B-1 Sectionals, 1992)

just happened amid the chaos and excitement in the arena. I was in a somber mood holding my warmup shirt and thinking about our season being over.

As I turned to walk off the court to join my teammates, a singular line of gold shot out of nowhere on the periphery of the court, rushing, almost like a stream of fire. It was the LaSalle Explorers, the team that handed us our most lopsided loss of the season. In a strange way, I was happy to see them.

When they dashed towards me on the edges of the court, I noticed their star guard, Carlos Bradberry, led the charge. I extended my hand out to give him some *dap*. With a look of urgency on his face, holding a basketball, he saw me and returned the gesture before leading his team into their pre-game warmup routine. I did not think much about it beforehand and just did it. Unlike Adonis, who could not stand Carlos, I respected him, and I hoped to play against him next year.

The locker room was quiet after our loss to Grand Island. The game was within reach, unfortunately, we just could not close the gap. Our guys fought hard, but just as in the McKinley and Riverside games, we could not pull it out in the end. Some of the guys would never put those thick nylon maroon and gold jerseys on ever again, and it was our last time being together as a team like this. I looked around and saw the seniors looking off into space. Adonis had that frustrated look on his face, and Chris Souter had a look of disbelief on his face.

"Well, we fought hard, guys, but we just came up a little short. Sometimes it happens like this. You put your all into it, and you just come up a little short," Coach Jones said in his low, grandfatherly voice, with a hint of scratch in his throat. "You have nothing to feel bad about. In a season full of adversity, you all fought and went much further than anyone thought that you would go."

"You are such a *Nanny Goat*," Coach Jones said, reaching out and gently tickling the hairs on Jermaine Fuller's chin, causing Jermaine to give a slight grin. Nanny Goat was a nickname that Coach had come up with for Fuller, probably because he was skinny and he had that little bit of hair on his chin. It was a glimmer of humor in an unhappy moment. The class of 1992 seniors took off their Hutch-Tech basketball uniforms for the last time, and they would forever pass into history: Michael Mann, Dion Frasier, Chris Souter, and Adonis Coble.

"They are a patient team on offense. They are a good club, and they are one of the more patient clubs in the city," Coach Jon Roth said in his postgame interview with the *Buffalo News*, paying homage to the way Coach Jones ran our team.[253] The featured image for those sectional final games caught Chris Souter and Chris Tassy battling for a loose ball as Andre Higgins looked on with Anthony Scott and Dion Frasier in the background also looking on.[254]

---

253 (Usiak, Grand Island wins championship; plays Fredonia next, 1992)

254 (Usiak, Grand Island wins championship; plays Fredonia next, 1992)

Once we put on our street clothes, Coach Jones asked if we wanted to hang around and watch some of the LaSalle-Williamsville North game. Terrance Collison, Andre Higgins, Carlton Ford and I all raised our hands. The rest of the guys got on the bus and went home. I told Mom that Coach Jones would drop me off. The four of us sat up in the stands watching the Class A final. Andre clowned and picked at me about something as we consumed snacks and refreshments. I got a little ticked off and just wanted to watch the game.

We watched LaSalle battle Williamsville North. The No. 1-seeded LaSalle Explorers were 22–0. The No. 2-seeded Williamsville North Spartans, whose colors were green and gold, were riding a nineteen-game winning streak of their own and did not look afraid of LaSalle, though they trailed them in the first half. It was a true battle between the gold-colored Explorers and the green Spartans. Williamsville North had an athletic team of their own. They were led by a sharpshooting guard, No. 13, Jonathan Parks, and No. 45, Marvin Hollie, who punctuated one of LaSalle's turnovers with a two-handed slam dunk in the first half. They also had a 6'8" big man named Brett Stanwich, a white kid with goggles. Like many of the Yale Cup big men, while he was tall, he did not seem to be of the caliber of Turner/Carroll's Kevin Sanford skill-wise.[255]

Consistent with most Section VI teams, Williamsville North had a hard time dealing with LaSalle's defensive intensity and hustle, their 1-3-1 zone defense, and their ability to slash to the basket. We only stayed until halftime where LaSalle led 36–15. After we left, Williamsville North battled back and made it a game in the fourth quarter before LaSalle finally pulled away for good, winning the game 62–52. They won the Section VI Class A Championship for the third consecutive year behind Carlos Bradberry's 21 points and Curtis Ralands' 14 points.[256]

Coach Jones took us all to McDonald's that evening, which I really enjoyed, before dropping us off one by one. I pondered that loss for a while. We were close to winning the Section VI Class B-1 final again, but just came up short. Fortunately, we had a lot of players coming back the next year, and our prospects for making another deep run were good. It was early March, and that Monday, we went to school and continued with the rest of our 1991–92 school year.

---

[255] (Committee S. V., 1992)

[256] (Harrington, LaSalle topples Spartans for fifth straight crown, 1992)

Chapter 26. The 1992 Far West Regionals, Bigger Fish, and the 1991–92 Engineers' Final Time Together

"The game with Greece Athena was unbelievable. We just had no answer for 'DA MAN', John Wallace!" —**Pat Monti, Head Coach, the LaSalle Senior High School boys' basketball team, 1975-2000, May 2018**

My basketball education continued after our loss to Grand Island in the Section VI Class B-1 final. My green sectional book likewise became glued to my eyeballs and hands after the season-ending loss.[257] It all fascinated me as I was one for new details and information. While the Yale Cup had fourteen teams, not all of the teams played in the same sectional class. Some schools in Section VI played in Class A, while others played in Classes B or C. None of our schools were in Class D. Ours was just one of many leagues in the larger basketball ecosystem that was Section VI.

Grand Island, LaSalle, and Niagara Falls all played in the Niagara Frontier League. There was a Niagara Orleans League with a bunch of schools I did not recognize. I did recall Newfane. It was the school that Coach Jones took us to for the George Lehman workshop in October. There were four Erie County Interscholastic Conferences (ECICs) where most of the suburban schools in the county played. Clarence, who we defeated in the Class B-1 semifinal, played in the ECIC II. Williamsville North, whom LaSalle dispatched in the Class A final, won that conference. Gabe's Cleveland Hill Eagles played in the ECIC IV. There were three Chautauqua conferences. Fredonia, who won the Class B-2 Championship, was from the Chautauqua I Conference. Finally, there was a Cattaraugus Conference and two independent schools, Allegany and Portville.

The inside of the cover of the sectional listed the classes each school played in. At the top of the page, there was language which read verbatim:

"The New York State Basketball Championship involves the eleven Sections that make up the New York State Public High School Athletic Association. In each section, schools are placed in a classification according to the total enrollment, boys, and girls in grades 10–12."

---

257 (Committee S. V., 1992)

Class "A"—801 and up, Class "B"—401-800, Class "C" 215-400, and Class "D"—214 and below

The schools from each conference were grouped for postseason play based on enrollment from grades 10–12. That meant that even within the Yale Cup, there was variability in school population sizes. Thus, we would not see Riverside or Buffalo Traditional in postseason play unless our enrollment decreased or theirs increased. The same was true for LaSalle and Cleveland Hill.

I studied all the pages of that book. There was a Section VI Boys' Basketball Committee that organized the tournaments and represented the teams in each conference/league. There were pages upon pages of sponsors on the inside, and there were pictures and rosters for each team that made the semifinal rounds. LaSalle fascinated me. Their picture was very dark in the program, so you couldn't see them clearly. I could make out Carlos Bradberry, Shino Ellis, Jody Crymes, Curtis Ralands, and Tod Guetta. I also spent a lot of time looking at Clarence, Grand Island, Buffalo Traditional and Riverside. I studied their records, coaches, and players—everything.

In the back of the book, the playoff brackets for the year were listed. Consistent with what the *Buffalo News* reported about McKinley, our Class B-1 bracket only had seven teams. There was also a list of the Western New York All-Time Scoring Leaders. That year the list was headed by Ritchie Campbell, Marcus Whitfield, Curtis Aiken, Christian Laettner, and Damone James. The final page had the sectional winners per class going back to 1952. Sure enough, Coach Jones' 1990–91 Hutch-Tech Engineers were listed for Class B-1, with Kensington being the winner the year before.

LaSalle won the Class A sectional each of the previous four years. Interestingly, in 1988 they won the Class B-1 sectional, meaning they switched classes. It was probably because of an increased enrollment. There was one school that I did not recognize called Trott Vocational High School, which seemed to have disappeared altogether along with other area schools I heard of only through stories, such as the former East High School in Buffalo. Later, I heard stories of private schools no longer existing, like Cardinal Doherty. There were many others.

There was a whole history and lore to Section VI. It was much bigger than our singular program at Hutch-Tech. I got excited thinking about the next season and what was to come. I would get to contribute to the legacy of another Hutch-Tech boys' basketball team. I would be a part of history in future Section VI playoff books. Going on a run like Curtis Brooks and the 1990–91 Engineers excited me like a kid anticipating his new toys on Christmas morning.

* * *

Chapter 26. The 1992 Far West Regionals, Bigger Fish, and the 1991-92 Engineers' Final Time Together

While the 1991–92 Engineers' season ended, the quest for Glens Falls for some teams continued. Four teams from Section VI still hoped to journey east to the Final Four and have a chance at history. Standing in the way of our four Section VI champions were the four Section V champions from the Rochester area. These matchups between the Section V and Section VI champions were called the Far West Regionals. Some called them Super Sectionals.

The regional games were the qualifying games for the state tournament. The winners advanced to the Final Four in Glens Falls and competed with the champions from other regions of New York State for the Public School Championships. The host for the Far West Regionals alternated every year. They were held at the Rochester War Memorial Stadium the previous year.[258] That was where the 1990–91 Engineers suffered their heartbreaking and lopsided season-ending loss to Newark. In 1992, they were held in Steele Hall at Fredonia State College.

For teams and players hoping to go to the next level, attending the Far West Regionals would have made sense if for no other reason than to know how to set your goals. I do not remember Coach Jones, or any of the senior players, suggesting going to the Far West Regionals the next week to watch the Section VI Class A, B, C, and D champions attempt to advance to the Final Four in Glens Falls. Because I thoroughly enjoyed seeing the 1990–91 Engineers' play, had someone recommended it or put a group of us together, I would have jumped at the chance to go to Glens Falls.

"Hey, turn on the TV to the Empire Sports Network. Riverside is playing against a team from Rochester, and they're getting torched by a kid named Matt Verkey," Gabe said over the phone. It was December when he alerted me to Duke matching up with Canisius. There was an excitement in his voice. He was probably happy to see Riverside getting beat. They allegedly talked trash to his Cleveland Hill boys' basketball team prior to their narrow 62–61 victory over the Eagles in the Class C quarter finals weeks earlier. The same Riverside team won the Yale Cup with their close victory over the Engineers in our gym a month earlier. They also narrowly edged out Buffalo Traditional for the Section VI Class C Championship.

I was just lazing around the house that Saturday, March 14th, not long after our season-ending loss to Grand Island. No one else was watching the big TV in the living room, so I turned it on and quickly flipped to the Empire Sports Network to see what all the commotion was about. The schedule for the Far West Regionals was actually listed on the back of my green sectional book; and in hindsight, what we were watching was actually a replay of those regional games, as the games were

258 (Committee S. V., 1991)

played on TV pretty much back-to-back. The Class A Regional, for example, started at 7 p.m., but I did not watch it until late into the night.

Sure enough, the Class C Far West Regional was on when I turned to the station. As I watched the TV with the phone still in my ear, Gabe went on about how Riverside could not stop this Matt Verkey, who played for a school I had never heard of called Mynderse Academy. Verkey was a 6'4" versatile guard-forward, and he and the entire team looked like any team of white suburban kids from the area; the complete antithesis of Riverside.

Our old friends, the Riverside Frontiersman, were still in the hunt, but they were barely hanging on. They had run up against a proverbial *freight train* in the form of the Mynderse Blue Devils from Seneca Falls, New York. Consistent with what Gabe said, Matt Verkey was debilitating Riverside, which was down by 20 points or more with little hope of staging a comeback. They were within one game of advancing to Glens Falls, but seemed powerless and unprepared against this opponent.

No. 5, Matt Verkey, was given any shot he wanted and made pretty much all of them. I tuned in partway through the first half and saw him participate in warmups at halftime. He wore a warmup shirt that said 'Assassin' on the back. Several times the cameras cut to where his family sat, and his grandmother wore a shirt that said, 'Matt's Grandma.' He must have been the town hero or something. While Verkey and his Mynderse Blue Devils were all new to us, this snowball had gained momentum all season. As described by his Coach, Scott Smith, in the postgame write-up in the *Buffalo News*, Verkey was a 'triple threat' who could beat you by driving the ball, posting you up, or with his outside shot.[259]

The same Riverside team that beat us in the last seconds of our game in late February looked confused, and they lacked any kind of rhythm on offense. They randomly fired up shots, hoping anything would fall and get them back in the game. They went 17-for-68 from the field by the end of regulation. Watching that game, it was clear that Mynderse was prepared for the stage, more so than Riverside, who in some ways, was fortunate to get there based on their string of narrow victories. Matt Verkey put on a clinic and thrashed the Frontiersman, scoring 34 points and leading his team to a 64–45 victory.[260]

"He is a great player, really strong," said Coach Bill Russell from Riverside. "But we did not help out as much on him defensively as I had hoped. Nobody came to get a charge or step into the lane."[261] Coach Russell cited things his

---

[259] (Harrington, WNY boys swept out of boys' cage regionals; Mynderse act too powerful for Riverside, 1992)

[260] (Harrington, WNY boys swept out of boys' cage regionals; Mynderse act too powerful for Riverside, 1992)

[261] (Harrington, WNY boys swept out of boys' cage regionals; Mynderse act too powerful for Riverside, 1992)

Frontiersman could have done to give them a chance to win, fundamentals that took time to impart that were instinctually executed in big games.

Mynderse went on to win the NYSPHAA Class C State Championship against Malverne and the federation title against Manhattan-Regis.[262] Coincidentally Manhattan-Regis defeated the Turner/Carroll Chargers in the Catholic School Tournament, the team that decisively ousted Hutch-Tech twice at the start of our season.[263] It was a dream season for the Blue Devils. All their seniors happily rode off into the sunset, leaving behind lofty but achievable goals for the underclassman succeeding them.

Gabe called me during the Mynderse-Riverside game, so I was also able to watch the Class D, B, and A matchups. For some reason, the Class D game was scheduled after the Class C game, so I watched Section V's Notre Dame of Batavia defeat Franklinville 67–61.[264] Again, we never played any of the D schools, so the game did not have much meaning for me. Like the Riverside-Mynderse game, I recognized two of the teams playing the Class A and B games.

The next game involved the Grand Island Vikings. After defeating the Engineers, the Vikings defeated the young Fredonia Hillbillies 59–55 in the overall Section VI Class B final the following Tuesday night at Lockport High School.[265] They advanced to the Class B Far West Regional and were routed 66–46 by the Palmyra-Macedon Red Raiders, another team I was not familiar with. They were called 'Pal-Mac' for short. They were led by their senior guard No. 20, Geoff Von Weigen, and their center No. 22, Dan Drews, who was 6'7", and again they were a more suburban team.[266]

Like the Class C game, Pal-Mac had a level of comfortability that Grand Island did not. Whatever lightning the Vikings rode into the Far West Regionals on, they seemed to have lost it. It was that, or Pal-Mac was in a totally different class. Bob Bojarski was not much of a matchup for Dan Drews, and the Vikings had no answer for Geoff Von Weigen, who penetrated their defense at will, repeatedly attacking the basket. In the second half, Anthony Scott attempted to put the Vikings on his back and shot them out of the contest, missing numerous three-pointers as his Vikings fell steadily further behind.

The next week in the Final Four, the Pal-Mac Red Raiders defeated Elmira Free Academy 71–68 before falling to Syracuse-Fowler 79–61 in the Class B state final.[267] Watching that game it occurred to me that with a few favorable bounces

---

[262] (Wilson, Perfect season is reality as Mynderse wins C crown, 1992)

[263] (Wilson, Perfect season is reality as Mynderse wins C crown, 1992)

[264] (Siuda, 1992)

[265] (Harrington, Scott paces Grand Island by Hillbillies, 1992)

[266] (Siuda, 1992)

[267] (Schopp, 1992)

and a basket here and there, it could have easily been us playing against the Red Raiders. I could have been down on those sidelines.

The final game involved the mighty golden LaSalle Explorers, the home team. They were playing team in black and gold that I hadn't heard of called the Greece Athena Trojans. They were led by a highly skilled and athletic center named John Wallace. You had to really be plugged into high school basketball at the state level to know who all the stars and Division I prospects were outside of Western New York. I had not heard of him or his legend.

The 6'8" Greece Athena star was Syracuse University-bound and was a Parade All-American. According to what the commentators said as the game unfolded, he was a highly coveted recruit for many Division I schools. While No. 44 had NBA height, his body was just filling out, so he still looked kind of wiry in terms of how his jersey fit him and how his feet looked relative to the rest of his body. He was brown-skinned and had a laidback look about him, though he oozed confidence. His head was bald except for some large letters on the back, which his barber skillfully cut, spelling out 'DA-MAN'. The announcers also picked up on it.

Because both teams were 22–0, the game was nicknamed 'The Meeting of the Perfect Strangers' and viewed as a clash of the Titans. Aside from John Wallace, the rest of Greece Athena's team looked unimpressive next to LaSalle's athletic roster. John Wallace's teammates looked like white suburban kids with average height and athletic ability. What they lacked in those areas, they made up for in intelligence, skill, and fundamentals. The game turned out to be quite a spectacle. It was the biggest and toughest fish in Section VI versus the biggest and toughest fish in Section V, with the winner going to Glens Falls.

From the opening tip, it was a close contest. Watching the game, I noticed that the Greece Athena Trojans were not crumbling under LaSalle's pressure defense the way that the rest of the teams in Section VI did. Their Head Coach, Don Brown, was an older, round white man with a black mustache and gray hair around the sides of his balding head. He wore a sweater and khakis and had clearly prepared his team for Coach Pat Monti's LaSalle Explorers.

Again, Greece Athena was calm against LaSalle's aggressive 1-3-1 zone defense, patiently passing the ball around the perimeter, reversing it to the other side, and then at the right moment lobbing it to John Wallace, who either scored or went to the free throw line. The Trojans reminded me of our team and what Coach Jones preached about *working* the ball for good shots. With a highly talented 6'8" All-American center, we could have easily been like Greece Athena.

Early in the first half, Wallace caught a lob pass in the middle of the lane. Todd Guetta of LaSalle fronted him. Wallace then turned, spun, and elevated off the floor, caught the ball, and authoritatively slammed it through the basket with two hands while his teammates and the Explorers looked on. It was a thing of beauty.

I do not think anyone had seen such an authoritative slam dunk on the best team from Section VI all season.

LaSalle also did not look afraid of No. 44 from Greece Athena, as both Carlos Bradberry and Curtis Ralands jawed at John Wallace, who gave it right back to them. The Explorers likewise used the same one-two punch of guards No. 50, Carlos Bradberry, and No. 30, Shino Ellis, the combination that got them there. Bradberry and Ellis went out and gashed the Trojans in the open court every chance they got. Whenever the Trojans got back on defense, the Explorers ran their offense, which involved passing the ball to the wing and then cutting away. After several passes, open shots were created for Shino Ellis who sank jumpers from all over the floor with beautiful form. Driving lanes to the basket were also created for Carlos Bradberry. The duo scored 25 of LaSalle's 27 points going into halftime of the tied game.

In the second half, Greece Athena came back and played their slow and patient game offensively, while LaSalle tried to play their up-tempo game. While Carlos Bradberry and Shino Ellis powered the LaSalle offense in the first half, Don Brown made an adjustment in the second half that seemed to make the Explorers' star guards disappear in the halfcourt. Also, as Greece Athena ran their offensive game plan to perfection, LaSalle seemed to run less and less in the open court. While production from their star backcourt seemed to drop off, LaSalle did get scoring from their supporting cast of Chris Frank, Curtis Ralands, Todd Guetta, O'Neal Barnett and Willie Cole. They kept LaSalle in the game, but could not push them past the Trojans. Todd Guetta hit several huge 15-footers from the free throw circle in the second half for LaSalle. He had excellent shooting mechanics.

During that second half of the game, the camera and the commentators often focused on LaSalle's Head Coach, Pat Monti. I did not remember him from our game with them, probably because it was not close, and I was so focused on the action on the court. Coach Monti was a competitive, studious-looking gentleman who looked to be in his late forties or early fifties. He had a brown mustache with short, curly brown hair. He wore a button-down shirt with jeans or khakis and was very animated on the sidelines, just like one of the famous Big East Conference coaches of the time. He grimaced, yelled at the refs and players, and paced back and forth while often standing up and sitting back down in his seat.

On a key play as the game ground down to its conclusion, Coach Monti turned and threw his rolled-up papers into the air after a LaSalle player threw Carlos Bradberry a pass that zipped right between his legs out of bounds. The star guard turned and dove on the floor to try to stop it. The camera immediately zoomed in on Bradberry walking away in his gold jersey and Series VII Air Jordans. He turned around with the scared expression of a child who thought he might get a whipping.

While LaSalle seemed to unravel, Greece Athena continued patiently playing its slow game. Sometimes, John Wallace punished the Explorers inside. Other times, their patience created open shots by their outside guards like No. 10, Jake Lenhard, who hit a back-breaking three-pointer late in the game, which pushed the previously invincible Explorers to the brink of elimination. In the end, it was the timely free throw shooting by their point guard, No. 30 Brian Pratt, that iced the game for them. The truth is that all the guards and supporting players contributed to that win, including Jeff Murphy, Mike Davey and Eric Schmidt.

By being patient on offense and capitalizing on Wallace's height and versatility on the inside, Greece Athena prevented LaSalle from getting out and running and defeated them 55–43, en route to the Class A State Final Four in Glens Falls.[268] I videotaped most of that game and watched it repeatedly over the spring and summer of 1992. It was a brilliant performance, showing that sometimes you can outclass and beat a more athletic team. Or you just need one player that your opponent cannot match up with.

Section V dominated the Far West Regionals that year. It looked like a lot of fun to be able to make it to that level and beyond. It took a lot of hard work for all the teams involved. Perhaps with what we had coming back at Hutch-Tech, we could get back there the next year and contend for a berth in the state final four.

* * *

The next week after our season-ending loss to Grand Island, we turned our jerseys into Coach Jones, who in turn gave us our deposits back. Aside from those couple of junior varsity games I had participated in, I did not sweat up my No. 52 jersey very much that year. I had much fun putting it on and watching our team battle from the end of the bench. Making the varsity team was my goal at the beginning of the year, and I achieved it. After the summer of 1991, and almost blowing my focus, it turned out to be a bit of a miracle.

All our winter sports teams were honored at an assembly in late March before the spring sports developed into full swing. It was the last time the 1991–92 team would assemble for the school to see. All the sports teams gathered in the gym and were called onto the stage one by one. It was what I saw the 1990–91 team do the previous year, and I was a bundle of nerves getting ready to go out on stage in front of the entire school.

The gym had much commotion as all the teams waited to be called. Someone on the hockey team caught my attention as we waited. It was Josh Gallagher, Bill Gallagher's older brother. He had put a balloon over his head and blew it up. Once

---

268 (Harrington, WNY is swept out of boys' cage regionals: SU-bound star single-handedly ousts LaSalle, 1992)

it was filled up, it shot off and flew away onto the hardwood floor of our little old gym, causing an eruption of laughter from everyone. The bowling team went out, followed by the swimming, hockey, and girls' basketball teams.

When it was our turn, we filed out of the gym to the rear entrance of the auditorium. The seniors went up on stage first, followed by the juniors and then the sophomores. I felt nervous with the eyes of the whole school on us. Coach Jones stood at the podium dressed in one of his signature blazers, a button-down shirt and tie, khakis, and running sneakers and read off the following summary of the season in his raspy, grandfatherly voice:

"The Engineers enjoyed another good basketball season, finishing with a very strong showing in the Section VI Class B-1 playoffs, only losing in the finals to the top-seeded team.

"Considering the strength of the schedule and the numerous injuries and illnesses the team incurred, the season was successful. Major injuries were sustained by Dion Frasier, Jamar Moore, Mike Mann, and Jason Majchrowicz. Illnesses to several team members throughout the season took its toll as well.

"Big wins were the overtime game against Seneca High in the 'Tip-Off Tourney' and the 66–65 overtime game against Kensington High to gain a berth in the sectionals for the third straight year. The season was highlighted by the excellent teamwork and defense displayed in the 56–53 victory over Niagara Falls High in the sectional quarter-final game and the 65–57 win over Clarence High School in the semi-final game.

"The entire squad was awarded certificates. Adonis Coble, Dion Frasier, Jermaine Fuller, Keith Herron, Jason Holman, Andre Huggins, Mike Mann, Roderick Peoples and Chris Souter were awarded Varsity Letters as players. Damion Alexander, Leroy Copeland, Jon Koval and Monica Peterson were awarded letters as managers.

"The following players were awarded coach's trophies in the following categories:

1. Best Intra-Squad Free Throw Shooter- Jason Hellerman
2. Best Free Throw Shooting % in Games- Jermaine Fuller
3. Best Rebounding Average Per Game- Chris Souter
4. Best Field Goal % in Games- Keith Hearon
5. Best Assists Average Per Game- Chris Souter
6. Best Defensive Player- Andre Huggins and Chris Souter
7. Best Practice Player- Anwar Dunbar

I was surprised to get my trophy and felt a little overwhelmed walking across the stage to accept it in front of everyone. It was like my receiving the Most Improved Player Award back at Campus West. I had not done anything heroic like Andre. I did not make any spectacular plays like Adonis and had not played enough to earn a varsity letter. Still, Coach Jones saw fit to honor my devotion to our practices, the program and learning the game. Coach continued:

"Chris Souter was named to the 'All Tourney Team' for the Hutch-Tech Tip-Off Tournament, and Jermaine Fuller was selected to the Festival of Lights All Tourney Team."

"We have two players who are candidates for the 'All-High' basketball team. They are Adonis Coble and Chris Souter. We will have a difficult task replacing the graduating seniors, especially our tri-captains: Dion Frasier, Mike Mann, and Chris Souter who have been with the team for four years.

"We would like to thank all the students and faculty for their cooperation and support. Congratulations Engineers on another great season."[269]

It was an up-and-down season plagued with injuries and unforeseen twists and turns, including suspensions of some of our key players. Our team persevered and stayed together even when things were at their darkest. It was in large part because of our senior leaders, and we came within a few plays of repeating as the Section VI Class B-1 Champions. After the last assembly, I did not have conversations with many of my teammates to a large degree besides Terrance Collison for the rest of the year. We saw each other around the school halls, but I didn't associate with any other guys much after the season ended.

I think that typified our 1991-92 team, which contrasted with the 1990-91 team in several fundamental ways. It was evident in the team pictures. The 1991-92 yearbook, which we received roughly a month later, featured a picture of the 1990-91 Engineers in an early section.[270] Like the official picture from the previous year, it was a cohesive and disciplined unit with a battle-tested core. The 1991-92 team, while having some similar parts, was a rebuilding project that faced many adversities. It was a unit consisting of more youth than experience, and it looked like an assembly of several incongruous parts that were cobbled together into a functional unit. I always looked back on our 1991-92 team with love and fond memories. It wasn't always perfect, and there were sometimes arguments, disagreements and personality clashes. However, there was enough cohesiveness

---

[269] (Jones, Hutch-Tech Boys' Basketball Team 1991-92 Season Awards and Summary, 1992)

[270] (School, Impressions: Stepping Into 92, 1992)

to stick together. It was a family and a brotherhood, and many said the players on our team were like Coach Jones' sons.

* * *

On April 11, 1992, the *Buffalo News* announced the 1992 All-Western New York (All-WNY) High School Basketball Team. To make the All-Western New York Basketball Team was a tremendous honor, and it meant that you were one of the best players in the area. It meant that you consistently scored a lot of points and produced in other categories, such as assists and/or rebounds. You were the leader of your team, you probably won your league, and you had led your team on a deep post-season playoff run. The players on the first team had either been dominant the previous year and made a repeat appearance on the team, or they rose to the top of the field in the current year. Usually, the members of the first team were Division I college prospects.

In his article entitled, *Big men pull down top spots on News' 1992 All-WNY team*, Mike Harrington described the class, which consisted of three players taller than 6'6".[271] I was familiar with some of them. The previous year, Mike Mitchell from Williamsville South matched up with Curtis Brooks and company in the overall Class B final. He would play at Buffalo State College the next year. Carlos Bradberry from LaSalle held the other guard position.[272] He averaged 20 points and led the Explorers to an undefeated record before running into John Wallace's Greece Athena Trojans in the Class A Far West Regional. He was the only junior in the group.

All the big men Mike Harrington wrote about were from private schools. One was a 6'8" kid named Bob Fitzgibbons who attended the Nichols School. I had not heard about him. Nichols had a mediocre season at 10–12, but Fitzgibbons had a breakout year. The article said he was headed to an Atlantic Coast Conference school, though it did not specify which one.

The player who played a major role in our first two losses also made the team, Turner/Carroll's Kevin Sanford.[273] He suffered a season-ending knee injury, which sidelined him for post-season play, and his Chargers advanced all the way to the Catholic Schools Class C final. He was headed to St. Peter's University, a private school in Jersey City, New Jersey which played in the Metro Atlantic Athletic Conference, the same league as Canisius College.

---

[271] (Harrington, Big men pull down top spots on News' All-WNY Team, 1992)

[272] (Harrington, Big men pull down top spots on News' All-WNY Team, 1992)

[273] (Harrington, Big men pull down top spots on News' All-WNY Team, 1992)

The final player on the All-WNY team was No. 44, Eric Eberz of the St. Joseph's Collegiate Academy.[274] The 6'7" Eberz made the All-WNY First Team the previous year and had been a star for the Marauders, leading them to a record of 77–4 his three years on the team. That season, he led them to the Manhattan Cup title and the semifinal final round of the Catholic School State Tournament. The next year he was going to play at Villanova in the Big East Conference.

That year the first teamers all posed in what looked to be a studio. Carlos Bradberry stood cradling a basketball in his right arm, dressed in his gold home jersey. Bob Fitzgibbons sat in a reversed chair in the middle of the group, dressed in his visiting green and white jersey. Eric Eberz stood behind him, cradling a basketball at his side in his left arm, wearing his home jersey. Mike Mitchell knelt beside him in his visiting dark blue jersey, and Kevin Sanford sat on the ground with one leg completely extended and the other bent with his arms wrapped around it like a model. A basketball rested on the floor right in front of him. There were Second and Third teams and similar All-League teams for each conference.

It was a cool picture. Coach Jones cut it out and posted it on the bulletin board outside of the coaches' offices where the other materials were posted. He left it there for a short while, before taking it down after about a week or so. Sometimes, I would stop to look at it and dream. I knew that next year, I might get to play against Carlos Bradberry. I thought about how cool it would be to be one of the top players in the area, though in hindsight, I did not understand how to get there.

* * *

The All-Western New York Team was an assembly of the greatest players in our area, but that was just *our* area. The high school basketball world was much bigger than Western New York. I did not completely understand how big the basketball *ocean* was, but Coach Jones left us all a sample of it on the bulletin board outside of the coaches' offices. In addition to following the *Buffalo News*, he kept his eyes on the national stage and who some of the great and up-and-coming players in other states were. *USA Today* compiled a postseason list of the top high school basketball players and coaches from across the United States and honored them. Again, this was all pre-internet and social media, so unless you were a college scout, sports reporter, or a top college recruit, you did not necessarily know who the best guys were in other states.

The *USA Today* No. 1 high school player for the 1991–92 season was a player named Jason Kidd from Alameda High School in the Bay Area of California. He was a 6'4" point guard, which did not register in my mind at the time. He looked like a biracial kid, and in his picture, he was hunched over, dribbling a basketball,

[274] (Harrington, Big men pull down top spots on News' All-WNY Team, 1992)

and looking away at something. His coach was quoted as saying, "Jason is at his best when he is out in the open court leading the break and making his teammates better!" He was going to play at the University of California at Berkeley the next year, which I mistook for the legendary school in Los Angeles, UCLA.

Multiple players on that first team were featured and may have also been the No. 1 high school players in their states. Donta Bright from Dunbar High School in Baltimore comes to mind, who was going to go on and play at the University of Massachusetts at Amherst. He was coached by an older black gentleman named Pete Pompey, a legendary high school coach who won High School Coach of the Year honors that year. The title of his feature said something like, *Pete Pompey does it the hard way*.

The other top players included Othella Harrington, who went on to play at Georgetown, Corliss Williamson, who went on to play at the University of Arkansas, and two other players named Jamaya Jones and Bryan Adams. Further down the list was John Wallace, who led his Greece Athena Trojans to their victory over the LaSalle Explorers. There were other names I did not recognize like Tony Delk, Rodrick Rhodes, Serge Zwikker and Chris Collins.

I did not understand that all the NBA Players whom I watched and admired were once great high school basketball players; unless they had a growth spurt and a rare opportunity to develop after high school and made it to the pros. Dennis Rodman comes to mind. Most were high school phenoms and prodigies who were courted, handpicked, and recruited by the National Collegiate Athletic Association's (NCAA's) greatest Division I coaches.

The next tiers of players were recruited by the smaller schools, such as nearby Canisius College, Niagara University, St. Bonaventure, and the University at Buffalo. You had to be great for coaches like Jim Boeheim, from Syracuse, to be interested in you. After that you had to be recruited by Division II or III schools, following that, you really had not distinguished yourself enough to play anywhere and had to figure out how to continue playing the best way you could, if at all.

"WHO WILL BE MY FIRST ALL-AMERICAN FROM HUTCH-TECH?" Coach Jones scribbled next to the newspaper clippings. He asked us this question verbally at times as well. I did not fully grasp what it would take to be the first, and I do not know that my teammates did either. A lot would have to come together for just one of us to get there, and it would start with stringing together multiple seasons like the one the 1990–91 Engineers had.

Chapter 27. The Underclassmen's Revolution: The Coming of the Fab Five, and Their Changing of the Basketball Landscape

"I felt like right away I should have been starting!" —**Reggie Hokes, Player, the Hutch-Tech boys' basketball team, 1992–95, February 2015**

After the high school basketball season ended, basketball continued at the collegiate and professional levels. As such, the basketball education continued for me and other kids around the country and the world. There was great basketball being played on both levels, and a change was taking place that would impact the game for years to come. It had been taking place that entire 1991–92 college basketball season in plain sight. I did not notice it until the 1992 NCAA Men's College Basketball Tournament. The epicenter of this revolution was the University of Michigan in Ann Arbor.

* * *

It was a cold Western New York Friday night, which as usual, found me in the house. Because she was in the living room watching the big TV, I was in Mom's room watching the East Regional Final in the 1992 Men's NCAA Basketball Tournament. That year it took place at the Spectrum Arena in Philadelphia, Pennsylvania. This contest was potentially the greatest college basketball game ever played. It was a matchup between Rick Pitino's No. 2-seeded Kentucky Wildcats and Mike Krzyzewski's No. 1-seeded Duke Blue Devils.

Years earlier, Coach Pitino left the New York Knicks in the NBA to resurrect the storied men's basketball program at the University of Kentucky, which was mired in scandals and recruiting violations. He gradually built a contender with less talented players like No. 32, Richie Farmer, No. 34, John Pelphrey, No. 11, Sean Woods, No. 12, Deron Feldhaus and No. 44, Gimel Martinez, who were all left behind by the previous coaching staff. He had one prized recruit, the 6'8", multitalented No. 24, Jamal Mashburn, out of Cardinal Hayes High School in the Bronx, New York. Feldhaus, Pelphrey, and Woods were the lone seniors from the previous regime, and they were now out to make history on their final ride as Wildcats.

The Duke Blue Devils were marching towards their second-straight National Championship on the shoulders of No. 32, Christian Laettner. Laettner was the Blue Devils' beloved star and golden boy, though he was hated by most other fan bases and sometimes his teammates. He led a stellar supporting cast consisting of No. 11, Bobby Hurley, No. 33, Grant Hill, No. 12, Thomas Hill, No. 23, Brian Davis, No. 21, Antonio Lang and No. 44, Cherokee Parks. On his bench, Coach Mike Krzyzewski, also known as 'Coach K', had another crop of players who would log significant minutes for him in the years to come.

Though they were the top two seeds in the East Region, Duke was predicted to blow out Kentucky and cruise to the Final Four. Because I hated Duke, I rooted for the smaller and lesser talented Kentucky team. Along with many other spectators, I hoped the Blue Devils would get sent home after knocking off the UNLV Runnin' Rebels in Indianapolis in the national semifinal the previous year.

Much to my liking, the predictions for this game were wrong. From the outset, it was a heavyweight slugfest where Kentucky unexpectedly came out and immediately punched Duke in the mouth. Early on, the Blue Devils were in a fight for their lives as Kentucky played very aggressively and matched them basket for basket. Brilliant play after brilliant play by Kentucky suddenly introduced the possibility that Duke might get beaten.

The battle between the two teams, whose colors were both dark blue and white, was a thing of beauty. Kentucky used Rick Pitino's famous pressing style on defense in addition to deadly accurate three-point shooting on offense. Duke stayed in the game due to their veteran experience and their height up front. I had not seen the two teams play much that year personally, but I was on the edge of my seat rooting for Kentucky. Even though he was from Western New York, like almost everyone else outside of Durham, I did not like Christian Laettner or Duke. They were like Larry Bird and the Boston Celtics in that they were perceived as being a privileged all-white team in spite of having a significant number of black players.

Heroic shots from Christian Laettner, John Pelphrey, Jamal Mashburn, and others sent the game into overtime. It turned in Duke's favor when Jamal Mashburn, Kentucky's sole shot creator and NBA talent, fouled out by getting called for a blocking foul on Christian Laettner. I and numerous other viewers had hoped that Christian Laettner would have been thrown out earlier when he stomped his foot into the chest of Kentucky's freshman No. 25, Aminu Timberlake; the refs let him stay in the game.

The game came down to two heroic shots in the overtime period. The first was by Kentucky's senior point guard Sean Woods, who penetrated the lane and threw up a one-handed floater from the front of the rim. The shot banked off the square on the backboard and ricocheted perfectly through the net, putting the Wildcats up by one point, 103–102. "OHHHHHHH," I yelled out in my mother's bedroom, pumping my fist as the ball went through the net.

With only seconds left on the clock, everyone pretty much thought Duke was dead. During the timeout, Coach K drew up the legendary play that had Grant Hill take the ball out of bounds near Kentucky's basket on the baseline. In a crucial tactical decision, Kentucky, which was undersized height-wise, decided not to guard Grant Hill out of bounds while double-teaming Christian Laettner at Duke's foul line at the other end of the court.

In the historic play, Grant Hill threw a perfect baseball (or football) pass down to Christian Laettner, who caught the ball at Duke's free-throw line. The ball arced perfectly in the air from Hill's fingertips to Laettner's. Laettner took one dribble in place and then spun around to his left side and shot up a ten-footer which cleanly sailed through the basket as time expired. The basket gave Duke the 104–103 victory and propelled them to the 1992 Final Four in Minneapolis. The Kentucky Wildcats and their fans were sent home in despair, wondering what had just happened.

"NOOOOOOO!" I felt the emotion of the shot in my own way and shared my own disbelief in the back of the house. It was history, but not the only history being made in the 1992 tournament.

* * *

Elsewhere, another team was making its way to the Final Four, the University of Michigan Wolverines. Coach Steve Fisher magically won the NCAA Tournament three years earlier in 1989. He took over for Bill Frieder, who had been fired by legendary Head Football Coach and Athletic Director, Glen 'Bo' Schembechler for not being a 'Michigan Man'.[275]

According to Mitch Albom's account in his book, *The Fab Five*, just before the 1989 tournament started, Schembechler discovered that Frieder intended to take a job at Arizona State University and wanted him out immediately.[276] In a magical run, Fisher took the helm and coached the senior-laden team to victory at Seton Hall in the final game. No. 41, Glen Rice, No. 52, Terry Mills, No. 35, Loy Vaught and No. 21, Rumeal Robinson, led the Wolverines that season. They were all seniors, and all four went to the NBA.

Late in the 1991–92 season, the Wolverines were led by a band of freshmen who had become known as the 'Fab Five'. It was the same Michigan team that had almost upset Duke in early December, the week after Duke's defeated Canisius.

---

275 (Albom, 1993)

276 (Albom, 1993)

While most of the story of the Fab Five involves the five freshmen, the other important part is what led up to their recruitment. After the 1989 national championship, Steve Fisher and his coaching staff were unable to repeat the magic that won them the title, creating inevitable pressure for coaches when losses steadily mounted.

Despite their lack of success following the championship, Fisher and his assistants recruited a highly touted class of freshmen led by the No. 1 high school player in the nation, the 6'8" Chris Webber from Country Day High School in Detroit. No. 4 was a man-child athletically, with versatility skill-wise and a combination of size, quickness, and grace. When I think about Chris Webber, I always think about his ability to make the game look fun, easy, and effortless.

Michigan also landed the 6'7" Jalen Rose from Southwestern High School in Detroit, a powerhouse for generating Division I basketball players led by Head Coach Perry Watson. The son of Providence College great and NBA ball player Jimmy Walker, Jalen Rose was a *hybrid* player like Magic Johnson. He wore No. 5 and was tall with *guard* skills, and he could play all five positions if necessary.

Fisher's very first recruit in that class was the 6'10" Juwan Howard from the south side of Chicago, who wore No. 25. Howard was another athletic, very skilled, and graceful frontcourt player who was highly sought-after just like Webber. Howard wore the No. 25 in honor of the legendary but tragically slain Chicago basketball phenom Benji Wilson. Finally, Fisher's staff rounded out that recruiting class by going into the state of Texas and recruiting the 6'6" Jimmy King from Plano, Texas and the 6'5" Ray Jackson from Austin, who wore Nos. 24 and 21, respectively. All five players were among the top 100 high school players that year. They were all NBA talents who could have been the cornerstones of any Division I program.

In the Legend of the Fab Five, all five of the freshmen did not break into the starting lineup immediately. Only Chris Webber, Jalen Rose and Juwan Howard started the first game that season. It was a hard pill to swallow for the seasoned veterans, most notably No. 3, Rob Pelinka, No. 42, Eric Riley, No. 14, Michael Talley and No. 32, James Voskuil. As the season went on, Jimmy King entered the starting lineup, and then finally, when Michigan played a non-conference game at Notre Dame, Ray Jackson started, and the five of them never looked back as a unit.

The all-freshmen lineup quickly made a name for themselves with their cockiness, confidence, and the way they blended their games together. They masterfully combined the playground and organized styles of basketball. Chris Webber made the game look easy and fun. He effortlessly dunked the ball from almost anywhere on the floor, either by himself or off alley-oops from teammates. I did not watch the game against Notre Dame, but in one of the highlights from ESPN's *30 for 30* documentary, *The Fab Five*, Ray Jackson is shown throwing

Webber an alley-oop pass on a fast break. In that footage, Webber effortlessly catches the ball with one hand, dunks it, and then runs up the court flashing his signature childlike grin. It was extraordinary.

They did not win the Big Ten Conference Championship that year, but No. 6, Michigan made a legendary run to the Final Four in 1992 Men's NCAA Tournament. On their way to Minneapolis, they knocked off John Cheney's No. 11-seeded Temple Owls 73–66, Eddie Sutton's No. 2-seeded Oklahoma State Cowboys 75-72, and Randy Ayers' senior-laden No. 1-seeded Ohio State Buckeyes 75–71 (OT) in the Southeast Regional Final. They did have some luck on their side, as No. 11-seeded East Tennessee State Buccaneers upset Lute Olson's No. 3-seeded Arizona Wildcats, who would have surely given the Wolverines a tougher game in the second round. Michigan won that game 102–90.

I watched that Southeast Regional Final matchup between the Wolverines and the Buckeyes. Still ignorant of most college sports, I was unfamiliar with the history between the two schools, which was particularly storied on the football field. The CBS broadcast did a good job of letting the viewers know that it was a battle of youth versus experience. You felt it, too, as the game unfolded in Lexington, Kentucky. While the Wolverines were led by the Fab Five, the Buckeyes were led by their sharpshooting senior guard, No. 22, Jimmy Jackson, and their long and athletic junior, No. 34, Lawrence Funderburke.

Michigan wore their navy blue uniforms which they wore from the third round on. They also wore the Nike Air Zoom Hauraches, and some of them shaved their heads bald for post-season play. The Buckeyes wore their home solid gray jerseys with matching red and gray Nikes. It was a tight game, and Chris Webber fouled out late in the contest. James Voskuil, a junior, came off the bench and made some very timely baskets, which in addition to clutch shots by Jalen Rose and Jimmy King, lifted the Wolverines to their 75–71 victory.

For its 1992 Final Four preview, *Sports Illustrated* used a photo from that game where Chris Webber dunked the ball with two hands with his legs cocked up and a crazed look on his face. Ray Jackson is in the background smiling, watching the whole thing. I had only seen Michigan play once that year, and that was in December when they almost beat the Duke Blue Devils at home in overtime. That was before all five freshmen had ascended into the starting lineup. Even then, it was evident that there was something special about them. I started watching their NCAA Tournament run during the Oklahoma State game and kept my eyes on them from then on.

With their talented and experienced upperclassmen now coming off the bench, the Wolverines found ways to win each game. Though I had not strongly rooted for them, I was on the edge of my seat, pulling for them as they battled Ohio State for that Final Four berth. It just felt like this was a team of destiny, and they had to win, and they did.

In the national semifinal game in Minneapolis, the Wolverines matched up against Coach Bob Huggins' Cincinnati Bearcats, whose colors were orange and black. The team featured a bunch of junior college transfers, including No. 31, Nick Van Exel, No. 33, Terry Nelson and No. 34, Herb Jones. The Bearcats played a trapping and physical style on defense and an up-tempo game on offense. In the Midwestern Regional Final, they knocked off Anfernee 'Penny' Hardaway's Memphis State Tigers 88–57 to advance to the Final Four.

The light blue and gray Memphis State Tigers were also a team I watched closely once the tournament started. They upset the Arkansas Razorbacks in the second round, 82–80. I purchased the issue of *Sports Illustrated* that captured the opening rounds and read it religiously. There was a picture in it where No. 11, Arkansas's Lee Mayberry, tried to get a shot off against Memphis State's No. 50, David Vaughn, in front of him and No. 25, Penny Hardaway, who was looking to block the shot from behind. Images like this are forever etched into my memory.

Going back to the University of Michigan Wolverines, at the beginning of the national semifinal game, CBS created a cartoon where a grinning Steve Fisher dropped milk bottles into the crib of the Fab Five. The bottles had the names of each of their previous four opponents on them. After the fourth bottle, five fingers reached up into the air, each spinning basketballs.

It was a tight game and, after seeing how Cincinnati ended Memphis State's run, I thought they might do the same to Michigan. The Wolverines were poised and used their superior size and athleticism to edge the Bearcats 76–72. The victory set up a rematch in the national championship game with Duke, that had defeated Bobby Knight's Indiana Hoosiers in the other semifinal 81–78, in a battle of master and apprentice coaches, Bobby Knight and Mike Krzyzewski, respectively.

In the national championship game, the Michigan Wolverines got the better of Duke early on. The Blue Devils were in a bit of an early funk, particularly Christian Laettner. In the first half, the Wolverines had fun and made the game look easy once again as Chris Webber dunked the ball and threw no-look passes to teammates like Rob Pelinka, who, on one play, caught the ball and made a 360-degree layup. Numerous times, Webber trotted up the court, showing his infectious childlike grin.

Other players made plays, too, like Jalen Rose, who either scored himself or dished out assists. Jimmy King hit shots from three-point range and caught alley-oops, and Eric Riley, who came in off the bench, hit turn-around jump shots with ease. At halftime, Michigan held a slim 31–30 lead. I felt confident that they would complete the upset, but it was just the first half.

Even during the first half, when nothing seemed to go right for Christian Laettner and Duke as a whole, they got production from Bobby Hurley, Grant

Hill, Thomas Hill, Antonio Lang, and their freshman big man, Cherokee Parks. Legend has it that in the locker room both Coach K and Bobby Hurley verbally lit into Christian Laettner. Whatever they did worked because Duke came out of the locker room a new team and blew the game wide open.

The biggest difference in the second half was Christian Laettner, who snapped out of the funk he was in and remembered who he was. He hit shots from everywhere, three-point range, close to the basket, and on fast breaks. With the production from his supporting cast, like Grant Hill, who penetrated for dunks, and more all-around play by Bobby Hurley, they shot out ahead of the Wolverines, who could not answer the more experienced Blue Devils and fell steadily further and further behind.

Duke cruised to their second-straight national championship, winning 71–51. The young Wolverines and the rest of us were stunned, wondering what had happened. While that game was the end of the Christian Laettner-led Duke unit, it was not the end of Duke's domination. It was also not the last we would hear from the Fab Five or the movement they had started in the basketball world.

* * *

The Fab Five made a huge impact on the basketball landscape that year. They would go on to become cultural icons, and they would be relevant in other areas of society besides basketball. On the court, however, their play inspired underclassmen everywhere and challenged the notion that you had to *wait* before getting a chance to play. For some coaches, it was easy to put incredibly talented young players on the floor over seasoned veterans who had put time into their program over the years and were ready to assume their would-be rightful roles. That prospect was agonizing for other more structured and traditional coaches who valued seniority and time in their programs. Those coaches were fiercely loyal to their players and wanted to see them play if they waited their turns over the years and did what was asked of them for the greater good. Change was coming for everyone, as it always did.

Chapter 28. A Spring Sport, the Empire State Games Tryouts, and Offseason Instructions

"Players in the program should look to play a fall and a spring sport!"
—Ken Jones, Head Coach, the Hutch-Tech boys' basketball team 1988–1993, April 1992

Sometime after the conclusion of the 1991–92 season, Coach Jones posted a note that he wanted all of us to see on the bulletin board outside of the coaches' offices. It must have been in April after the All-Western New York teams were announced. It was like the postings he left for the 1990–91 and 1991–92 teams. It was printed in the same capitalized letters and the top of it had the word LOOK scribbled in his handwriting. The Os had smiley faces drawn on them. All the text was highlighted in yellow. The letter read as follows:

DEAR PROSPECTIVE BASKETBALL CANDIDATE FOR THE 1992–93 SEASON

JUST A NOTE TO LET YOU KNOW THAT TRYOUTS FOR THIS SUMMER'S EMPIRE STATE SCHOLASTIC BASKETBALL TEAM WILL BE HELD AT CANISIUS COLLEGE'S KOESSLER ATHLETIC CENTER MAY 10TH AND 24TH STARTING AT 9:00 A.M.

WE ARE ENCOURAGING ALL PROSPECTIVE BASKETBALL CANDIDATES TO TRY OUT FOR THE TEAM.

WE HAVE ALSO BEEN WORKING ON AN EXCELLENT AND CHALLENGING SCHEDULE FOR NEXT SEASON WHICH INCLUDES A NON-LEAGUE GAME AT GATES CHILI, THREE TOURNAMENTS (HUTCH-TECH "TIP OFF," "PEPSI" AND "HOLIDAY FESTIVAL") PLUS THE TOUGH YALE CUP LEAGUE.

PREPARING FOR THIS TOUGH SCHEDULE MEANS EMPHASIS ON OUR **SELF IMPROVEMENT PROGRAM** (WHICH INVOLVES):

1. STUDYING AND GETTING READY FOR FINAL EXAMINATIONS.
2. PARTICIPATING IN A SPRING SPORT.
3. A SYSTEMATIC WEIGHT TRAINING PROGRAM.
4. A SELF PRACTICING PROGRAM. (MIKAN DRILL, ETC.)

5. PARTICIPATING IN BASKETBALL INTRAMURAL PROGRAMS.
6. PLAYING IN THE SUMMER BASKETBALL LEAGUES.
7. ATTENDING OUR EXCELLENT SUMMER BASKETBALL CAMP. (BE WITH US BY GETTING YOUR REGISTRATION IN **NOW**.)
8. PLAN ON PARTICIPATING IN A FALL SPORT.

IF YOU HAVE ANY QUESTIONS, SEE ME OR CALL.
KEEP IN TOUCH AND BEST TO ALL.

YOURS IN GOOD SPORTS,
COACH JONES

It was just like everything else Coach Jones did involving the great game of basketball. It was well-organized and highly thought out. The 1992–93 season was roughly nine months away, but he was already looking to the horizon at what was coming. It is worth noting that 'SELF IMPROVEMENT PROGRAM' was both bolded and underlined in red. He expected improvement in our games. We were not to return the same players we were at the final buzzer of the Class B-1 final game against Grand Island. Coach Jones was already thinking about assembling the 1992–93 team. I intended to be a part of it, and thoughts of starting on that team began dancing through my head.

* * *

Coach Jones encouraged his returning players to play a spring sport and to try out for the Empire State Games basketball team for our region. Theoretically, both would make us better basketball players and put us in better shape for the 1992–93 season. There were only a couple of spring sports for us to choose from. They included tennis, baseball, and track and field. I never tried tennis, and I had not played anything resembling baseball since I played T-ball ten years earlier. There were also those sporadic times when I would throw baseballs back and forth with Dad in Schenectady over the summertime.

Growing up in New York City, Dad was a baseball player. Had we grown up under the same roof, I might have become one too. Instead, I did not pay much attention to baseball as a youth, only basketball and, eventually, football. Baseball was less glamorous to me than basketball and football. Whenever I would see baseball on TV, it seemed slow and boring. Still, I noticed that my then Uncle David Simpson was always excited about watching his Atlanta Braves whenever he came to Buffalo with my Auntie Tracey.

Chapter 28. A Spring Sport, the Empire State Games Tryouts, and Offseason Instructions

Later, I learned that football, baseball, and football were like the 'Holy Trinity' of boys' sports. While many kids *specialized* in one sport at the time, there was still lots of value in learning to compete in multiple sports and then choosing one later at the college level. Coach Jones wanted us to maintain our cardiovascular fitness, but even big-time college football coaches like Jim Harbaugh at the University of Michigan years later admitted to enjoying playing the big three sports, and he actively sought out kids who were doing it in modern times.[277]

Hutch-Tech had a boys' baseball team, but I had no interest in joining it. That left track and field, which was a reasonable choice at the time as it would keep my cardiovascular fitness high into the summertime. I was not passionate about playing a spring sport, but I wanted to prepare for the 1992–93 boys' basketball season. Thus, if this were something I had to do, then I would do it. I did not want to have to play my way into shape early in the season, as I saw some of my teammates do early in our 1991–92 boys' basketball season. For completeness, it's also worth noting that Hutch-Tech also had a girls' softball team.

The Hutch-Tech boys' and girls' track teams were coached by Mr. Thomas Pressley. He taught the electrical engineering students. Mr. Pressley was a studious-looking middle-aged black man. He was husky in build with a gentle spirit. He had a 'salt and pepper' goatee with short curly hair. His glasses made him look like a lawyer or a professor. I think he might have also been a minister at a church. I heard that from multiple classmates.

The track team was run much differently than the basketball team. In contrast to Coach Jones' tightly run and highly structured basketball program, the track team was very laid back, a reflection of Mr. Pressley himself. There were no formal tryouts, and everyone participated in some way. Likewise, I do not remember any fear of going out for the track team.

Mr. Pressley attended practices dressed in his own sweatsuit after school. He did not micromanage his teams like Coach Jones did the basketball program and team. After school, for those early practices, he would come down and meet with the captains on the Johnson Park side of Hutch-Tech and tell them how much to run the rest of the team. The captains gathered around him, and the rest of us gathered around them. It was very informal, and he would stand there among us, figuring out what we would do right there on the spot.

"Run a half mile. Run a mile and a half," he would say off the top of his head and then disappear.

It was a different experience than being on the boys' basketball team. The overall energy was different, and winter had transitioned to spring. Instead of being

---

[277] (Bacon, Endzone: The Rise, Fall, and Return of Michigan Football; Reprint Edition, 2016)

cooped up in our little old gym for the afternoon, we were outside, breathing the fresh Buffalo air and sometimes rolling around in the grass. All I remember about those first track practices was the stretching on the Johnson Park grass. There were also lots of pushups and arm circles.

In between the arm circles, we had to hold our arms up in place for minutes at a time, which was painful. After that, we would run around the park, and at other times, we would run around the neighborhoods surrounding Hutch-Tech. Sometimes, we would do a drill called 'Last Man' where we would all run in a single file line, and the last man would have to sprint to the front. Everyone had to push themselves and keep pace.

Amahl liked running sports. Like the cross country team, he and our friend Dorian Johnson, participated on the track team. I think he had done it in three of his four years. It was the only time in our two years at Hutch-Tech together that we were teammates of any kind. The track meets were divided into multiple events, and my brother did the hurdles that year while I was assigned to some of the long-distance running events, probably due to my lack of quickness and speed.

Just as with the basketball team, Mr. Pressley eventually handed out uniforms to all of us. Like our basketball uniforms, they were all made by the company Champion. The track uniforms were less spectacular to me than the basketball uniforms. There were no visiting or home variations, just solid maroon tank tops with three gold numbers on the front and back. In addition to receiving tank tops, we also received shorts. Some guys might have called them 'coochie cutters'. Coochie cutters was a silly and vulgar name for ridiculously short shorts. They were not designed to make us look cool per se, but to provide us with the least amount of wind resistance in our running events. Mom got me a pair of green and gold Nike Air Pegasus running sneakers to compete in.

All our meets took place behind Bennett High School's 'All-High Stadium', the old broken-down stadium where many of the Harvard Cup football games were played on fall Saturdays. All-High Stadium was symbolic of the facilities in the Buffalo Public School system in that it was old and decrepit. It had bleachers on both sides though the uncovered side was weathered and crumbling. The covered side was also to some degree, even though it was where most of the fans gathered for the football games and track meets.

While the other sports were pretty much unique to certain ethnic groups and demographics, the track team was a mixture of boys and girls of all races. Some of the guys from the cross country team naturally came over due to their expertise with distance running like Darryl Strickland and Chris Szaba. Some of the football players came out as well due to their quickness and, in some instances, their strength. By far, most of the student-athletes on the team during my sophomore season were black. In addition to myself, from the boys' basketball team, Andre Higgins came out and ran along with Terrance Collison.

Chapter 28. A Spring Sport, the Empire State Games Tryouts, and Offseason Instructions

By far our track team was dominated by the class of 1993 juniors, many of whom were in the aforementioned crew, the 'Mack Daddies'. They were guys like Theron Sanderson, Theory Hayward, Paul Easton, also known as 'EJ', and many others I will not name. True to their group, there were plenty of jokes and pranks taking place. One funny joke took place one day when Theron Sanderson ran a race and came down the stretch towards the finish line. As he tried to finish the race first, he developed a painful grimace on his face.

Paul Easton joked and said he looked like the rapper Busta Rhymes from the Tribe Called Quest's hit song, *The Scenario*, which they recorded with another group called Leaders of the New School. At the end of the song, Busta Rhymes famously says, "GROWWWW-WOWWWW, LIKE A DUNGEON DRAGON," and he had a similar grimace on his face in the video to Theron. It made all of us laugh on the sidelines.

Our strongest runner on the team that year, at least speed-wise, was Dwand Henderson, a dark-skinned black senior. You would not think it to look at him, but he was a fast sprinter who won most of his races. Someone jokingly nicknamed him 'Black Magic'. Unlike the other runners, he ran upright and slightly tilted to the back, but it worked well.

A big matchup at one of the meets was against Kensington's runner, Robin Harris, who was equally as fast, if not faster than Dwand. He ran with his arms and hands pointed out straight to the side and with his fingers together like he was going to karate chop someone. One day they matched up against one another in the 100 meters. It was a day when Dwand was visibly sick. Everyone watched in anticipation of the gun firing off.

Within seconds, Robin Harris had won the race, and as he came up to the finish line, he slowed down to show off. At the last minute, he tripped and landed face-first in the gravel while Dwand charged on to win the race. Everyone burst out laughing. Harris got up with his face and jersey covered with gravel wondering what had happened.

* * *

What was cool about the track meets was that there were more than two schools there at once. At any track meet, three to five schools could compete, so you were sure to see someone from the other schools that you knew. One day, Chuck Huggins' friend Reggie Reese from Martha Avenue, was running the Four by One Relay. He ran the 'anchor' leg for McKinley, which is reserved for the fastest runner. Due to his bulky size, I did not know Reggie was that fast, and I was amazed at how he accelerated around the curve of the track that day to win the race for his team. I don't know what position he played, but he also played football at McKinley. Either way, he was fast.

Other vivid memories of being on the track team were seeing my brother run the hurdles and seeing Andre Higgins run the relay races. I think Terrance Collison ran the relay races as well. Terrance was a very gifted athlete, and he was extremely fast in terms of sprinting. He was usually the first of us to finish the wind sprints at the end of our basketball practices.

I ran in one race that year. I think it was the one- or the two-mile, one of the longer races. Mr. Pressley thought I would be most useful doing a distance event since I was not as fast as the other guys were. Normally running around a track like that, I would go at my own pace and slow down whenever I felt my heart and lungs working too heavily. In a race, you must push your body to its limits to try to beat your competitors. As I crossed the finish line, I did, in fact, feel like my body had been pushed to its limits, and I thought that I was about to collapse.

And that was my track and field experience at Hutch-Tech. My motivation was in large part due to Coach Jones' insistence that we do it. Nothing satisfied my appetite the way that basketball did. I gradually realized that many of the best basketball players in Western New York played other sports, and it was commonplace. Athletes were athletes, and most liked that feeling of competition, no matter what the arena was.

If you look in the 1991–92 yearbook, you will not see me or any of the other guys who were there. The season took place well after our yearbooks were printed, bound, and published. My picture for the track and field team would thus be in the 1992–93 yearbook. Again, that 1991–92 team was the only time my brother and me competed in an organized sport together.

* * *

In addition to playing a spring sport, Coach Jones also encouraged us to try out for the Empire State Games Western New York boys' basketball team. He continued putting messages on the bulletin board outside of the coaches' offices about it to catch our attention and encourage us to try out for it. The Empire State Games were like an Olympics for the best amateur athletes in New York State. The best high school kids (and some college) from their region competed to see who the best was in their sport in the state.

The state was divided up into multiple regions for the games: the Adirondack, Central, Westchester, Hudson Valley, and the Western Regions, to name a few, and of course, New York City. Our area fell under the Western Region like the sectionals, though in this case, a team would be created with players from Buffalo and Rochester. Thus, only the best of the best from each city would make it. This meant that only a handful of players from Buffalo would be taken onto the team depending upon who was selected from the Rochester area. That explained why a familiar face was front and center at the tryouts that Saturday morning.

The Buffalo tryouts for the Western Region team took place at the Koessler Athletic Center on the campus of Canisius College. It sat on the corner of Delavan and Main streets across from the Delevan/College Metro Rail Station and diagonal from the Forest Lawn Cemetery. The tryouts took place on a Saturday morning, around 9:00 or 10:00 a.m. We were some of the first prospects to get to the main gym, which was initially empty. I wondered Gabe and I were in the right place. It gradually filled with boys from all over Western New York ranging from grades 9–11.

I recognized some of the guys, but there were lots that I did not. From our Hutch-Tech boys' basketball team, Jason Wardlawer came out, as well as Andre Higgins and Jermaine Fuller. Ed Harris from Riverside was there too. Two of LaSalle's players, whom I recognized immediately, had also come out, Curtis Ralands and Jody Crymes. I paid close attention to them for most of the tryouts. They were competitors who had beaten us handily, and in my mind, they were royalty. None of their other guys showed up, most notably their star all-purpose scoring guard, Carlos Bradberry.

"See, even white kids act like they are Jordan! They try to run like him and try to shoot their jump shots like him," Gabe lamented and shook his head, complaining as we shot baskets warming up. He pointed out a white kid who wore a No. 23 Chicago Bulls replica jersey, had a crew cut/high-top fade, the No. 23 etched into his hair, and a pair of Air Jordan Nike sneakers. Like today, race was a large part of our thought process, and it was funny hearing Gabe take issue with this kid who had no idea we were talking about him. I did not care. I just wanted to see if I could make the team.

Before long, all the prospective players were shooting on the baskets of the main court reminiscent of the Ken Jones Basketball Camp. Multiple basketballs bounced and hit the baskets in addition to the chatter among the players. My jump shot was off that morning and was not falling into those college-style baskets that hung from the ceiling of the Koessler Center over its main court. With every miss, I got steadily more frustrated. I started wondering if I belonged there with the rest of the players.

"FINALLY," I said out loud as one of my shots sailed through the net. A couple of the guys turned, looked at me, and laughed.

Once we warmed up for a while, we were all called to the bleachers, where we were addressed by the coaches and given instructions. I do not remember who most of the coaches were, but there was one that I recognized, Coach Gary Oehlbeck from Gates-Chili High School and the Ken Jones Basketball Camp. He was probably a representative from Rochester who was there to help determine who from Buffalo would make the team.

"Hey, Coach Oehlback," I said, happy to see him feeling some kinship from the camp the previous summer.

"Hey, Anwar. It is good to see you. How are you?" He was cordial but also short with me as he was there to determine who the best potential additions to the team were, not to fraternize with specific players.

"We are going to give you numbers and put you on teams," Coach Oehlbeck said, holding his clipboard and whistle. "We are going to watch you guys play a quarter against one another and then call out the names of the players who we want to keep!"

Those tryouts were fierce as everyone tried to put their best games on display. For the really good players, there was the challenge of being *too* selfish and being a team player. For players like myself, the challenge was just keeping up with everyone else or breaking out and exceeding expectations. I wound up on a team with Jody Crymes, the baby-faced freshman point guard from LaSalle. I quickly found out that he played as fast as he did as a teammate as he did as an opponent.

On one play, Jody used his crossover dribble on his defender and drove down the lane. I followed close behind him as he drew several defenders. I was just trying to position myself to get an offensive rebound off the shot I thought he was about to take. He jumped up in the air as though he was going to shoot the layup himself, but instead threw a no-look behind the head pass that caught me by surprise and sailed right past me. Had I caught his beautiful assist, it would have been an easy layup. I would have scored, and it would have been a spectacular play for both of us. He turned around smiling, looking for the fruits of his beautiful assist with an expression that I interpreted as his saying, "Hey, what happened?"

Jody had many spectacular plays after that, but a score by me would have increased his chances of making the team also. Instead, it may have looked like a careless play on his part. A score also would have boosted my own confidence and made me play harder. When playing with players like Jody, you had to anticipate the assists coming. I had not played with any guards like him, and Coach Jones did not encourage that type of improvisation from his guards. That is my most vivid memory of those tryouts, besides not having my name called at the end.

After a few rounds of scoping out the talent pool, Coach Oehlbeck and the other coaches huddled up and figured out who they wanted. They called out the names of the kids who made it to the next round, kind of like the way basketball tryouts were held at most other schools on TV. My name was not called, and neither was Gabe's. Neither was Jason Wardlawer's.

"I accidentally smacked Curtis Ralands on the head as we went up for a rebound," Gabe said jokingly afterward as we left the gym with Jason Wardlawer. "He turned around slowly and gave me a look through his goggles. I told him, 'My bad, man,' and he just nodded his head and said, 'OK.'" Gabe always had a funny story to tell, no matter where we went. This story was funny because Curtis Ralands, at only 6'1", had a particularly intimidating and menacing look about him facially with his goggles, his bald head, and his muscular frame.

I think Coach Jones wanted us to try out, thinking that one of us making the team was the best-case scenario. He probably also thought that the experience would be good for us in terms of seeing where we needed to develop our games and what our peers in Section VI were doing. I was not good enough to make the team, but in hindsight, unfortunately, it did not make me angry in a way that motivated me to improve and return with a vengeance. It did not motivate me to approach my off-season development with more of a sense of urgency. I just knew that the guys whose names were called played at a higher level that day.

To make your region's team, you had to be at the top of your game and at an elite level, and the guys who did, paid the price to get there. That experience should have been a barometer for me going into the next year, letting me know where I needed to take my game going into the summer of 1992. Instead, it was only a blip on my radar.

What also stands out about those tryouts for the Empire State Games that year is that Gabe and I went one way when they were over, and Jason Wardlawer went his way afterward. I would obviously see Jason back at Hutch-Tech, but we did not exchange phone numbers or make plans to play together over the summertime at courts around the city. In hindsight, I find it odd and would approach it differently today.

In the last days of the 1991–92 school year, Coach Jones left specific instructions for those of us who played on the boys' basketball team that year. The previous bulletin was for all the prospects for the 1992–93 team. These directions were specifically for us. It related to our development and improvement as individuals and as a group over the summer months, the summer leagues, and his basketball camp. Unlike his previous note to prospects for the 1992–93 team, this page was written out by hand and read as follows:

For Summer League Games

1. Acting Captains, contact players each week to ensure attendance (if you can't make it, call acting captains)
2. Workout Rides- GET THERE! Carpooling, Transits
3. USE MAN FOR MAN (DEFENSE)
4. USE A 3-2 OFFENSIVE ALIGNMENT (Give & Go, Screen away, Flash Post, Use Motion)

5. Use The Substitution Schedule (Equal Time For All) WE WANT TO DEVELOP ALL PLAYERS FOR NEXT SEASON)
6. HAVE FUN
7. SEE YOU AT BASKETBALL CAMP (BASKETBALL'S OUR GAME AND YOURS CAN BE THE SAME!)

*SEE ME OR CALL IF YOU HAVE ANY QUESTIONS

Coach Jones: 834-1160, 763-8675

Again, Coach Jones left us clear instructions for what to do. Aside from the summer league games he organized for us at Nichols and Bishop Timon, a few of us from the 1991–92 Hutch-Tech boys' basketball team organically got together as teammates to play and mesh our individual games together going into that summer of 1992 or throughout it. Pockets of our team might have done it like Andre Higgins and Jermaine Fuller, who were personally tight, but none of the rest of us did. I also had no idea who was considering attending Ken Jones Basketball Camp. Despite his instructions, we all just largely wandered into that summer of 1992 in different directions, not knowing what our teammates were doing to develop individually or as a unit.

Epilogue. The Games Played Both Inside and Outside of the Lines

"Sports are a microcosm of life!" —**Alice Jones, Coach Jones' Wife, 2012 and Onward**

The great game of basketball never stops truly calling out to you if you've ever played it meaningfully. They all call out to you – the court, the ball, the competition, defending your man, the potential of making a play, and the potential of making a basket. There is always something special about making a basket and seeing it go through the hoop from one of *your* shots. That's true if you're just shooting by yourself or when you're playing in a game. Sit by a court sometime when a game is being played, and the thoughts will organically start crossing your mind, even when you're older and even after having surgeries that forbid you from playing. *Can I still do it? Can I play? Should I?* The game calls you, and it continues teaching you. It also compels you to reflect on the lessons you learned when you seriously played it, no matter where you've settled in your later years. You never forget those lessons…

If you have humored me and read part one of *The Engineers: A Western New York Basketball Story*, I thank you and hope you enjoyed it. I also hope that you will read part two. As the author of this tale, I think it is important for me to say, when possible, why this story matters. One way in which it matters involves something that Alice Jones, Coach Jones' wife, reminded us of numerous times when discussing this project. She often said that, "Sports are a microcosm of life!"

There is the game within the lines that we all see–the final score, the standings, who is going to what college, etc. There is also the game behind the game, which is the game of life itself. In many instances, I have learned personally that the game of life greatly impacts the game within the lines. Thus, while this story is grounded in the great game of basketball, its themes and lessons apply to all other arenas of life. My blueprint for navigating the world, personal relationships, graduate school, and my current federal regulatory career started with those innocent basketball dreams at Hutch-Tech High School in our little box of a gym.

During my sophomore year, I achieved my goal of making the Hutch-Tech boys' varsity basketball team. In hindsight, it is kind of laughable, as my goal was to *make* the team and not necessarily get on the floor and play as a sophomore. That mindset was a symptom of many things, a major one being not having someone in my personal camp to *stress* the distinction between the two—just making the team versus getting onto the floor to play, even as an underclassman.

My research showed me that I was not the only one on the 1991–92 team with this mindset, though, in terms of that first year on the team being a *learning* year. Several other guys on the 1991–92 team also approached it that way. In hindsight, with Coach Jones' style and system, it was easy to default to that setting.

In addition to not having any men regularly in my home ecosystem, whispering in my ear to try to get on the floor with Adonis Coble and the rest of the veterans, we also did not have full-time assistant coaches around. Assistant coaches to complement what Coach Jones taught us would have been valuable in terms of giving other perspectives and filling in some of the gaps inevitably created by having only one teacher. At the end of the day, approaching the game was so much about context and perspective.

In hindsight, I would have pushed myself harder and the class of 1992 seniors to get myself on the floor to play with them. I would have pushed for 20 points in a game instead of my two against Performing Arts. I would have, "Attacked each day with an enthusiasm unknown to mankind," as the University of Michigan Head Football Coach Jim Harbaugh famously stated.

I'll have to rejigger part two of *The Engineers* to capture this, but Coach Harbaugh and the Michigan Wolverines won the 2023-24 College Football National Championship. It culminated three years of gradual progress, following five to six years of disappointment and heartbreak for the team and us as Michigan Football fans.[278] Coach Harbaugh, the players, the athletic department, and the school persevered, just as Coach Jones taught us back at Hutch-Tech and they were rewarded for it. Coach Harbaugh persevered and became a champion and a legend like his mentor Coach Glen 'Bo' Schembechler.[279]

* * *

Going back to the 1991-92 Hutch-Tech boys' basketball team and my approach to that season, much of that year was my mindset at that time. The same was true for my summer fling with Maria Harrison, which nearly derailed everything. Someone reading this story may wonder why it was important for me to weave that thread into the main story. First, I have protected her identity as Maria Harrison is not her real name. The same is true for James Anthony Forrester.

But I have speculated numerous times afterward how much better I would have been going into my sophomore year had I just focused on honing my craft that summer of 1991, especially after attending the Ken Jones Basketball Camp for the first time. In our interview, the legendary Buffalo Traditional point guard and now

---

278 (Bacon, OVERTIME: Jim Harbaugh and the Michigan Wolverines at the Crossroads of College Football, 2019)

279 (Bacon, BO'S LASTING LESSONS, 2007)

Coach Jason Rowe called this 'tunnel vision'. Getting good and then great at something requires tunnel vision, which is basically focusing on a singular goal and not getting distracted. Coach Rowe appears in part two of *The Engineers*, where I first witnessed his tunnel vision and the fruits that it bore on the basketball court.

As Coach Jones constantly told us, "Basketball is a game of fundamentals!" Thus, once you get them down and gain confidence in your skills, the fear of competition largely goes away, something I did not figure out until later. Once you do the *work* and know you have done it, it speaks for itself through your play.

"Half of basketball is confidence. Once you get your confidence, you can go anywhere!" Damien Foster gave another spin on learning the great game of basketball in our interview. The game was largely about confidence and not restricted to the vast and impressive expanse of fundamentals Coach Jones taught us. Damien Foster is also a legendary guard from Buffalo Traditional. Damien and others also appear in part two of *The Engineers* and help reaffirm that this is a 'Gladwellian' story, as described in the preface of this book.

A lot of time was wasted that summer of 1991 on my fling with Maria Harrison, time that could have been spent on my jump shot, dribble moves, hook shots, and other fundamentals. I just did not know how to stay focused on my larger goals at the time, and there are costs for not staying focused. I also did not understand that a major key to making leaps and bounds in whatever craft you are interested in requires a level of passion and even ruthlessness.

In my case, the craft was the great game of basketball. I did not know how to approach it that way at that time, and there were reasons for that. I might sound like a broken record, but I attribute that to not having a mentor, particularly a male mentor around in my home ecosystem to encourage me to, "Stay focused," or to say, "You will meet plenty of girls in your lifetime," and that, "You all just spent $300–$400 to go to camp, and now you are focused *only* on this girl?"

I have also speculated on numerous occasions as I have worked on this story what would have happened had I had to tell Coach Jones that I did not make the minimum grades for eligibility for the second-straight year. Not only would there have been no story to tell here, but it would have also been very embarrassing. I would have participated in the practices as a freshman and then spent the time and effort to go to his basketball camp, only to not qualify academically for tryouts.

He probably would not have given me a chance as a junior and would not have taken me seriously going forward. Ironically, my *making* the grades just barely that year, could be credited to Maria and her parents, Maria especially for giving me that final talking to and setting my young and fragile feelings free while I could still salvage my first-quarter grades. So, thank you to Maria.

* * *

Going back to the game itself, as I wrote the story and revised it, I realized that exposure is a major key to one's development, not just practicing drills or playing pickup basketball games. Those certainly have their place, but seeing the game and being around other players in a particular system like the one Coach Jones ran also matters. What I am saying is that, in hindsight, I stunted my growth by not being able to participate more in the program as a freshman. Had I participated from the start of the season, I might have gotten to be around the 1990-91 Yale Cup and Class B Sectional Championship team more and absorbed more from them.

After interviewing him, I think the same thing is true for the 6'5" Keith Hearon. Being eligible to play on the 1990–91 team would have been a major win for himself, the team, and Coach Jones. In my opinion, it would have changed the trajectory of both his junior and senior seasons just as participation in the program during the 1990–91 season would have done mine.

I learned so much from interviewing players like Curtis Brooks and Jerrold 'Pep' Skillon and their teammates from the 1990–91 team. They readily spoke about the blueprint for their winning the Yale Cup and the Section VI Class B sectional that 1990–91 season. What would have happened had this information been transferred to me (and others) directly from them in that time when we were trying to succeed them? The truth is that none of us will ever know, which is always one of the dilemmas when having discussions like this. What I do know is that the transfer of knowledge, no matter what arena or field you are in, is critical to the maintenance of success. Furthermore, when that knowledge is not smoothly transferred, there are more mistakes to be made by the successors.

My research revealed that the LaSalle Explorers in Niagara Falls did not have this problem. Based upon the size of their city, the outlets for learning basketball in their neighborhoods and the program that Coach Pat Monti and Frank Rotundo built, there was almost a built-in continuity and set of expectations from class to class. There was a built-in brotherhood and transfer of knowledge.

My research for *The Engineers* also revealed that Coach Pat Monti's LaSalle Explorers in Niagara Falls had been whipping most of the teams in Section VI for four to five years before I saw them play that December of 1991. They won the Class B Federation Championship in 1988, as David Lorenzo Glover described in the foreword of this book. This is why Jason Hellerman felt that we wouldn't beat them, as described in Chapter 20. It's also why the two girls' basketball players silently smiled when either me or Terrance Collison said that we would beat their boys' team at that 1991 Festival of Lights Tournament.

It did not come up in any of my interviews with Coach Pat Monti, Carlos Bradberry or Tim Winn that LaSalle won the Corning Cup Tournament Championship out in Albany, NY, a month before playing our 1991-92 Hutch-Tech boys' basketball beam. They defeated Albany High School 68-48 behind

Carlos Bradberry's 27 points.[280] I found the article and box score when researching the *Buffalo News* at the Central Buffalo Public Library. It was the weekend after our team got smashed by Turner/Carroll the day before Thanksgiving 1991. They had a history of winning, which was a way of life for them. I just didn't know about them because I hadn't been exposed to Section VI-Western New York high school basketball and its history up to that point. Exposure mattered in that arena as it does in other arenas in life.

How much would that transfer of knowledge have mattered for our Hutch-Tech teams if there were *not* cohesive groups of selfless players coming after the 1990–91 Hutch-Tech boys' basketball team? I will argue not much, as that was a major part of the formula for what they did too. They were a group of players who really wanted to play together, who all endured Coach Jones' temperament during the building of the program, and who were not going to give up for any reason.

Players like Curtis Brooks and Pep Skillon revealed that most of the players on the 1990-91 team *liked* each other, which isn't a given on every team. They were a group of players who genuinely cared about one another and played together for the good of the team and not individual benefit and recognition, something many players (and people) don't understand. Despite hearing stories of the core of that team being jokers, they also all listened and submitted to the structure Coach Jones implemented, something many had gotten at home from their parents and families.

The success of that 1990–91 team and the qualities that allowed them to work together could arguably be attributed to the homes they grew up in. They were further able to galvanize even those players who came from broken homes. This was another key to LaSalle's sustained dominance. The players were, for the most part, a brotherhood. They liked each other and accepted their roles as noted by Carlos Bradberry in our talk. They also bought into Coach Monti's teachings.

I intentionally highlighted Michael Mann, Dion Frasier, and Chris Souter for the leadership they showed. It held our 1991–92 team together when it could have easily broken apart. They were the final holders of the culture and the values that Coach Jones established in the program when he arrived in the 1988–89 school year. You will have to read part two to see what happened to our program for the remainder of my years at Hutch-Tech after they graduated, of course.

As I have written this story, I did speculate that none of the 1990–91 seniors came back to talk to us that next year. This would've been extremely helpful, especially for players like me who were *projects* and did not have the blueprint for developing hardwired into my brain. I do not know if Coach Jones even asked them. Many of them went off to college in other cities and probably did not have time. Some were local, though, and were around for the holiday season. This all returns to the mentoring theme and its role in achieving and maintaining success.

---

[280] (Staff, Bradberry sparks LaSalle to Corning Cup crown, 1991)

My research revealed that a key roster decision Coach Jones made for the 1991–92 team, my sophomore year, impacted one player's immediate willingness to come back and mentor us. That player was the above-mentioned Jerrold 'Pep' Skillon. He was the older brother of Jermaine 'J-Bird' Skillon from the class of 1992, who Coach Jones cut from the final roster. This was an unintended consequence of Coach's roster decision, perhaps a gamble he may or may not have pondered before doing it. We at least had Michael, Dion, and Chris that year to keep things together and create a sense of brotherhood and family, even when the team was losing. Talking to the 1991 seniors would have been tremendous.

* * *

My research revealed that the John Wallace-led Greece Athena Trojans team that defeated the 1991-92 LaSalle Explorers in the Far West Regionals lost its last game. For years I thought they completely ran the table. Just like stumbling upon the Explorers' winning the 1991 Corning Cup Tournament, I stumbled upon the Trojans' 68-57 loss to Bishop Laughlin from New York City in the 1992 Class A federation championship game when trying to finalize the references for this book. I saw Allen Wilson's write-up in the *Rochester Democrat and Chronicle* when looking for something else.[281] They were a remarkable team that went on a magical run, and I'll always see them that way. Seeing this led me to rename chapter 26 to include the term 'bigger fish' as this was always the case in athletics and life.

I did not formally interview my Uncle Scott McKinney, who appeared in part one of *The Engineers* in the preface and early chapters. He bounced from Buffalo down to Atlanta to follow my Auntie Melva and then back to Buffalo before leaving again. He played a little bit at Hutch-Tech and then at his school in Atlanta. When he returned to Buffalo, he allegedly didn't want to back up the great Curtis Aiken at Bennett and didn't play his final year of high school.

Through his storytelling, he was informally a part of my research as he shared that my Uncle John 'De Pody' Harris was the best shooter amongst the uncles. Uncle John, in fact, gave me my first formal lesson on shooting the ball. He passed away in 2021 after being estranged from the family. Uncle Scottie also shared that he, Uncle Tony, Uncle John, Uncle Jeff and my father, the baseball player of all people, beat lots of teams at the community centers on the west side of Buffalo. I had no idea. Once again, the research matters.

Part one of *The Engineers: A Western New York Basketball Story* ends with optimism, hope, mystery, and uncertainty. After earning a roster spot in my sophomore year, I assumed that I would get on the floor and play significantly as a junior. I would start building my legacy like the players and teams before me.

[281] (Wilson, Athena falls in state A title game, 1992)

Terrance Collison would be alongside me as would Jason Wardlawer. We were, after all, the *future* of Hutch-Tech basketball.

But how would we do it? Would it come from going to the Ken Jones Basketball Camp? Would it come from all of us going down to Delaware Park every day over the summer of 1992 to continuously sharpen our skills against the best players in the city? Would it come from searching out all the other courts in the city for competition? Would it be playing in the summer leagues Coach Jones had his teams play in at Bishop Timon and the Nichols School? Would it be from practicing the Mikan drill every day?

Aside from going to his basketball camp and participating in the summer leagues, Coach Jones gave us recommendations going into the summer of 1992. There was, however, no weekly supervision, and thus, our development was left up to us as players individually. I just knew that it was going to happen somehow. It was all going to come together for the 1992–93 and the 1993–94 seasons, my final two seasons. It would all come together somehow.

"If you want to play basketball in college, Anwar, you're going to have to be prepared to practice a lot. It's like a *job* at the college level, and the basketball players I know at the University of Georgia practice all the time while also having to do their coursework," My cousin Monica Willis said in her commanding, forceful, and stern way of communicating, an extension of her personality. Monica, an attractive, highly intelligent, dark-complexioned young woman, was my Grandma Lena's oldest grandchild and grew up mostly in Atlanta. She was also a well-accomplished athlete who competed in multiple sports, including track and field, at a high level in high school. She earned a scholarship to run track at the University of Georgia at Athens (UGA), a major Division I school.

UGA produced notable athletes in multiple sports. Two that come to mind for basketball are No. 10, Vern Flemming of the Indiana Pacers, and the once *King* of Atlanta, No. 21, Dominique Wilkins. 'Nique', also known as 'The Human Highlight Film', wore the UGA Bulldogs' red before wearing his beautiful red and yellow 1980s Atlanta Hawks uniform with the diagonal color scheme and names. They still give me goosebumps, and I loved it when the Bulls played the Hawks.

Monica was the sole Division I athlete in our wing of the family. Both Amahl and I looked up to our cousin, whom we only saw a few times a year because of the geographical distance between us. That said, I didn't fully grasp her words. With the number of college athletes she knew who were knocking on the doors of both the Olympics and professional sports, she certainly knew what she was talking about. The same was true when she corrected me when I tried wearing my ankle weights continuously after watching the movie *No Retreat, No Surrender,* starring Jean-Claude Van Damme.

A lot of kids have *said* they wanted to be basketball players. She was communicating that this dream was going to take a lot of effort, focus, and work.

Some luck or good fortune would be involved, too, depending upon your spiritual beliefs. I was gradually figuring this out, and it's safe to say that I didn't fully appreciate what went into playing basketball at a high level back then.

* * *

I intentionally chronicled the college basketball and professional sports of the time, mostly basketball and football, because a part of learning your craft is studying it. I got a late start in playing sports and watching and comprehending them. I did not understand it at the time, but in watching the ascension of the Buffalo Bills, the Chicago Bulls, and the Duke Blue Devils, and the coming of the Fab Five at the University of Michigan, for example, I was learning *about* competition.

It was not just those teams but also the teams around them, the injuries, the opening and closing of competitive windows, the coaching changes, and player trades—all of it. I did not understand everything, but it was a part of my learning in addition to what Coach Jones was teaching us. Like what he taught us, I would not understand all of it in its entirety until much later in my journey through life. It is worth noting that some kids learned all of this before getting to high school.

So, I will close this epilogue by once again thanking you for coming along on the first part of my basketball journey, a story that others and, as a result, I have questioned its need and significance. Each time I have personally questioned whether this story is necessary, I have come to a resounding, "Yes," as this story is very much a coming of age, rite of passage, and manhood story. It is particularly important in today's age, where masculinity is arguably under attack and when many boys are being left with no blueprint for becoming men, as described in the preface. It is also an era where the definition of manhood has become blurred and diminished. In my journey, I continually stated that there were few men consistently around, and that was intentional as it had consequences for my early basketball journey as it did in other areas of my life.

While so much of what we do in life starts with dreams, whether it is playing basketball, writing a book, getting married and starting a family, going to medical school, etc., there comes a time when we must pursue those dreams, which is where the real adventure often begins. We must act on our dreams. Even when we act, the outcome is never certain, as life contains many variables. We likewise may only have control over a few of those variables, if any at all.

Thus, while we may have equality of opportunity, the outcomes are often never equal. To learn about what happened to my innocent basketball dreams in my junior and senior years at Hutch-Tech High School, please join me for part two of *The Engineers: A Western New York Basketball Story*. I can promise that it will also be worth the read and the ride. Best regards and yours in good sports!

Bonus Chapter 1. The 1990–91 Hutch-Tech Boys' Basketball Team

"On our first possession on offense, Brooks immediately drove the ball to the basket without setting up the offense. I told him to come and have a seat next to me and watch the game for a little while. It took him sitting on the bench a couple of times before he learned to play within our offenses!" **—Coach Ken Jones, Head Coach, the Hutch-Tech boys' basketball team, 1988-1993, June 2014**

This bonus chapter was originally part of the main story of *The Engineers: A Western New York Basketball Story*. When editing the third draft, I decided that stopping to tell the entire story of the 1990–91 Engineers disrupted the overall flow of the book. The story I was constructing was one of constant discovery and, in large part, ignorance.

I did not know much of what I discovered during my research for *The Engineers* as a freshman, and this is partially why the journey unfolded the way that it did. What I learned could only be fully appreciated by someone who had followed sports for years and understood its many dynamics, intricacies, and nuances. I only learned much of what I now know about the 1990–91 Engineers from my research years later. There were also the forty-three interviews I conducted. There was also studying Coach Jones' notes and the scrapbooks he created from issues of the *Buffalo News* and the *Rochester Democrat and Chronicle*. Still, though, the 1990–91 Engineers were, in part, the basis for my story, and in honor of them, they deserved their own chapter. GO TECH!

* * *

"When I heard you wanted to interview us, I was thinking, man, we were not a special team," Curtis Brooks said at L' Enfant Plaza in Washington, DC. It was the summer of 2017. It was my *compressed* day at my job, and he agreed to meet me on his lunch break. Since I started working on *The Engineers: A Western New York Basketball Story*, I wondered if I would get to talk to No. 13 from the class of 1991. 'Curt' Brooks, as some called him, was also the leader of its 1990-91 Yale Cup and Section VI Class B Championship teams.

Fate would have it that I would get to talk to him, and there we were. Curtis Brooks looked about the same. He was now a veteran federal worker and a family man, but it was still him, and he was almost as tall as me. His hair was cut short, and he wore glasses, a short-sleeved white button-down shirt with a black tie, slacks, and shoes. His work attire reminded me of that of Michael Douglas' character, William Foster, in the movie *Falling Down*.

It was three years before the Coronavirus/COVID-19 pandemic hit our shores, and we sat outside with everyone at the plaza. In the background, you could hear the horns of the trains sounding off as they arrived and departed the above-ground L' Enfant Plaza train station. As I sat down and talked with Curtis Brooks, I could not believe it.

Tracking him down was similar to how I tracked down the other Hutch-Tech boys' basketball players. It started with Adonis Coble. That led me to Coach Jones and Michael Mann. My road to Curtis Brooks started on Facebook with his class of 1991 teammate No. 11, Quincy Lee. Like Coach Jones, Quincy would not see the final book, just the promotional materials I generated up to October 2022. He passed away from a heart condition during my final edit of the book.

Like Chuck Thompson, Paul Saunders, and Dion Frasier, Quincy also attended Campus West prior to going over to Hutch-Tech for high school. He agreed to an interview when I reached out to him using direct messaging on Facebook. That led to my interviews with Jerrold 'Pep' Skillon, Chuck Thompson, and then Curtis Brooks.

"When you look back at what we did, we raised the bar in terms of the basketball history at Hutch-Tech. Now when you look back and have a larger landscape in terms of other high schools and other students, you realize that what you did was a nice *chapter*," Curtis said, starting off our second discussion. Our first interview got cut short, and he graciously agreed to meet me a second time. There was a lot that Curtis shared in both parts of our interview that surprised me. In the opening of our second discussion, I expressed my surprise at his nonchalance regarding what the 1990–91 Engineers accomplished.

I understood what he meant. Maybe it was a *flash in the pan*, as they say, and the years after their dream season were indicative of that in terms of the Hutch-Tech boys' basketball team. It was one great year compared to the dominant decade the LaSalle Explorers had put together and the series of years the Buffalo Traditional Bulls had put together. There was also the run that Christian Laettner and his Nichols teams went on before the 6'11" star went to Duke.

That was just in Western New York. There were powerhouse high schools across the United States regularly sending players to Division I colleges to play basketball. From that group, the lucky select few who had the ability, health, and work ethic played in the NBA, which most boys playing basketball dreamt of. Only one of the 1990–91 Engineers, Chuck Thompson, played major Division I basketball. He went to play for the University of Pittsburgh Panthers. None went to the NBA. Still though, for that year, the 1990–91 Engineers took the entire school on a ride and made some of us dream of doing it, too. Some of us had not extensively played the game yet and did not appreciate what it took to do what they did.

"Why does water run downhill and not uphill? Because it is easy!" If I were to add it all up, me and Curtis Brooks spoke for almost two hours, mostly about Hutch-Tech basketball and Coach Jones, but about life as well. I did not know the Curtis Brooks in the early 1990s, but he was now incredibly wise in terms of life, relationships and being successful overall. I could have sat and talked with him for hours if we had time.

"We had the Randy Smith League, which was really about athleticism. Who was the fastest? Who was the most skilled? It was more one-on-one, and you never learned the concepts behind what you were doing," he said, discussing the basketball taught in the Randy Smith League versus what he learned playing for Coach Jones at Hutch-Tech. "You just learned, hey, this is my man, and basketball is about a team—knowing your position, knowing your man, knowing how to box out, knowing who needs help. There was so much more than beating *your* man.

"The same thing was true on the offensive end. There was ball movement, kind of like how Golden State does it. They have so much movement going on that eventually if you move the ball, it gets somebody out of position so that someone ends up with an easier shot off a missed assignment. That is what his (Coach Jones) structure was. We did not really have a pro-style offense where we were just going to dump the ball into one player and let him do his thing. It was like that, but it was not designed for that. He never told one player to shoot. He said if you are in that area and you are open, that is your shot. He never said, 'Brooks, I want you to get ten threes this game!' It was not a star system!"

As it relates to the Hutch-Tech boys' basketball team, several things stood out to me. Curtis Brooks had nothing but praise and respect for Coach Jones and how he did things, regardless of how his teammates or anyone else felt about him. Also, going back to his humility about what they had done that magical year, Curtis simply described basketball as something he was interested in, which kept him out of trouble. He just happened to be one of the more talented players at our school who wanted to play and got a chance to play. There was little ego involved and no lofty plans of leading the team in scoring. There was preparation involved, such as his going to the courts early in the morning in the summertime to work on his jump shot and wearing a weight vest in pickup games, but it was all genuinely to help his team win though and not about his own ego.

"It was like Hoosiers!" No. 11, Quincy Lee was the first of the class of 1991 players I interviewed. This was one of the many memorable things he said about Coach Jones and his system. There were some surprising things he shared about our coach too, that I never would have equated with him. He described Coach Jones' program and style of play as being like that in the movie *Hoosiers,* starring Gene Hackman, in terms of its structure and discipline. There were other aspects as well that I would never have known about the program and the class of 1991 seniors had I not done the research.

"I had to get back to playing *my* game!" Amidst all of Coach Jones' structure, Quincy Lee had to learn to play his own game within the framework the new coach established—something many players struggled with over the years and something I did not understand until afterward. Quincy further shared that most of his time playing for Coach Jones was a battle in and of itself, as the two constantly seemed to be at war. An initial point of contention was Lee's wiry frame which Coach Jones allegedly initially scrutinized. While other players would have quit, Quincy loved the game and his teammates, both of which compelled him to stay and endure it all. The Coach Jones he described was much different than the one I knew most of my time as a player, but as I learned, people can be different things to different people. I actually wrote a promotional essay about that.

"Our sophomore year, we got blown out at Buffalo Traditional. I will never forget it. We had fresh haircuts and everything!" Potentially my most fun interview for this project was with No. 32, Jerrold 'Pep' Skillon. I could hear the joy in his voice as he reminisced on his days playing in the maroon and gold. He said so much in our discussion. He shared his *quitting* experience in Little League football and the regret afterward. This was something many of us also had to learn in our journeys. He discussed playing for Mr. Shea during his freshman year on a team of veterans along with classmates Chuck Thompson and Quincy Lee. The seniors on the team that year were guys like Kevin Roberson and Kevin Lee. He talked about his junior year injury and their magical senior year, which involved their seventeen-game winning streak and their upset victory over the Turner/Carroll Chargers at their gym.

"Jones did not really teach you the one-on-one style of basketball. Any kind of handle or any of the moves I used on offense, I learned by watching games on TV!" Perhaps the most valuable piece of information Pep shared with me was his acknowledgment of his own game and skill level. It was the same thing I learned about my own offensive game as I crafted this story.

Coach Jones was about the fundamentals of basketball and doing things by the book. Though his teams needed it at times, he was not about the street game and developing individual moves. It is what my teammate Earl Holmes meant when he told me that my game was *basic*. I was just doing what I was taught to do and did not know how to expand beyond what Coach Jones was teaching us and how to blend the two. This is where a second set of eyes from a mentor would have been valuable. Pep was fortunate to be in a unit and a group that had all learned the system together, bought in, and made it work.

"Jones ruled the roost," Pep also jokingly said when discussing the level of discipline and martial law that Coach Jones established when he took over the program in the fall of 1988.

* * *

In the fall of 1990, as I was finding my way through high school, the Hutch-Tech boys' basketball team was gearing up for its 1990–91 season. Around the end of October, Coach Jones announced tryouts for his third team since taking over the reins in the 1988–89 school year. He reassembled his collection of players, most of which he had nurtured from day one and which he had watched come of age over the previous two years.

The 1989–90 team just barely qualified for sectional postseason play off a last-second three-pointer by junior No. 11 Quincy Lee. His buzzer-beater lifted the Engineers over the Buffalo Traditional Bulls 72–69 and into the Section VI Class B-1 playoffs.[282] The 1989–90 team overcame losing its first five league games before surging to win seven of its last eight to achieve the necessary greater than 0.500 record to qualify for sectional play.

Studying my brother's yearbooks, I saw that the 1989–90 team consisted of a nucleus of juniors and seniors, the bulk of which was on the 1988–89 team, Coach Jones' first group. The class of 1990 seniors were No. 22, Jerome Freeman, No. 42, Frankie Harris, No. 20, Derrick Herbert, and No. 23, Ed Lenard. There was also their 6'5" big man No. 33, Michael Brundige, who stood tall in the back line of the 1989–90 team's yearbook photograph. I did not see him on the 1988–89 team which meant that he was either injured or Coach Jones cut him. Freeman, Harris, Herbert, and Lenard all looked like nice enough guys. They were all brown complexioned and wore high-top fades as most black males did in that era.

The juniors were No. 13, Curtis Brooks, No. 32, Jerrold 'Pep' Skillon, No. 30, Paul Saunders, No. 11, Quincy Lee, and No. 55, Charles 'Chuck' Thompson. Chuck stood shoulder to shoulder with Mike Brundige in the back row. Both were stone-faced with their arms folded behind their backs. In the 1989–90 team photo, Pep Skillon wore his jersey, but he also wore jeans and sneakers. My brother Amahl said he severely injured his ankle that season which sidelined him for the latter stages of it.

Underneath them were the class of 1992 sophomores. They were No. 21, Michael Mann, No. 24, Dion Frasier, No. 34, Jermaine 'J-Bird' Skillon, and No. 44, Christain Souter, the only white kid on the team during Coach Jones' first three years. J-Bird looked like his older brother Pep, but just more massive and stockier. I recognized Dion Frasier and J-Bird around the halls of Hutch-Tech but not so much Michael Mann and Chris Souter, both softer-spoken and more preppy guys who you could miss if you were not looking for them.

---

[282] (Staff, Hutch-Tech captures game and playoff bid, 1990)

The 1989–90 team was close to Coach Jones' ideal makeup of a team but slightly off, having five seniors, five juniors, and four sophomores instead of two. There was a logic to this ideal team make-up. He was building his program as a series of classes and then grooming them as groups so that they all learned and trained together. They would all understand the culture and values of the program. The classes of 1990, 91 and 92, each was a group. Other coaches just put together teams of the best players they could get and ignored this continuity aspect, but not Coach Jones. There was a logic and reason to most everything he did basketball-wise.

That year, the 1989–90 team wore their white trunks with their white tank tops at home. In my brother's 1989–90 yearbook, there were pictures of Curtis Brooks shooting the ball from long-range and Jerome Freeman crouched low in his defensive stance guarding an opposing player. Both wore the 1988–89 black and white Series IV Nike Air Jordans, the pair Michael wore when he hit 'The Shot' against the Cleveland Cavaliers and in his Mars Blackmon commercials with Spike Lee. Those were my favorite edition of Jordans, by the way.

There was also a picture of Michael Brundige dunking the ball with one hand. That dunk appeared to get the crowd hyped up in the picture, as some of the Hutch-Tech students could be seen in the background dancing with their hands up in the air. Whoever took that picture must have taken it from the ground because it seemed to have been right under Brundige as he threw the ball through the basket. I wanted to be at that game every time I saw that picture.

The 1989–90 Hutch-Tech boys' basketball team entered the Section VI Class B-1 playoffs as the No. 9 seed.[283] In the pre-quarterfinal, they knocked off No. 8-seeded Depew 60–40 behind Chuck Thompson's 13 points. In the quarterfinal round, they knocked off No. 1-seeded Clarence 78–58 behind Curtis Brooks' 27 points and 12 rebounds. The team went 23-of-32 from the free-throw line in the fourth quarter.[284] This would be a hallmark of Coach Jones' teams at Hutch-Tech. If they qualified for sectional play, they were always good for winning at least their first two games just off defense, disciplined offense, and consistent free throw shooting.

In the Class B-1 semifinals, the Engineers lost to No. 4-seeded Kensington 74–59. They also lost to the Knights 81–62 earlier that season in league play. They watched along with everyone else as Kensington defeated the No. 3-seeded Grand Island Vikings and their Tulane-bound star Carlin Hartman 68–66 in the Class B-1 final.[285] Bob Mitchell's team, led by their star Taka Molson, then defeated the

[283] (Staff, Hutch-Tech captures game and playoff bid, 1990)
[284] (Staff, J.F. Kennedy sweeps 'twin bill', 1990)
[285] (Harrington, Kensington knocks off No. 1 Grand Island, 68-66, 1990)

Class B-2 Champion Lackawanna 52–50 in the overall Class B final.[286] The Knights advanced to Far West Regional, where they were met by Newark from Section V. In a hard-fought contest, the Knights fell to the Reds 76–66 at the Erie County Community College-South gym.[287]

Knocking off the No.1 seed and then losing to the eventual sectional champion, Coach Jones' Engineers had much to look forward to going into the next season. The core of the 1990–91 team had gotten significant minutes, and the players were battle-tested. Having two years of seasoning made them much stronger during their senior season, and great things were on the horizon for the maroon and gold.

* * *

In the late 1980s and early 1990s, there were multiple ways to put together winning basketball teams. One way was to put together a group of players who were more athletically gifted and talented than their opponents and just let them play. Another way was to train a team in the fundamentals of the game so they could use their skills and smart play to make up for what they lacked athletically. You could also have a mixture of the two, athleticism and fundamentals, which was the ideal case.

Training teams up required continuity, the players staying together for consecutive years and collectively growing and embracing a common philosophy. Staying healthy and avoiding injuries also helped. Injuries are the great equalizer of sports which have ruined many careers and seasons for players and teams and have changed whole lives.

The 1990–91 Engineers were led by the 5'11" No. 13, Curtis Brooks, the team's floor general, shot creator, and one of its best long-range shooters. With his quickness and strength, he was one of the team's top two *on-the-ball* defenders. In the backcourt, he was joined by the 6'2" No. 40, Paul Saunders. The frontcourt was anchored by the 6'2" No. 32, Jerrold 'Pep' Skillon, and the 6'5" No. 55, Charles 'Chuck' Thompson. That starting lineup would be rounded out by the 6'2" senior No. 11, Quincy Lee, also an elite shooter and on the ball defender, while at times Coach Jones would start some of his juniors in the final spot.

Through the eyes of a bright-eyed and bushy-tailed freshman, all five guys looked like grown men. Pep Skillon and Chuck Thompson looked massive when I saw them around the school. Chuck Thompson especially looked older. Curtis Brooks wore glasses and looked studious and a little preppy. Paul Saunders had a

[286] (Harrington, Knights rally to claim 'B' title, 1990)

[287] (Harrington, Newark wins 'B' title as Kensington cools, 1990)

bit of a baby face, and Quincy Lee had a smoothness about him. At least in my eyes, they were all royalty and God-like in a way.

Playing under the class of 1991 seniors were the class of 1992 juniors, some of whom had played for Coach Jones since they were freshmen. There was the 5'8" backup point guard, No. 21, Michael Mann, the 6'2" forward, No. 24, Dion Frasier; the 6'2" forward, No. 44, Chris Souter; and once again, the 6'2" forward, Jermaine, No. 34, 'J-Bird' Skillon. While Brooks, Thompson, and the Skillon brothers came over from the football field, Chis Souter spent his fall seasons as one of Mr. Shae's top runners on the cross country team. Three juniors who played on the junior varsity team the previous year were the 6'1" No. 23, Adonis Coble, the 6' No. 25, Jason Paris, also known as 'J-Paris', and finally, the 6' No. 10, Juno Patterson.

The two sophomores on the team from the class of 1993 were the 5'8" No. 15 Andre Higgins and the 6'3" and the skinny No. 42 Jermaine Fuller. Andre Higgins was a shorter dark-skinned kid who I barely noticed my freshman year around the school. Jermaine Fuller was light-skinned taller kid, and I knew of him in passing.

* * *

"Throughout the story, I describe you guys like the Spartans in the movie *300*," I told Curtis Brooks. "Did you ever see the movie *300*?"

"I did, but I do not remember it," Curtis Brooks said, laughing.

As a freshman, I looked upon the 1990–91 team with reverence, like King Leonidas and his Spartans in the movie *300*. They were big and strong, and it seemed like they could not lose. Like Leonidas and his Spartan army, though, the 1990–91 Engineers left for battle one last time to match up against a formidable foe that they would not defeat, just like the God-King Xerxes' vast army of Persians and Immortals in the legend and the movie.

Unless you lived in the Rochester area or followed the 1990 Far West Regionals, you would have only associated the name Newark with the city in Northern New Jersey across the Hudson River from Midtown Manhattan. Sure enough though, just southeast of Rochester in Wayne County, lay the village of Newark, NY, which has one sign on the New York State Thruway. Unless you are looking for it, it is easy to miss. In the early 1990s, the village had something special basketball-wise going for it, which made its name known and remembered for many years to come.

Years later, when I pieced the whole series of events back together, I found that for the second-straight year in 1991, the Newark Reds, coached by Ron Ceravolo, emerged as the Section V Class B Champion. The Reds were a veteran team who had been to the Far West Regional the previous year and had knocked off the previous Section VI Class B Champion, Kensington from the Yale Cup

76–66 to advance to Glens Falls.[288] They lost to Jamesville-Dewitt of Section III, the Syracuse area, 60–52 in the state semifinal.[289] In 1991, they once again won the Section V Class B Championship by knocking off Wilson-Magnet High School for the second straight year, 56–52 in double overtime.[290] They were battle-tested, experienced, and tough.

Like the 1990–91 Hutch-Tech Engineers, the Newark Reds returned a veteran squad of players. The Reds had five players 6'5" or taller. There was No. 24 Jason Williams, and No. 20 Mike Hennesey, who stood 6'5". No. 30 Jon Dubler, No. 31 Todd Rohlin, and No. 32 Brent Oakleaf were all 6'6". They also returned a senior at point guard, No. 12 Nester Hernandez.

I did not see the 1991 Section V Championship souvenir program until years later.[291] Coming from a small town, the Reds ethnically looked to be what one would expect. They were mostly white. They looked especially stout and, to some degree, intimidating in their team photo, particularly Brent Oakleaf, who looked menacing in the back row.[292] Just by eye, one could predict that the Reds would provide matchup problems for Coach Jones' smart, disciplined, but undersized team.

As described by Mike Harrington of the *Buffalo News*, Newark lost the opening tip but went on to dominate every other aspect of the game against the Engineers to go on to win 77–47 and advance to the state tournament for the second-straight year.[293] The Reds relentlessly pounded the ball inside to its powerful trio of seniors, Todd Rohlin, Brent Oakleaf, and Jon Dubler, who combined for 48 points.[294] Oakleaf led all of the Reds scorers with 21 points and grabbed 7 rebounds.[295] He scored all 10 of his second-quarter points during a 14–5 run that helped Newark turn a 17–11 first-quarter lead into a 39–26 halftime lead.[296] The Reds put the game away with a 20–9 burst in the third quarter when they shifted to a 1-3-1 zone which the Engineers could not penetrate.[297] The Engineers went scoreless for the first 5:51 of the third quarter, which also helped the Newark Reds put the game out of reach.[298]

---

[288] (Harrington, Newark wins 'B' title as Kensington cools, 1990)
[289] (Conner, 1990)
[290] (Slater, 1991)
[291] (Committee S. V., 1991)
[292] (Committee S. V., 1991)
[293] (Harrington, Newark overwhelms Hutch-Tech, 77-47, 1991)
[294] (Harrington, Newark overwhelms Hutch-Tech, 77-47, 1991)
[295] (Harrington, Newark overwhelms Hutch-Tech, 77-47, 1991)
[296] (Harrington, Newark overwhelms Hutch-Tech, 77-47, 1991)
[297] (Harrington, Newark overwhelms Hutch-Tech, 77-47, 1991)
[298] (Harrington, Newark overwhelms Hutch-Tech, 77-47, 1991)

"If Newark keeps playing as well as they did today, it has to be considered the favorite in Class B in Glens Falls," Coach Jones said in the *Rochester Democrat and Chronicle* in the aftermath of his beloved 1990–91 team's lopsided, season-ending defeat.[299]

"The big guys really hurt us," Coach Jones said in a postgame interview with the *Buffalo News*. "I think one of the problems is that we allowed them too much ball handling when they got the ball inside, and we did not beat them to the spot on defense."[300]

"We became impatient on offense, and we got very few second and third shots," he continued regarding his team going 14 out of 59 from the field. "Everything was a first-shot situation, and in those cases, it must be a good one. Your shot selection had to be almost perfect."[301]

"There is really no way to play with us," noted Newark Coach Ron Ceravolo. "Our style is to pound it inside. There was nothing they could do."[302]

Not surprisingly, the Engineers' *Big Three* each had subpar games. Chuck Thompson led the Engineers with 14 points, and Pep Skillon added 10 points.[303] Curtis Brooks, perhaps the most dynamic player on the team and the engine that powered the maroon and gold for the entire season, ended the game with only 8 points.[304] Thompson, Skillon, and Brooks led the Engineers the entire year, and it was not surprising that the three of them being neutralized spelled doom for the team.

"Two rebounds, Skillon only got two rebounds the entire game against Newark," Coach Jones said to me twenty years later after the loss to Newark. We were on his back porch in Amherst, NY. You could still hear the pain and agony in his raspy and scratchy voice. "I do not want to pick on Skillon, but Grandma Jones could have gotten more than two rebounds in a game!" Coach Jones usually used his Grandma Jones jokes when he thought one or more of his players underperformed or were not tough enough. The joke was usually, "Grandma Jones could have done *this* or done *that*," which usually drew laughs from his players.

Without looking at the statistics from the season, one would think that Coach Jones was just getting bent out of shape over nothing. Looking at the formula from their 17-game winning streak though, it is easy to see why he was fired up about it. Pep Skillon was one of the Engineers' leading rebounders along with Chuck Thompson. This is what made his low rebounding total so glaring. While one would think that height usually wins out, there have been instances when the

---

[299] (Staff, Newark 77, Hutchinson Tech 47; Class B Far West Regional Box Score, 1991)
[300] (Harrington, Newark overwhelms Hutch-Tech, 77-47, 1991)
[301] (Harrington, Newark overwhelms Hutch-Tech, 77-47, 1991)
[302] (Harrington, Newark overwhelms Hutch-Tech, 77-47, 1991)
[303] (Harrington, Newark overwhelms Hutch-Tech, 77-47, 1991)
[304] (Harrington, Newark overwhelms Hutch-Tech, 77-47, 1991)

basketball gods have rewarded shorter, disciplined, and highly determined teams with unlikely victories based on discipline, effort, and execution.

After the Newark loss, rumors circulated around our school about the players being out the Friday night before the game partying instead of resting and saving their strength for the Far West Regional game. My research revealed that they went to the movies late at night to see *New Jack City*. Why would they do this? It could have been for any number of reasons. Though they were seniors, the core of the team were still teenagers. Furthermore, they had not advanced to the regional before and potentially did not understand everything that came with a potential berth to the state tournament.

Were the Newark Reds that much better than the 1990–91 Hutch-Tech Engineers? They certainly had a height advantage. They had also advanced to the state tournament the previous year and had the experience. In sports and life, there is no substitute for experience. Instead of being out the night before the game, they were probably at home in bed, sleeping and getting ready for the battle the next day in front of their home crowd.

"On the way back from the game, the players were on the bus playing cards," Coach Jones lamented as well. His players were not visibly disappointed by their missed opportunity to advance to Glens Falls. Stories about the postgame card games also circulated around the school. Years later, my interviews revealed that the players were, in fact, disappointed about the loss but showed it in their own way. It hurt them just as much as it hurt Coach Jones. In a way, they may have also felt a sense of relief that the whole thing was over.

It was a long season, and they had been together going to practices since late October. The players who had been on the football and cross country teams had been in organized sports since August and September and may have been burnt out as well. For some young people, making those kinds of commitments for that long a period of time is difficult, and eventually, in some way, shape, or form, they show that they are young people again.

* * *

In *The Engineers: A Western New York Basketball Story*, to a small degree, I chronicled the rise of our hometown Jim Kelly-led Buffalo Bills alongside my basketball journey at Hutch-Tech. As I revised the story, its themes gradually came more into focus, I realized that it was one big journey of discovery involving life, athletics, and competition. Just like the Hutch-Tech Engineers, the Buffalo Bills were not particularly good for a long stretch and then gradually coalesced into a winning unit with the right players and the right leadership. They had a distinct four- to five-year window to win the Super Bowl. They did not, and then their window closed. For most teams, there is a window for them to win, which opens and then closes.

As I worked on this story, I realized that the Hutch-Tech boys' basketball team and the Yale Cup generally operated similarly. Everything happened at the right time and under the right circumstances for the 1990–91 team. That year I got to Hutch-Tech, Coach Jones had been grooming the team for two years. Furthermore, a whole crop of stars who had dominated the Yale Cup had graduated. They included the great Ritchie Campbell and Marcus Whitfield from Burgard, and players like Chris Williams from Buffalo Traditional. A vacuum was created, allowing teams like Coach Jones' Engineers to win the Yale Cup in 1991, followed by Coach Bill Russell's Riverside Frontiersman in 1992.

In 1993, the league title was shared by the McKinley Macks and the Seneca Indians. Afterward, Jason Rowe and Damien Foster led the re-ascension of the Buffalo Traditional Bulls, who became the kings of the Yale Cup for the next three years. The 1993-94 City Honors Centaurs could have been the *2.0* version of our 1990-91 Hutch-Tech boys' basketball team. Their team just so happened to mature as the Buffalo Traditional Bulls ascended to their throne in the Yale Cup and the Class C sectional. The Bulls would not relinquish their thrones until their core players graduated.

Our academic rival, City Honors, in fact, fielded a team in the 1993–1994 season like our 1990–91 team. The 1991–92 Centaurs featured a group of young players led by Larry Gilbert, Shaun Nelms, and Carlos James Gant. They had their own cast of supporting players who donned the burgundy and gray as freshmen, and they literally grew up together over the next four years into a championship-caliber unit. During my junior year, the 1992–93 Centaurs had visibly matured and taken that next step like Coach Jones' 1989–90 Engineers team. Again, they just peaked when another arguably younger and more talented time was ascending.

What was also notable was that both Hutch-Tech and City Honors were schools where the students had to academically qualify for admission. Curtis Brooks pointed this out during our interview, which was that academics were the focus at Hutch-Tech. Excelling at sports was as great as was any magic it created, but the students were there for academics first, with the expectation that they would go on to college for academics.

And this is what I meant about things coming together just right for Coach Jones and his 1990–91 Engineers. He had a philosophy and a structured way of doing things, but he also had a crop of mentally tough kids and a nucleus that wanted to play basketball, develop, and get better. His core group listened and eventually bought into what he taught. They had the right amount of athleticism, skill, and basketball IQ to go undefeated in the Yale Cup and then to almost advance to the state final four. Only the Bennet Tigers went 13–0 in the fourteen-team Yale Cup four years earlier in 1987, and the next team to do it after them was the Buffalo Traditional Bulls in the 1995-96 season.

"You have to be good to be lucky and lucky to be good!" This is another one of Coach Jones' signature quotes, and there is truth in it. It is worth noting that some luck was involved in the 1990–91 team's run. They were able to stay healthy that season. Also, the team who they beat in a 93–90 thriller and could have upset them in postseason play, the Grover Cleveland Presidents, were academically ineligible for the sectionals that year.

* * *

"On the news at night, they started calling us the '*Mighty* Hutch-Tech'," Quincy Lee said happily, reflecting on the local nightly news coverage of the results of their games.

Ultimately, No. 13, Curtis Brooks was right in that it was all a nice chapter, a magical one that did not end the way that its participants had hoped. While magical for some, it could also be seen as a blip on the radar, a flash in the pan, or even a non-story, as I discovered when I told numerous people I was working on this. But there is a story in everything, and from my vantage point, this is one of the greatest stories, a story about the great game of basketball, life, dreams, growing up, and making the best of your circumstances.

What Curtis Brooks and the 1990–91 Engineers could not have known is the effect they had on others. While the rest of our school was excited to see their boys' varsity basketball team go undefeated in its league and then come within one game of the state final four, there were other kids who they inspired to dream. They created something that matters years later. I have personally thought about coaching and getting involved with basketball somehow myself. Maybe before I die, I will get to experience coaching the great game of basketball and molding young players myself.

Not being immersed in the game now, I do not know what it is like today. From my vantage point though, basketball is not the same as in the late 1980s and early 1990s in Western New York in our old, rickety, and underfunded Yale Cup gyms. It is not the same as when Coach Ken Jones had us practicing early in the mornings and then after school in the wintertime. It is not the same as when the 1990–91 Hutch-Tech boys' basketball team ran through the Yale Cup 13–0 unscathed and into the history books. This was all in the basketball outpost that was Western New York and in the Far West Region which was dominated by the Rochester schools at the time. I was there at the school to witness it, to see the players, to dream, to go on my own up-and-down basketball adventure, and to have it impact the rest of my walk on this planet Earth.

Bonus Chapter 2. Not Just a Basketball Team, a Basketball Program

"He strategically picked people for different reasons, and the first year was like the movie *Hoosiers.* We weren't that good, and we wound up finishing 3-15. The personalities and play styles didn't gel. We had a bunch of football players that didn't really play basketball. We had track runners that didn't really play basketball, and then we had basketball players who were spending more time on the bench than they were on the court." **—Quincy Lee, Player, the Hutch-Tech boys' basketball team, 1987-1991, May 2017**

This chapter about Coach Jones and the basketball program he created at Hutch-Tech was in the first draft of *The Engineers: A Western New York Basketball Story*. When I edited the third draft, I realized that stopping the story to describe the program Coach Jones built would disrupt the flow of the overall story. I set out to use the *show-and-don't-tell* approach I learned in the many writing classes I had taken. That is, I wanted to tell the story in such a way that the reader could see and discover what is happening through the elements of the story itself instead of blatantly explaining things.

I realized that the readers should see and discover the program Coach Jones created at Hutch-Tech High School as I did. It was a gradual process where I did not understand everything until much later. If I have written the story correctly, readers will be able to see that our team and practices were not simply something where kids could just show up, dribble, and shoot the ball every day. Hell, not every kid could try out for the team, as Coach Jones used an invite list for prospects.

"Ken *ministered* to his players through the game of basketball," said Father Jacob Ledwon when delivering the homily at Coach Jones' memorial service in January 2019. He was right, and if I have written the story correctly, readers will see that our team, our practices, and our program were very much like a classroom, an organized classroom where life and values were also taught to us in addition to the great game of basketball. The goal was to win as many games on our schedule as possible, but there was so much more.

* * *

"Your *ATTITUDE* determines your *ALTITUDE*! I have never heard that before. I like that," said the woman helping me at the Horace B. Rackham

Graduate Studies Building at the University of Michigan. It was the summer of 2005. She was a middle-aged black woman. I was submitting the pages of my graduate thesis to be bound into hard copies. The quote was the front piece for the book of research I had generated over the previous four years.

The pages that followed dealt not with the great game of basketball but instead with something called 'drug metabolism', specifically *The Ubiquitination and Proteasomal Degradation of Neuronal Nitric Oxide Synthase*, the title and subject of my graduate thesis. This one quote had been imprinted into my brain thirteen years earlier. It served as a guide and a reminder of my first attempt at something meaningful and the results of that attempt.

"My high school basketball coach used to tell us that all the time. It has stayed with me all these years," I told her as we momentarily bonded over the quote.

"Your *ATTITUDE* determines your *ALTITUDE*," my graduate advisor said with a grin as he examined one of the hard copies of my thesis. We sat in his research lab. I could not tell if he was amused or impressed by the quote. In the previous four to five years, Dr. Yoichi Osawa, an Orchard Park native, served as a coach of sorts for me and the rest of his research lab in the game of science. The science world was another arena that required the same personal skills Coach Jones taught us years earlier.

"Your *ATTITUDE* determines your *ALTITUDE*!" Many long and hard hours were spent in Dr. Osawa's lab, and there were plenty of days when I felt like quitting. It was this one quote, though, in the front of my graduate school thesis that helped me climb up off the proverbial mat every day in Ann Arbor, MI. It was my days suiting up in the maroon and gold in that old rickety, undersized gym at 250 South Elmwood Avenue that helped keep me going. It was those experiences playing on my high school basketball team and not achieving my hoop dream that fueled my perseverance for my doctoral studies.

* * *

Being two years older than me, my brother Amahl went off to high school first. He went off to Hutchinson Central Technical High School. 'Hutch-Tech' was one of the top two high schools in the city. In the late 1980s, it was recently named a 'National School of Excellence', which created a Camelot-like aura around the school. Hutch-Tech was royalty in the late 1980s and early 1990s. My desire to attend Hutch Tech stemmed strictly from my brother going there. I saw how proud my relatives were of him, and I wanted them to feel the same way about me.

Hutch-Tech has a rich academic history and a reputation for producing accomplished and competitive students. Academically, our only competition was the City Honors School, or 'City Honors' for short. City Honors was located on Best Street in the Masten District near what we called the 'Fruit Belt', a then dangerous crime-ridden neighborhood where the streets were literally named after fruits. It was close to downtown Buffalo and the world-famous Roswell Park Cancer Institute, today the Medical Campus of the University at Buffalo. City Honors was a smaller school in terms of population, and from the outside, it felt more like a small liberal arts college versus our larger high school at the corner of Elmwood Avenue and Chippewa Street.

In the fall of 1988, Amahl entered a whole new world. He was in high school, which seemed to be galaxies away from Campus West, though it was only further south down Elmwood Avenue. When he went off to Hutch-Tech every day, I wondered what it was like to go there. Still in middle school myself, it seemed like a magical place.

At the end of his freshman and sophomore years, when he brought his yearbooks home, I curiously flipped through the pages, asking him who this girl was and who that guy was. I asked him about the faculty. I asked him about the Principal, Mr. Gentile, a serious-looking man with a beard and olive-colored skin. He ruled Hutch-Tech with an iron fist in the stories I would hear about the school.

Having dreams of playing basketball, I eventually flipped through to the Hutch-Tech boys' basketball team's page. I could not see their beautiful maroon- and gold-colored jerseys, but I recognized some of the players instantly. Some of them went to Campus West, including Charles 'Chuck' Thompson, Quincy Lee, Paul Saunders, and Dion Frasier. I did not recognize: Adrian Brice, Curtis Brooks, Jerrold 'Pep' Skillon, Jermaine 'J-Bird' Skillon, Jerome Freeman, Frankie Harris, Derrick Herbert, Ed Lenard, Abraham Mungro, Chris Souter, Michael Mann, and Michael Brundige. Collectively they looked like a well-trained and disciplined team.

In addition to the team photo, there was usually a short summary about the season, and action shots. The managers were also in the team photo, including Monica Peterson, Geoff Alexander, Frankie Williamson, Hillary Pearson, Ebony Carson, and Jonathan Koval. As an eighth grader, I thought the female team managers were cute even though they were out of my reach then.

Finally, there was the orchestrator of it all, Coach Ken Jones. He was distinctly referred to as *Dr.* Jones by Coach Kathy Garcenea. He had earned his PhD in Physical Education from the University at Buffalo. She also affectionately referred to him at times as 'Jonesy'. He stood at attention in the team's pictures with the players, looking on through his glasses. He usually wore a blazer, khakis, and running sneakers. He was an older man in his late 50s or early 60s. He had thinning hair on the top of his head with thicker, curly hair around the sides. He could have easily been the stereotypical Eastern European physicist from some prestigious university.

In his own personal photo in the back of the yearbooks with the other faculty, he wore a white polo shirt that said 'Ken Jones' over his heart, which was probably from his Ken Jones Basketball Camp that he ran in the summertime. He looked like a very peaceful, wise, and mild-mannered man. I would later find out that though he was wise, he was anything but peaceful and mild-mannered, especially when it came to his passion, the great game of basketball.

I did not know in junior high that this man would have a lasting impression on my life. He would teach me lessons that would guide me to greater success years after playing for him. His team appealed to me from what I could see in the yearbook pictures. Thus, besides attending Hutch-Tech for academics and to impress my family, I also wanted to be an Engineer and play for Coach Jones.

* * *

"YOUR *ATTITUDE* DETERMINES YOUR *ALTITUDE*!" Coach Jones often told us this quote with lots of enthusiasm and vigor. In many ways, he reminded me of Rocky Balboa's fictional trainer, Mickey Goldmill. Like Mickey, Coach Jones was tough, gritty, older, and grizzled, and he was also a master of his craft. He frequently told us this quote about our attitudes to keep our spirits high. It reinforced that our feelings towards the challenges of life often impact the outcome of the situations we face. He taught us in the context of basketball, but it was advice that would apply in our lives off the court as well. It was one of the many motivational quotes he told us during those years. He *ministered* to us, as the clergyman said at his memorial service in January of 2019.

"More so than becoming good basketball players, I want you all to become good people," was something else he frequently told us at practices. He had forty to fifty years of life experience over us and had seen a lot both on the basketball court and in life. Most of us understandably only cared about playing time, our personal statistics, and winning games. In addition to all the basketball theory and science, there was a definite character-building element to his program. All that being said, he still wanted to win.

It seemed that the words that he passed onto us, he lived by himself. Coach Jones had experienced his own trials, tribulations, and tragedies in his life before I met him. Growing up in Edwards, NY, on the St. Lawrence River, he lost his father at an early age, for example. He also tragically lost his first wife to cancer in the late 1970s. Perhaps it was these two events that solidified his messages about perseverance through adversity that he steadfastly passed on to us.

I have often wondered if I would have played varsity basketball had I gone to one of the other Yale Cup schools. Entering Hutch-Tech, as a freshman, I was raw and untrained. I needed lots of development as a player, even just to play at the junior varsity level. I had never been to a basketball camp and had only played games of Twenty-One and pickup basketball around neighborhood courts, city parks, or at the William-Emslie YMCA. I furthermore did not know the first thing about developing my fundamentals for organized basketball.

Most of the other schools in our league had basketball teams with little structure where anyone could play strictly based on their talent levels. The teams in our league were not known for running offensive sets or even for playing disciplined team defense. This is something that made the boys' basketball program at Hutch-Tech unique in the Yale Cup regardless of our record every year, and it made me lucky to have chosen to go there.

* * *

At Hutch-Tech, we had a basketball *program* where certain kinds of kids were preferred and where others were less desired, no matter how talented they were. Coach Jones' program emphasized talent, character, and coachability on the part of the players. Some students at Hutch-Tech at the time and other Yale Cup coaches will probably scoff at this because having a basketball program was not necessarily popular.

"The best guys in the school do not always play on the team for one reason or another," my father told me once. I think my Uncle Jeff said the same thing. At Hutch-Tech I can honestly say that they were right. Over my four years in high school, I saw guys who were incredibly talented and who did not play for the varsity team for one reason or another, whether it was grades, behavior, or a lack of desire. Some incredibly talented players were practicing Jehovah's Witnesses and could not play due to their religious principles.

When done right, organized basketball requires tremendous commitment from all involved, which, depending upon the household you come from, is not easy. It also is not easy to commit to something four months out of the year, and to continue to improve in the offseason. You really must love what you are doing and take it personally. Most of the suburban and Catholic schools ran organized programs and had the funding and infrastructure to do so. This organized style of basketball was often thought of as playing the game the way the *white* boys played it in the suburbs, though there was no racial component to it. It was just a matter of where you were and what you were exposed to.

Interestingly, Ken Jones was not the only coach who ran a structured system in an inner-city school. Years later, in ESPN's *30 for 30* series, where the tragic story of Benjamin Wilson from Chicago was documented, the producers showed that Wilson's coach, Bob Hambric, at Simeon Vocational High School, ran a highly structured program. Coach Hambric was an older black man who seemed to eat, sleep, and breathe basketball the way Coach Jones did, though maybe a little more reserved.

"Coach Hambric was a stickler for discipline, you know. They used to call us *robots* because he wanted perfection in everything that you did," said Ben Wilson's teammate Tim Bankston in the documentary.

It was interesting to see a similar system run in another inner-city school, especially by a coach of color. Hearing Tim Bankston's statement made me feel good inside about our program at Hutch-Tech years later. It was much maligned, especially in Coach Jones' last year at the helm. Nevertheless, I enjoyed playing in the program, and it was one of the most magical times of my life, especially my sophomore year, even though I did not play much.

What was so good about this program? I could talk about the Mikan Drill, the Foot Fires, the Truck and Trailer Drill, the offensive sets, the full-court presses, and the press breakers. I could talk about the scouting reports, the practice jerseys that were washed for us every single night after practice, and the chewing gum handed out to us in the locker room before every game. I could talk about the early morning free throw shooting competitions and the trip to McDonald's after our season-ending loss in the sectionals to the Grand Island Vikings my sophomore year.

The truth, though, is that it was Coach Jones himself who made the program what it was. The Yale Cup coaches did not get paid significantly more money for coaching the boys' varsity basketball teams, and he arguably did the most for his players of all the Yale Cup coaches. It was his love for the game of basketball that permeated throughout everything. It was all the extras that he gave us and how he did more than he had to do. It was all the motivational quotes that he gave us that made us try just a little bit harder for him. It was what was at the core of his being and how basketball was not the same once he left Hutch-Tech.

Some classmates rejoiced when Coach Jones retired. Some students held grudges against him. Some of us mourned the loss because it was Coach Jones who made the program what it was. It was Coach Jones who made showing up every day in the mornings and those two to three hours after school worth the while.

* * *

"COACHES COACH AND PLAYERS PLAY! YOU CONCENTRATE ON THE GAME AND LET ME TALK TO THE REFEREES!" Coach Jones frequently told us this to keep us focused on the game itself and not the officiating. It was *his* job, and he did it well.

"COME ON GUYS, YOU *CAN'T* BE TIRED!" This was something else Coach Jones said to us in practice which came back to me in the latter stages of this project. Our cardiovascular fitness was critical in the basketball program and he readily challenged us when we showed signs of getting tired in practice.

"In a good program, kids who are not as good will win games for you that they should lose," Coach said. Though teams are ultimately measured by wins and losses, the effectiveness and success of a program cannot always be measured that way. A good program (and coach) gets the most out of the talent that it has and can often do the unexpected, such as our 1991–92 Hutch Tech boys' basketball team. Our team made a relatively deep run in the sectionals despite having an undersized team and a season plagued by injuries. Our offensive and defensive fundamentals and team play took us much further than we should have gone. We were furthermore one bad shooting day at the end from going much further.

There were several hallmarks to the program Coach Ken Jones established at Hutch-Tech High School, which set it apart from the other Yale Cup schools during those years. The key hallmark was aggressive and disciplined man-to-man defense in a league with a reputation for not playing any defense at all. Likewise, no zone defense was allowed.

"How do you get your kids to consistently play man-to-man defense?" Coach reflected on a question another coach from Section V (the Rochester area) asked him. "It is not hard if they know it is what they are going to play," he replied. Coach brought this philosophy to the Yale Cup. Disciplined man-to-man defense, it was the way he had done it since his days at McQuaid Jesuit School twenty years earlier.

"I knew that your teams would always be in the sectionals at the end of the season based upon the way that your kids play defense," he was told by several onlookers. It was one of the best compliments a coach could receive. This was in the era before Section VI completely opened postseason play to include even the most underachieving teams. Prior to that change, you had to have at least a 0.500 record in your league to qualify for sectional play.

In addition to not playing defense, the Yale Cup as a league was also not known for running offensive sets and plays. It was known for playing a racehorse style of basketball, which took advantage of its players' speed and, in some instances, size. The league was thus known for playing more of an undisciplined and up-tempo street game. That was normal in the Yale Cup. This was another thing that set Hutch-Tech basketball apart.

Coaches from the suburban leagues were amazed by Coach Jones' teams. He had rosters of mostly black kids running motion offenses, zone offenses, and offensive sets to inbound the ball. Up to that point, when our Yale Cup teams won, it was usually because they were longer and faster or more talented than the competition, not because of Xs and Os or basketball IQs.

"In the fourth quarter, fatigue sets in, and most players' legs are tired, so I had a no dunking rule which some players did not like. One player dunked in the fourth quarter, and I pulled him out of the game," Coach said, describing a rule he instated along the way to prevent missed dunks in crucial late-game situations. It was a rule that made sense but also that robbed his teams of the back-breaking power of a late-game dunk to electrify themselves and to get the crowds hyped up.

"At night, when Ken got home after games, it would take him a little while to wind down and relax," said Alice Jones, Coach Jones' wife, in her soft, motherly voice. She taught Spanish at Riverside High School briefly before teaching at the Herman Badillo School not far from Hutch-Tech. "He tended to lose a couple of pounds during the season," she added, discussing the physical toll the games took on him.

He was not out there playing the games himself, but he was fully invested in them before, during, and afterward. It was late at night after the games when he would analyze the statistics and write his summaries for the morning announcements. He also must not have needed much sleep as he was one of the first ones at the school each morning, particularly for our morning practices.

After both sitting in the stands as a spectator and watching him coach from our own bench, it was easy to conceive that he would have to wind down after the games. I do not remember any of the other coaches on the teams we played against, pacing the sidelines or getting as animated or passionate during the games as he did. Coach Jones was a show all by himself, yelling at our players and the referees and then living and dying on every possession. I could easily see him further analyzing, agonizing, and deliberating over the postgame statistics at home before calling in the box scores to the *Buffalo News* at nighttime.

One of the final hallmarks of his tenure was the intramural program he ran. Just like the basketball program itself, the intramural program was a well-oiled machine. In the fall of every year, Coach Jones organized early morning intramurals which were open to the entire student body. When I got to Hutch-Tech, the freshmen played on Friday mornings, while the upperclassmen played on Tuesday and Thursday mornings. He must have made that change when I got to Hutch-Tech because Jerrold 'Pep' Skillon told me that during his time, the freshman played with the upperclassmen.

The intramurals were for the students, but they were also a way for Coach Jones to scope out the talent in the school and *prospect* players. It was strictly voluntary, and Coach Jones did not get paid anything extra for running his intramurals in terms of pay. When they got wind of what was happening over at Hutch-Tech, some of the other Yale Cup coaches allegedly complained to the Athletic Director Willie Evans that Coach Jones was doing something illegal and that he was gaining some unfair competitive advantage.

This would be the hallmark of his tenure at Hutch-Tech. He sought to mimic the programs that were run for years in Section V, such as the one he ran at McQuaid Jesuit High School twenty years earlier. He sought to create a basketball program like those at the private and suburban schools in a city league with basketball teams and no programs. This also involved preparing a make-shift junior varsity team. He and a handful of other Yale Cup coaches realized that some kids needed preparation for ascension to the varsity level. None of them got paid anything extra from the Buffalo Public Schools for addressing this need.

"You all are going to miss Jonesy," Coach Kathleen Garcenea said the year after Coach Jones left. She was with him daily in the athletic department and knew how hard he worked for our school and its kids. Much of his efforts were likewise unappreciated. Once he was gone from our H-shaped building, it and basketball were never the same. Those of us who worked with him were incredibly lucky. They were some of the best times of my life. That goes for the ups and the downs, all of it.

While Coach Jones was a true student of the game and meticulously built our basketball program at Hutch-Tech High School, he couldn't control everything. The opening quote for this bonus chapter is from a discussion we had days after meeting up with Adonis Coble and Michael Mann at Louie's in Tonawanda in 2014. That 1991 loss to Newark in the Class B Far West Regional still hurt him years later because he thought his team didn't play up to its potential.

Michael Mann shared something interesting that day we met up regarding that loss, something Coach Jones surprisingly never mentioned. It turns out that there was a backup of some sort on the interstate on the way out to Rochester to play Newark. It caused the Engineers to arrive at that game literally just before tipoff. They had to change on the bus and prepare to play immediately upon arrival at the venue. Quincy Lee also shared a story during our interview. He recalled not having his signed permission slip that day when it was time to leave Buffalo for the game, which may have also confounded what happened.

I wanted to include this story because it underscores a theme discussed throughout the book, and that is that we don't have control over all the circumstances in our lives, though we often must deal with the aftereffects and outcomes. No matter how much we plan things out, our lives are often subject to circumstances that are out of our hands. We have control over some things, but other things we don't, and some of them impact our outcomes. Coach Jones lived for the great game of basketball and teaching it. He didn't have control over everything, though. He genuinely cared about his players and teams even years later, and he made a difference. In summary, Coach Garcenea was right.

Bonus Chapter 3. Our Little Old Gym on South Elmwood Avenue

"It would have been nice to have that new gym when we were working out as opposed to having that dinky piece of shithole we had to practice in until the girls got done!" **—Coach Francis Daumen, Head Coach, the Hutch-Tech boys' basketball team, 1993-94, November 2016**

Like the other bonus chapters for *The Engineers: A Western New York Basketball Story*, this chapter regarding our Hutch-Tech gym was in my original manuscript. Once again when I started my revisions, I realized that having a chapter just talking about our gym was disruptive to the flow of the overall story. Furthermore, I determined that the details about it could be woven into my narrative, more *showing* instead of *telling*, which is a popular modern tool in the writing world.

In writing *The Engineers: A Western New York Basketball Story*, it was important to me, at least for my creative process, to write something about where we played our home games and practiced. Likewise, the bulk of those years for me centered around our undersized gymnasium which only now exists in the memories of those of us who were there at the time and in pictures. Hutch-Tech, along with most of the other Buffalo Public Schools, underwent renovations, and like the private and suburban schools, it now has a regulation-sized basketball court. Our little old gym was undersized and not ideal, but it was special, nonetheless.

* * *

It had been almost twenty years since I had set foot in the old H-shaped building on the corner of South Elmwood Avenue and Chippewa Street. I had been back to Buffalo countless times between the late 1990s and in 2013, but not to my alma mater, Hutchinson Central Technical High School, 'Hutch-Tech' for short. It was the school I followed my older brother Amahl to and where I embarked on the first meaningful journey in my life. As with most of the Buffalo Public Schools in the system, Hutch-Tech had undergone renovations and was not open to anyone for a period. Hutch-Tech was a surviving school in the old Yale Cup basketball league of the early 1990s.

"You can come by, but only around 3 p.m., when all of the students are gone," Principal Sabatino Cimato wrote me in an email. I scheduled a visit with him for the day before Thanksgiving in 2013. We had never met, and he was nice enough to allow me back into my alma mater for a tour of the new facilities. I think

Principal Cimato had either attended St. Joe's, had been the principal there, or both. He was the next principal after Dave Greco, who himself succeeded my second principal, Mr. Joseph Gentile.

Much of the old Hutch-Tech was still there, but much had also changed. The principal's office had received a complete makeover and was now enclosed by glass windows. Just over those glass windows to the principals' offices, there were pictures of all of Hutch-Tech's past principals. I recognized Ms. Schnell, Mr. Gentile, Mr. Grecco, and now Principal Cimato. Principal Cimato was an Italian man who was a little older than me. He wore a button-down shirt, tie, and slacks. He wore a mustache with a beard. He was one of many children of Western New York who decided to stay and plant roots while many others left. He was a very pleasant man, and he and one of the assistant principals escorted me around the school.

The ambiance of the building had changed. The hallways felt darker, probably due to the black and white checkered floors. We might have had ceiling tiles before, but I cannot remember. The library had been moved from the first-floor bridge to the northwest corner where some of the computer labs, other classrooms, and lockers were previously located. Instead of a tiny library, it was now massive and took up the whole northwest wing of the building on the first floor. That was the corner of the building where I squeaked by my computer programming class as a freshman with a final 65% grade.

"And this is the new gym," Principal Cimato said as we stood on the first-floor bridge. In place of the old library now was a window overlooking a gym that I did not recognize. It had a regulation-sized basketball court with multiple glass backboards and breakaway rims, just like those in suburban and private schools. It was beautiful, but it was not the gym I played in.

"Wow, this is the new gym?" I marveled, looking on, remembering the old box that we practiced and played in, which now existed only in black-and-white pictures in yearbooks from the early 2000s and earlier.

"Yes, as I mentioned before, this is where the old library used to be. If you look up, you can see more room overhead. They tore off the top of the courtyard where the skylight was. They literally lowered a box down on top of that space to create the new ceiling," Principal Cimato said, smiling. "They also removed the swimming pool to create more length for the gym. They knocked the western wall out and pushed the gym further back closer to the boiler room."

"Wow, this is amazing," I said, taking pictures, trying to be subtle, though the new coach and some of the players probably wondered who I was and what I was doing.

"What happened to Coach Rappl?" I had met him several years earlier. Coach David Rappl was a shorter white man with a black mustache, black hair, and glasses who mostly wore sweatsuits. He became the boys' basketball coach after my cousin, Coach Phil Richardson, relocated to North Carolina.

"He retired last year," Principal Cimato said. "That is the new coach down there, Coach Nieves. Come on. I will show you the other renovations to the building."

Coach Nieves was clearly Hispanic based on his name. He was slim and wore a sweat suit of some sort, and his hair was short. His players looked like kids to my thirty-seven-year-old eyes, which is probably how we looked to adults in the early 1990s. Even though Curtis Brooks and the 1990–91 Engineers looked like grown men to me as a freshman, they probably looked like kids to all the adults. It turned out that age was all relative to your station in life.

It turned out that Coach David Nieves and I overlapped at Hutch-Tech, and I remembered him. He was a part of the notorious class of 1993. He was not involved with our basketball program though. He had gotten involved with Western New York high school basketball through refereeing later on after graduating from Hutch-Tech. We talked briefly about it a year or so later when I returned to catch the Engineers' matchup with the Riverside Frontiersman.

Everything had changed so much. The play on the court seemed so different from the way we played. The gym also was not packed. One of the parents told me that it was normal as there was violence at some of the schools. It seemed anyone could come to the games at Hutch-Tech if they paid their $3, though. It was all so different from our Yale Cup from the early 1990s. It was a little less gritty and somehow a little less tough.

It was no longer the era of Michael, Magic, Larry, and the original Dream Team. This was the era of LeBron James, Dwayne Wade, and Stephen Curry. It was the era of one-and-done players in college, little to no physical play, lots of points, and lots of three-point shots from halfcourt. It was also the era of tattoos. Coach Nieves touched upon that briefly when we talked as well.

There was a familiar face on the Riverside bench. Coach Bill Russell, who led the Frontiersman to the 1991-92 Yale Cup and Section VI Class C Championships, sat at the end of the bench with a clipboard, giving his input to the young Riverside players. He was a student of the game, just like Coach Jones. He also ate, drank, and slept the great game of basketball.

He had not changed much. He was still shorter with a mustache and beard, balding on the top, and the long gray mullet. We talked briefly after the game about his Riverside teams, the success they could not reproduce that fateful 1992–93 season, and the changes from the Yale Cup of the late 1980s and early 1990s to the current era. I asked him about an interview then, but it would not come until eight years later. It was well worth the wait, as it was both fun and educational.

* * *

So much had happened in that old H-shaped building to make me the man that I had become. So much growth took place in that little box of gym that no longer existed. That little old gym was Coach Ken Jones' classroom for life and his passion, the great game of basketball. For five years, he taught the game there to his teams of players with varying ability levels and personal backgrounds. He worked hard to galvanize them into a single winning unit, a challenge at our technical school.

"Your *ATTITUDE* determines your *ALTITUDE*! Success breeds confidence, and confidence breeds success! You have to be good to be lucky, and you have to be lucky to be good!" Twenty years later, I could still hear his raspy voice molding us, pushing us, and encouraging us along. The time I spent with him in that little old gym from fall to early spring in the early 1990s shaped the rest of my life, and it was one of the best times of my life.

* * *

"I remember coming to play you guys in your gym at Hutch-Tech in the basement like, 'What is *this* thing?' But it was live. It was live. I think we lost to you guys that year, too," said Coach Samuel 'Quinn' Coffey of the class of 1992 from Kensington High School. We played some intramural basketball together during my one year at the SUNY College at Brockport. Now a coach in Baltimore, he had lots of stories and reflections on his time playing in the Yale Cup. One of his most vivid memories was coming to our little old gym his junior year, the year that Curtis Brooks and the Engineers went 13–0 in the league.

Our little old gym was multiple things. It was a venue for volleyball matches in the fall and basketball games during winter. It was a classroom for basketball which now only exists in pictures and the memories of those who stepped foot in it, ran around in it, and who sweated in it. Lessons, both happy and sad, were imparted upon me there that shaped my future, important lessons about perseverance, toughness and how to compete in the world. Many of those lessons bore fruit later in my life.

The first time I set foot in the Hutch-Tech gym was my eighth-grade year at Campus West. It was the 1989–90 school year. Hutch-Tech was hosting an open house and was accessible after hours for parents and prospective students to tour the school. Mom took both me and my best friend Gabe on this tour. Gabe's father, Kenneth Bernard Smith, and some of my uncles and an aunt attended Hutch-Tech from the 1940s to the 1970s when their generation was our age. Gabe took the entrance exam as well, and we were both going to potentially continue our family's legacies.

Gabe and I both wore our Chicago Bulls jackets. His was a popular Starter brand, and mine a less popular Swingster. If I recall correctly, my brother Amahl was in one of the architectural design labs drawing with other current students as parents and prospective students toured the school. Hutch-Tech was the only school that I applied to and had I not gotten accepted, I may have wound up at my district school, Kensington.

I saw pictures of Coach Ken Jones and his Hutch-Tech boys' basketball teams in my brother's yearbooks from his first two years at the school, but I had never seen them in person. This gave the open house added meaning for me. That night, Coach Jones and the team were in the gym scrimmaging, and families were allowed to peek inside and observe them.

I recognized him immediately. The team was playing as shirts and skins. Coach Jones sprinted up and down the floor with his players, readily blowing his whistle to call fouls or to stop and teach them something. He wore what I learned would be his signature gym attire. It, in part, consisted of one of his signature Ken Jones polo shirts. Also, even though we were in the Michael Jordan era, where baggy shorts were popular, he wore the shorter John Stockton-length shorts instead. Basketball fans would know the significance of this distinction. He also wore white socks with colored stripes and a pair of Converse sneakers.

His voice was strong and gritty. I did not understand anything he was saying to his players, but he had their collective attention. To the onlookers, it was clear that he was a natural teacher and that his basketball program was a well-oiled machine. Unfortunately, we only stayed and watched for a few minutes. What I saw gave me butterflies. I walked away, wondering if I could play for Coach Jones. I wondered if I would get to don the maroon and gold and if I would play in that gym.

* * *

With its peeling paint, old bricks, caged industrial clock, and antiquated accessories, our little old gym was as much an old industrial storage room as it was a space for high school basketball and volleyball games and practices. It was only a fraction of the size of our gym at Campus West. A regulation high school basketball court is eighty-four feet in length and fifty feet in width. The length of the Hutch-Tech court was somewhere between fifty and sixty feet, and the width was roughly thirty feet. In hindsight, it is amazing that we played in such a facility. With its small size and its acoustics, you could easily hear the balls bouncing off the hardwood, the referee's whistles, and the buzzer down the halls of the basement.

We were not the only school in our league with less-than-optimal facilities. Both Lafayette and South Park High Schools had basketball courts that were narrow and had running tracks around the top of them making it impossible to shoot corner three-pointers. The gym at the Buffalo Academy for the Visual and Performing Arts was not much better. It was so narrow that it could not encompass a complete three-point arc. Its floor also seemed to be concrete or some sort of marble.

In our interview, Buffalo Traditional basketball legend Damien Foster jokingly referred to the Performing Arts gym as a bowling alley. In that regard we were lucky to have our gym at Hutch-Tech. Speaking of Buffalo Traditional, I think Damien also stated that they did not have the corner three-point line in their gym either. This was the Yale Cup we played in, and we just made it work.

The largest gyms in our league belonged to City Honors, Grover Cleveland, McKinley, and maybe Riverside. Kensington and Seneca might be in this group too. City Honors and Riverside's gyms were nearly identical. They were large and cavernous. City Honors did not have its own gym and played at the Buffalo Vocational and Technical Center, the old East High School. Because of my tumultuous junior year, I never got to play official games in the McKinley or Riverside gyms. I did scrimmage in the Riverside gym once, though.

None of the Yale Cup gyms were completely modern like those in the suburban and private schools in terms of seating and overall comfort for fans. Except for Buffalo Traditional and Emerson, the Yale Cup gyms had basic rims with V-shaped welded metal supports underneath the hoops. This was probably due to the lack of resources in the Buffalo Public Schools. Similarly, most of our buildings were old and built decades earlier.

Within the circle at the center of our court where the tipoffs took place, there were the two letters HT, the initials of our school. Just diagonally above the Johnson Park-side basket was our lone scoreboard with the high school-style buzzer. Just below it, there was a stairway that led upstairs. Near the doorway for the stairs, there was the area where the person selected for the role of public announcer gave the starting lineups from a mobile podium. During my junior year, water leaked from the ceiling and warped the floor near the Chippewa side entrance causing it to bubble up. The maintenance staff quickly came and leveled it back off with new floorboards.

Like most of the schools in our league, our gym did not have state-of-the-art hoops or backboards. The backboards at Hutch-Tech were made of wood, painted solid white, and held up with black metal pipe extensions. They were attached to the brick walls of the gym with long strips of plywood and chains, as opposed to the suburban and private schools with window-style backboards with breakaway rims that hung from the ceilings and were retractable.

Whenever the basketballs hit the backboard or someone authoritatively dunked on the Johnson Park-side basket, you could hear the mounts on the backboard rattle, chains, etc. In the equipment room, which sat adjacent to the Johnson Park-side basket across from the coaches' offices upstairs, you could see the cinder blocks cracking from the basket's support structures pulling on them over the years. It was probably also due to the drastic swings in the Western New York temperatures that crept into the foundations of the building.

Our gym had small bleachers on both sides of the court. When retracted, they did not look like they could accommodate many fans. Come game time, though, large crowds packed into them somehow, mostly on the Elmwood Avenue side. There were three entrances. Two were on the Johnson Park side. The entrance on the Elmwood side led up to the visitors' locker room, which was adjacent to the coaches' offices and a spare room that eventually became our weight room.

The entrance closest to the boiler room was gated by two wooden doors. Behind them was a passage that led past the swimming lockers and onto a winding stairwell. This led back up to the coaches' offices and the locker room utilized by the Hutch-Tech football and boys' basketball teams. Padding between each of those passages prevented students from colliding with the brick wall.

On the Chippewa Street side of the gym sat another entrance near the vending machines. There was also a gated storage area on that side of the gym, which was the main weight room for a time. A mirror in the weight room allowed you to see your reflection whenever you were on the main court. Above that weight room was a seating area where the band played before games. Due to the solid white backboards, spectators never sat there.

The ceiling of our little old gym had ropes for climbing, which we never used during gym class, probably for health and safety reasons. A skylight with two windows sat on the rear courtyard of our H-shaped school. If we looked up, we could see the snow accumulating there during the winter when we practiced or when nighttime set in.

During my first year on the basketball team, I practiced in that gym twice daily. I was there early in the morning before school and then late in the afternoon after school. I would only see daylight through the windows during classes, and my trips to and from school would be in darkness. It was great.

One of the students created collages on the walls of the gym to celebrate the Hutch-Tech boys' basketball teams under Coach Jones. I believe it was Frank Williamson of the class of 1991 who drew cartoons of a player dunking a basketball, a basketball with all the players' hands touching it, and the Yale Cup itself. Everyone associated with the program signed those drawings.

Those collages stayed on the walls for a couple of years after I graduated from Hutch-Tech. One of the newer coaches who wanted to erase previous traditions had his players take them down and throw them away one day at practice when I just happened to be in town. I salvaged them and took them home, though they were lost with many other items once my mother's second marriage dissolved.

Our little old gym was actually our big gym, and we had a smaller one, if you can believe it, the 'shithole' described in the opening quote of this chapter. It sat on the Chippewa Street side near the boiler room near the school's rear entrance. The second gym was nothing more than a box with one hoop and an uneven ceiling. When it got too hot in there, Coach Jones would open the cage screens and then slide the windows open allowing the cold winter air in. Coach Jones and Coach Boyleston, who coached the girls' team, worked it out so that the boys would practice in that tiny gym for the first hour after school, and then we would swap for the final hour and a half of practice. It was not ideal for either team.

Both gyms had a distinct smell, an odor or an aroma generated by competition, where mass amounts of carbon dioxide and the scents from sweat, salts, and urea are sent into the air. Without efficient ventilation systems, those smells stayed in those spaces and combined with the other industrial smells from the basement and those of the cleaners our custodians used. You could smell it as soon you descended into the structure, just as you could hear basketballs hitting the hardwood floor and echoing out to those nearby.

Before and during practices, and while the players scrimmaged, Coach Jones would often walk through with a wide push broom, trying to remove the dust on the floors. If left there, players would slide all over the place when playing offense and defense. In between plays and during free throws, for example, many of us would also reach down and wipe the bottoms of our shoes off for more traction.

We practiced and played in those facilities, unbeknownst to the students who have never seen them. Nowadays the Buffalo Public Schools' athletic facilities are more on par with their suburban and private school counterparts. Our little old gym is no more, and neither is the little box on the Chippewa Street side. They are relics of the past, just like the old fourteen-team Yale Cup league from the late 1980s and the early 1990s. They live on in pictures, rare video footage, and in the memories of those of us who were there at the time.

Bibliography

Albom, M. (1993). *The Fab Five.* Grand Central Publishing.

Anderson, W. H. (1998). *The Art Of Grant Writing.* Buffalo: WORDS Publications.

Bacon, J. U. (2007). *BO'S LASTING LESSONS.* New York: Hachette Book Group USA.

Bacon, J. U. (2011). *Three and Out: Rich Rodriguez and Michigan Wolverines in the Crucible of*. Farrar, Strauss and Giroux.

Bacon, J. U. (2016). *Endzone: The Rise, Fall, and Return of Michigan Football; Reprint Edition.* St. Martin's Griffin.

Bacon, J. U. (2019). *OVERTIME: Jim Harbaugh and the Michigan Wolverines at the Crossroads of College Football.* New York: HarperCollins Publishers.

Berger, J. (2013). *Contagious.* New York, NY: Simon & Schuster Paperbacks.

Clarey, A. (2013). *Enjoy the Decline: Accepting and Living with the Death of the United States.* CreateSpace Independent Publishing Platform.

Committee, S. V. (1991, March). Section V Basketball: Championship Souvenir Program. *Section V Boys' Basketball Playoffs.* Rochester, New York, United States of America: Section V.

Committee, S. V. (1992, March 7). Section VI Basketball: Boys' Championship Playoffs 1991-92. *Western New York: Section VI.* Amherst, New York, United States of America: Section VI.

Conner, D. (1990, March 16). Counter Nottingham's speed Newark hopes big men will. *The Post Standard*, pp. D-7.

Davis, K. (2022). *Reclaiming The Black Feminine: The Lies Of Feminism And The Road To Recovery.* Murrieta, CA: Black Star University Publishing.

Early, G. (1994). *Daughters: On Family and Fatherhood.* Da Capo Press.

Eberstadt, N. (2022). *Men Without Work; Second Edition.* Templeton Press.

Frazier, W. (2013). *Rockin' Steady: A Guide to Basketball & Cool; First Edition.* Triumph Books.

Gaughan, M. (1991, December 8). Duke cruises to a 96-90 victory over Canisius; Laettner nets 19 and enjoys homecoming. *Buffalo News*, pp. D-1.

Gaughn, M. (1991, December 7). No. 1 Duke in Aud - a night to remember; Laettner shocked by near sellout for Blue Devils. *Buffalo News*, pp. B-1.

Gladwell, M. (2011). *Outliers: The Story of Success; Reprint Edition.* Back Bay Books.

Gladwell, M. (2015). *David and Goliath: Underdogs, Misfits, and the Art of Battling Giants; Reprint Edition.* Back Bay Books.

Glover, D. L. (2014). *Cocktail Conversations.* Baltimore: XLIBRIS.

Glover, D. L. (2019). *No Friday Foolishness.* Baltimore: DG Enterprises.

Glover, R. (2003). *No More Mr. Nice Guy: A Proven Plan for Getting What You Want in Love, Sex, and Life.* Running Press Adult.
Greene, R. (2013). *Mastery; Reprint Edition.* Penguin Books.
Greene, R. (2019). *The Laws of Human Nature; Reprint Edition.* Penguin Books.
Greene, R. (2023). *The 48 Laws of Power; First Edition.* Viking.
Haley, A. (1990). *The Autobiography of Malcolm X; Second Edition.* Ballentine.
Harrington, M. (1990, March 4). Kensington knocks off No. 1 Grand Island, 68-66. *Buffalo News*, pp. C-10.
Harrington, M. (1990, March 7). Knights rally to claim 'B' title. *Buffalo News*, pp. D-5.
Harrington, M. (1990, March 11). Newark wins 'B' title as Kensington cools. *Buffalo News*, pp. C-8.
Harrington, M. (1991, February 19). February Madness starts for WNY basketball powers. *Buffalo News*, pp. D-4.
Harrington, M. (1991, February 24). High School Basketball: Class B-1 Quarterfinal. *Buffalo News*, pp. C-8.
Harrington, M. (1991, March 2). Hutch-Tech holds off Kenmore East upset bid. *Buffalo News*, pp. B-5.
Harrington, M. (1991, March 6). Hutch-Tech tips South to capture Class B crown. *Buffalo News*, pp. D-5.
Harrington, M. (1991, March 10). Newark overwhelms Hutch-Tech, 77-47. *Buffalo News*, pp. C-8.
Harrington, M. (1991, February 16). Presidents forfeit playoff berth. *Buffalo News*, pp. B-5.
Harrington, M. (1991, March 5). Tech, South to meet in Class B title game. *Buffalo News*, pp. D-5.
Harrington, M. (1992, April 11). Big men pull down top spots on News' All-WNY Team. *Buffalo News*, pp. B-1.
Harrington, M. (1992, March 8). Defense propels Franklinville to familiar top of the class, 66-48. *Buffalo News*, pp. C-8.
Harrington, M. (1992, March 8). LaSalle topples Spartans for fifth straight crown. *Buffalo News*, pp. C-8.
Harrington, M. (1992, February 12). Parker layup ices title for Riverside. *Buffalo News*, pp. D-5.
Harrington, M. (1992, March 8). Rice's late free throw ices win for Frontiers. *Buffalo News*, pp. C-8.
Harrington, M. (1992, March 11). Scott paces Grand Island by Hillbillies. *Buffalo News*, pp. C-5.
Harrington, M. (1992, February 25). Section VI basketball teams beginning journey for the state tourney. *Buffalo News*, pp. D-4.

Harrington, M. (1992, March 15). WNY boys swept out of boys' cage regionals; Mynderse act too powerful for Riverside. *Buffalo News*, pp. C-8.

Harrington, M. (1992, March 15). WNY is swept out of boys' cage regionals: SU-bound star single-handedly ousts LaSalle. *Buffalo News*, pp. C-8.

Johnson, T. H. (2023). *Solutions For Ani-Black Misandry, Flat Blackness, and Black Male Death (Leading Conversations on Black Sexualities and Identities); First Edition.* Routledge.

Jones, K. (1990, November 29). Boys' Cathedral High School vs. Hutch-Tech High School; The Hutch-Tech Tip Off Tournament. *Hutch-Tech Boys' Basketball Game Summaries.* Amherst, New York, United States of America: Ken Jones.

Jones, K. (1990, December 10). Hutch-Tech High School vs Turner/Carroll High School; Non-Leauge. *Hutch-Tech Boys' Basketball Summaries.* Buffalo, New York, United States of America: Ken Jones.

Jones, K. (1990, December 12). Hutch-Tech High School vs. Depew High School; Non-League. *Hutch-Tech Boys' Basketball Game Summaries.* Amherst, New York, United States of America: Ken Jones.

Jones, K. (1990, December 18). Hutch-Tech High School vs. South Park High School. *Hutch-Tech Boys' Basketball Summaries.* Amherst, New York, United States of America: Ken Jones.

Jones, K. (1990, December 17). Lafayette High School vs. Hutch-Tech High School; Non-League. *Hutch-Tech Boys' Basketball Game Summaries.* Amherst, New York, United States: Ken Jones.

Jones, K. (1990, December 3). Niagara Falls High School vs Hutch-Tech; Hutch-Tech Tip Off Tournament. *Hutch-Tech Boys' Basketball Summaries.* Buffalo, New York, United States: Ken Jones.

Jones, K. (1991, January 10). Bennett High School vs. Hutch-Tech High School; Yale Cup. *Hutch-Tech Boys' Basketball Game Summaries.* Amherst, New York, United States: Ken Jones.

Jones, K. (1991, January 31). Buffalo Traditional High School vs. Hutch-Tech High School. *Hutch-Tech Boys' Basketball Game Summaries.* Amherst, New York, United States of America: Ken Jones.

Jones, K. (1991, January 14). Burgard High School vs. Hutch-Tech High School; Yale Cup. *Hutch-Tech Boys' Basketball Game Summaries.* Amherst, New York, United States of America: Ken Jones.

Jones, K. (1991, February 27). Clarence High School vs. Hutch-Tech High School; Class B-1 Sectionals. *Hutch-Tech Boys' Basketball Game Summaries.* Amherst, New York, United States: Ken Jones.

Jones, K. (1991, February 11). Emerson High School vs. Hutch-Tech High School; Yale Cup. *Hutch-Tech Boys' Basketball Game Summaries.* Amherst, New York, United States of America: Ken Jones.

Jones, K. (1991, October). Hutch-Tech Boys' Basketball Team 1991-92 Tryout Informational Materials. *Hutch-Tech Boys' Basketball Team 1991-92 Materials and Information*. Amherst, New York, United States of America: Ken Jones.

Jones, K. (1991, December 18). Hutch-Tech High School vs Emerson High School; Yale Cup. *Hutch-Tech Boys' Basketball Game Summaries*. Amherst, New York, United States of America: Ken Jones.

Jones, K. (1991, December 9). Hutch-Tech High School vs Grover Cleveland High School; Al Pastor Tournament. *Hutch-Tech Boys' Basketball Game Summaries*. Amherst, New York, United States of America: Ken Jones.

Jones, K. (1991, December 23). Hutch-Tech High School vs. Bennett High School; Festival of Lights Tournament. *Hutch-Tech Boys' Basketball Summaries*. Amherst, New York, United States of America: Ken Jones.

Jones, K. (1991, January 7). Hutch-Tech High School vs. City Honors High School; Yale Cup. *Hutch-Tech Boys' Basketball Game Summaries*. Amherst, New York, United States of America: Ken Jones.

Jones, K. (1991, February 5). Hutch-Tech High School vs. Lafayette High School; Yale Cup. *Hutch-Tech Boys' Basketball Game Summaries*. Amherst, New York, United States of America: Ken Jones.

Jones, K. (1991, January 16). Hutch-Tech High School vs. McKinley High School; Yale Cup. *Hutch-Tech Boys' Basketball Game Summaries*. Amherst, New York, United States of America: Ken Jones.

Jones, K. (1991, March 11). Hutch-Tech High School vs. Newark High School; Class B Far West Regionals. *Hutch-Tech Boys' Basketball Game Summaries*. Amherst, New York, United States of America: Ken Jones.

Jones, K. (1991, February 13). Hutch-Tech High School vs. Performing Arts High School; Yale Cup. *Hutch-Tech Boys' Basketball Game Summaries*. Amherst, New York, United States of America: Ken Jones.

Jones, K. (1991, February 7). Hutch-Tech High School vs. Riverside High School; Yale Cup. *Hutch-Tech Boys' Basketball Game Summaries*. Amherst, New York, United States: Ken Jones.

Jones, K. (1991, February 4). Hutch-Tech High School vs. Seneca High School; Yale Cup. *Hutch-Tech High School Boys' Basketball Summaries*. Amherst, New York, United States of America: Ken Jones.

Jones, K. (1991, January 22). Kensington High School vs. Hutch-Tech High School. *Hutch-Tech Boys' Basketball Game Summaries*. Amherst, New York, United States of America: Ken Jones.

Jones, K. (1991, February 23). Maryvale High School vs. Hutch-Tech High School; Class B-1 Sectionals. *Hutch-Tech Boys' Basketball Game Summaries*. Amherst, New York, United States: Ken Jones.

Jones, K. (1991, December 11). Regina Pacis High School vs. Hutch-Tech High School; Hutch-Tech Tip Off Tournament. *Hutch-Tech Boys' Basketball*

Game Summaries. Amherst, New York, United Sates of America: Ken Jones.

Jones, K. (1991, December 13). Seneca High School vs. Hutch-Tech High School; Hutch-Tech Tip Off Tournament. *Hutch-Tech Boys' Basketball Game Summaries*. Amherst, New York, United States of America: Ken Jones.

Jones, K. (1991, January 2). The 1990 Festival of Lights Boys' Basketball Tournament Results. *Hutch-Tech Boys' Basketball Game Summaries*. Amherst, New York, United States of America: Ken Jones.

Jones, K. (1991, March). The 1990-91 Hutch-Tech Boys' Basketball Team Season Summary. *Hutch-Tech Boys' Basketball Game Summaries*. Amherst, New York, United States of America: Ken Jones.

Jones, K. (1991, November). The 1991-92 Hutch-Tech Boys' Basketball Varsity Team Roster. *Hutch-Tech Boys' Basketball Materials and Information*. Amherst, New York, United States: Ken Jones.

Jones, K. (1991, December 5). Turner/Carroll High School vs. Hutch-Tech High School; Al Pastor Tournament. *Hutch-Tech Boys' Basketball Game Summaries*. Amherst, New York, United States of America: Ken Jones.

Jones, K. (1991, March 6). Williamsville South High School vs. Hutch-Tech High School; Class B Sectionals. *Hutch-Tech Boys' Basketball Summaries*. Amherst, New York, United States of America: Ken Jones.

Jones, K. (1992, January 27). City Honors High School vs. Hutch-Tech High School. *Hutch-Tech Boys' Basketball Game Summaries*. Amherst, New York, United States: Ken Jones.

Jones, K. (1992, April). Hutch-Tech Boys' Basketball Team 1991-92 Season Awards and Summary. *Hutch-Tech Boys' Basketball Game Summaries*. Amherst, New York, United States of America.

Jones, K. (1992, January 9). Hutch-Tech High School vs. Buffalo Traditional High School; Yale Cup. *Hutch-Tech Boys' Basketball Game Summaries*. Amherst, New York, United States of America: Ken Jones.

Jones, K. (1992, March 4). Hutch-Tech High School vs. Clarence High School; Class B-1 Sectionals. *Hutch-Tech Boys' Basketball Game Summaries*. Amherst, New York, United States of America: Ken Jones.

Jones, K. (1992, March 8). Hutch-Tech High School vs. Grand Island High School; Class B-1 Sectionals. *Hutch-Tech Boys' Basketball Game Summaries*. Amherst, New York, United States: Ken Jones.

Jones, K. (1992, January 16). Hutch-Tech High School vs. Grover Cleveland High School; Yale Cup. *Hutch-Tech Boys' Basketball Game Summaries*. Amherst, New York, United States of America: Ken Jones.

Jones, K. (1992, February 4). Hutch-Tech High School vs. Kensington High School; Yale Cup. *Hutch-Tech Boys' Basketball Game Summaries*. Amherst, New York, United States of America: Ken Jones.

Jones, K. (1992, January 22). Hutch-Tech High School vs. Lafayette High School. *Hutch-Tech Boys' Basketball Game Summaries.* Amherst, New York, United States of America: Ken Jones.

Jones, K. (1992, March 1). Hutch-Tech High School vs. Niagara Falls High School; Class B-1 Sectionals. *Hutch-Tech Boys' Basketball Game Summaries.* Amherst, New York, United States of America: Ken Jones.

Jones, K. (1992, February 8). McKinley High School vs. Hutch-Tech High School; Yale Cup. *Hutch-Tech Boys' Basketball Game Summaries.* Amherst, New York, United States: Ken Jones.

Jones, K. (1992, January 14). Performing Arts High School vs. Hutch-Tech High School. *Hutch-Tech Boys' Basketball Game Summaries.* Amherst, New York, United States of America: Ken Jones.

Jones, K. (1992, February 12). Riverside High School vs. Hutch-Tech High School; Yale Cup. *Hutch-Tech Boys' Basketball Game Summaries.* Amherst, New York, United States of America: Ken Jones.

Jones, K. (1992, January 18). Seneca High School vs. Hutch-Tech High School; Yale Cup. *Hutch-Tech Boys' Basketball Game Summaries.* Amherst, New York, United States of America: Ken Jones.

Jones, K. (1992, January 6). South Park High School vs. Hutch-Tech High School; Yale Cup. *Hutch-Tech Boys' Basketball Game Summaries.* Amherst, New York, United States of America: Ken Jones.

Jones, K. (2013). *FIGHTING BACK: A WAY OF DEALING WITH NEUROLOGICAL DISORDERS.* Amherst, NY: Ken Jones.

Jones, K. (2018). *DEFENSE: The Greatest Equalizer in the Game.* Amherst, NY: Ken Jones.

Kiyosaki, R. T. (2000). *Rich Dad Poor Dad What The Rich Teach Their Kids About Money--That The Poor & The Middle Class Do Not.* Business Plus.

Kiyosaki, R. T. (2014). *Rich Dad's Conspiracy of the Rich: The 8 New Rules of Money.* Plata Publishing.

Murray, D. (2022). *The War On The West.* Broadside Books.

Northrup, M. (1991, December 7). No. 1 Duke in Aud - a night to remember; NCAA champions have a shot at lasting fame. *Buffalo News*, pp. B-1.

Press, A. (1991, December 15). Experience helps Duke hold off Michigan's OT upset bid 88-85. *Buffalo News*, pp. D-1.

School, H.-T. H. (1991, May). *Impressions: Stepping Into 91.* Buffalo, New York, United States of America: Wadsworth Publishing Company.

School, H.-T. H. (1992). *Impressions: Stepping Into 92.* Buffalo: Wadsworth Publising Company.

Schopp, M. (1992, March 29). Fowler runs away from Pal-Mac, 79-61. *Rochester Democrat and Chronicle*, p. 1C.

Siuda, B. (1992, March 15). WNY is swept out of boys' cage regionals; Drews; Von Weigen pace Raiders by Vikes. *Buffalo News*, pp. C-8.

Slater, W. (1991, March 8). Wilson falls in two OTs: Newark advances in 56-52 thriller. *Rochester Democrat and Chronicle*, p. 5D.

Staff. (1990, February 16). Hutch-Tech captures game and playoff bid. *Buffalo News*, pp. B-5.

Staff. (1990, February 25). J.F. Kennedy sweeps 'twin bill'. *Buffalo News*, pp. C-11.

Staff. (1990, December 30). The Buffalo News' Cage Poll. *Buffalo News*, pp. B-11.

Staff. (1991, December 4). Billies face Chargers in tourney final. *Buffalo News*, pp. C-4.

Staff. (1991, December 1). Bradberry sparks LaSalle to Corning Cup crown. *Buffalo News*, pp. C-13.

Staff. (1991, December 11). Buzzer-beater sends Hutch-Tech to defeat. *Buffalo News*, pp. C-4.

Staff. (1991, December 7). Fitzgibbons nets 54 for Nichols. *Buffalo News*, pp. B-6.

Staff. (1991, January 5). Hutch-Tech rallies to top Grover. *Buffalo News*, pp. B-4.

Staff. (1991, January 30). Hutch-Tech's free throws sink Traditional, 92-85, in Yale Cup; Intrasquad contests pay off in 42-of-45 day at line. *Buffalo News*, pp. D-5.

Staff. (1991, February 23). Lackawanna struggles but wins. *Buffalo News*, pp. B-5.

Staff. (1991, December 22). LaSalle extends Falls mastery. *Buffalo News*, pp. D-12.

Staff. (1991, December 21). LaSalle Senior High School vs. Hutch-Tech High School; Festival of Lights Tournament. *Buffalo News*, pp. B-5.

Staff. (1991, March 10). Newark 77, Hutchinson Tech 47; Class B Far West Regional Box Score. *Rochester Democrat and Chronicle*, p. 10E.

Staff. (1991, February 24). Riverside ousts top-seed Wilson. *Buffalo News*, pp. C-8.

Staff. (1991, January 29). The Buffalo News' Cage Poll. *Buffalo News*, pp. D-4.

Staff. (1991, November 28). Turner/Carroll High School vs. Hutch-Tech High School; Non-League Box Score. *Buffalo News*, pp. C-10.

Staff. (1991, December 4). Turner/Carroll High School vs. Hutch-Tech High School; Non-League Box Score. *Buffalo News*, pp. C-6.

Staff. (1992, January 4). Burgard scores 87-75 victory to snap Hutch-Tech win streak: Engineers had won 16 straight in Yale Cup series. *Buffalo News*, pp. C-14.

Staff. (1992, March 4). Explorers, Spartans battle for Class A title. *Buffalo News*, pp. D-2.

Staff. (1992, January 11). Hutch-Tech High School vs. Bennett High School; Yale Cup Box Score. *Buffalo News*, pp. C-6.

Staff. (1992, January 9). Hutch-Tech High School vs. Buffalo Traditional High School; Yale Cup Box Score. *Buffalo News*, pp. D-4.

Staff. (1992, February 5). Hutch-Tech High School vs. Kensington High School; Yale Cup Box Score. *Buffalo News*, pp. D-4.

Staff. (1992, March 1). Hutch-Tech High Schools vs. Niagara Falls High School; Class B-1 Sectionals. *Buffalo News*, pp. C-11.

Staff. (1992, March 4). Hutch-Tech vs. Clarence; Class B-1 Sectionals Box Score. *Buffalo News*, pp. D-4.

Staff. (1992, March 1). Hutch-Tech vs. Niagara Falls; Class B-1 Sectionals Box Score. *Buffalo News*, pp. C-11.

Staff. (1992, January 11). JFK hands Holland first defeat: East Aurora survives Eden rally; Yale Cup. *Buffalo News*, pp. C-6.

Staff. (1992, February 8). McKinley High School vs. Hutch-Tech High School; Yale Cup Box Score. *Buffalo News*, pp. B-4.

Staff. (1992, January 16). Riverside Edges McKinley to take over first. *Buffalo News*, pp. D-6.

Staff. (1992, February 12). Riverside High School vs. Hutch-Tech High School; Yale Cup Box Score. *Buffalo News*, pp. D-6.

Staff. (1992, March 1). Riverside, Traditional post narrow wins. *Buffalo News*, pp. C-11.

Staff. (1992, January 18). Seneca High School vs. Hutch-Tech High School; Yale Cup Box Score. *Buffalo News*, pp. B-7.

Staff. (1992, February 8). St. Joe's extends win streak: Yale Cup. *Buffalo News*, pp. B-4.

Sullivan, J. (1991, December 8). Duke cruises to 96-90 victory over Canisius; Fans get chance to visit Aud's cage past. *Buffalo News*, pp. D-1.

Usiak, D. (1992, March 8). Grand Island wins championship; plays Fredonia next. *Buffalo News*, pp. C-8.

Usiak, D. (1992, March 8). Hillbillies tip Billies in double OT. *Buffalo News*, pp. C-8.

Walker, B. S. (2005). *Why Should White Guys Have All The Fun: How Reginald Lewis Created A Billion Dollar Business Empire.* Black Classic Press.

Wilson, A. (1992, March 29). Athena falls in state A title game. *Rochester Democrat and Chronicle*, p. 1E.

Wilson, A. (1992, March 29). Perfect season is reality as Mynderse wins C crown. *Rochester Democrat and Chronicle*, p. 3E.

A Chapter Excerpt from The Engineers: A Western New York Basketball Story Part Two

Chapter 2. Basketball Camp Year Two and the Summer Leagues

I quickly realized that this new team was great for me because I had a defined role. On my previous team, I was not sure where I was supposed to be. It was now clear that the low block was all mine. I would also grab rebounds and start the fast breaks. If I could rebound the ball, Bobby could quickly advance the ball up the floor to create shots for himself or for our teammates, many of whom were shooters. It was a perfect marriage.

In the half-court, Coach Ford once again installed a few motion offensive sets to play against the man-to-man defenses we would face. Coach Jones did not allow zone defenses at his camp. In those motion sets, I would methodically come down the lane and set up on the low block and call for the ball. My teammates were all well-trained and unselfish. They readily looked for me inside. After catching the ball, I made strong moves to the basket for layups, or I drew contact and fouls. At the free-throw line, I shot a high percentage.

If I did not catch the ball on the low block, I flashed at the top of the key. After catching the ball, I put my head down and drove to the basket for layups or I got fouled and went to the free-throw line. If I did not drive the ball to the basket, I launched 15-foot jump shots which were falling for me. I slowly but surely began developing confidence in my jump shot and my game in general, both of which did not exist before.

I started enjoying myself. The best basketball I ever consistently played was at that 1992 Ken Jones Basketball Camp with Bobby Markel and the other players on that team. They all played hard, were unselfish offensively, and had good team chemistry. We were not playing the playground isolation-style basketball that we played back in Buffalo. We were playing more of an organized suburban game. It was the style that Coach Jones sought to blend with the street style we learned in inner-city Buffalo…

Contributors to the Engineers: A Western New York Basketball Story

…Continued from the frontcourt of this book

"You could tell by how he (Coach Ken Jones) was running the tryouts that he was going to judge you by your play, not by what grade you were in and not your social status. It was strictly can you do this drill or not? So, I was thinking, I might have a level playing field here, so that was good to know. He was going to choose the team strictly based on merit. You know? Another thing I noticed was, and I think this goes back to him being in shape, but I noticed how he paid attention to that, too. Who was in shape? Who was tired? When he said to drink water, who was drinking water? Who was tired? Being in the tryouts, though, knowing you would be chosen based on your merits wasn't surprising, but it was definitely gratifying. And then, knowing that, I wasn't surprised at the end of the day who he chose for the team because a lot of guys were coming out because they were seniors and had their own agendas, so I wasn't surprised at the end of the day that certain people didn't make it."

—Derrick Herbert, Player, Hutch-Tech High School

"Coach Jones really changed my game a lot. As a freshman, when I was trying to make the team, he was more of a *traditional* coach. He didn't like all of the flare and the flash. He was basically like, make one move and pass or you won't play on my team. You won't play! So, he turned me into a *smarter* player. He made me a smarter player. He was one of the only coaches who was really big on teaching fundamentals and skill sets. Out of all my three coaches, he was the best at that, in terms of working on your game."

—Reggie Hokes, Player, Hutch-Tech High School

"I didn't have a problem with that either. I had a cousin who went to Hutch-Tech. I think that was the year they went to the states with Curt Brooks and the Skillon boys. I didn't know that much about Ken Jones. Do you know how they had the summer program? Actually, me and Chiquita Howard were shooting around with the basketball. Coach Jones came up to me and said, 'You've got pretty nice form there. Are you thinking about coming out for the team?' I said, 'Yes, I'm thinking about it.' I was adamant in telling him that football was my thing, and he said to me, 'Football players play basketball too!' And I said, 'Okay, well, I'll make sure that I try out.' And that's what it was."

—Earl Holmes, Player, Hutch-Tech High School

"I used to go play rec-ball at Campus East, so a lot of those guys would be up there. They were legends to us—Ritchie Campbell, Marcus Whitfield, and, like I said, Kevin Roberson and Jerrold Skillon, to name a few. Absolutely, I was aware of what was going on, and then over at Turner/Carroll, you had some people going off. I was definitely aware of what was happening in the high school scene."

—Ronald Jennings, Player, Campus West and Turner/Carroll High School

"It was controlled chaos. Here are some rules. Just don't break them. It was the first time I ever and maybe the only time—because I played for Dick Bihr later on at Buff State, and he was pretty rigid—it was the only time I played for what you would call a *player's coach* today. He was, in many respects, one of us (Coach Phil Richardson). He would tell Hargrove, 'You know what. If you don't like it, then dunk on him!' He would encourage things that I think other basketball coaches would look at as being not okay. That didn't matter to him. He had rules, and you couldn't be foolish, but when we got in between the lines, we were encouraged to play hard and play through whistles, even against each other. He would encourage Callahan and Hokes to go at each other and Dre and Randy to go at each other. He knew, just like those Cowboys teams we talked about or 50 other teams we could name, that it would make you better when it really mattered—you could rely on the guy next to you!"

—Brandon Jones, Player, Hutch-Tech High School

"Jones shook things up when he came in. We learned about the coaching change when the school year started. He started with the invite list, and I think he started with the people that were on the team the previous year. He gave some other people a chance from the freshman class. It was us the sophomores, whoever else was on the team, and then he opened it up to people he saw in the hallways or maybe gym class. They were pretty much *closed* tryouts—invitation only. He let everybody know that being on the team the previous year meant nothing! He made that clear from the beginning."

—Quincy Lee, Player, Hutch-Tech High School

"'We're going to play man-to-man,' the Lancaster coach said, and I was thinking, 'We're going to come out and toast this team!' I showed the clip to my kids because I'd taped it—I used it as fodder for them. The score was something like 37–15 at halftime. They pressed us full-court, Anwar. All I did was what I now call the 'One-Breaker', where I had my point guard taking the ball out every chance we could after a dead ball. I had my twos and threes in the corner and my fours and fives at half-court—basically, it was a '1-2-2 press-breaker.' When we passed it into the two or the three which were both also guards who probably could've played the point—I'm trying to think if it was a Timmy Winn team or a Modie Cox team–. We just passed it into the corner, and Modie shot up the middle, and my fours and fives, which were just small forwards, both pinched in, and it was a bounce pass and a layup to either side. It was like a layup drill. They should never have been pressing us, and they shouldn't have been playing us man-to-man!"

—Pat Monti, Coach, LaSalle Senior High School

"I think Brooks was the best player at Tech ever. He and my brother were tight. He lived a few houses down from us on Thatcher. He was unstoppable. We would go to the courts, and he never missed his jump shots."

—Jamar Moore, Player, Hutch-Tech High School

"Coach Jones ran a great program. It had structure and taught character, not to mention it helped your skills come about even when you didn't realize it."

—Roderick 'Spanky' Peoples, Player, Hutch-Tech High School

"One thing we would do growing up is go to the parks and recreation. They always had a lot of fun community activities. There was one right there in Armor, NY, and we would head over to Green Lake, and we spent a lot of time growing up just doing that. I know it was similar in Hamburg. Reading your article, I know the kids from Niagara Falls were playing basketball at the Boys Club and playing early. Growing up where we did, little league baseball was the kind of thing that we all did. Some of the kids played little league football. Basketball was something we didn't talk about until later. A lot of kids were 11 or 12 years old before they started playing basketball, and it really didn't become a big deal until middle school. That's what I noticed from some of your interviews regarding how some of the kids grew up north in the cities of Buffalo and Niagara Falls."

—Brian Reith, Player, Hamburg High School

"The Yale Cup was basically—I think it was thirteen high schools in the public school system. We didn't go outside of the Yale Cup to play anybody for basketball. We didn't play in Section VI. We didn't scrimmage St. Joe's, Williamsville North, or anything like that. We were just playing right there in the Yale Cup. It was a twelve-game schedule, and I think the top four teams made the playoffs. You played the first round and the second round, and the second round was the championship. After the Yale Cup, that was it. The season would end around the beginning of February, and everyone got ready for baseball and track. It was an altogether different picture from when you played at Hutch-Tech. Now it's even more of a different look for the kids who are playing in the Yale Cup. Back then, the Yale Cup was not represented in Section VI. There was no state title representation or anything. This was in the late 1960s. I think they went to Section VI in 1971, but our group of athletes and the kids the year after me—we were really upset that in 1971 or 1972, they allowed the Buffalo Public Schools to play in Section VI and compete for the state championship. It was around 1971 and 1972 or something like that."

—Phillip Richardson, Player, Bennett High School and Coach, Hutch-Tech High School

"Our goal was to win the state championship. It was my personal goal and the team's goal as well. When you have that goal, you get that 'tunnel vision'. We used to say, 'Get to Glen! Get to Glen! You've got to get to Glens Falls!' That's where the state championship was held. For some time, the Buffalo teams were having a hard time getting past the Rochester teams in the Far West Regional. We wanted to get past Rochester. For us, we had a lot of confidence because we played against the top-notch competition in Buffalo. We were confident enough to get past Buffalo's competition, and we just had to beat the Rochester teams. It was step by step."

—Jason Rowe, Player, Buffalo Traditional High School

"Well, along with what you're saying, in addition to being done at 6 p.m., you can also say done on February 15. Coaches didn't have so much contact with the kids after the season was over. There are some, then and now, who have the kids in a rec league in the spring or the fall, so they at least get a once-a-week connection with the kids. It's not much, but it's enough to know what's going on in the kid's life, somewhat. I worked with my kids over the summer. I worked with Ed Harris, doing drills and workouts with him. When you have a kid like Ed—I used to say that coaches get credit for motivating players. I like to turn that around and say that players motivate coaches, and if you know what kind of kid Ed was, you would know why I would say that. Ed would be a cause for me to research and educate myself on a new drill for when we'd meet up at some park in July. He motivated me to spend a little bit more time on my practice plan and get a better plan ready for that day's practice or the next day's practice. So, I think players motivate coaches."

—Bill Russell, Coach, Riverside High School

"Xs and Os. Like I said, the fundamentals, I'll give it to Jones (Coach Ken Jones). He drilled those fundamentals into you, and there would be two-hour practices where you wouldn't shoot the basketball once. You might get to shoot it in the last fifteen minutes. He drilled the fundamentals into you, so that was just the way he was. To me, he would do camp stuff. He wasn't a good Xs and Os coach to me. He didn't adjust too much, but he drilled the fundamentals—the Mikan Drill, everybody had to be able to use both hands. He was a good *fundamentals* coach! We were doing the same thing offensively and defensively. It wasn't rocket science. If they ran a zone, we had zone offenses, and we ran motion. He wanted to *work* the ball, and we kept working it, and working it, and working it, and someone might break free for a layup. There weren't a lot of intricacies in it, but he drilled it into you, kind of like Jim Boeheim and the 2-3 zone, but if someone shoots them out of that zone, they're stuck, like a fish out of water. That's how I view Jones. But he drilled that into us. We would practice that first hour in the small gym with no ball. That was just it."

—Jermaine 'J-Bird' Skillon, Player, Hutch-Tech High School

"On a side note, my favorite game from that year was the Turner game (Turner/Carroll High School). Mone (Damone James) was always the guy in our age bracket. Turner was always ranked, and they came in with all the hype. We were the underdog, and the gym was packed—ah man. The hair is standing up on my arm, thinking about that game. It was a Friday night, and the energy from that game was off the chain. Everybody knew that a lot of girls went to Turner, and we all tried to get cuts before the game. This was different—it was a Friday night game. Turner was in the hood. They had Kev Sanford and the Ortiz kid, along with Mone, and they got so much hype. They might've been ranked No. 1. No. 1, or 2—they were ranked higher than us. Man, we just HANDLED them—HANDLED them—shut them right on up. We took ya'll manhood and ya'll women! Quincy stayed right around the corner from Turner, so I know he would say the same thing. Your kicks, your uniform—everything had to be right before that game. Pregame there was music—it was standing room only. I was so hyped for that game. That was THE GAME. We shut everybody right on up. That's what let everybody know that we were for real that year. It was that game. Because everybody was there. And when we mopped Turner. That put everybody on notice! That was the game that put everybody on notice that, 'Uh Oh. Tech might be for real,' because we smacked them. OHHHH, we smacked them. That's where the confidence came from. That game. We put the whole town on notice after that game!"

—Jerrold 'Pep' Skillon, Player, Hutch-Tech High School

"I would say that as the tryouts continued, I would say I was less surprised than I would have been at the beginning of the tryouts. Because looking back on it, and you look at it—he kept five freshmen, five sophomores, and five juniors, or maybe four juniors, I can't remember—and he kept one senior. Yes, it was Adrian (Brice)—he was the only senior on the team, and he was the point guard, but I don't think he was what you would consider a typical point guard—speedy with the ball and pushing, pushing, pushing, where he had to be more methodical with the ball. That's what Coach Jones wanted, right? He wanted someone who would bring the ball up, wouldn't lose it, and put the team into an offensive set. We'd run it, and we'd run it until we got an open look."

—Christain J. Souter, Player, Hutch-Tech High School

"Oh, absolutely. Their coaching and their culture were totally better than hours (LaSalle's). It was totally structured and consistent. Pat Monti was their coach, and he was like the Greg Popovich (of the NBA) of high school basketball back then. That was the biggest thing. Talent and body for body and person for person, we had some players, but they were just coached tremendously well. We used to sum it up by saying that they knew their roles and we didn't."

—Darris Thomas, Player, Niagara Falls Senior High School

"We kept each other balanced. That's what I think our thing was. The egos were there, but we balanced each other. We always just kept pushing each other. I can always remember Curt (Brooks) and I in the backyard pushing each other. He's pushing me to be a better rebounder and a post-up player. I'm pushing him to be a better shooter because he had to shoot over me and stuff like that. When you had these people always playing against each other and competing, it always made you better. But we knew the bigger picture, which was that it was all about the team and not about the individual. We pushed each other. Because we all knew that we were good!"

—Charles 'Chuck' Thompson, Player, Hutch-Tech High School

"I wanted to play basketball, so I felt like Turner/Carroll was a basketball school. Throughout the 1980s, Turner/Carroll was known for basketball. I spent a lot of time in that neighborhood. I went to School 81, which was in that neighborhood, and I used to go to Tops near Turner/Carroll. My mother always used to play Bingo at Turner/Carroll, so you just enjoyed those things, and I said when I get older, I want to go to that high school. I was a smart student so in terms of the testing, I didn't have to worry about it much. Honestly, at that time, we probably couldn't afford it, which is ultimately why I left. But it was ultimately what I wanted to do and play basketball. Yes, it was mostly black, and it was small. My father went to

Turner too—he graduated in 1969 or 71—I can't remember which year he graduated. But he went and played basketball."

—Dennis Wilson, Player, Turner/Carroll High School and Riverside High School

"After Carlos Bradberry's senior year, we graduated eight or nine seniors. No one gave us a chance to come back the next year and do any work. It was the perfect opportunity for guys like me, entering my sophomore year, and Jody, entering his junior year, to take our claim. We didn't care about being better than St. Joe's or Buffalo Traditional. Could we be better than the team we were on last year? The only way you would get props in our city and our program was if you were one of the best teams within that program, and that was our motivation. Could we be better than Carlos' team the year before, who had the *Buffalo News* Western New York Player of the Year on it? Could we get back to Glens Falls?"

—Tim Winn, Player, LaSalle Senior High School

"I met Coach Jones in 1984. I was almost eighteen years old. We were just knocked out when I was playing with the national basketball team of the Netherlands. I was playing in the under-18 team, and we were knocked off in the qualification game by Finland. We didn't go to the European Championship that summer, so my summer was free. My brother played in the American professional games, and he played with Paul Zeretzky, who was coming from Rochester. My family said, 'Ron, it's about time. You spent some time with the national team. You've traveled with the team. Now it's time to go to the United States by yourself.' That was great and exciting. I stayed with Paul and his parents at his house. The first camp I worked out at was the Nazareth Camp. The second camp was the Ken Jones Basketball Camp in Hamilton, NY. That was my first introduction to Mr. Ken Jones. That was the love of my life. He was such an inspirational and passionate coach. He stayed with me forever, so that's the story about Ken Jones. He had 300 campers that week and by the end, he knew all their names. He was so into it with every camper, and he had a passion with the energy he had. I was a big fan of him right away."

—Ronald Wolfs, Coach, Wolf Pack Nation, The Netherlands

To see the print and video promotional content created for *The Engineers: A Western New York Basketball Story*, scan the QR code above or visit this URL:
www.bigwordsauthors.com/theengineersawnybasketballstory

Made in the USA
Columbia, SC
24 April 2025

38245bcb-cdcb-480c-ae03-22e2bc09c81dR01